Voices Prophesying War

Voices Prophesying War

Future Wars 1763–3749

I. F. CLARKE

SECOND EDITION

Oxford   New York

OXFORD UNIVERSITY PRESS

1992

Oxford University Press, Walton Street, Oxford OX2 6DP
Oxford New York Toronto
Delhi Bombay Calcutta Madras Karachi
Petaling Jaya Singapore Hong Kong Tokyo
Nairobi Dar es Salaam Cape Town
Melbourne Auckland
and associated companies in
Berlin Ibadan

First edition published 1966 with the title
Voices Prophesying War 1763–1984
Second edition published 1992

British Library Cataloguing in Publication Data
Data available

Library of Congress Cataloging in Publication Data
Clarke, I. F. (Ignatius Frederick)
    Voices prophesying war, future wars, 1763–3749/ I.F. Clarke.
        p. c.m.
    Rev. edn. of: Voices prophesying war, 1763–1984. 1966.
    1. War stories—History and criticism. 2. Science fiction—
History and criticism. 3. Imaginary wars and battles in
literature. 4. Imaginary wars and battles—Bibliography.
5. Science fiction—Bibliography. 6. War stories—Bibliography.
7. Prophecies in literature. 8. Future in literature. 9. War in
literature. I. Clarke, I. F. (Ignatius Frederick). Voices
prophesying war, 1763–1984. II. Title.
PN3448.W3C58 1992 809.3'9358—dc20 92–8583
ISBN 0–19–212302–5

Set by Hope Services (Abingdon) Ltd
Printed in Great Britain by
Butler & Tanner Ltd.
Frome, Somerset

For my grandchildren
Rosalind, Jonathan, and Stephen

May they live all their days in peace

Contents

List of Illustrations   ix

Preface to the Second Edition   xi

Chapter One   The Warfare of the Future: The Opening
                 Phase, 1763–1871   1

Chapter Two   The Break-in Phase: The *Battle of Dorking*
                 Episode   27

Chapter Three   Science and the Shape of Wars-to-Come,
                 1880–1914   57

Chapter Four   Politics and the Pattern of the Next Great
                 War, 1880–1914   93

Chapter Five   From the Somme and Verdun to
                 Hiroshima and Nagasaki   131

Chapter Six   From the Flame Deluge to the Bad
                 Time   164

Notes   218

Checklist of Imaginary Wars, 1763–1990   224

Index   263

List of Illustrations

1. *Result of the invention of aerostatic machines*. Engraving by J. M. Will. From François-Louis Bruel, *Histoire Aéronautique* (Paris 1909), No. 146.

2. 'AN ACCURATE REPRESENTATION of the FLOATING MACHINE Invented by the FRENCH for INVADING ENGLAND'. From a copy in the National Maritime Museum, Greenwich, by permission of the Trustees.

3. An artist's impression based on the specifications for a 'Locomotive Battery with steam engine' in the 1855 patent taken out by James Cowen and James Sweetlong.

4. The 'British Tar' of the Future, as seen by *Punch*, 1862, vol. 42, p. 147.

5. Front-page illustration to the Scientific American, 1885, p. 406.

6. Armoured fighting vehicles from *La Caricature*, 27 October, 1883.

7. Underwater warfare, as foreseen by Albert Robida in *La Caricature*.

8. The images of the war-to-come in Albert Robida's *La Guerre au vingtième siècle* first appeared in *La Caricature* in 1883 and were published in book form in 1887.

9. The Martian fighting machine in action. From the Belgian edition of the *War of the Worlds*, 1906, illustrated by the Belgian artist, Alvim-Correa.

10. Artist's impression of the air war of the future in *Black and White Budget*, 24 February 1900.

11. A fully illustrated account of a German invasion opened on 13 February 1909 in the popular middle-class magazine *Black and White*.

12. The Lord Mayor's *Proclamation* in William Le Queux's *Invasion of 1910*, 1906, aimed at total realism.

13. Submarine warfare as described in the *London Magazine*, August 1909.

14. A double-page spread on the air-sea warfare of the future in *Black and White*, 19 October 1907.

15. The dangers of air warfare presented in *Die Vierte Waffe*, 1913, a translation from the Danish original.

16. Albert Robida foresees rocket-powered aircraft.

17. During April and May 1910, readers of the *Sketch* had the pleasure of seeing Heath Robinson's anticipations of *Der Tag*.

18.   Artist's impression of the robots in R.U.R.. From the author's collection.

19.   The Daily Hate scene from Michael Anderson's version of *1984*, 1955.

20.   Jet-packs for infantry: one of four projections in the US Army Material Command display, 'Army Mobility Looks to the Future'.

21.   Artist's impression of jet-borne cavalry. Author's collection.

22.   The end of the world draws nigh in Kubrick's classic *Dr Strangelove*, 1963 by permission of Columbia Picture Industries Inc.

23.   Wars continue far off in space and time in George Lucas's *Star Wars*, 1977 by permission of 20th Century-Fox.

Preface To The Second Edition

A QUARTER-CENTURY has passed since this book first appeared. In that time many hundreds of writers have described the various phases of the third world war between East and West in the greatest outpouring of these tales of future warfare in the history of the genre. Then came the arms reduction treaties and the astonishing events that transformed the political situation in Eastern Europe and Russia. These entirely unexpected and extraordinary changes so altered relationships between the two major power blocs that by 1990 the tale of the war-to-come had gone into rapid decline. And so, in the last decade of the twentieth century, when there are now good reasons for thinking that the insects and bacteria may not inherit the world, a new edition of this book will acquaint readers with the most recent innovations in the fiction of future wars. The original text has been completely revised and new material added. The fifth chapter has been largely rewritten, and the new sixth chapter surveys the many changes in this fiction during the last three decades.

The new subtitle, *Future Wars 1763–3749*, sets out the theme of the book. The date of 1763 refers to the publication of *The Reign of George VI*, the first of many tales of future warfare, and the date of 3749 signals the beginning of the end in Walter Miller's classic *A Canticle for Leibowitz* (1959).

I take this opportunity to record my gratitude to all those who helped in the preparation of this book. This new edition owes much to the unfailing assistance of librarians everywhere; and I thank in particular the Storage and Delivery Branch of the British Library, the Staff of the Bodleian Library, the London Library, the Library of Congress, the Bibliothèque Nationale, and the Katalogabteilung, Deutsche Staatsbibliothek.

My grateful thanks go to those friends, colleagues, and correspondents who added to my information: Dr Eric Grove enlarged my understanding of modern naval warfare; Dr William Fortescue, University of Kent, added greatly to my knowledge of the French political situation in the 1840s; and Neil Barron, an eminent bibliographer, gave invaluable advice in the early stages of preparing the new edition. I owe much to Professor Paul Brians, Washington State University, who most generously sent me a list of the post-1984 additions to his admirable bibliography, *Nuclear Holocausts*; and I have had good reason to be grateful for the unfailing advice of Jeremy Lewis, who knows so much about books and publishers. Finally, and most of all, I thank my wife for her great patience in reading the various drafts of this book and for her always perceptive and kind criticism.

I.F.C.

Milton under Wychwood

Chapter One

The Warfare of the Future
The Opening Phase, 1763–1871

DURING the evening of 2 September 1871, the British Prime Minister, William Ewart Gladstone, spoke to the Working Men's Liberal Association at Whitby in Yorkshire. His theme was the state of the nation and of the world; and towards the end of his speech he warned his audience and the country against the dangers of alarmism. The occasion was most unusual in British politics, since the cause of the warning was a piece of fiction that had appeared four months earlier in the May issue of *Blackwood's Magazine*, one of the most influential of the Victorian monthly journals. It was an even more remarkable moment in literary history. One of the greatest of British prime ministers was paying unwilling tribute to the effectiveness of *The Battle of Dorking*, a short story about an imagined future German invasion of the British Isles which had alarmed the nation and had astounded innumerable readers throughout the world. Gladstone, however, was not to know that the extraordinary success of *The Battle of Dorking*, read everywhere from Canada to New Zealand, had established the tale of the war-to-come as the most favoured means of presenting arguments for—or against—new political alliances, changes in the organization and equipment of armies, technological innovations in naval vessels, or even schemes for colonial expansion. The anonymous author had written the first hot story in the first cold war of new armaments and conscript armies. Before the end of 1871 many more pamphlets had appeared, sometimes to support, but more often to deny, the possibility of a successful invasion of the British Isles as Lieutenant-Colonel George Tomkyns Chesney had described it; and by April 1872, when the period of alarmism had ended, the fortunate author had received a handsome sum from *Blackwood's* in final payment of the large profit made from the many reprints and translations.

The *Battle of Dorking* episode was far more than the major publishing event of 1871, for the author had hit upon a new and most important area in the then new business of mass communications. Chesney the soldier had understood the military consequences of technological progress as these had appeared during the War of 1870, and, like his countrymen, he had seen how the German victory in that war had altered the balance of power in Europe.

So, without fully realizing the exceptional novelty of the means and methods, he chose to present his fears for the future of his country in a highly dramatic and totally realistic projection. And then, after the excitement had died down, Chesney's admonitory tale of disaster and defeat went on to provide both form and technique for the many forecasts of coming wars and future battles that began to appear in ever-increasing numbers throughout the new industrial nations. British, French, German and Italian propagandists learnt from the English colonel how to deliver forceful lessons on naval policy or warnings about the dangers of military unpreparedness in a pattern of fiction that the middle classes and—later on in the 1890s—the new literate masses could readily comprehend. In 1887, for instance, an anonymous French author brought out a fiercely anti-British story, *Plus d'Angleterre*, in which he related the coming French conquest of the British Empire in the style first developed, as a Frenchman had to admit, 'by that ingenious fiction called *The Battle of Dorking*'.

In fact, the French had long memories of Chesney's story. As late as March 1900, at a time when anti-British feelings were particularly violent in France in consequence of the Fashoda Incident and the Boer War, the editor of *Le Monde Illustré* devoted a whole number of the magazine to *La Guerre Anglo-Franco-Russe*, a detailed, fully illustrated, and most enthusiastic account of the defeat of the British in a future war. He thought that 'this tale should not be displeasing to the British. Have they not themselves already published *The Battle of Dorking*, in which Germany crushed the United Kingdom, and the *Naval War of 1887*, in which France defeated them?' Later on, when the outbreak of the First World War caused some Americans to turn to fiction as a means of warning their countrymen against the dangers of remaining unprepared in a warring world, they found their model in the Chesney story. In 1914 the American publisher George Putnam bought the copyright of *The Battle of Dorking* for publication in the United States; and in the introduction he wrote for *America Fallen*, an imaginary invasion story published in 1915, Putnam devoted several paragraphs to a commentary on Chesney's story. It was, he wrote, 'the work of a man who was a great staff officer and an accomplished student of military history'. The situation of the United States in 1915, so Putnam thought, was similar to that of Great Britain in 1871: '*America Fallen* is a very cleverly presented bit of possible history, and the book makes an appeal for the realization on the part of American citizens of the risk of invasion which is very similar to that made in *The Battle of Dorking*.'

And yet Chesney was certainly not the first writer to describe an imaginary war of the future or even a projected invasion of the British Isles. Long before 1871 there had been a succession of occasional pamphlets and satires that had used the description of future wars and battles as a means of propaganda. Few of these attracted more than a passing interest, and not one of them ever enjoyed success on a scale that could bear any comparison with the world-wide notoriety of *The Battle of Dorking*. The fact is that before Chesney's innovatory story the tale of the war-to-come was generally presented in political rather than military terms. Writers looked on war as a customary and acceptable process in European society. In their imagination they projected the weapons and tactics of their time into a future that was simply the old world reshaped to suit their individual purposes. Before *The Battle of Dorking*, no author of an imaginary war of the future ever suggested that the deliberate use of new weapons and technological devices could have a decisive effect on the outcome of a battle or a war.

It will be evident, therefore, that any account of the origin and course of these imaginary wars will also be a history of the changing attitudes to war itself. Because all these stories have been immediate responses to the perceived dangers or promising opportunities that awaited the nations-in-arms, they present a remarkable record of the arrival and departure of favoured assumptions and dominant expectations. These begin with the nationalistic, often aggressive, and generally heroic tales of coming battles and future campaigns in that last age of innocence before the first great technological war in world history. They end in fear and trembling with the post-Hiroshima projections of the horrors that threaten all living things in tales like *On the Beach*, *Die letzten Kinder von Schewenborn*, *The Coming Self-Destruction of the United States*, and *Hakobune no Sakura*. So, all that follows will relate the rise, decline, and sudden disappearance of the idea of armed conflict as a traditional practice readily accepted by Western industrial nations.

During the first main period in the course of the new fiction between 1871 and 1914, the deciding factors were the effects of technology on the conduct of war and the coming of universal literacy. After the Franco-German War of 1870 had changed the power system in Europe, and after the first ironclads and the first breech-loaders had started off the arms race, the tale of imaginary warfare came into its own. As the new elementary schools taught the masses of the major industrial nations to read, the numbers of these future war stories increased rapidly until they had become a stock feature of the popular press by the 1890s. Almost all of them took it for granted that the next war would be fought more or less in the manner of the last, and they assumed that future wars would continue to be conducted in a relatively restrained and humane fashion. This unfortunate failure in anticipation was an inevitable consequence of the now familiar problem of knowing how best to adapt to the scale and the rate of change. 'Future shock' was a concept beyond the worst imaginings of the many earnest patriots who wrote about 'The Next Great War'. For them there was no time-lag between traditional attitudes to war and the rapid development of increasingly destructive weapons. Not a single writer—not even

H. G. Wells—ever guessed that industrialism plus mass conscription would make it possible for a Falkenhayn to plan the Battle of Verdun with the intention of bleeding the French armies to death.

Today there is no comparable failure of the imagination. The world knows only too well what the effects of another total war could be. A succession of special studies, from the Rand Corporation's *Report on Non-Military Defense* (1948) to Jonathan Schell's *Fate of the Earth* (1982), have made everyone familiar with the jargon of overkill, of nuclear and thermo-nuclear explosions, and of the many dangers of biological and chemical warfare. The brutal facts of the new military technologies present the disaster of nuclear warfare in terms that fiction cannot make more horrifying. Indeed, one expert writer in this field has claimed that:

even writers of fiction have failed to give us a deep impression of the nature and extent of the catastrophe. Perhaps even they cannot truly visualize what it would mean to the survivors to see fifty, eighty, or a hundred million people killed within a few days or hours and tens of millions grievously ill, living without hope in hovels amidst poisonous radio-active debris.[1]

Once, and it is difficult to believe that it was only a hundred years ago, it was generally agreed that the advance of science would put an end to all strife on earth. Many echoed the sentiments of the Scottish poet Charles Mackay, who believed that universal peace would follow the spreading railway networks of the mid-century:

> Lay down your rails, ye nations, near and far
> Yoke your full trains to Steam's triumphal car;
> Link town to town; unite in iron bands
> The long-estranged and oft-embattled lands.
> Peace, mild-eyed seraph—Knowledge, light divine—
> Shall send their messengers by every line.
> Men, join'd in amity, shall wonder long
> That Hate had power to lead their fathers wrong;
> Or that false Glory lured their hearts astray,
> And made it virtuous and sublime to slay.

The coming conquest of the air raised similar hopes. In 1864 Victor Hugo wrote in joyful phrases to the French balloonist Nadar that the invention of the aircraft would mean the end of warfare. Out of science would come peace. Aircraft would bring about 'the immediate, absolute, instantaneous, universal and perpetual abolition of frontiers. Armies would vanish, and with them the whole business of war, exploitation and subjugation. It would be an immense peaceful revolution. It would mean the liberation of mankind.'[2]

Two world wars changed that simple faith. It was shattered in the First World War when the great artillery battles and the grinding attrition of trench warfare demonstrated the power of the applied sciences in the *Material-schlacht*—the new kind of conflict that killed men and squandered material at a rate and on a scale never known before. But it took another world war and the invention of nuclear weapons before men gave up hoping that the advance of science would bring in the millenium.

A fact central to human experience today is that, although a nuclear war will undoubtedly be the most terrible war ever fought, it would be the first in which there could be little real fighting. The struggle of man against man, of battery against battery, could never take place. After the last bombs had fallen, after the fire storms, and after the survivors had waited ninety days in their shelters to escape the worst dangers of local fallout, they would emerge to face devastation and destruction never known before in human history. Ever since Hiroshima a common fear has united the peoples of planet Earth, and an immense literature has developed to describe how the end could come for all humankind. One familiar stereotype follows the swift sequence of events in *Warday* (1984)—Russian ICBMs suddenly detonating over the North American landmass, then the retaliatory strikes, and then the end of the first nuclear war thirty-six minutes after the first flash in the sky. One million years afterwards, so Kurt Vonnegut foresees in *Galàpagos* (1985), Nature will have made good the disastrous experiment with *Homo sapiens* by reshaping the remote descendants of the few who survived the final catastrophe. 'Thanks to certain modifications in the design of human beings,' Vonnegut reports, 'the Law of Natural Selection did the repair job without outside assistance of any kind.' The new-model earthlings will at last be in harmony with themselves and with their world. They will inhabit the Galàpagos Archipelago, the ideal environment for sea creatures that have flippers for hands, prognathous jaws for catching fish, and small bullet-like skulls.

All this has come about in little more than two centuries. The earliest account of a future war appeared in *The Reign of George VI, 1900–1925*, an anonymous story of 1763. That utopian fantasy was one of the earliest experiments in futuristic fiction and the first to project an ideal state into the centuries-to-come. The unknown author had turned to the vacant area of the future in order to reveal a perfect Patriot King toiling away for the good of his country. The story was, in fact, a demonstration of the political theories set out in *The Idea of a Patriot King* which Henry St John, Viscount Bolingbroke, wrote for the instruction of the Prince of Wales and published later, in 1749. The author follows the Bolingbroke thesis in most of the details. The hero of his story is the energetic, wise, heroic King George VI, a constitutional monarch who restores the greatness of his country and conquers all before him. There is a curious unpremeditated irony about the description of the many marches and battles that make George VI master of Europe and the admired King of France; for the narration is so much taken up with the best of all possible eighteenth-century systems that time has not moved on. All the battles in the European War of 1917–20 are old-style affairs of infantry advancing in the oblique order of Frederick the Great and of naval battles hammered out by frigates and ships of the line. The kings of Europe still lead their troops into battle, and at sea the secret weapon is the fire-ship. This the Duke of Grafton uses with devastating effect in 1920, when he discovers a Russian fleet in Stockholm: 'On a dark night he sent in six fire-ships among their squadron; eleven ships of the line were burnt and seven frigates, four sunk and seven taken.'

The unwitting disjunction between the fictional future and the later reality appears even more strikingly in the account of George VI's greatest victory before the gates of Vienna in May 1918, at a time when—in the real course of history—millions of men were in action along the Western Front and the Ludendorff Offensive was grinding to a halt before the Americans at Château-Thierry. Contrast the scale of those facts in 1918 with this projection of 1763:

The Russian army had a superiority of above sixty thousand men, consequently their numbers were two to one; but no danger could depress the heart of George. Having, with moving batteries, secured the rear and wings of his army from being surrounded, he placed his artillery in the most advantageous manner; and dividing his front into two lines, at the head of the first he began the attack, after his artillery had played on the enemy an hour, with great success. The Russian infantry, animated by the presence of their Czar under whom they had so often conquered, repulsed him with some loss. . . . George flew like lightning to his weakened troops; and, placing himself at the head of six regiments of dragoons, made such a furious attack on the eager Russians as threw them into disorder with great success.[3]

It is easy enough to find something quaint—even comic—in the contrast between the unprecedented scale of operations during the First World War and this would-be prophet's expectation that there could be no change whatever in the conduct of warfare. In projecting the battles of the eighteenth century into the year 1918, however, the author had been as true to the expectations of his time as so many later writers would in their turn hold fast to nineteenth-century expectations of future aeronautical developments in their descriptions of air attacks by enormous airships propelled by steam, or electricity, or by more mysterious sources of power. In fact, the total failure to foresee the true shape of coming things in *The Reign of George VI* was no discredit to the author. A natural ignorance of the world-changing powers of technology had made it impossible to guess that the tactics and weapons of the eighteenth century might not continue into the imagined twentieth century.

That first English tale of the future had appeared on the eve of momentous developments—political, social, and technological—which were to alter the pattern of civilization as surely as the discovery of agriculture and the domestica-

tion of animals had begun the process of civilization. Even as the history of
the future George VI was being read, many factors were already at work that
were soon to change the European attitude to time and, in consequence, would
open up a new dimension for the imagination.

The advance into the future begins with the rapid success of the first balloon ascents, which date from the spectacular triumphs of the two Montgolfier
brothers and of Jacques Charles during the second half of 1783. Their public
demonstrations of the results of the new laboratory sciences, especially in the
hydrogen balloons of Jacques Charles, were a most powerful stimulus to the
imagination. As vast crowds watched the first aeronauts take off for the skies,
it seemed evident that, in the words of Louis XVI, a new epoch in human history was beginning.[4] The Montgolfières and the Charlières were evidence of a
new-found human capacity for great achievements. This growing awareness of
the powers of technology was still further extended by the enthusiasm that followed on the increasing use of Watt's steam engine during the closing decades
of the eighteenth century. Changes of this order had a decisive effect on the
development of that singular Western sense of the future as a distinct and
desirable period of time. And out of the growing sharpness of the new vision
of the future there came the new habit of describing the shape of things to
come.

The new balloons were all the rage during the 1780s. For a time it seemed
that the aeronauts would soon realize the ancient dream of travelling through
the air. Thoughts about the use of balloons in warfare came as naturally as
anticipations of transatlantic air crossings. There were plays on both sides of
the Channel—jolly farces like *Aerostation; or The Templar's Stratagem*, which
delighted audiences at the Theatre Royal in Covent Garden in 1784. Scene III
opens with the comic hero 'discovered sitting in deep thought'. He declaims:

I think I could make a devilish good bargain for myself, and do my Country at the
same time essential service. [*muses*] Let me see, let me see; fourteen first-rate balloons, each carrying twelve cannonades, ten bombs, and four twenty-two- and
forty-pounders. Ay! fourteen would do it. Suppose I undertake to contract with
the Government for paying off the national debt, on condition that they grant me
and my heirs for ever an exclusive patent for the bombardment of Algiers.

Across the Atlantic, the readers of the *Freeman's Journal* for 22 December
1784 found similar entertainment in a poem on 'The Progress of Balloons'
from the American Patriot, anti-British satirist, and one-time sea captain
Philip Morin Freneau. Long before Tennyson's famous lines about the 'airy
navies grappling in the central blue', the American poet had foreseen the air
battles of the future:

> How France is distinguish'd in Louis's reign!
> What cannot her genius and courage attain?

Thro'out the wide world have her arms found the way
And art to the stars is extending her sway.
At sea let the British their neighbours defy—
The French shall have frigates to traverse the sky,
In this navigation more fortunate prove,
And cruise at their ease in the climates above.
If the English should venture to sea with their fleet,
A host of balloons in a trice they shall meet.
The French from the zenith their wings shall display
And souse on these sea-dogs and bear them away.

This distinctive attitude to time and technology made a spectacular contri-
bution to the visual fantasies that exploited the novelty of the first balloon
ascents. The imagination of many engravers had made the leap from the facts
of flight by balloon in the 1780s to the possibility of balloon battles and even
balloon journeys to the moon in time-to-come. The result of this shift in the
imagination—the first since the utopias of the Renaissance—appeared in
numerous prints produced throughout Europe. These showed French and
British vessels in close combat and vast Charlières with several decks of cannon sailing majestically through the air to bombard helpless infantry from
above. And these appeared some twenty years before Robert Fulton made the
first attempt to apply the new science to the art of war, when he demonstrated
his 'plunging boat' to the French in 1803. Already the sense of the new potential in science had begun to act upon the imagination. Men were beginning to
see that warfare might one day be very different from the tight squares and
charging cavalry of their times. In this way the first rudimentary impressions
of future wars had outrun the course of development years before Admiral St
Vincent declared that Fulton's invention of the submarine and torpedo 'was
laying the foundation for doing away with the Navy on which depended the
strength and prestige of Great Britain'.

The emergent technology of the industrial revolution was one factor that
helped to establish the tale of imaginary warfare as a political and literary
device. This joined with the anxieties aroused by the dangers of an invasion
during the war against Napoleon to produce the earliest English war fantasies
in print and prose. The prints began in the last years of the eighteenth century
and they continued until Nelson's victory at Trafalgar ended the Great Terror
caused by fear for the safety of Britain in the event of a French invasion. The
purpose of the engravers was to attack Napoleon and to stiffen the British will
to resist by showing the horrors to be expected from a French conquest. And
in like manner on the French side there were plays and prints to encourage the
nation in its efforts against the perfidious islanders. Some of these prints
showed extraordinary contrivances reputed to have been designed for the invasion of England: large rafts, capable of transporting thousands of men and their

equipment, with a windmill to provide motive power. Others displayed troop-carrying Montgolfières loaded with infantry and cavalry in the act of passing over Dover Castle; and some engravers bent hopeful fantasy to its limit in visions of a French army on the march through a newly constructed Channel Tunnel while up above a fleet of Charlières moved towards England.

In poetry and drama, writers on both sides of the Channel produced visions of a triumphant Britain repelling the invader, or of the invading French triumphing over the British. The *Anti-Jacobin* for 1798 gave excerpts from a play then running at the Théâtre des Variétés in Paris. This was *La Descente en Angleterre: Prophétie en deux actes*, an interesting piece which already contained many of the stock characters and incidents that were to be a feature of the imaginary war fiction of the 1890s. The scene is Dover and the hero is that well-known figure of chauvinistic literature, the enemy citizen whose passion for a just cause makes him work for the other side. The part is played by Fergusson, a tavern-keeper, who organizes a group of conspirators to seize Dover Castle in order to assist a French landing. But the course of a patriotic drama can never run smoothly, and the author brings on a useful means of suspense in the person of 'a traitor sold to the party of Pitt'. He reveals all. The conspirators are apprehended by the Governor of Dover Castle and condemned to death, but at the last moment the French land, save their friends from the scaffold, and set off at the double for London, the general officer in command crying out: 'Englishmen! Now is your time to destroy the British Government which has caused all your misfortunes, desolated your neighbours, and set Europe on fire. It is time that the fate of the people should no longer depend on the caprice of an individual.'

These sentiments have nothing to do with the fantastic technology of the invasion rafts and the projects for invading Britain by balloon. They spring from the universal desire to see the enemy as contemptible, inferior, and already defeated. As the course of these imaginary wars unfolds it becomes clear that, no matter who is the author and no matter what is the period of the story, these great wars of fiction are invariably directed by the internal principle that the greater the passion, the greater is the element of nationalistic fantasy. An indication of this can be seen from the dialogue of the conspirators in the first act of the *Descente en Angleterre*. The chief conspirator begins:

GORDON. My friends, I will not remind you of the crimes of the English Government: the long tyranny which it has exercised upon the seas; the disasters which it has carried into the Colonies; the perfidiousness which it employs to perpetuate the scourge of war. I will not talk of Pitt. You all know that cunning is his instrument, deception his element, and that his infernal policy would sacrifice all the belligerent nations to his ambition.

FERGUSSON. Yes, it is time to put a stop to the murderous plots of that destroyer of the human race.

A Conspirator. Philosophy has already devoted him to the execration of the people.
Gordon. English Patriots, you have already heard the thundering eloquence of
    Fox. He summons you to assert your rights.
Fergusson. We shall know how to defend them.
Gordon. His voice invokes liberty.
Fergusson. We will gain it at the expense of our lives.
Gordon. But let us not stop for idle talk; let us think of carrying out our plan.
    You are all decided in favour of a French descent that will shatter your chains,
    and bring freedom to your degraded country?
Conspirators. Yes! Yes!
Fergusson. We swear it.
Gordon. The guarantees of victory are Fox and his friends; our courage and
    Buonaparte. The genius of liberty watches over the people, and will soon crush
    their tyrants. [*He unfolds a large piece of paper*] In two hours the descent will be
    made. The regiment in this town is commanded by the brave Houssey. We can
    count on him; but we have everything to fear from the Commander of the Port;
    he is sold to Pitt and his infamous agents. We must anticipate him and strike
    the first blow.[5]

There is little difference between this fantasy of the Napoleonic period and
the mass production of British and German visions of future wars in the years
before 1914. What the dramatist had written in *La Descente en Angleterre*
would be repeated in the new setting of cruisers and torpedo boats in a tale
like Karl Bleibtreu's *Die 'Offensiv-Invasion' gegen England* of 1907.

Hope or fear, a desire to teach or to warn—these are the shaping influences
behind all these tales of future warfare. They are not the product of long med-
itations. Indeed, they come hot from the debates of their day and are little
more than projections of the talk going round the clubs, or of the most recent
pronouncements in the magazines and newspapers. For instance, as the British
marched and drilled for the day when they would oppose the expected French
landings, pamphlets and proclamations appeared everywhere to tell the nation
what could happen if the French ever managed to cross the Channel. Their
titles warned of coming terrors: *Buonaparte in Britain; A Warning Voice! or,
The frightful examples and awful experiences of other nations; The Warning Drum;
A Call to the People of England to resist Invaders; A Warning to Britons against
French Perfidy and Cruelty*. Some of them affected a direct approach that was
close to the realistic style of the contemporary plays and invasion stories.
There were, for example, the many lurid details in *The Prospect; or, A Brief
View of the Evil which the Common People of England are likely to suffer, by a
Successful Invasion from the French*. That pamphlet piled terror upon terror:

In every corner of the streets of Paris, papers are stuck up for the purpose of raising volunteers for the invasion of England; and as an inducement to enter into this
service, the paper states that

A FREE PILLAGE

shall be granted to every soldier that engages in the expedition.

But there is another reason, likewise, to be assigned for their endeavouring to invade us. Don't you see that Buonaparte wants to rule over Europe? Don't you see that he has already got a good way towards having it all under his power?

Propagandists on both sides of the Channel were united in exploiting the simple mechanisms of the new futuristic literature for the encouragement of their countrymen. In 1803 the French looked forward to a successful invasion of Great Britain, and equally sturdy British patriots foresaw a total defeat for the French.

One anti-French forecast appeared in a play of 1803, *The Invasion of England*. The author's purpose was quite simple: he wanted to show how British courage, resolution, and soldierly ability would triumph over the dastard French invaders. The theme of the play was to become very familiar in the imaginary wars published between 1871 and 1914: 'Better for us to fall than our country.' It had all the trappings of patriotism and sentiment. A young mother laments over her innocent children, and a handsome 'Lieutenant of the Navy' comes in with the news that the main French invasion forces had been defeated: 'They had slipt out of Boulogne, with a parcel of their flat boats full of troops, in a dark night—they had given our sloops of war the slip; but on daylight, being half-channel over, some of our frigates fell in with them.' That vision of future victory sprang from the mood of anger and alarm that had swept the country in 1803, when it was learnt that the First Consul had ordered the construction of invasion craft at Dunkirk and Cherbourg.

When the thousands of pinnaces, sloops, gunboats, and other craft were ready, the scheme was for the flotillas to assemble at Boulogne. From there, weather and the Royal Navy permitting, they would transport the invasion force across the Channel for the great task of stamping out British resistance to the French domination of Europe. The menace of a French invasion produced attitudes and responses that recall the more recent mood of 1940. 'Does haughty Gaul invasion threat?' wrote Robert Burns. 'Then let the louns beware, Sir!' The popular songs were far more forthright in what they had to say about the reception waiting for the enemy:

> Our vengeful blades shall reach those hearts
> Which seek our country's ruin;
> And night and morn our song shall be
> 'O give us Death—or Victory!'
> When with French blood our fields manured,
> We'll sing the dangers we've endured,
> The blessings we've defended.

As rumours of dead Germans and wrecked invasion barges had produced an imagined victory out of real anxieties in 1940, so the comparable situation during the time of the expected French invasion had fathered similar fantasies of a British victory in verse, in engravings, and in drama. Here, for instance, is the comforting vision of victory as it was reported in *The Armed Briton* by William Burke. A dragoon enters with the news for the heroine:

DRAGOON. The enemy, madam, after their landing, having pushed on and taken possession of this place, halted to arrange themselves for further operations— but our generals, aware of the intention and that this was only a division of the enemy, resolved to attack without delay, and by that means prevent their being joined by any other bodies of the invading force. With this view, they lost not a moment, but, collecting and forming the troops as they arrived, led them bravely on, the officers pointing out to the men [*imitating with his sword*] with their swords the enemy entrenched in front, and reminding them that in all probability the events of that day would give forever their country a prize to the conquerors. Four times our brave soldiers assaulted the enemy's works, but were as often compelled to retreat before a tremendous fire of grape-shot from their batteries. [*Georgiana appears terrified*] The carnage was now becoming dreadful—the ardour for attack slackened for the moment—but 'British courage was not to be subdued'. [*Looking fierce*] A few heroes were seen everywhere, flying sword in hand through the broken ranks, exhorting Britons 'not to abandon tamely their country.' In an instant the fatigued troops became re-animated—the unjust attack and danger of their country filled them with fresh indignation; and, nobly rallying in the midst of the enemy's shot and shells, those brave men once more rushed furiously on to the assault, over heaps of their slain countrymen.[6]

Nevertheless, the impartial observer has to report that on at least one occasion the French gave better than they got. If there are any prizes for patriotic drama, then *Les Prisonniers français en Angleterre* must take them all. As an opera in two acts, it scores well above average for originality; and it must have given the French audiences all they wanted to see and hear, since a printed version appeared soon after the first performance at the Théâtre des Variétés on 19 Germinal, Year VI, of the French Republic. In 1798 events in Europe were a guarantee of success for any projection of the victories-to-come. On 26 October 1797 the Directory had begun to prepare for the possibility of invading the United Kingdom by appointing Citizen General Bonaparte to be Commander-in-Chief of the Armée de l'Angleterre; and in February 1798 Napoleon had made a rapid inspection of the Channel ports to supervise military preparation and, in particular, to speed up the construction of invasion craft. Two months later, when *Les Prisonniers français en Angleterre* opened in Paris, Napoleon had to miss the first night because he was fully engaged with his plans for the assault on Egypt. By 19 May, however, when the main part of the French invasion fleet had sailed from Toulon, the Parisians could read the text of the new opera which carried a fulsome dedication *Au Général Buonaparté:*

YOUNG HERO! Terror of the English!
Graciously cast your eyes on this work,
And welcome it as the poor praise
Which the French render to your greatness.
Here we present the innumerable sufferings
Of our soldiers in their misery!

The curtain rises on a dark prison scene, French prisoners are sleeping wretchedly on the floor, and the time is eleven o'clock at night. Valcour, a French officer, begins a recitative in which he laments their sufferings—without food, without clothing, but never without hope. Scene II opens with the appearance of Clarice, the beauteous daughter of the brutal gaoler Varton, who declares her love for the prisoner Florival. Although her father hates the French, she knows they can look for help to the deputy-gaoler, Williams; and he appears promptly on cue in Scene V with news of the imminent arrival of French troops. Act II opens on a British coastal defence position: from the distance a sound of gunfire; in the foreground the British commander, a melancholy bass called Milord Smith, sings gloomily of disaster as he prepares to receive the enemy. By Scene VI he surrenders to *Le Général en Chef Français*: Clarice pleads successfully for her father: and all exeunt in pursuit of the craven British to a rousing chorus of 'Let us follow the path of glory!'

More striking than this, however, were the prints and caricatures that poured out in the United Kingdom during the period of the war against Napoleon. It was a time of intense patriotic activity for the many outstanding artists who regularly turned out satirical prints against the hated Bonaparte. One of the first of these anti-French prints appeared in 1796, the work of the brilliant caricaturist James Gillray. It was called the 'Promised Horrors of the French Invasion'; and it showed what many people were already forecasting: French troops barbarously slaughtering the inhabitants of London, and Pitt bound ready for execution.

The print-shops and the taverns filled with pictures that displayed 'Boney in Time for the Lord Mayor's Feast', where a gallant sailor leads in the hated Corsican before the Lord Mayor of London. Another popular variant was 'The Grand Triumphal Entry of the Chief Consul into London'. This showed Bonaparte riding through Westminster, bound hand and foot and sitting back to front on a dejected horse. The most frightening anticipations, however, must have been the various artists' impressions of the vast invasion craft, said to be waiting for a fair wind in Boulogne harbour. One of these claimed to be 'A Perspective Representation of the Raft, and its APPARATUS as invented by the FRENCH for their proposed INVASION OF ENGLAND'. The text below gave the ominous details:

This machine, which extends 2,100 feet in length by 1,500 in breadth, is to be navigated by four wheels, turned in the water by the action of the wind, and

moving with equal facility from whatever point it may blow. In the middle is a
Fort: this encloses mortars and perriers, for the defence of the troops in their
disembarkation; the Raft is armed on each side and at both ends with 36 and
48 pounders; the whole composing a battery of 500 pieces; and it is intended
to carry 60,000 men, etc.

*London, Published by Messrs. Laurie and Whittle, Fleet Street, January 22nd,
1798.*

If the prints were not enough to display the terrors-to-come, there was always
the opportunity of a visit to the enormous 'Panoramic Picture of Boulogne',
3,804 square feet of canvas painted by the celebrated marine artist John Serres.
The spectators stood in the central viewpoint, which represented '*The Leopard*,
the Flag Ship of Rear Admiral Louis . . . from the Stern Gallery of which the
Spectators view the Panorama'. In a circle round them they could see tomorrow's battles in the making—the principal buildings in Boulogne and the
'Encampments called the Army of England' in the far distance; French coastal
batteries and invasion craft in the middle distance; Bonaparte and Mamelukes
approaching the mortar battery in the foreground; and the Rear Admiral actively
engaged in 'persuing [*sic*] the affrighted flotilla which is taking refuge in the harbour of which Bonaparte is himself a spectator'.

The panorama, the plays, and especially the engravings produced by Gillray
and his contemporaries reveal the other point of origin for the new habit of
showing the dangers of the day fully realized in an imaginary future time of
terror. Indeed, only a different enemy and different circumstances distinguish
the purpose behind these prints and plays from the objectives that shaped
Saki's account of the German occupation of the United Kingdom in *When
William Came*. In their various ways all these earnest patriots were using the
art at their command to warn their countrymen to prepare, while they still had
time, against the dangers that might come.

But before the prose fiction of the imaginary war could begin to attract the
attention of a nation or of an entire continent, as *The Battle of Dorking* was to
do in 1871, new literary habits had still to emerge. The *Anti-Gallican*, for
instance, which was constant in its attacks on the French, gave most of the
space to addresses by bishops, generals, and gentlemen on the perils of invasion, and to poems that breathed defiance to the enemy. It was unusual to find
in one number a brief sketch of *London* under French occupation:

An Invasion Sketch

London, 10 Thermidor, year—
General Bonaparte made his public entrance into the Capital over London Bridge,
upon a charger from HIS BRITANNIC MAJESTY'S stables at Hanover, preceded by a
detachment of Mamelukes. He stopped upon the bridge a few seconds to survey
the number of ships in the river; and beckoning to one of his Aid-de-camps
ordered the French flag to be hoisted above the English—the English sailors on

board, who attempted to resist the execution of this order, were bayonetted, and thrown overboard. When he came to the bank, he smiled with complaisance upon a detachment of French grenadiers who had been sent to load the bullion in waggons, which had been previously put in requisition by the prefect of London, Citizen MENGAUD, for the purpose of being conveyed to France.[7]

But propaganda forecasts of this type were very brief and appeared very rarely before *The Battle of Dorking* and the beginnings of the arms race altered matters in Europe. Until 1871, and certainly during the first half of the nineteenth century, the anxieties of the nation still found their usual means of expression in satirical prints as well as through the customary channels of the public oration, the tracts against the peril of the day, and especially through the traditional medium of poetry. Burns, Coleridge, and Scott all wrote verses on the theme of the invasion danger. In 1803, when Napoleon was assembling his Armée de l'Angleterre across the Channel, Wordsworth wrote a prophetic poem of rejoicing over the destruction of the French invasion force that never appeared. Very appropriately it was called 'Anticipation':

> Shout, for a mighty Victory is won!
> On British ground the Invaders are laid low;
> The breath of Heaven has drifted them like snow,
> And left them lying in the silent sun,
> Never to rise again! The work is done.

There is no fundamental distinction between anxieties at a possible French invasion in 1803 and the detection of similar German plans in Erskine Childer's admirable *Riddle of the Sands* in 1903. Armaments, the size of population, and the power of European countries had all changed beyond precedent since Wellington's 70,000 troops had formed square and prepared to receive cavalry at Waterloo. In the space of one hundred years, the population of the United Kingdom had come close to trebling and the British people had employed all the contrivances of the new technology to establish an immense empire throughout the world. But no matter how great had been the change in circumstances, the situation of the island race remained unchanged. From Cecil to Marlborough, from Pitt to Asquith, the national policy had been grounded on the principle that the United Kingdom could never allow any single nation to be predominant in Europe, and that, in all operations affecting the security of the British Isles, the Royal Navy had to have decisive superiority. From Shakespeare to Churchill, it had been the constant refrain of poets and politicians that the narrow seas served the country in the office of 'a moat defensive to a house'. As Coleridge put it:

> And Ocean, 'mid his uproar wild,
> Speaks safety to his Island child!
> Hence for many a fearless age

Has social Quiet loved thy shore;
Nor ever proud Invader's rage
Or sacked thy towers, or stained thy fields with gore.

But that was in the days of sail, when it was easy to maintain British naval superiority. In an epoch of wooden ships, there was little to fear until steam and armour-plating revolutionized the nature of naval warfare, and conscription plus railways did the same for land warfare.

Out of these developments came a central paradox of the nineteenth century. While a poet like Tennyson could find reason for immense hope 'in the ringing grooves of change', the admirals and the generals only too often could see nothing but disaster in the coming of the steamship and the railway. As invention followed on invention in that hectic epoch, from the first screw propeller to the devastating use of the shell projectile at the Battle of Sinope in 1853, the exuberant delight in the new myth of progress covered a multitude of anxieties about the future of an island people in a time of unending technological advance. The generation of the Reform Bill and the Great Exhibition had been born under the twin sign of Watt and Napoleon. Steam power and continental militarism appeared to make a nightmare of the future for many thoughtful people—especially for the military. Some felt that the recent invention of the steamship had made the war against Napoleon a very close-run affair. That was the view of Robert Southey, the poet and the biographer of Nelson. He observed in 1829 that it was 'worthy of especial remark, and more especial gratitude, that if steam ships had been rendered manageable only ten years earlier—nay, even a less time—our deadly struggle with Buonaparte must have been decided upon our own soil: and in that case London might easily have shared the same fate as Moscow'.[8]

Southey's remarks throw light on the ceaseless give-and-take that has always provided both material and motive power for tales of the future in all places and at all times. His 'must have been' marks the intimate, operational connection between any contemporary frame of reference and the projection of the major hopes or the great fears of the day as writers have imagined these would be realized—sooner or later—in the years ahead. The primary obsessions in this most purposive literature give the committed writer a strictly limited range of possibilities on which to draw—a Patriot King bent on uniting all Europe, the repulse of French invaders, the celebration of future French victories in the war against the British, and so on over the years to the many nuclear catastrophe tales of the last four decades. Throughout all the varieties of futuristic literature, the unwritten formula has always been: Tomorrow begins Today. In the more prescriptive areas, where duty and necessity are the formative influences, the slogan is: What you have sown, that shall you reap.

All the evidence shows that any reading of the national interest must always generate its own unique message of inevitable disaster or glorious victory. That factor has already been evident in the invasion myths of the Napoleonic period, and it is most instructive to see how it has operated in the New World context of the first American anticipations of the war-to-come. Long before Chesney wrote his *Battle of Dorking*, the differences between North and South in the United States had already found their proper shape in two tales of the coming war between the states. The first was *The Partisan Leader*, a work of treason to some, published secretly in Washington with a false imprint and given the false date of 1856, twenty years in the future. The name of Edward William Sydney was intended to conceal the true identity of the author Nathaniel Tucker, who came from a distinguished Virginian family and was Professor of Law at William and Mary College. Tucker was totally dedicated to the rights of the Southern states, and in his tale of *The Partisan Leader* he set out to show how Virginia might secede from the Union. Although Edgar Allen Poe called it '*the best* American novel', the story failed to achieve its true potential as a tale of future warfare. Had Tucker succeeded, this history would have to talk of American inventiveness, and Chesney would make his appearance later on as a successor in the great tradition and not as the true originator he was. No doubt the world had to wait for a soldier to demonstrate the concentration of effort that maintains the rolling barrage in the successful tale of the war-to-come.

Tucker, however, took Sir Walter Scott as his model, and in imitation of the master he spread his story over two books, 392 pages, and some 110,000 words. Had Tucker limited himself to the main business of a war between the states, he might have produced an interesting book. Unfortunately, he had failed to understand that his task was to devise a pattern of fiction that would be emblematic of the identity, aspirations, and ideal future of Virginia. In consequence, he introduced long and irrelevant romantic interludes which affected both the coherence and the pace of the narrative. It is realistic enough, since the story accurately reflects the contemporary debate between Northern and Southern states and the malign activities of Martin Van Buren in the story are not unfair to the man who was to become the eighth President of the United States in 1837. There are no major confrontations, no great set-piece battles. The future of the South depends on a few heroic individuals and their small units of volunteers who ambush the federal troops not far from Lynchburg. The narrative hurtles onward with great speed; and, somewhat breathlessly, Tucker concludes in his grandiloquent way by noting how the projected engagement was the start of 'that gallant contest, in which Virginia achieved her independence, lifted the soiled banner of her sovereignty from the dust, and once more vindicated her proud motto which graces my title page—SIC SEMPER TYRANNIS!'

That first clash near Lynchburg proved to be a minor engagement in comparison with the battles of another civil war which Edmund Ruffin related at great length in *Anticipations of the Future, to serve as Lessons for the Present Time*, first published in Virginia in June 1860. If Tucker wrote too little about the coming war between the states, Edmund Ruffin wrote far too much. Like Tucker, he belonged to the old gentry and is now remembered for the work he did to raise the standards of farming in Virginia and South Carolina before there were colleges of agriculture. Out of his devotion to the Southern cause, Ruffin looked into the future and created a wish-fulfilment fantasy of 424 pages in which the Southern Confederacy was seen to triumph in the coming struggle. The prospects are most agreeable. By the end of the future war in 1870, the Southern states could expect 'to thrive and flourish, drawing growth and vigor and wealth from nearly all the sources which had heretofore supplied the whole former United States, and of which the former benefits were retained mostly by the northern portion, and especially by New England'.

This tale of battles long ago makes unhappy reading in the late twentieth century. The great issues of the American Civil War—the right to secede from the Union, slavery, land grants, navigation of the Mississippi—have their place in the *ante bellum* account of the future war. This begins with a forecast that came close to the later reality: the Confederate attack on Fort Sumter in Charleston harbour (12 April 1861 in the historical record) would start in the Ruffin story on the night of 24 December 1867. The rest of his imaginary war is a luckless reversal of the true course of events, as the South goes from victory to victory. By 27 January 1870 he reports that readers of the London *Times* had news that the war was coming to an end, and that New England was likely to be abandoned by the other north Atlantic states:

And when the other northern Atlantic states (New York, Pennsylvania, New Jersey and Delaware) shall be left united with New England only, it is not probable they will consent to continue in that baleful connection, and then very feeble political position. These four states, bordering upon the great confederacy of not only the southern but the north-western states, will doubtless desire to be re-annexed to the great and prosperous body, even if yielding, as the necessary condition, all power for the future action of anti-slavery fanaticism. Then New England will be left alone, as it ought to be, without any political associates to rob of their wealth, or to hate and annoy or persecute, because of their diverse opinions, or preferred policy.

As these first American projections show, the shape of the future in the tales of future warfare will always conform to the pattern of contemporary expectations. Before the 1880s American propagandists did not turn out any accounts of wars with the British, the Canadians, or the Japanese for the good reason that the United States had not reached that point in its evolution when earnest patriots would begin to find potential enemies in other countries. That is equally true of the French. After all the plays, poems, and prints of the Napoleonic period, there was little talk of future wars until the events of 1870 directed the attention of the nation to the lost provinces and the great war that must come. For decades after 1815 the absence of any foreign danger was a licence for French writers to speculate as fancy suggested. So Louis Geoffroy took the opportunity to rewrite the course of recent events in his *Napoléon et la conquête du monde* (1835), an ingenious work of fiction and an early example of the alternative history. In it, Napoleon did not retreat from Moscow: he turned aside to Saint Petersburg, seized the Czar, restored the ancient kingdom of Poland, and by 1813 ruled all Europe—save for Britain, Sardinia, and Turkey. In the following year the Emperor finished off the British without any difficulty, although his plan of campaign ignored his main lines of communication. The invasion began with Bernadotte storming north from his bridgehead to capture Norwich, and it ended with Napoleon destroying the main British force, Duke of York commanding, in a great battle at Cambridge on 4 June 1814. The French then entered London. Napoleon would have nothing to do with the British plenipotentiaries, Castelreagh and Liverpool. The Emperor wanted his new subjects to know who was their master; and they learned their future in the *Decree of London*, a document in which Geoffroy displayed the most admirable malice, great inventiveness, and a sound understanding of imperial ambition:

We, Napoleon Emperor of the French, King of Italy, Protector of the Confederation of the Rhine etc., etc.
We have decreed and we decree all that follows:
Art. 1 The seas are free, and the different European states may recover the colonies they possessed before 1789.
Art. 2 England is reunited to the French Empire.
Art. 3 The House of Brunswick has ceased to reign over England.
Art. 4 King George III will take the title of feudatory king of the united kingdoms of Scotland and Ireland, paying an annual tribute of 5,000,000 francs to France, and furnishing troops and money as will be decided later.
Art. 5 The English parliament is suppressed.
Art. 6 The English constitution is that of the French Empire to which it belongs.
Art. 7 England is divided into twenty-two *départements*.

That was one French way of changing the world for the better. Another was to bring in the Cossacks and make a fresh start, as Ernest Coeurderoy arranged in his *Hurrah!!! Ou, La Révolution par les Cosaques* of 1854. That tumultuous story was an anarchist's tribute to the good society and to friendship between nations; for Coeurderoy anticipates the modern space invasion story by calling in the Cossacks to wipe out the infamy of monarchical government. The Cossacks lay about themselves with immense success, and quite soon *L'Europe de Papa* has vanished from history.

Real dangers, however, have always served to concentrate attention on the possible combinations that might form against any nation and on the technological developments that could change the balance of military or naval power. This sense of new dangers was behind the first invasion scares to alarm the United Kingdom after the defeat of Napoleon. It began with the growth of the French navy, and in particular with the Prince de Joinville's pamphlet of May 1844. The Prince was a son of Louis Philippe and an ardent supporter of French naval development. In his *Notes sur les forces navales de la France* of 1844 he sought to drive home the importance of the French fleet by describing how France could use the new steamships to reduce the naval superiority of the British. 'A fact of great importance,' he told the French, 'which has for some years been realized, has given us the means to raise up again our decayed naval power; to cause it to re-appear in another form, admirably adapted, to our resources and national genius. This fact is no other than the establishment and progress of navigation by steam.'[9]

Since the imagination had not yet mastered the scale of the changes then taking place at sea, de Joinville's account of the damage that could be done to British commerce and his indication of the way the steamship could facilitate operations against Britain were together responsible for a major panic over the possibility of invasion. The danger had been stated all too clearly by de Joinville: 'With a steam navy an aggressive war of the most audacious nature may be carried on at sea. We are then certain of our movements, at liberty in our actions; the weather, the wind, the tides will no longer interfere with us.' In consequence, the nation began to lose faith in the abiding principle, so well put in Blackstone's famous dictum, that 'the royal navy of England hath ever been its greatest defence and ornament'. Thus, in 1845 Palmerston was for a time ready to believe it possible for the French to convey a large force across the Channel on a favourable night. He told the Commons: '. . . the Channel is no longer a barrier. Steam navigation has rendered that which was before impassable by a military force nothing more than a river passable by a steam bridge.'[10] And in 1848 Wellington himself unwittingly added to the general anxiety when a letter of his on national defence to Sir John Burgoyne, Inspector-General of Fortifications, was published in the *Morning Chronicle* without his knowledge. The letter was a considerable shock, since the public for the most part ignored the limiting conditions Wellington had been careful to write into his opinion. They forgot his point that 'if it be true that the exertions of the fleet alone are not sufficient to provide for our defence', and they saw only the terrible warning that 'we are not safe for a week after the declaration of war'.

The many profound changes in the pattern of warfare since the 1840s make it difficult for us to appreciate the full extent of the shock caused by Wellington's letter. His great prestige only served to confirm the worst fears that the days of Britain's insular security were over; for the Duke had said that, apart from the Dover area, there was 'not a spot on the coast on which infantry might not be thrown on shore at any time of the tide, with any wind, and in any weather'. The characteristically blunt statement from Wellington caused a major panic in many papers. It seemed to deny many accepted ideas consecrated by centuries of repetition. The poet Campbell had boasted in some famous lines that Britannia required no bulwarks—'no towers along the steep'. But the new steamships seemed to destroy this natural order of society; and for this reason many found it difficult to make the necessary mental adjustment from the traditional picture of Nelson's weather-beaten ships on perpetual watch outside the French ports to the new era of steamships and possible invasions.

It was certainly no simple matter of steamships moving secretly by night across the Channel. And the Prince Consort was only revealing half the story when he announced in 1850 that 'nobody who has paid any attention to the peculiar features of our present era will doubt for a moment that we are living at a period of most wonderful transition'. For the steamship panic of the 1840s marked the beginnings of a process of transition and rapid development in every aspect of warfare that has not yet ended.

One immediate effect was that naval tactics of a sudden became a matter of guesswork and the signal books had to be rewritten. Technology had come bearing many gifts that were to prove dangerous, and as early as the 1840s anxious questions were being asked about the state of the national defences and about the best equipment for the armed forces. At times even the Duke of Wellington did not know the right answer, as Lord Hardinge discovered in 1815, when he argued in favour of issuing the new Minié rifle to the infantry. The Duke would not consent. The arms race had started and Hardinge feared that in the course of the next three or four years there would be a general war in Europe: 'we shall be involved in it, and we shall be beaten unless we have a rifle'.[11]

From the steamship episode of the 1840s to the many alarms in the years before 1914, not a decade passed without a national commotion of some kind. At times the alarm would sound on an incident such as the engagement between the ironclad *Monitor* and the Confederate *Merrimac* during the American Civil War. According to *The Times*, it meant the end of British naval supremacy, since the performance of the new ironclad had made all but the *Warrior* and the *Ironside* obsolete. And at once the press began to cry: 'We are actually without a war fleet. We shall be outstripped to a certainty by America, and possibly by France, if we do not move at once. Already America is preparing to finish her Stevens battery, which promises to be to the *Monitor* what that was to the *Merrimac*.'[12]

On other occasions the panic would start from a political development like the *coup d'état* by Louis Napoleon in December 1851. This made him dictator of France, and at once all the worst memories of the first Napoleon revived to make the year 1852 another time of anxiety. In the January of that year the Prince Consort told Prince William of Prussia that the public was 'occupied and bothered by the idea of a possible French invasion'. Then, in the May of the same year Queen Victoria wrote to the Earl of Derby that 'all the Foreign Powers have to be careful about is to receive an assurance that the *Empire* does *not* mean *a return to the policy of the Empire*, but that existing treaties will be acknowledged and adhered to'.[13] Month by month there was an unbroken series of pamphlets, books, and articles in the press which anxiously examined the state of the national defences. One of these was an anonymous prediction of twenty-three pages, *A History of the sudden and terrible invasion of England by the French in the month of May, 1852*. It foretold how 'that little Corsican, Louis Napoleon Bonaparte', improved on his uncle by launching a successful invasion of Britain. The story anticipated several of the devices Chesney was to use twenty years later in *The Battle of Dorking*. The author concentrated on the supreme danger of not being prepared for the new kind of steamboat warfare; and in the Chesney manner he pointed to the many failings on the British side. Thus, national indolence and the inadequate equipment of the troops brought on the final disaster, when 'the whole of the English army was annihilated before they could come within shot of the enemy'.

The French invasion follows the pattern of contemporary fears. Louis Napoleon makes secret preparations to attack Britain, and when all is ready a French fleet of fourteen steamers crosses the Channel and lands the advance guard on the Sussex coast. In little more than a fortnight the French have crushed all opposition, seized London, and imposed an enormous indemnity. The author mixes anger with ridicule in order to make the reader see the dangers threatening the country:

When parliament met, some talked like old women of the Law of Nations, and Declarations of War; forgetting that he who had stolen the liberties of his country, like a thief in the night, would not be very likely to hesitate where only his enemies were concerned; others, no less like old women, vaunted the courage of the people, and spoke in the true Bobadil style of swallowing a disciplined army of Frenchmen like so many oysters, forgetting that an English mob, which is all that could be raised at a short notice, and which may easily be repulsed by half-a-dozen policemen, was not likely to stand firm very long against the deadly fire of the Tirailleurs de Vincennes; while a third party, more foolish than either, pointed triumphantly to the fortifications of Portsmouth, and hinted historically at Tilbury and the Spanish Armada, just as if the French generals knew nothing of the science of war, and would invade England through a strong fortress or by a dangerous river, rather than, as they actually did, force the position in the centre, whence the road to London was the shortest, and where the people were utterly and entirely destitute of the means of defence.[14]

The chief device for commenting on a crisis, however, was still the book, the pamphlet, and the article in the monthly or quarterly journals. They poured from the presses year by year: *Thoughts on National Defence; The Defensive Position of England; On National Defence in England; A Memoir on the Defence of East Suffolk; System of National Defence; Measures for the Defence of England; The National Defences; The Invasions and Projected Invasions of England; A French Officer's Ideas upon the Defence of England; Political and Legislative Considerations on National Defence; On the Defence of England: Naval, Littoral and Internal; The Defences of London; The Perils of Portsmouth; The Fleet of the Future; National Defences: The Great Question of the Day.*

These and hundreds like them filled the decades between 1840 and 1880 with their forecasts of disaster, with complaints, denunciations, plans, and counter-plans for the defence of the British Isles. All of them were variations on the Prince Consort's theme of 'most wonderful transition', and all of them were trying to find some effective and final answer to the problem of adapting the armed forces and their equipment to the new dynamics of warfare. For one writer, the only hopeful fact in a gloomy future was that, 'if scientific discoveries have increased the faculty of attack, and diminished that of defence in general, exception has to be made in reference to the attack of maritime fortresses by floating vessels'.[15] Here at least the invention of hollow shot gave the shore batteries every advantage. The guessing game had begun. Would new weapons have a decisive effect in the next war? Would the advantage lie with the attack or the defence? One distinguished officer thought that the odds were certainly on the side of the invader:

It is a question that has been considered, whether the introduction of more rapid means of locomotion through the adoption of steam, and of more speedy methods of the communication of information through the adoption of electricity, will be more favourable in future wars to the attack or the defence. Both will no doubt to a certain extent be benefited, but as the essence of the success of an attack in most cases depends upon surprise, and in all cases on rapidity of action, it appears certain that the assailant will derive more advantage from these improvements than those who have to resist his assault. In case of an invasion being at a future time directed against our shores, it will not now be necessary that the transports or the armed vessels that are to convey them should be assembled in any particular port, or collected beneath some well-marked feature of the shore where their concentration must be known to the cruisers of the enemies. It will be only necessary that a certain point should be fixed upon the chart as the rendezvous for their flotilla, and only known to the commanders who have to direct the operations. These, too, would not necessarily be acquainted with the spot, until they had already left their ports, and were out of sight of land. The power of steam would allow these vessels to be collected at a certain point without danger of delay, or of being blown back to friendly harbours by unfavourable breezes. The introduction of the electric telegraph would allow various descents to be made on

different parts of the coasts simultaneously, and would thus prevent the great
advantage which has hitherto accrued to the defence of acting on interior lines in
such a manner as to allow different parts of an assailant force, attacking at intervals
to be overwhelmed by the superior force of the defendant thrown judiciously on
particular points, while other points of assault were watched and defended by weak
detachments.[16]

For many of these writers, the problem resolved itself into the facile solution of new ships for the navy, or new weapons for the army, or new
fortifications along the coast from Plymouth to the Thames. But these did not
answer the really crucial question of what was to be done if great continental
armies did manage to establish a bridgehead on this side of the English
Channel. How was an island nation to defend itself against the danger of
attack by immensely superior land forces? As Sir John Burgoyne had pointed
out to the Master-General of the Ordnance in his memorandum, *Observations
on the possible Results of a War with France, under our present system of Military
Preparation*, there were in 1846 some 30,000 regular troops in the whole of the
United Kingdom; and, when the troops needed for reserves and for garrison-
ing Ireland had been subtracted, there were at the most perhaps 10,000 left to
face an invading force ten times their number. The point was developed by
the Royal Commission on National Defence of 1859. As the commissioners
saw the matter the great danger was that

[if the Fleet,] from whatever cause, be unable to keep the command of the
Channel, it appears to your Commissioners that the insular position of the kingdom, so far from being an advantage, might prove a disadvantage for defensive
purposes, in as much as it would enable any superior Naval Power or Powers to
concentrate a larger body of troops on any part of our coasts, and more rapidly
and secretly than could be done against any neighbouring country having only a
land frontier; and an army so placed could maintain its base, and be reinforced,
and supplied with more facility than if dependent on land communications.[17]

One solution much favoured at this time was to establish special
fortifications in such vital areas as Portsmouth and Plymouth. Some of them
are still there, close to the anti-tank ditches and air-landing obstacles devised
against another threat of invasion. But, in fact, there were only two possible
answers to the problem: one was for Britain to find some acceptable means of
increasing the number of trained men available for home defence; the other
was to choose between the advantages of following the Prussian system of universal military service and the more distasteful French practice of using a bal-
lot system to augment their large regular forces. The one was unthinkable and
the other was impossible. And so a temporary answer was found in the expedient of directing the Lords-Lieutenant to establish formations of Volunteers
when there were fears of a French invasion in 1859. They were to consist
mainly of artillery batteries and engineers for coastal defence, as well as

infantry battalions organized in brigades for home defence. The First Lord of the Admiralty called on the Commons 'to restore the naval supremacy of England'; and in the debate on the National Defences Lord Lyndhurst warned the country of French intentions: 'the French are at the present moment building steamers for the purpose of transporting troops, each of which is being constructed to carry 2,500 men with all the necessary stores'.[18] The Poet Laureate rose to the occasion with a special poem on the Volunteer movement for *The Times* of 9 May:

The War

There is sound of thunder afar,
Storm in the south that darkens the day,
Storm of battle and thunder of war,
Well, if it do not roll our way.
Storm! storm! Riflemen form!
Ready, be ready to meet the storm!
Riflemen, riflemen, riflemen form!

Let your reforms for a moment go,
Look to your butts and take good aims,
Better a rotten borough or so
Than a rotten fleet or a city in flames!
Form! form! Riflemen form!
Ready, be ready to meet the storm!
Riflemen, riflemen, riflemen form!

The Volunteer system, however, in spite of all the rhetoric and the fashions it generated, could not be the final answer, since the role of the Volunteers was to supplement but not replace the regular forces. What these part-time troops might have to face was revealed in a succession of wars that suddenly flared up in Europe. For the Italian campaign of 1859, the French mobilized an army of 120,000. In the wars against Denmark in 1864 and against Austria in 1866, the Prussian General Staff showed a formidable capacity for using the railway, the telegraph and the mass forces of their conscript system to make the change from peace establishments to large armies in a brief space of time. Then came the war of 1870 and the stupefaction that followed on the rapidity and completeness of the German victories. For most observers would have agreed with Matthew Arnold, Professor of Poetry at the University of Oxford and Inspector of Schools, in his 'conviction as to the French always beating any number of Germans who come into the field against them. They will never be beaten by any nation but the English, for to every other nation they are, in efficiency and intelligence, decidedly superior'.[19] Convictions of this kind explain the astonishment of all who watched the rapid progress of the Franco-German War. What everyone had imagined to be the greatest military power in Europe had been crushed in a series of dazzling victories. The speed and scale of the operations seemed so unprecedented that the *Annual Register* for 1870 was at a loss for comparisons: 'Only by becoming, in imagination, the readers of some future historical work, and comparing it with any or all of the histories that now stand upon our shelves, can we form an idea of the place that must be found in the world's annals for the catastrophe of Sedan and the siege of Paris.'

But suppose the Fleet were absent one day, and suppose that the Prussian General Staff had secretly concentrated several armies close to railheads and North Sea ports: what could the Volunteers do when the German veterans stormed ashore somewhere on the South Coast? That was a hidden fear after 1870; and it was the starting-point for a sudden run of imaginary wars that followed on the warning vision at the end of Chesney's *Battle of Dorking*. It had happened to France and it could happen to Britain. But, Chesney wrote, the consequences would be even more terrible:

When I look at my country as it is now—its trade gone, its factories silent, its har- bours empty, a prey to pauperism and decay—when I see all this and think what Great Britain was in my youth, I ask myself whether I have really a heart or any sense of patriotism that I should have witnessed such degradation and still care to live.

Chapter Two

The Break-in Phase
The *Battle of Dorking* Episode

ON 18 January 1871 the Hohenzollerns took over the palace of the Bourbons and in the Galerie des Glaces at Versailles the German princes hailed the King of Prussia as the first Emperor of the new German Reich. The splendid ceremonies and sonorous proclamations marked the end of French military dominance in Europe and the emergence of a new political power. There was already a suggestion of coming changes in the Emperor's declaration: 'We undertake the Imperial dignity, conscious of the duty to protect with German loyalty the rights of the Empire and its members, to preserve peace, to maintain the independence of Germany, and to strengthen the power of the people.'

Ten days later, at the German headquarters, one of the French delegates, General de Valdan, signed the articles of an armistice between the two nations. And eleven days after that a distinguished officer of the Royal Engineers, writing from the India Office, sent John Blackwood the outline of a short story. He believed that if *Blackwood's Magazine* published his story it would drive home the need for a complete reorganization of the British military system. It was the starting-point for 'that wonderful and stirring romance', as Admiral Colomb called *The Battle of Dorking*.

The would-be contributor was Sir George Tomkyns Chesney, who had begun his military career as a second-lieutenant in the Bengal Engineers and after outstanding service in India had been recalled to establish the Royal Indian Civil Engineering College at Staines. Chesney, a colonel at this time, was an enterprising and energetic man, one of the new race of educated soldiers to be found in a specialist branch like the Royal Engineers. He had first written for *Blackwood's* in 1867; and on his return from India in 1870 he renewed his connection with the magazine in a letter in which he offered to review the second volume of Kaye's *History of India*. This made him a regular contributor and led to his suggestion for a story 'describing a successful invasion of England, and the collapse of our power and commerce in consequence.'

Chesney was fortunate enough to have found the right moment for discharging his frightening forecast upon the British people, since most of the year 1871 was passed in a mood of foreboding and anxiety for the future. In fact, Chesney's success owed everything to the moment and to his capacity for showing contemporary fears fully realized in an imaginary future. The accident of an effective style and the fact that *The Battle of Dorking* had appeared in a widely read magazine made Chesney the true begetter of the new fiction of imaginary warfare, although he was not the first in the field. In 1851 there had been the earlier publication of *A History of the . . . invasion of England by the French* which anticipated some of Chesney's methods; and there was the much more recent invasion story from Alfred Bates Richards, the editor of the *Morning Advertiser*. He had long campaigned for an improved system of national defence and had played a leading part in the establishment of the Volunteers in 1859.[1] In August 1870 Richards had a pamphlet printed for private circulation, *The Invasion of England (A possible tale of future times)*. It described an enemy invasion in which incompetent regulars and heroic Volunteers die in familiar English surroundings. It is possible that Chesney may have seen the pamphlet; but since he denied that he had copied from Richards, and since he had sent his sketch of an imaginary invasion to Blackwood twelve days before Richards had his own story printed in the *Morning Advertiser*, it is unlikely that Richards's story had any influence on him. He had nothing to learn from Richards. He was a far better writer and had an unusual imaginative capacity for transforming the facts of a military situation into an alarmingly realistic narrative. No matter who was first in time, there is no doubt at all that the whole of Europe considered that Chesney's *Battle of Dorking* had introduced a new type of purposive fiction. 'It is as vivid as Defoe,' so one contemporary thought, 'and I have done nothing but dream of invasion all the night through. The effect is almost too vivid.'[2]

The nation was a ready victim for a tale of terror that would realize its fears and the ominous predictions then being made. According to the *Pall Mall Gazette* of 9 January, 'most Englishmen believe that at present the country is not properly secured against attack, that its purely defensive forces are not sufficiently large or sufficiently organized to make invasion virtually impossible'. On 21 January Lord John Russell bore out this claim in a letter to *The Times* in which he recommended that a force of 200,000 troops, regulars and militia, should be retained in the United Kingdom. Once again, the general alarm began to sound throughout the press; and then, as news arrived of the entry of the German troops into Paris, the sense of anxiety increased markedly. Many feared that the event was symbolic—even prophetic—of what might yet happen to the British people. They thought that, but for good luck and the English Channel, those long lines of German infantry might have been moving through London on that grey and cheerless morning of 1 March, instead of parading past the veiled statues in the Place de la Concorde. The alarm even penetrated to the usually placid pages of *All the Year Round*: 'Half a million men, who have trodden down France and threatened England, may pine for fresh conquests. It may suddenly appear necessary for United Germany to win colonies, and a foothold in Central Asia, Persia or India.'[3] That was the mood of the year 1871. The *Annual Register*, looking back on the events of the year, saw it as a time of chronic anxiety, when Britain

was in one of her fits of periodical alarm about herself, and, to believe those who should know best, she was never in so fatally unprepared a condition as now, at a moment when the Prussian armaments were secretly gathering against her, if indeed the French war, as some of our journals more than insinuated, had not been undertaken chiefly as a prelude to the working-out of some sinister design upon ourselves.[4]

Chesney was indeed fortunate in the timing of *The Battle of Dorking*; he was still more fortunate in his gift for writing a vigorous narrative and in his experience as a military specialist. He followed in the tradition of the numerous army and navy officers who had been turning out pamphlets on the problems of national defence ever since the appearance of the steamship had revolutionized the conduct of warfare. But he broke with this tradition by presenting his arguments in fictional form. Moreover, although precedents for the story of imaginary warfare had existed long before Chesney, he owed little to them—despite many obvious affinities of mood and intention. His effectiveness as a writer owed everything to the new realistic technique he had borrowed deliberately from the stories of Erckmann-Chatrian, as well as to the imaginative procedure of attempting to assess the intentions of an enemy. In this sense the imaginary war is older than Alexander and Hannibal. Soldiers have always had to plan their campaigns on the basis of what they consider the enemy would do in certain circumstances. Add the methods of the realistic narrative to the practice of the military assessment, and the product is a full-scale story of imaginary warfare.

Chesney's most telling contrivance, however, was to transform the old-style military tract into a vivid narrative by presenting all his propaganda through the experiences of the Volunteer who tells the story. Chesney begins: 'You ask me to tell you, my grandchildren, something about my own share in the great events that happened fifty years ago. 'Tis sad work turning back to that bitter page in our history, but you may perhaps take profit in your new homes from the lesson it teaches. For us in England it came too late.' From that ominous start the narrative goes on its way, as the Volunteer tells of one disaster after another. He represents the well-intentioned Volunteer, the typical middle-class gentleman who meant well to his country, provided that he was not asked to pay what he thought was too high a price for national safety. In this way Chesney contrives to condemn both the nation and the system of defence. He achieves a double take, since the Volunteer stands for and comments on the follies that have allowed the enemy to invade and conquer. The story opens with his bitter reflections on what might have been—the 'if only' gambit of the purposive writer; and it advances from the first moments of apprehension through rising anxieties to the final terror and despair of total defeat.

The Volunteer is certainly not the hero of the story. His sole function is to play the part of narrator and lamenting chorus. The tragic hero is the nation itself, and in the manner of high tragedy the nation brings on its own doom; for, being neither completely good nor totally evil, it provokes the final disaster by an error of collective folly. It is a tragedy of them and us, set in black and white, a political myth for a period of nationalism, designed to excite feelings of pity and terror. As an unhappy Britain makes the swift change from apparent security and happiness to defeat and humiliation, the moral and military purpose of the story comes out in the lamentation of the closing lines:

The rich were idle and luxurious; the poor grudged the cost of defence. Politics had become a mere bidding for Radical votes, and those who should have led the nation stooped rather to pander to the selfishness of the day, and humoured the popular cry which denounced those who would secure the defence of the nation by enforced arming of its manhood, as interfering with the liberties of the people. Truly the nation was ripe for a fall.

The disaster was complete. There was no hope for a revival of national greatness, whereas a poem on similar themes, published anonymously in 1871, found consolation in the certainty of an ultimate victory for Britain:

> The German and the Muscovite
> Shall rule the narrow seas;
> Old England's flag shall cease to float
> In triumph on the breeze.

> The footstep of the invader
> Then England's shore shall know,
> While home-bred traitors give the hand
> To England's every foe.

> Disarmed before the foreigner,
> The knee shall humbly bend,
> And yield the treasures that she lacked
> The wisdom to defend.

> But not for aye—yet once again,
> When purged by fire and sword,
> The land her freedom shall regain,
> To manlier thoughts restored.

> Taught wisdom by disaster,
> England shall learn to know
> That trade is not the only gain,
> Heaven gives to man below.[5]

Chesney was too good a soldier and too sensible a writer to make the mistake of weakening his story with the anticlimax of producing hope out of disaster. In fact, the only weakness in the story is the device he uses to get rid of the Royal Navy and so arrange for the Germans to land their invasion forces without hindrance. He introduces an ingenious variation on the doctrine of 'the absence of the Fleet', which had dominated military thinking on home defence ever since the Duke of Wellington had written his famous letter to Sir John Burgoyne. The fear was that some accident—a storm or a naval war overseas—might lead to the dispersal of the Fleet; and this Chesney arranged to demonstrate in his prologue to the invasion:

I need hardly tell you how the crash came about. First, the rising in India drew away a part of our small army; then came the difficulty with America, which had been threatening for years, and we sent off ten thousand men to defend Canada—a handful which did not go far to strengthen the real defences of that country, but formed an irresistible temptation to the Americans to try and take them prisoners, especially as the contingent included three battalions of the Guards. Thus the regular army at home was even smaller than usual, and nearly half of it was in Ireland to check the talked-of Fenian invasion fitting out in the West. Worse still—though I do not know it would really have mattered as things turned out—the fleet was scattered abroad; some ships to guard the West Indies, others to check privateering in the China Seas, and a large part to try and protect our colonies on the Northern Pacific shore of America, where, with incredible folly, we continued to retain possessions which we could not possibly defend.[6]

The Germans seize the moment of our maximum weakness to launch the war they had been secretly planning for many years. Chesney shows in so many words how the new forces of the centralized nation-state and of modern technology had made possible a sudden and overwhelming attack. It is a restatement of that War of Surprises in 1870. Telegraphic communications are suddenly cut off; embassies and legations are sent packing at an hour's notice. But the difference is that in the ports from the Baltic to Ostend troops hurry aboard the waiting transports. The Volunteer reports the preparations for war and in his other role as commentator directs the devastating cannonade of Chesney's criticism upon the frightened reader:

But everything had been arranged beforehand; nor ought we to have been surprised, for we had seen the same Power, only a few months before, move down half a million men on a few days' notice, to conquer the greatest military nation in Europe, with no more fuss than our War Office used to make over the transport of a brigade from Aldershot to Brighton.

This is the strategy of Chesney's military moralizing on the duty of national defence. *They* show enterprise, discipline, and exceptional military abilities: *we* are feckless, unprepared, and have been imprudent enough to send off the best part of the Fleet on a fool's errand to the Dardanelles. There are even secret weapons to change the course of European history and allow the author to bring the enemy ashore without interference from the Royal Navy. What is left of the Fleet in home waters sails to seek out and destroy the would-be invasion forces; but the enemy fleet very sensibly 'evaded the conflict at close quarters, and, sheering off, left behind them the fatal engines which sent our ships, one after the other, to the bottom'. The Government, it appears, had received warnings of the invention; but to the nation this stunning blow was utterly unexpected. These secret weapons—presumably mines or torpedoes— were the only weakness in the story. They caused Charles Yriarte, who trans- lated *The Battle of Dorking* into French, to exclaim upon the 'affair of five lines' by which Chesney had so conveniently disposed of 'a force without rival in the world'.

But once that improbability has been accepted, then the whole narrative moves forward with great vigour through vividly described incidents, which tell the sad story of a nation's failure to prepare for the evil day. The reader experiences the disaster in a succession of personal and national tragedies as they are related by Chesney. The Volunteer recounts the effect of the news on his family—father, mother, brother, sister; then comes the confusion at the office and the anxiety in the City; and then the difficulties of joining his unit and the hopeless incompetence of the attempt to destroy the invading force on the beaches. The story of the defence is a long tale of administrative chaos and inefficiency, made worse by the presence of large hordes of half-trained Volunteers, but relieved by attractive descriptions of familiar English scenery which make each disaster seem more terrible.

The commissariat fails to provide rations for the Volunteer's unit; and when they buy food in a village they discover that the regiment is without cooking equipment. But—far worse—when it takes up its position 'on the extremity of the ridge which runs from Guildford to Dorking', the regiment has no information whatsoever about the progress of the battle. The Volunteers deploy along their section of the line and wait for the enemy to arrive—without fear and without information. The least military-minded reader of *Blackwood's Magazine* could see that, in contrast to the German troops engaged in the war of 1870, the Volunteers were still prepared to fight in the manner of Waterloo. Chesney's description of a review by the com- manding general suggests that the army is commanded by old-style generals ready for an old-style war:

At last the whole line stood to arms, the bands struck up and the general com- manding our army corps came riding down with his staff. We had seen him several times before, as we had been frequently moving about the position during the morning; but he now made a sort of formal inspection. . . He was a tall thin man, with long light hair, very well mounted, and as he sat his horse with an erect seat, and came prancing down the line, at a little distance he looked as if he might be five-and-twenty; but I believe he had served more than fifty years, and had been made a peer for services performed when quite an old man. I remember that he had more decorations than there was room for on the breast of his coat, and wore them suspended like a necklace round his neck. Like all the other generals, he was dressed in blue, with a cocked-hat and feathers—a bad plan, I thought, for it made them very conspicuous. The general halted before our battalion, and after looking at us a while, made a short address: We had a post of honour next her Majesty's Guards, and would show ourselves worthy of it and of the name of Englishmen. It did not need, he said, to be a general to see the strength of our position; it was impregnable, if properly held.[7]

These fine last words to the troops are the prelude to Chesney's demonstration of heroic failure and monumental incompetence. In a quick succession of brilliantly observed incidents, he shows that the Volunteers are brave fellows, but are not trained for a modern war. They leave their positions at the end of an engagement, and a staff officer has to drive them back with a cry of 'Gentlemen, do, pray, join your regiments, or we shall be a regular mob.' Towards the end, as Chesney begins to hammer home the lesson, they realize where the fault lies: 'We felt, indeed, our need of discipline, and we saw plainly enough the slender chance of success coming out of troops so imperfectly trained as we were; but I think we were all determined to fight on as long as we could.'

There had never been anything to compare with this in English fiction before Chesney wrote *The Battle of Dorking*—neither in method nor in quality. For Chesney has the unusual distinction that his success helped to launch a new type of purposive fiction in which the whole aim was either to terrify the reader by a clear and merciless demonstration of the consequences to be expected from a country's shortcomings, or to prove the rightness of national policy by describing the course of a victorious war in the near future. The strong or weak points of a situation—moral, or political, or naval, or military— were presented in a triumphant or in a catastrophic manner according to the needs of the propaganda.

This technique was so well suited to a period of increasing nationalism and incessant change in armaments that writers in Europe and the United States were happy to apply the Chesney formula of defeat and disaster to their own versions of the next great war. First in the long line of variants was *La Bataille de Berlin en 1875* (1871) by Édouard Dangin, who transformed Chesney's Volunteer into an 'Old soldier of the Landwehr' and set him to describing the coming defeat of the Prussians. Another early application of the *Dorking* technique appeared in *The Invasion of 1883* (1876), where the anonymous Scottish author kept closely to Chesney's account of the secret assembling of the enemy troops:

Without a word of warning, large masses of men were conveyed in a single day from almost every part of the German Empire to Hamburg and Bremen, put on board the many large steamers secretly collected there for the purpose, and on a dark night, while the bulk of our fleet was lying off the Scheldt, watching another army which was known to be collecting under the walls of Antwerp, a force of 70,000 men of all arms left the shores of North Germany, and avoiding the Firth of Forth, which the Government had at last been induced to fortify, sailed up the Tay, and effected a landing in the neighbourhood of Dundee.

That borrowing from *The Battle of Dorking* is evidence of the colonel's originality. Before Chesney there had been little effective method in the few tales of the war-to-come that had appeared. After Chesney there were very few of these tales that did not employ the devices that had alarmed a nation, amazed a continent, and annoyed the Prime Minister.

Gladstone had good grounds for feeling annoyed at the upheaval created by *The Battle of Dorking*. Hitherto it had always been the crisis that had been responsible for the flood of pamphlets on the state of the Fleet or of the national defences; but in 1871 it was the publication of *The Battle of Dorking* in the form of a pamphlet that had caused the commotion. To a politician like Gladstone, who had begrudged money for ships and fortresses, it must have seemed decidedly improper and unjust that a colonel of engineers should have caused a political sensation with a short story in a respectable middle-class monthly magazine. He paid unwilling tribute to Chesney's skill as a writer and to the effectiveness of his story when he felt it was necessary to warn the nation against the dangers of alarmism. In a speech at Whitby, on 2 September 1871, he attacked *The Battle of Dorking* and all whom it had aroused. It was a heart-cry from the Treasury:

In *Blackwood's Magazine* there has lately been a famous article called 'The Battle of Dorking'. I should not mind this 'Battle of Dorking', if we could keep it to ourselves, if we could take care that nobody belonging to any other country should know that such follies could find currency or even favour with portions of the British public; but unfortunately these things go abroad, and they make us ridiculous in the eyes of the whole world. I do not say that the writers of them are not sincere—that is another matter—but I do say that the result of these things is practically the spending of more and more of your money. Be on your guard against alarmism. Depend upon it that there is not this astounding disposition on the part of all mankind to make us the objects of hatred.[8]

Gladstone could talk with some heat about the effects of Chesney's story, since it had set in motion a series of counter-attacks that lasted from May until September, when the success of the autumn manoeuvres showed that an invading force had little hope of leaving its beachhead. During those five months the episode attracted international attention. Coming so soon after the

German victories in 1870, and appearing in the midst of the greatest maritime power on earth, it was taken seriously outside the country. An indication of what *The Battle of Dorking* meant abroad can be seen in the editions immediately printed in Australia, Canada, New Zealand and the United States, in the numerous translations, and in the thirty-six pages Charles Yriarte wrote for his preface to the French edition. If there was amazement abroad, at home the feeling ranged from satisfaction to alarm and indignation. Kinglake, the historian of the Crimean War, wrote to congratulate John Blackwood and hoped that the story would prove 'a really effective mode of conveying a much-needed warning'. From the Carlton it was reported that no one could take up *Blackwood's* for five minutes without a waiter coming to ask if he had finished with it. By June the story had been reprinted as a sixpenny pamphlet, and in a month over 80,000 copies had been sold, mostly to readers for whom it had never been intended. This fact impressed foreign observers. They regarded the appearance of the story in bookshops and on railway bookstalls as an indication that the whole nation was involved in the alarm, and not simply the readers of the select monthlies. In fact, the press became a battlefield, as the counter-attacks and the anti-Chesney articles appeared in the papers and in the bookshops. Most of these began as short stories or articles in dailies like *The Times* and *St James's Gazette*. All of them employed Chesney's methods against him in their attempts to prove there had never been a German victory at Dorking, or that after the initial disaster the Fleet had returned from overseas and had routed the enemy. The number of these pamphlets and tracts, and the fact that they attacked Chesney's theme, are a remarkable sign of the alarm and indignation *The Battle of Dorking* had caused. They appeared by the week and by the month with their stories of victory: *After the Battle of Dorking, or What Became of the Invaders?*; *The Battle of Dorking: A Myth*; *The Battle of the Ironclads*; *The Cruise of the Anti-Torpedo*; *The Second Armada*; *What Happened after the Battle of Dorking*; *The Other Side at the Battle of Dorking*; *Chapters from Future History*. For Chesney's tale of defeat they substituted victories; they show how the Volunteers, who had failed so signally in Chesney's story, prove to be as good as the best regulars. For example, in *What Happened after the Battle of Dorking* the anonymous author dwells on the good discipline and the excellent training of the Volunteer forces. On several occasions he goes out of his way to describe how regular officers marvelled at the efficiency of the Volunteers. When a battalion carries out a difficult flanking movement, the regulars stand by: 'The old general and his staff had watched the admirable coolness with which this manoeuvre was executed. "Gad, colonel," he said to our commanding officer, "the smartest regiment of the Line couldn't have done that movement better."' Not even the veterans of Sedan could hope to conquer troops like these.

These counter-attacks produced some extraordinary pamphlets. One army officer, Lieutenant-Colonel William Hunter, published an *Army Speech dedicated to those who have been frightened by the Battle of Dorking*. He wrote 'to revive the drooping courage, to calm the shattered nerves of those who have been too lightly alarmed by the predicted woeful results of the phantom *Battle of Dorking*'. He attacked 'the extraordinary invasion panics' and showed that the British people were well able to take care of themselves. Anything could have happened during this period when the excitement was still running high. One enterprising publisher produced a faked issue of the *London Gazette*, which set out 'The official despatches and correspondence relative to the Battle of Dorking, as moved for in the House of Commons, 21st July 1920.' But by the time Chesney's story had been set to music, it was clear that the panic had begun to subside, for the music halls were singing:

> England invaded, what a strange idea!
> She, the invincible, has nought to fear.
> John Bull in his sleep one day got talking,
> And dreamt about a battle fought at Dorking.

And then in September there was the first of what subsequently became the annual army manoeuvres. They were a considerable novelty, for the German successes in the war of 1870 had been attributed in part to their practice of training troops in fire discipline and large-scale operations by means of annual manoeuvres designed to test both staff and troops. In 1871 Cardwell, who had done so much for Britain as Secretary for War, introduced a Bill to make it permissible for troops to be assembled in large numbers for the purposes of manoeuvres. The first of these began in September, and the innovation was closely watched by press and public, since the aim of the exercise was to test the co-operation between regulars, militia, and volunteers. The scheme was for the home forces to engage and repel an invading enemy. The results were felt to be very encouraging. The press gave signs of satisfaction, and *Punch* celebrated the success of the manoeuvres with a full-page drawing of Mr Punch reviewing members of the Army, the Militia, and the Volunteers. The caption was *All's (Pretty) Well!* That summed up the feeling of a country recovering from the alarm of the *Battle of Dorking* episode. As the *Daily News* wrote: 'If the supposition on which these manoeuvres were planned should ever become reality—if the fleet should be dispersed, the Channel crossed by an invading force, the armies along the coast defeated and scattered, and the enemy should have penetrated to the neighbourhood of the Hog's Back, on his way to London—some Sir Hope Grant of the time will render a very admirable account of himself.'[9] That was the end of the *Battle of Dorking* episode for 1871. The last state of the affair was that it became a stock joke to ask anyone with a trifling injury: 'Weren't you wounded at the

Battle of Dorking?' The country had decided there was little danger of an invasion; and Chesney could now look forward to fame, reputation, and eventually a seat in the House of Commons. In January 1872 he was writing to Blackwood asking for a higher rate of pay; in February he was asking Blackwood to use his good offices in his election to the Athenaeum; and in April he sent Blackwood his grateful thanks for the sum of £279 8s. 10d. in final settlement for *The Battle of Dorking*.

The colonel of engineers had earned his money. Chesney had revealed the workings of a new literary device, which was admirably adapted to the mood and methods of the new epoch of belligerent nationalism. But he had not won a military victory, since there is no evidence that his story had any influence on the reorganization of the Army. Chesney had gained a great literary success, since his story established the pattern for a predictive epic on the victory or defeat of a nation-species in the international struggle to survive. It was a narrow and limited form of fiction; but it could be effective to the point of causing a national panic, if an earnest patriot could describe telling incidents in the Chesney manner, making actions speak with far greater force than lengthy arguments about the state of the nation's defences. It was for this reason that the form of *The Battle of Dorking* became dominant in its field throughout Europe and its influence lasted until the outbreak of the First World War. As late as the year 1900, that astute publisher Grant Richards calculated that the reputation of Chesney's story was still powerful enough to sell a book for him. His project was *The New Battle of Dorking*, an account of a successful French invasion, which he had commissioned from Colonel Maude 'in the hope that it might have the same kind of success that its predecessor had had three or four decades earlier'. Then there was the American publisher, George Putnam, who paid a visit to England shortly before the outbreak of war in 1914. He went over the site of Chesney's battle with a copy of the story in his hand, and was amazed to find how closely Chesney had kept to the topography of the area. Finally, in 1940 the Nazis brought out a special edition under the menacing title of *Was England erwartet!*

There was the same interest in France. In August 1871 Charles Yriarte wrote his long preface to the translation, *Bataille de Dorking*, in which he made a detailed study of the reasons for the effectiveness of Chesney's story. He was so impressed by the vigour and ingenuity of the narrative that he wondered 'if such a book, published here in 1869, might not have had an influence on our future'. And, again in 1871, another Frenchman produced the first foreign imitation of Chesney when he recounted his comforting vision of a defeated Germany in *La Bataille de Berlin en 1875*, the first of many French fantasies of a war of national revenge for the humiliations of 1870. The author, Édouard Dangin, found considerable satisfaction in the hope that the burden of conscription and the indemnity paid by France would lead to the swift decline of Germany. His desire to make the Germans suffer for what they had done to France shapes the course of his imaginary war, which comes to a brisk finish with a proclamation designed for French readers rather than a conquered enemy: 'Germans! We do not come to conquer you. It is not you on whom we make war, but your ruler who for four years has kept Europe in a state of war and troubled the peace of nations. Our sole desire is to break those iron fetters that oppress you and set you free.' The First World War, it would seem, had been desired and described long before it took place.

From 1871 onwards, Chesney's story showed Europe how to manipulate the new literature of anxiety and belligerent nationalism. Between 1871 and 1914 it was unusual to find a single year without some tale of future warfare appearing in some European country; for, wherever certain conditions existed, there would also be these tales of coming war. The conditions were that a nation should be actively concerned in the international manoeuvring of the time. Big-power—or nearly big-power—status alone qualified for entry into the new club. Spain and Serbia, for instance are innocent of the new fiction; and Ireland appears only when Irish patriots from North or South are involved in the internal political struggles of their great-power neighbour. The other conditions were that a nation should be troubled by naval or military problems, and that that nation should permit a free press to operate. Thus, the United States (at the start) and Russia (for most of the time) are outside the conflict of the imaginary wars for different reasons. The United States lacked the strong and permanent sense of a foreign menace required to touch off tales of future wars, and Russia lacked the free press and the free play of opinion that alone could produce private solutions for public perils.

Wherever these factors operated, the name and the method of Chesney were remembered. Both Italy and Germany offer an excellent illustration of this connection between the *Battle of Dorking* technique and the problems of a nation. About the end of the nineteenth century these two powers were both taken up with the question of their navies. On the Italian side it was a brief history of sharp decline, since the Italian fleet had failed to maintain its place at a time of rapid naval expansion. This was the characteristic Chesney situation; and in order to emphasize the danger to Italy, the Lega Navale Italiana in 1899 published a story of future naval defeat, *La Guerra del 190-*. The story reveals the influence of the Chesney tradition. The author explains that he has taken for his model the *Racconto di un Guardiano di Spiaggia*, which was *The Battle of Dorking* translated and transposed to an Italian setting in 1872. The introduction indicates both the tradition and the intention behind the story: 'At a distance of thirty years the *Racconto di un Guardiano di Spiaggia* lives again in *La Guerra del 190-*. They are two signals of alarm, two cries of dismay, two invocations to the sea, to the nation, and to all who still believe in the Fatherland.' The author certainly carries out his promise of alarm and dismay, since he foretells how the French are able to destroy the Italian fleet, bombard La Spezia with impunity, and land in force at Viareggio.

There was a comparable propaganda situation in Germany at this time, when Tirpitz had called for a further expansion of the navy. The enabling bill was passed by the Reichstag in the June of 1900, after the Centre Party had forced the government to cut the number of cruisers. While the argument about the size of the fleet was in progress, a German patriot, Gustav Erdmann, wrote his warning to the nation, *Wehrlos zur See*. The story was composed in the mood of the statement by von Bülow, the Foreign Minister, that 'in the coming century the German people must be either the hammer or the anvil'. For the purpose of his propaganda, Erdmann chose to show that an inadequate navy accounted for the fact that 'Germany's sons rested with their ships at the bottom of the sea.' He describes a future war in which Russia, France, and Italy attack Germany, Austro-Hungary, and Turkey. Like Chesney before him, he relates in detail such moments of national humiliation as the destruction of the Baltic fleet, and a naval blockade that leads to starvation, typhus epidemics, and mass suicides. The responsibility for this disaster rests with the guilty party in the Reichstag: 'Through the fault of the Reichstag Germany has fallen inexcusably behind other maritime nations in the expansion of her fleet.' And, again like Chesney, he ends the long tale of disaster by describing how Germany would be reduced to the level of a small power:

British and American industry seized the German markets throughout the world for themselves; and once their rival had been overthrown, they were strong enough to keep him down. That German industry, which a few weeks earlier had a dominant position in the world, to which Germany owed its wealth, saw itself suddenly reduced to the level of a small-state economy.

From all that has been said so far, it will be evident that Chesney's ability as a writer was in part responsible for the continental success that made *The Battle of Dorking* a model to be copied by all who had something to say about the state of a nation. But this is a literary explanation that does not answer the far more important question: Why does the mass production of this type of fiction begin in 1871, and why does it become a standard device for many writers in Britain, France and Germany? Part of the answer would seem to begin from the fact that the publication of *The Battle of Dorking* had coincided with the coming of a new mood throughout Europe. In one way this appeared as a general realization that the German victories in 1870 had altered the European power system, and that in consequence, as Matthew Arnold wrote in January 1871, 'one may look anxiously to see what is in the future for the changed Europe that we shall have'. One result of the change was that in France after 1871, for example, a succession of tales about future wars began. They appeared almost every year, growing in detail and in length, until they reached a climax in the large-scale epic forecasts of French victories written by Capitaine Danrit during the 1890s. The authors generally described how the enemy of the day—Germany, or sometimes Britain—was soundly defeated by the superior abilities and resources of the French troops.

Another reason for the rapid growth of the new literature of imaginary future wars was the extraordinary development in every type of armament that took place during the last quarter of the nineteenth century. The frequent changes in military equipment and the often spectacular advances in the design of quite new naval craft posed questions about the conduct of the next war which at times could cause considerable anxiety. Further, with the coming of universal literacy and the emergence of the popular press towards the end of the century, it became a general practice in the major European countries for writers to appeal directly to the mass of the people in order to win support for the military or naval measures they advocated.

The service writers were very clear about their objectives—the right votes for the right military or naval policies. Colonel John Frederick Maurice, for instance, wrote often and at length in *Blackwood*'s on the defence requirements of the nation, and in 1888 he published these articles as *The Balance of Military Power in Europe*. In the preface he was entirely candid about his intentions: 'The audience to which I am anxious to appeal are the lawyers, the business men, the doctors, the numbers of intelligent working men whom I know to be interested in the concerns of their country.' His reason was that the politicians could not 'ensure the efficiency of our small army and the necessary supremacy of our navy without your support, sir, or madam, who chance to be reading this. . . .':

There is no man living who, for the reasons I have named, is so directly your representative and mine as taxpayers as the Permanent Secretary of the Treasury. It is as you feel that he will act. If you choose to have such a navy and an army so mobile that you can by their aid ensure the support of the Central Powers in keeping Russia quiet, then you will have no war with Russia for India at all, in all human probability. At the worst, if you do, it will be a short one, for you will have some of the greatest Powers in the world on your side. There are few facts more certain in the world than that within the next ten years the fruits of your decision will have been gathered.

Chesney had by chance introduced a new device in the communications between a specialist group and a nation. As an engineer, he belonged to the then still small group of well-educated officers to be found in the British Army of the period: he could move from the direction of a large engineering college to a seat in the Commons, and he was as much at home with a staff paper as he was with writing an article for *Blackwood's*. He was in touch with the political and military thinking of his time; and when he suggested to John Blackwood that his idea for a tale about an imaginary invasion might be 'a useful way of bringing home to the country the necessity for a thorough reorganization', he was looking for a suitable medium through which he could communicate the convictions of a professional to an influential section of the community represented by readers of a monthly like *Blackwood's*.

Thereafter, once the tale of imaginary warfare had established itself as a natural propaganda device for the period before the First World War, it quickly became a favourite instrument with eminent persons, whether they could write effectively or not. Admirals, generals, and politicians turned naturally to telling the tale of the war-to-come, since it so conveniently allowed them to draw attention to whatever they thought was wrong with the armed forces. The rate of development in this field can be gauged from the fact that in 1871 an unknown colonel considered the middle-class *Blackwood's Magazine* to be a suitable channel for his ideas. By 1906 all the varied effects of the new mass dailies, universal literacy, the growth of armaments, and the ending of British isolation came together in the episode of the *Invasion of 1910*. With the agreement and active encouragement of Lord Northcliffe, Field-Marshall Lord Roberts worked in close association with the popular journalist, William Le Queux, in preparing a story about a German invasion of Britain in 1910 for serialization in the *Daily Mail*. Lord Roberts saw it as an opportunity to spread his conviction that Britain must be better prepared for a modern war. As he wrote in his commendation of the *Invasion of 1910*, 'The catastrophe that may happen if we still remain in our present state of unpreparedness is vividly and forcibly illustrated in Mr. Le Queux's new book which I recommend to the perusal of every one who has the welfare of the British Empire at heart.'

The world learnt certain lessons of technique and method from Chesney and his successors. Wherever a patriot feared that France, or Germany, or the United States was falling behind in the cold war of armaments and military organization, the tale of warning followed the example set by Chesney. Thus, in 1874 an English writer followed in the master's footsteps with a story of German aggression. He arranged that 'England was to learn, though happily not at so terrible a price, the bitter lesson taught to the French in 1870, that no amount of enthusiasm, nor temporary self-sacrifice, will make up for pre-arrangement and steady discipline'. The story, *The Carving of Turkey*, started off from an account of the dangers to be anticipated if ever Germany went to war again. It was an object lesson for the British people on the need to be prepared for the swift warfare of great armies. When Germany quarrels with Austria, there is no breathing-space for the victim:

The conflict began. The German troops were mobilised with a speed and accuracy even greater than that displayed in 1870. Nor was this surprising. No day had passed since that eventful time which had not seen them more prepared for future war. There was not a country in Europe the invasion of which had not been worked out in detail by their generals. There was not a railway carriage unnumbered and undestined. There was not a man in the whole enormous army whose billet for each successive day had not been determined, assigned, and registered—a feat which would never have been possible but for the facilities of information afforded by the wide-spread employment of German waiters. It had become in fact the business of Germany to make war; and that Germans are excellent men of business is well known to all the world. Such was the finish of that exquisite engine of despotism that at the slightest touch each citizen became a soldier; and without noise, without confusion, almost without enthusiasm the entire nation revealed itself as a compact and disciplined army.[10]

The nationality of the writers does not in any way affect the medium of communication. Germans and French use the device of the imaginary war to advance the interests they have most at heart. Indeed, the similarity of the peril produces stories with so much in common that a simple change of names would make them useful propaganda for the country against which they were intended.

This principle held good on both sides of the Atlantic. Change the language, the contestants, and the geography of any future war story, and *La Guerre qui vient* or *Der nächste Krieg* could pass for an American tale of the war against the British, or the Canadians, or the Japanese. The literary traditions that American writers had inherited from Europe and the experience of life in a technological society they shared with Europeans—these made for a general uniformity in the description of their future wars and of their better worlds-to-come. Like the Europeans, whenever some major issue set American writers thinking about the future of the nation, they responded in their own characteristic ways. This was apparent in the earliest American tales of future warfare, where the possibility of a civil war decided what Nathaniel Tucker and Edmund Ruffin were to write in their anticipations of the war between the states. Their stories were a false start, however. The tale of the future did not begin to develop in the United States before the 1880s. For two decades after the Civil War the American people were fully engaged in the tasks of rebuilding the economy, settling the Great Plains, and developing the greatest railway system in the world. When they finally turned their attention to possible wars of the future, American writers had a far wider choice of potential enemies than the Europeans. The would-be combatants of the Old World gave their whole attention to the enemy of the day—France against Germany, Britain against France, Italy against Austria. At that time, however, the United States did not have any major external enemy to serve as the focus for future war stories. American writers were, therefore, free to declare war upon any nations they considered to be a threat to the future of the United States—British, Canadians, Chinese, Mexicans, Spanish, or Japanese. The first of the new American wars was the great disaster related in Pierton Dooner's *Last Days of the Republic* of 1880. It is an early example of the mortal blow dealt by the enemy from within, then a novel device that would become a universal stereotype before the end of the century. On this occasion Chinese labourers combine to take over the United States; the Imperial Dragon flag of China is raised over the Capitol; Washington falls to the merciless yellow men; and, in keeping with the unrelenting workings of these propaganda stories, the end comes for the United States.

After the Chinese there were the British: ferocious enemies who destroy all before them in Samuel Rockwell Reed's *The War of 1886, Between the United States and Great Britain* (1882). Then there was an Irish interlude; *Ireland's War! Parnell Victorious* (1882) was published in New York to give Irish immigrants the pleasure of reading about the coming end of the British Empire. By 1888 the first indications of new thinking about the American role in the world appeared in *The Battle of the Swash and the Capture of Canada*, where Samuel Barton made it one of his aims to demonstrate the maritime weakness of his country: British warships patrol the Atlantic seaboard, causing immense havoc, devastating New York and destroying that sacred icon of Yankee enterprise, the Brooklyn Bridge. The story was intended to demonstrate the need for a satisfactory naval policy; it was a condemnation of the failure 'to adopt defensive precautions, or to encourage the reconstruction of the American Merchant Marine'.

The United States was then approaching that point in its rapid advance to world power when it would require a large fleet to safeguard its many interests overseas. Twenty years after the *Monitor* had revolutionized naval warfare, the United States had one of the smallest and weakest fleets in the world. Work on the first steel warships began only in 1883, and it was not until 1889 that Congress began to consider a construction programme for battleships. So, it was a sign of new times that the first American tale of future warfare to arouse any general interest was an account of a war at sea. The British are the necessary enemy in *The Stricken Nation* (1890), for the Royal Navy is made the instrument of well-merited retribution. The author, who wrote under the pseudonym of 'Stochastic', was Henry Grattan Donnelly. Donnelly had already tried his hand at writing tales of the future. In 1880 he published *The Coming Crown*, which he arranged as a series of press cuttings from American newspapers for 1882 in order to describe the projected activities of General Grant; and in 1883 he published *'84: A Political Revelation*, in which he reported on the imagined proceedings of the Democratic and Republican conventions.

Donnelly applied what he had learnt from writing these stories to his history of the war-to-come between the Americans and the British. It is instructive to see how his account of an American catastrophe in *The Stricken Nation* employed all the narrative techniques developed by the European prophets of future warfare. There is no evidence that he had read any of their stories; and it was certainly not necessary for him to learn from the Europeans, since the business of describing 'what would happen if . . . ' has always generated uniform descriptive methods. The destiny of the nation is a theme that lends itself to dramatic treatment. So, Donnelly presents his imaginary war as a contest between darkness and light. On one side there are the British, as vicious and unscrupulous as an American propagandist of Irish descent can make them. On the other side there are the great American people—innocents in a hostile world, living in a peaceful people's democracy fated to learn the bitter lesson that only might can protect the right.

Like so many of his European counterparts, Donnelly prudently bases his propaganda on points of pure prejudice. His talk about 'the traditional envy and hatred of England towards the United States' was part of the American mythology that derived from the legends of the War of Independence and was kept alive in the absurdly anti-British textbooks used in the state schools. Similarly, the references to the commercial expansion of the United Kingdom, the subsidies for new British steamship lines, and the political pressure on South American countries were stock devices in the Republican campaign against President Cleveland in 1888. To abuse the British, especially before audiences of Irish immigrants, was reckoned to be good politics. It is evident from *The Stricken Nation* that Donnelly reckoned it made for good writing as well.

Donnelly arranges the future to provide the evidence that will allow him 'to arraign before the American people their representatives in Congress, who in their blindness and folly were responsible for the defenceless position of the great cities on this coast'. This is the characteristic Chesney theme in a transatlantic setting. Another similarity between the Old World and the New is the balance of evil: the British are as willing and ready to do their worst to the Americans as the Germans had done to the British in *The Carving of Turkey*. The British fleet sails across the Atlantic and destroys most of the cities on the East Coast:

With nothing to fear in Europe, she could concentrate all her forces for an attack, which she well knew the United States was powerless to resist. For years her spies and agents had been at work in every Department of the American Government. She knew the weakest of our weak defences better than even our own engineers. She had on file plans of every port, charts of every harbor, tables of the valuation of every sea-port town, particulars of our torpedo arrangements; and she had her own soldiers specially detailed for the duty, in the guise of enlisted men in every branch of our service. There were British on our ships, British spies in our arsenals, and British influence had for years been powerful enough to defeat every attempt made to get appropriations for defence. This was accomplished by American representatives whose election to Congress to perform this very duty had been secured by a lavish outlay of British gold.[11]

This is the transatlantic version of perfidious Albion. It demonstrates the patriot's principle that controls so much of the feeling released in these tales of future warfare: all other nations are perfidious, and the enemy nation of the moment is the most perfidious of them all.

Although this may show that *The Battle of Dorking* gave rise to an international practice in the composition of these imaginary wars, it fails to give a final answer to the question, Why does the device of the imaginary war spread throughout Europe from 1871 onwards? Although it is apparent that the starting-point for this new type of fiction is an urgent sense of anxiety over some problem of the day, it does not seem possible to account completely for the continental scale of Chesney's success by the simple technical explanation of a good story at the right time. Behind the European reception and imitation of *The Battle of Dorking* stand the varied and often concealed influences of the new sciences and the even newer technologies: first, in the facilities that the electric telegraph offered for the rapid dissemination of news; second, and more profoundly, in the general expectation of change engendered both by the fact of technological advance and by theories of progress and evolutionary development. Between the alarm caused by Louis Napoleon's *coup d'état* in 1851 and the flood of pamphlets following on the appearance of *The Battle of Dorking* in 1871, the new electric telegraph had brought all the cities of Europe—indeed, almost all the great cities of the world—within a single communications system. The world had become a much smaller place since those days in 1839 when the Great Western Railway had installed the first telegraph line and the crowds had queued at Paddington to see 'this marvel of science which could transmit fifty signals a distance of 280,000 miles in a second'.[12]

To meet the speed with which the news had begun to flash from one end of Europe to another, there were quicker and more efficient typecasting and composing machines, which helped to reduce the cost and increase the size of publications. More people read more news sent more quickly than ever before. The incident of one evening could be read the next day in all the capitals of Europe. This fact was well understood by the press. On the occasion of the finally successful laying of the Atlantic Telegraph Cable in 1865, the newspapers indulged in the favourite Victorian habit of imagining the shape of things to come. One of them declared that

instantaneous communication between America and Europe means, of course, in its ultimate development, instantaneous communication all the world over. And so we shall have daily before our eyes a bird's-eye-view of human affairs over the entire surface of the globe, and we shall be able to study all nations, as day by day they are making contemporaneous pages of history.

And so, when *The Battle of Dorking* affected nerves at home and curiosity abroad, it came to enjoy a notoriety that was not possible in the days before the rotary press and Wheatstone's automatic printing telegraph.

Technology was behind the whole process of advance as it was seen and felt by the Victorians. Technology provided the power and the equipment for incessant change; it was a major source from which the nineteenth century derived evidence for the gospel of progress; and it had a decisive influence on the establishment of the new futuristic fiction that began to spread throughout Western literature after 1800. All the great advances, from the steam engine and the railway to the laying of the Atlantic Cable, the opening of the Suez Canal, and the ending of cholera epidemics, had helped to convert the evident fact of change into the dogma of unending progress,

The realization of constant change carried over into the imagination to produce an entirely new literature of forecasts and enquiries about the future condition of mankind, as well as satires, ideal states, and romances placed in the centuries ahead. Within a generation of the first balloon ascents and the first steam engines, a new literature of futuristic fiction had begun to emerge in Europe: steam balloons, steam ploughs, passenger kites, and electrical road vehicles were to be expected, so writers imagined, in the very different world of time-to-come. 'Change', 'progress', and 'improvement' were the new catchwords. As Jane Webb explained in a Gothic romance of 1827, *The Mummy: A Tale of the Twenty-second Century*, the future would be a time when 'education became universal and the technical terms of the abstruse sciences familiar to the lowest mechanics'. Similarly, on the evening of 1 February 1827, Goethe told Eckermann that he was confident of continued change, because 'through my whole life down to the present hour one great discovery has followed on another'. For this reason, he felt like 'one who walks towards the dawn and, when the sun rises, is astonished at its brilliancy'.

Ecstasies of this kind were common to the emergent industrial societies of the West. Poets agreed with engineers that technological development undoubtedly meant social—and often moral—improvement. By the 1840s it had become accepted social doctrine that science had led mankind to a new and desirable order of existence. With this went the characteristically modern attitude to time as a process of development, and to the present as a necessary but preliminary stage on the way to a better and more advanced future.

This Goethean delight in the dawn of a new order of human existence is admirably expressed in the rhapsodic verse of Tennyson's *Locksley Hall*. Tennyson was deeply moved by his contemplation of the 'wondrous Mother-Age'. It was heaven to be alive at a time when technology was leading men to final beatitude in a realizable future:

> When the centuries behind me like a fruitful land reposed;
> When I clung to all the present for the promise that it closed:
>
> When I dipt into the future far as human eye could see;
> Saw the Vision of the world, and all the wonder that would be.

For Walt Whitman, the future could be seen in the making of the United States. The pulses of the world beat, he said, to the rhythm of the great Western movement which he celebrated in a famous poem, 'Pioneers! O Pioneers!':

> All the past we leave behind,
> We debouch upon a newer, mightier world, varied world,
> Fresh and strong the world we seize, world of labor and the march,
>   Pioneers! O Pioneers!
>
> We detachments steady throwing,
> Down the edges, through the passes, up the mountains steep,
> Conquering, holding, daring, venturing as we go the unknown ways,
>   Pioneers! O Pioneers!
>
> We primeval forests felling,
> We the rivers stemming, vexing we and piercing deep the mines within,
> We the surface broad surveying, we the virgin soil upheaving,
>   Pioneers! O Pioneers!

Since the rate of change and the scale of innovation were so different from all that had previously occurred in human history, comparisons have to be made in terms of geological time. The marvels of that first industrial morning, when science was revealing its powers in an explosion of inventions across the world, can compare with 'the abominable mystery' of the Cretaceous Period, as Darwin called it, when the flowering plants suddenly appeared upon the earth and changed the course of life as it was then developing on this planet. The two events are related in size and in consequences. Indeed, the Tennysonian phrase about the 'Triumphs over time and space' comes straight from the new awareness of unprecedented changes and from the general realization that there was a real future—distinct and discernible—before the human race. The Prince Consort had said it was 'a period of most wonderful transition'; and an American had told de Tocqueville in 1832: 'There is a feeling among us about everything which prevents us aiming at permanence; there reigns in America a popular and universal belief in the progress of the human spirit. We are always expecting an improvement to be found in everything.'

The epoch of extrapolation had commenced. Men knew that the modifications of one day would the day after give rise to the improved model. And this knowledge was in its turn responsible for the vast literature about the future that ranges from a serious analysis of the prospects before democracy in America, as in de Tocqueville, to tales of future warfare and Wellsian visions of better worlds to come. In keeping with the methodology of science, a new race of investigators began to examine the present so that they might discern the forces that would shape the future. Thus, in 1831 the French administrator and aristocrat de Tocqueville obtained leave of absence from his post of

Juge auditeur and set off to study the new world of the United States. He began from the central fact of the political situation which he wished to examine: 'It is evident to all alike that a great democratic revolution is going on among us.' In the manner of the social scientist, he considered it would be necessary to study the United States, because it was the model of the system to which all things were tending in Europe: 'I confess that in America, I saw more than America; I sought the image of democracy itself, with its inclinations, its character, its prejudices, and its passions, in order to learn what we have to fear or to hope from its progress.'[13] The answers he expected to find in his journey across the United States would throw light on the likely course of development in Europe: 'I have undertaken not to see differently, but to look further than parties, and while they are busied for the morrow I have turned my thoughts to the Future.'

This conviction of a completely different future meant that in politics the advocate of a new measure had to present his case in terms of the better state of affairs to be expected from the changes he wished to see introduced. And conversely, it meant that a forecast of coming disasters might be an even more forceful device for pushing through a desirable reform. From this came the new fiction that aimed to persuade the reader to support present changes so that something better might emerge in the future. It was a popular form of enterprise and effort that grew rapidly until in the last quarter of the nineteenth century it became one of the most favoured modes of commenting on the state of society.

The new literature of the future was the imaginative and adaptive response of a society that had learnt to think in terms of origins, growth, and evolutionary advances. In fact, the final consolidation of the new futuristic utopias, dystopias, and imaginary wars of the nineteenth century followed on a fusion of evolutionary and progressive ideas about the time of the publication of *The Battle of Dorking* in 1871. This was the final mechanism required for the smooth functioning of the tale of the future, since it brought the apparent certainty of scientific law to the general conviction of progress. And so the interest that followed on the publication of the *Origin of Species* in November 1859 had the effect of providing a biological explanation for the constant technological progress and social struggle that all knew to be going on around them. By 1868 the *Saturday Review* noted that the influence of the *Origin of Species* had been rapid and far-reaching: 'So rapid has been the hold that it has taken on the public mind that the language incident to the explanation of the "struggle for life", and the gradual evolution of the new forms consequent thereon, has passed into the phraseology of everyday conversation.'[14]

Evidence for this can be seen in the sudden flowering about this time of the new fiction of the future, which owed as much to Darwinian ideas of change and development as it did to the more general notion of progress. The first main phase opened in France in 1863 with the publication of *Five Weeks in a Balloon* by Jules Verne; and from that date until his death in 1905 there was only one year in which Verne failed to delight his readers throughout the world with his tales of high adventure beneath the sea, in the air, and under the earth. By 1870 he had already turned out seven books when the second phase in the development of futuristic fiction opened, with the appearance of *The Coming Race* by Bulwer Lytton in 1871 and *Erewhon* by Samuel Butler in 1872.

Unlike Verne, the two Englishmen did not aim at wonder for the sake of wonder. Their use of science was entirely subsidiary to the primary purpose of satire. Both writers obtained much of the material for their attacks on Victorian society from Darwinism. With Butler the idea of evolution is central to the thought and method of his satire: the inhabitants of his imaginary land had long ago forbidden the use of machines, because they discovered that 'machines were ultimately destined to supplant the race of man, and to become instinct with a vitality as different from, and superior to, that of animals, as animal to vegetable life'. This suggestion of a conflict avoided, of a struggle for survival between two groups, is developed more fully in Bulwer Lytton's story of the highly advanced Vril-ya. Like Butler, he deals with the future relative rather than with the future absolute; his subterranean race exists contemporaneously with the Victorian world of 1871, but it has gained a degree of scientific knowledge and a control over nature far in advance of anything the Victorians had achieved. It is Verne's world of technological marvels—from robots and flying machines to the mysterious fluid, Vril, which gave them control of 'the natural energic agencies'. But there all similarities with Verne finish, since the aim of Lytton's story is to apply Darwinian ideas to his theme of social evolution. He explains the superiority of the Vril-ya by 'the intensity of their earlier struggles against obstacles in nature amidst the localities in which they had first settled'. And he ends on a note of menace, as he looks forward to the day when the human race may have to wage a great war for survival against the more advanced species from below the earth. Lytton's parting shot comes straight from the *Origin of Species*: 'If they ever emerged from these nether recesses into the light of day, they would, according to their own traditional persuasions of their ultimate destiny, destroy and replace our existent varieties of man.'

The sudden emergence of tales about the future,[15] which were based on Darwinism and on the idea of progress, followed on the war of 1870; and in that war two great nations had demonstrated the fact of technological progress in a savage struggle to survive. In 1815 the infantry had used a smooth-bore musket which had a moderately effective range of fifty yards; in 1870 they had rifles which were accurate up to twelve hundred yards. The slow and clumsy muzzle-loading cannon had given place to the Prussian field batteries equipped with the new breech-loaders from Krupps, which gave such a devastating performance at the Battle of Froeschwiller. This was frightening evidence of progress. It makes it easy to see how Chesney's *The Battle of Dorking* could have shocked a nation and at the same time established a new literature of imaginary warfare; for the Franco-German War had taken place at the time when ideas of natural conflict and the struggle to survive were merging with the earlier dogma of unending progress. It was widely assumed that human society was an integral part of nature and that it would therefore be controlled by the universal mechanism of the struggle for life. Nature's first law for mankind seemed to be an extension of De Candolle's principle that 'all the plants of a given country are at war with one another'. Ideas about the universal process of war came as naturally out of the Darwinian discourse about man and society as they did from the popular kings-and-heroes history of the period. Had not the Normans conquered the English, and had not the warlike Arab race swept out of the desert to overrun an effete Byzantine civilization? In India and Africa the advanced and better peoples of Europe were subduing the lesser races by a natural right to conquer. When one looked at the war between the French and Germans, it seemed to bear out Darwin's conclusions at the end of the *Origin of Species* that 'from the war of nature, from famine and death, the most exalted object which we are capable of conceiving, namely, the production of the higher animals, directly follows'.

Ideas of this kind were in full circulation at a time when, after decades of argument and anxiety about the nation's ability to prevent invasion in an epoch of steamships and ironclads, the sudden destruction of what had been considered the greatest military power in Europe gave rise to grave doubts about the future. Chesney worked on these anxieties and gave a military twist to Darwinian ideas by showing that in the new warfare of conscript armies and high-speed artillery only the fittest nation could hope to survive. And fitness meant military preparedness. His story was presented in terms of progress, the need to be ready for a new form of warfare, and the fact of a natural conflict between groups. He began with a picture of the days when 'London was growing bigger and bigger'; he goes on to the clamour that 'the army ought to be reorganized, and our defences strengthened against the enormous power for sudden attacks which it was seen other nations were able to put forth'. He finished by showing how the great conflict, which ended Britain's day as a dominant power, turned ultimately on the internal struggle that led to the nation's decline and fall: 'Power was then passing away from the class which had been used to rule, and to face political dangers, and which had brought the nation with honour unsullied through former struggles, into the hands of lower classes, uneducated, untrained to the use of political rights, and swayed by demagogues.' This was a soldier's application of Walter Bagehot's principle, put forward in 1868, that 'those nations which are the strongest tend to prevail, and in certain marked peculiarities the strongest are the best'.

The period of 1870–1 represents a grand climacteric in international affairs and in the complex of the popular notions about progress and evolution that are behind the emergence of the tale of the future as a major literary device. The war of 1870 had altered the power system in Europe, and in a more general way it was considered to have revealed the working of the Darwinian mechanism for the rise and decline of species. In fact, on the Continent the war had an immediate influence on the development of Social Darwinism, since the struggle between the French and Germans had the apparent characteristics of a struggle for survival between two rival species. In Britain, according to Lord Wolseley, the lesson of 1870 was that the country would have to change the army system or cease to be a great power:

Before the Franco-German War we had rather modelled ourselves upon the French army. In the Crimea we had found our military system in all its methods and phases to be hopelessly out of tune with modern ideas, and were astonished when we realized that it was obsolete when compared with that of the army which the Emperor Louis Napoleon had sent into the field. . . . But yet, though all thoughtful men who had served before Sebastopol realized how much our whole Army System needed reform, none of any real importance was effected. The Franco-German struggle at last opened the eyes of our people to the real state of our out-of-date Army, and to our absolute military inefficiency.[16]

The German victory was considered a triumph for the ideal of the nation-in-arms and a demonstration of the fact that in modern warfare only those best adapted to the new conditions could hope to survive. It was thought that the Germans had won because they were better. Soldiers like Wolseley argued that their organization was better and that the training of their officers—especially of the general staff—gave them a decided superiority over the French. The consequences of this were profound and far-reaching. They ranged from the establishment of great conscript armies in most European countries to the general adoption of the new literature of imaginary warfare, which was dedicated to the task of preparing nations for the new type of war. That was the central point in *The Battle of Dorking*. Chesney took his facts from the German campaign, added the device of secret weapons, and showed what would happen to Britain if it did not secure 'the defences of the nation by the enforced arming of its manhood'.

Already in 1871 the First World War was being prepared in fact and in fiction. The terrible slaughter of the Somme and Verdun was the direct consequence of the lessons taught by the German victory; for the nations took note that if they were to survive they would have to have the biggest armies and the most murderous weapons possible. From 1871 onwards, the major European powers prepared for the great war that Bismark had said would come one day. And for close on half a century, while the general staffs and the ministries argued about weapons, estimates, and tactics, the tale of the war-to-come was a dominant device in the field of purposive fiction. For the most part, certainly from 1871 to the appearance of the mass press in the 1890s the writers were naval and army officers who had something they thought it important to say at a time of rapidly changing armaments. Like Chesney, they confined themselves to the areas of the influence and effective opinion represented by the middle-class journals and the more important daily newspapers. They turned out short stories designed for publication in *The Times, St James's Gazette, Le Journal des Débats, Blackwood's Magazine, Le Monde Illustré.*

Everywhere the method was the same: the authors composed a piece based on a few statistics in manpower, armaments, or organization. Usually they kept very close to Chesney's method of relating the disaster through the experiences of a survivor who picks out the causes—bad training, the construction of a Channel Tunnel, the lack of capable engineer officers in the Royal Navy—that brought on the catastrophe. It was a British export to Europe that became an international commodity, since the fears of one country were frequently translated to provide pleasant reading in another. In December 1884, for example, an anonymous English author brought out *The Siege of London*, in which he attacked Gladstone's policies by showing that 'those who for years had been frittering away England's power' were responsible for a successful French invasion. Such a view had considerable appeal to a French audience, and six months later there duly appeared a translation, *La Bataille de Londres en 188–*. In the preface there is a very interesting analysis of the purpose and workings of the new tale of future war:

Like *The Battle of Dorking*, which was first attributed to Disraeli and then to a general in the British army, and like *The Battle of Port Said*, the author of which is reported to be a senior officer in the Royal Navy, *The Siege of London* belongs to a type of publication in which the English seem to excel, especially since the War of 1870. It can be classed under the heading of *Batailles imaginaires*. The purpose of these stories is either to criticize the action of the party in power, or to exert enough influence on public opinion to oblige the government to take precautions against possible troubles or probable conflagrations, and by these means secure the increase and improvement of the means of defending the country.

The range of these stories goes from the strictly tactical examination of possible fleet actions or army movements to nationalistic fantasies in which French—and later German—writers describe the last days of perfidious Albion. Many of these tales went the rounds of the European publishing houses, often in the route followed by an account of a naval war between France and Britain which was written by Spiridion Gopčević, an officer in the Austro-Hungarian Navy. This began as a story which appeared between July and September 1886 in the *Internationale Revue über die Gesamten Armeen und Flotten*. The story was *Der grosse Seekrieg im Jahre 1888*, a flat and painfully detailed account of an imaginary engagement between British and French naval forces in the Channel. It was very much a staff officer's piece, for it had more to do with lectures on strategy in a naval training establishment than with the art of fiction. After its appearance in the *Internationale Revue* the story was published as a pamphlet, and it was then translated by a commander of the Royal Navy and published by a Portsmouth firm in 1887. After that it waited until 1891, when French naval policy in the Mediterranean was affecting relations between Britain and France, and the French then brought out a translation, *Comment la France conquit l'Angleterre en 1888*.

On other occasions the to-and-fro process of publication and translation started in France. This can be seen at work in the publishing history of a French tale of stupendous revenge. It began in 1887 with the anonymous *Plus d'Angleterre* which ran through six editions in the first year of publication. The following year it was translated into English as *Down with England,* and in the same year it provoked a counter-attack, *Plus encore d'Angleterre*. The original was an apocalyptic vision of triumph and revenge in which the British suffered a swift and humiliating defeat.

As in all these tales, the plot of *Plus d'Angleterre* started from a recognized fact in contemporary history. On this occasion the point of origin was the ill feeling between the French and British over the occupation of Egypt in 1882. 'Is it not clear enough,' the author wrote, 'especially since 1882, that the English oligarchy has resumed its old struggle to the death with France?' The rest of the story was composed according to a formula of vengeance and victory, an early specimen of the nationalistic fiction of future warfare that was to be very popular in France, Germany, and Britain between 1890 and 1914. The tone of these stories can be gathered from the opening pages of *Plus d'Angleterre*.

We admit that there is something great, even something enormous, about England; and that is her audacity. This island kingdom, as they call it, which exploits the whole world and works night and day to embroil the European powers, has only its talent for intrigue with which to defend its approaches. The three great European powers comprise 180 million people and have 3 million soldiers under arms. The mistress of 310 million subjects, the ruler of the empire on which the sun never sets, has not even 200,000 regular troops that could be deployed for action, and of these half are in India and the colonies. Any one of the great powers with a quarter of its effective forces could finish off the schemer in her den, because the famous silver streak is no longer a defence and at the decisive moment her scattered fleet would be inferior to that of France.[17]

At this distance from the passions and indignation of the French patriot writing in 1887, it is possible to see the comic side of an international dispute that caused an anonymous Frenchman to find in Britain both the form and the occasion for his attack. He based his style on that 'ingenious fiction called the *Battle of Dorking*'; and he planned his book as a condemnation of a 'certain boorish Chauvinism' that prevailed on the other side of the Channel. Forgetful of what was then being said in France about Britain, he protested with good reason against the arrogance of the British people: 'It was an axiom that one English soldier was as good as three of any other nationality, and that every foreigner was an inferior and contemptible creature. It was taught in their schools that Britain had beaten the Russians in the Crimea without the French Army.' But there is a justice in the tale of the future that arranges the destinies of nations according to an international system of rewards and punishments. The proud and fickle British are condemned to perpetual seclusion in what remains of their island kingdom and suffer the loss of all their overseas possessions. The French—virtuous and deserving much—are given Dover, the Channel Islands, Gibraltar, Malta, West Africa, the West Indies, Tasmania, New Zealand, and most of the British islands in the Pacific. There is a clause in the peace treaty that reflects French cultural interests: 'The Egyptian antiquities taken from France after the Battle of Aboukir, and at this moment in the British Museum, will be returned to France together with the Elgin Marbles.' And finally, after this best of all possible wars has made the Germans see the wisdom of returning Alsace and Lorraine to France, the epic closes on a chauvinist's vision of the world reorganized to suit French interests through an arrangement by which 'France and Germany agreed on the terms of a reciprocal disarmament. The active army of either nation was not to exceed 200,000 men, and each was to be allowed full liberty to choose her form of military organization.'

But there were not many like this before the 1890s. Most of these stories—British and foreign—were short and practical pieces. They confined themselves to a pamphlet of thirty or forty pages in which the authors dealt with a single matter. For the most part they were all 'little Europeans' until the 1890s. No doubt this was a result of thinking in one-topic terms of the Channel Tunnel, the state of the nation's morals, the dangers of Irish self-government, and the indifference, mismanagement, and parsimony so many naval writers complained about for so long and so bitterly. The greater themes of world-wide warfare only became general with the full-length stories that writers like Capitaine Danrit in France and Louis Tracy in Britain produced for the new literate masses.

But even before the 1890s there were occasional stories that had caught the theme of the great globe, world communications, and the need to arrange the human race to suit the convenience of a dominant group. One of these pictures of the future anticipates the later vision of H. G. Wells: *Three Hundred Years Hence*, first published in 1881 by William Delisle Hay. The story sums up many of the great aspirations of the period: a world state, the Sahara irrigated and under cultivation, the seas farmed by 'algoculturists', flying machines, television, and all the desirable goods of applied science. It is an epic tale on the great Victorian theme of unending progress; and yet there are elements drawn from Darwinism and the whole complex of evolutionary ideas that help a citizen of the post-Hiroshima world to understand how ordinary men could contemplate without a blink the tales of death and destruction that poured from the presses of Europe between 1871 and 1914.

The author has a whole chapter on what he calls 'The Fate of the Inferior Races'. After describing the development of a form of world socialism, he comes to the conflict between the white and the non-white races. His ideas look forward to the Nuremberg rallies:

The old idea of universal fraternity had worn itself out; or rather it had become modified when elevated into the practical law of life. Throughout the Century of Peace, gradually, but steadily and surely, men's minds had become opened to the truth, had become sensible of the diversity of species, had become conscious of Nature's law of development. The incompatibility of certain races of men with others, that prevented their admixture with the general mass, and that held them aloof from the advantages of civilization, was slowly recognised. The stern logic of facts proclaimed the Negro and the Chinaman below the level of the Caucasian, and incapacitated from advance towards his intellectual standard. To the develop- ment of the White Man, the Black Man and the Yellow must ever remain inferior, and as the former raised himself higher and yet higher, so did those latter seem to sink out of Humanity and appear nearer and nearer to the brutes. The Social impulse had blindly proclaimed the equality of these races with the highest, theo- logy had declared them equals of the Teuton and the Sclav, but Nature decreed these doctrines to be impossible, and showed the Inferior Races but a step above the beasts, a wide degree below intellectual man. It was now incontrovertible that the faculty of Reason was not possessed by them in the same degree as the White Man, nor could it be developed in them beyond a very low point. This was the essential difference that proved the worthlessness of the Inferior Races as con- trasted with ourselves, and that therefore placed them outside the pale of Humanity and its brotherhood.[18]

This truly Hitlerian act of semantic cheating and self-deception was native to the time; it had fed on the pseudo-science of so many ideas about the sur- vival of the fittest. When grafted on to the sense of mission in an imperial people and the natural vanity that came from belonging to a dominant power, these ideas issued into fantasies of the world made safe for the White Man. It was the most brutal self-interest masquerading under the convenient notion that 'the duty of a rising race is either to absorb or to crush out of existence those with which it comes in contact, in order that the fittest and best may eventually survive'. The solution is still the Stone Age remedy of slaughtering the enemy; and the author gives an account of the wars and the air battles that butcher all who stand in the way of the White Man. The air armadas fly across China and Japan, sending down beneath them 'a rain of death to every breathing thing, a rain that exterminates the hopeless race, whose long presumption it had been that it existed in passive prejudice to the advance of United Man'. *Dulce bellum inexpertis*.

Chapter Three

Science and the Shape of Wars-to-Come, 1880–1914

BEFORE the beginning of the 1890s the first phase in the growth of the tale of imaginary warfare had come to an end. Although the methods revealed by Chesney were not forgotten, the second and major phase of this literature began with a change in the direction and with a rapid expansion of the new fiction. An early sign of the new influences at work was the appearance in 1884 of the popular and aggressive French story, *Les Malheurs de John Bull*; and this was followed in 1888 by Arnold-Forster's attempt to describe the likely course of a future naval engagement in his story, *In a Conning Tower*. What had hitherto been a middle-class exchange between the service writers and the readers of the monthly reviews and *The Times* quickly became an open market in which distinguished admirals competed and sometimes co-operated with enterprising journalists for the attention of the general reader. Behind this change, and shaping the stories of the period throughout Europe, were the increasingly powerful forces of mass journalism, mass literacy, and the mass emotions of extreme nationalism. The new tales of future warfare had the marks of a raw and frequently brutal epoch. At times they were violent and vindictive both in matter and in manner; they were often nationalistic to the point of hysteria; and they displayed an eagerness for novelty and sensation at the level of entertainment provided by the new journalism in publications like *Answers* and the *Daily Mail*. The cool tone, the objective approach to contemporary problems, the controlled emotion of Chesney now gave way on many occasions to excited language, crude emotionalism, and an often foolish idealization of the nation as the sole source of justice and the supreme arbiter in human affairs.

At the same time, there was a corresponding change in the form of these stories. During the Chesney period the account of the imaginary war had usually appeared as a short story, designed to be one item among many for one issue of a newspaper or of a monthly periodical. By the 1890s, following on the great expansion of the daily and weekly press, the new stories very often began as serials and, if successful, were immediately reprinted as full-length books. In this way it was often possible to combine the interest of matters of immediate political importance with the demand for excitement and adventure. This fact was noted by a new race of popular journalists like Louis Tracy, George Griffith, and William Le Queux. They had a standard formula for dealing with every situation: a major anxiety of the moment plus a racy and exciting narrative plus the introduction of eminent contemporary figures who would talk to the reader in the intimate manner favoured by the columnists of the *Daily Mail*. These were the distinctive features of much of the new fiction; and in essence it was the Chesney technique adapted to include romantic interludes and the treatment of personalities as practised by the popular press.

Another change appeared in the way the new tales covered a wide field of national interests. The writers looked into every aspect of future warfare, from the effects of new and as yet untried weapons to wild fantasies of anarchist uprisings throughout the world. Thus, Hugh Arnold-Forster, later to be Secretary of State for War, set out in 1888 without any political intentions to give the readers of *Murray's Magazine* 'a faithful idea of the possible course of an action between two modern ironclads availing themselves of all the weapons of offence and defence which an armoured ship at the present day possesses'. His story, *In a Conning Tower*, was a simple exercise of the imagination; and it proved to be so congenial to the interests of the period that after it was published as a book in 1891 it went into eight editions and was translated into five languages. In complete contrast, there was the case of William Le Queux, the tireless exploiter of any scare or anxiety that would 'make a story'. Most of the war fiction he produced was extraordinarily successful, partly because he chose to write on matters of great national concern and partly because his handling of his themes never rose above the level set by the new mass newspapers.

A notable example is to be found in the history of his first really profitable venture, *The Great War in England in 1897*, which first appeared as a serial in *Answers* during the war scare of 1893. Then, having helped to increase the circulation of *Answers*, it came out as a book in 1894 with a preface by Lord Roberts. It sold five editions in the first four weeks of publication; and it drew letters of commendation from the Duke of Connaught, Lord Wolseley, and other eminent personages. By 1899 it had gone through sixteen editions and had been accorded leading articles in the Paris *Figaro*, the Rome *Opinione*, and the *Secolo* of Milan.

The variety and number of the new publications reflect many forms of opinion and interest. In fact, they differ so much in quality and subject-matter, from sober military forecasts to tales of demon scientists eager to destroy humanity, that it is impossible to contain them all within a single explanation, beyond noting that they display a far greater interest in the details of armed conflict than had ever appeared before. War in all its fascination and terror was one theme that found its way into even the most purposive and political tales of future warfare. At every level in the nation, the subject of 'the next great war' attracted constant discussion and description. The boys' magazines were filled with serial after serial describing invasions by every possible enemy—French, German, Russian, even Chinese. In this the boys were only following the interests and preoccupations of their elders, for the new journalism represented by *Answers* and the *Daily Mail* saw that the public got what the editors thought their readers wanted. In fact, the immense popularity of these imaginary war stories depended on an extraordinary failure of the imagination. They represented a comfortable accommodation with the arms race: their projected campaigns and battles-to-come could never lead to immense casualty lists, the mobilization of nations, trench warfare, and the rapid development of new weapons. The seeming modernity of their narratives and the careful precision of the illustrations concealed archaic habits of mind and a romantic attachment to the self-transcending glories of warfare. They encouraged entirely illusory expectations about 'the Next Great War' which had a major part in shaping a mental geography of the future.

Since Chesney first wrote to *Blackwood's* in 1871, the links between writers and editors had become ever closer. Out of the general desire to perceive and comprehend the changes-to-come there occurred a marriage of like minds. It was a true market relationship, in which the editors and the entrepreneurs of the new popular press decided on the commodities that would sell to advantage. As the Le Queux episode demonstrated, many writers were eager to compose their stories to meet the market demand.

Again, the business of providing the up-to-date and the sensational led to the recruiting of artists to add their exciting images to the printed page. So, from the 1880s onwards, as the illustrated newspapers and magazines multiplied, the image and the word combined to give the readers the most dramatic pictures of contemporary and coming events. In their treatment of war, the editors and their artists were obedient to popular taste and faithful to the high style of narrative painting set by renowned French artists like Jean Louis Ernest Meissonnier, Édouard Detaille, and Adolphe Yvon. One outstanding example of their treatment of the heroic mode is the painting by Antoine-Jean Gros of *Napoleon on the Battlefield of Eylau* (1805). It is a dramatic eye-catching composition; and it succeeds perfectly in transforming a murderous battle (25 per cent casualties) into a magnificent set-piece glorification of the great commander. Whole regiments lie upon the snow where they have been struck down by cannon-fire and cavalry charges. But the painting deceives: as Delacroix pointed out, 'all this is but a setting for the sublime figure of Napoleon'. The same discrepancy between the battle as experienced and the battle-scene as a military icon marks the paintings still preserved in the Salle des Batailles in the Palace of Versailles. They exhibit a mythology of the heroic—destiny, resistance, endurance, triumph—concocted out of a nationalistic history. They deal in victories, never in defeats. The dead receive little attention.

The best example of the British style of military painting is undoubtedly the work of Lady Butler. She began her immensely successful career as a painter of Army and Empire when she exhibited *Calling the Roll* at the Royal Academy in 1874. The painting was the artistic sensation of the year, singled out for praise by the Prince of Wales, principal guest at the Academy Banquet, and shown to millions when it went on tour after the exhibition had ended. The artist soon gained a major reputation with a succession of much admired battle scenes—*Balaclava, Inkerman, Scotland for Ever, Defence of Rorke's Drift*—for these presented striking images of war and victory that flattered the national pride in a proud contemplation of British heroism, British fortitude, and exemplary British vigour.

War was the greatest of dramas, and the images of war would always hold the front page of the illustrated magazines or take their proper place in a series of 'our artist's impressions'. It was, however, an imagery of war that differed from the realities of gunfire, sinking ships, and hand-to-hand fighting: it tended to ignore the casualties by concentrating attention in headline fashion on the heroic incident. This practice generated, and depended on, a form of visual rhetoric in which the enemy often appeared as vile or as menacing as an artist could make them. This was particularly evident in the illustrated reports on colonial wars, where our troops would often appear like demigods visiting planet Earth, unruffled and frequently in immaculate dress; opposite them in studied groupings were the enemy—Sikhs, Pathans, Afghans, Matabele, Zulus, Sudanese, and the rest—who would display the extremes of savagery and barbarism. This practice can be seen at work, for instance, in the contemporary accounts of the Zulu War when the British took on Cetywayo. There were set-pieces for the heroic defence of Rorke's Drift, for the relief of Eshowe, and for the repulse of the Zulu impi at Kambula; but the episode that caught the attention of the editors was the unfortunate death of the former Prince Imperial of the French, the son of Napoleon III, who was killed when out with a reconnoitring party. Although the only information was the news of his death, the illustrated magazines saw to it that their readers could look on that event as it might have been. Some magazines carried special one-page sepia prints which presented an idealized image of a proud, self-confident, and resolute young man, seen in half-profile, hand on sword, calm defiance on his face, and around him a band of the vilest, most frightening, and brutal savages imaginable.

From time to time there were protests from the regimental officers who deplored these calculated misrepresentations of reported actions. One of the most uncompromising and revealing of these came from Lieutenant-Colonel Maurice, a distinguished soldier and frequent commentator on military affairs. He condemned the editors of the illustrated magazines, because they sent out hard-working artists to a war zone and then failed to use their sketches.

Instead, he complained, they substituted 'productions drawn from the fancy of their excellent wood-engravers, which have less relation to anything which ever happened than Mr. Tenniel's cartoons have to actual scenes in Parliament or elsewhere'. As soon as some heroic action had caught the public interest—for instance, the Defence of Rorke's Drift or the Charge of the Heavy Cavalry at Massawah on 28 August 1882—then the trade went to work on their picture of 'Sir Baker Russell leading the Cavalry at Massawah, composed in the back rooms of Fleet Street or the Strand long before it would be possible for the most zealous correspondents to have sent home from Africa the slightest sketch'. They falsified the events of Wolseley's campaign in Egypt, and from his own direct knowledge of the Ashantee campaign the indignant colonel testified that the editors and the engravers had transformed it into a campaign that never was:

We had been travelling through a dense forest, with snatches here and there of beautiful glades of rampant, over-luxuriant flowers, rich in their colouring, their growth and their texture, but nowhere was there anything but crowding, close-packed foliage that seemed on all sides to choke the view. Of this the artist on the spot had given a faithful reproduction. The artist who had to reproduce his work at home felt the absence of distance and middle distance to be hopelessly inartistic, and looked upon it as the blunder of a young hand to have crowded the lines of soldiers densely in between the masses of tropical vegetation. Accordingly, wide space and breath and air were introduced in Fleet Street. All the characteristics of the scene had disappeared, and, except in the one facsimile so condescendingly given, we were none of us able to recognize the scenes we had passed through.[1]

In this way, the word had begun to give ground to the image, and the visual has ever since become an increasing element in the interchange of news, views, and propaganda. When the first fully illustrated accounts of future wars began to appear in the illustrated magazines of the 1890s, the artists sought to give the most realistic appearance to their studied interpretations of future battles. That prized facility gained both in range and in realistic effects with the coming of the film industry; and it has advanced still further with television and video machines. The triumph of electronics has been to domesticate warfare. Nowadays anyone can sit at home, switch on the computer, enter a disk, and enjoy all the excitement of hunting the enemy in *Red Storm Rising*, fighting the enemy in *Tank Attack*, or helping the US Air Force to clear the skies in *Retaliator*. The manufacturers of the video war games would undoubtedly feel themselves at home with the newspaper proprietors who developed the popular press a century ago. In the 1890s they knew that war made for increased sales. Indeed, it was a Harmsworth principle that 'war not only created a supply of news but a demand for it. So deep-rooted is the fascination in war and things appertaining to it that . . . a paper has only to be able to put on its placard "A Great Battle" for its sales to mount up.'[2]

If there were no wars going on, then Harmsworth would send for the man who could invent them. William Le Queux had done so well for *Answers* with his serial account of *The Great War in England in 1897* that Harmsworth recalled him to duty on the occasion of the visit of the Russian Fleet to Toulon in 1894. That event had set the experts talking about the new treaty between the French and the Russians, and what dangers might come from it. It was an ideal opportunity for Alfred Harmsworth to plan a new serial with William Le Queux in order to 'promote interest in the idea of a larger Navy'. War was to break out in 1897 in *The Poisoned Bullet*, when the French and Russians attacked the British. Three weeks after the serial began, there were complaints from the management about the small number of war scenes. In three instalments hostilities had advanced no further than the bombardment of Newhaven and Brighton. The call went out for far more battles and far less action from the hero and heroine. The author replied with new instalments on 'The Battle of Beachy Head' and 'The Massacre of Eastbourne'; guns thundered, beautiful women prayed, blood flowed, and then it was the turn of Birmingham and Manchester to face the enemy.[3]

This eager search for the most vivid tales of future warfare had nothing to do with the principles of Milton's *Areopagitica;* it had everything to do with the circulation figures of the newspapers and the magazines. Witness the case of the middle-class and imperialist illustrated weekly, *Black and White*, which started publication in January 1891. The editor, who had been selected for his enterprise, tried out many devices in an attempt to increase his sales during the early months of publication. His most spectacular and successful experiment started within twelve months of the first number. It was *The Great War of 1892*, which gave Harmsworth and Le Queux the model for their first venture in the business of future war stories. In fact, the serial story printed in *Black and White* was a major innovation: the editor hoped to achieve the greatest possible accuracy in the projected episodes by arranging for Admiral Colomb and other eminent experts to write their own separate forecasts—political, naval, military—and by introducing illustrations that were designed to give the impression of photography. It was to be the perfection of the new illustrated journalism, the last word in presenting the shape of coming things. The editor revealed his intentions in the editorial he wrote to introduce the serial in January 1892. It is evident that he expected an increase in circulation figures from a story that combined imperialist ambition with the novelty and excitement of the next war:

The air is full of rumours of War. The European nations stand fully armed and prepared for instant mobilisation. Authorities are agreed that a GREAT WAR must break out in the immediate future, and that this War will be fought under novel and surprising conditions. All facts seem to indicate that the coming conflict will be the bloodiest in history, and must involve the most momentous consequences to the whole world. At any time the incident may occur which will precipitate the disaster.

The Editor of *Black and White*, considering that a forecast of the probable course of such a gigantic struggle will be of the highest interest, has sought the aid of the chief living authorities in international politics, in strategy, and in war; and in the present number appears the first instalment of the suppositious record of this future War. In the construction of this imaginary but possible history, Admiral Sir Philip Colomb, Mr. Charles Lowe, Mr. D. Christie Murray, Mr. F. Scudamore, and other experts in military campaigns have taken part. From week to week the course of the events will be narrated as though an actual war were in progress, and the Proprietors have obtained the assistance of Mr. F. Villiers, their own War Artist, Mr. C. W. Wyllie, Mr. J. Finniemore, Mr. W. F. Calderon and other artists, for the purpose of illustrating the scenes and episodes incident to the War. The various campaigns and political crises involved in the scheme, will be treated by writers and artists who have a particular knowledge of their subject, and the whole narrative will, it is hoped, present a full, vivid and interesting picture of the GREAT WAR of the Future—as it may be.

Although the war of 1892 could not in any sense be described as 'the blood-iest in history', certainly not by modern standards, the editor's hopes were fully realized. As the story came out week after week, supported by vivid illus-trations, it aroused considerable interest and discussion. It quickly appeared in book form and was then translated into several European languages. By 1894 the German version, *Der grosse Krieg von 189–*, had reached its fifth edition. In an introduction to the German text, General von Bülow attributed the great interest shown in the forecast both to what was said and also to the eminence of those who said it, especially Admiral Colomb. The German general consid-ered that *The Great War of 1892* was an important work; and his reasons sug-gest an explanation for the general popularity enjoyed by these stories in Europe: 'So far there has been no shortage of stories about future battles in the German press. These stories have all aimed at describing the course of future battles and engagements from a military point of view . . . but this work has a higher aim. It concerns itself with the subject of international poli-tics in Europe.'

The widespread European success enjoyed by stories as different as the straightforward forecast of *The Great War of 1892* and the simple imaginative projection of *In a Conning Tower* shows clearly that Britain, France, and Germany were united in spite of themselves by an interest in tales of future wars that described how these nations fought and defeated one another. But behind this common interest, there were far more varied and unusual reasons than the simple anxieties that explained the excitement following on *The Battle of Dorking*. New drives and new forces began to reveal themselves in the 1890s, and these gathered strength until they exerted a decisive influence on the form and direction of many of the new-style stories produced in that decade. A taste for the exotic, a delight in the marvels of military technology, a desire for adventure, an aggressive spirit of nationalism, the constant appeals from demagogues in Press and politics—these were some of the discernible influences that began to play with increasing effect upon the pattern of the imaginary war. The result was a flood of new stories that ranged from the innocent curiosity of *In a Conning Tower* to the completely romantic attractions of a world at last subject to the British Empire as described in *The Final War* by Louis Tracy. His preface revealed the purpose behind the numerous romantic tales of future wars that came out during the 1890s: 'I have taken the whole world as my theme and its chief citizens are my characters. I can only hope that I have given no offence . . . I have tried to write a story of adventure.'

Although the contemporary interest in adventure provided the motive for many of these stories, there were quite different reasons behind the other types of the imaginary war as they developed in this period. Many of the stories fall into distinctive categories. They were deliberately shaped by their authors to present a military or a naval forecast, to teach a political lesson, or to give a demonstration of scientific marvels still to come. And they were all so taken up with the shape of 'the next great war', as it was so often called, that they had no space to display any interest in peace, except by way of conquest and the domination of other peoples. This is the one great ironic fact that must strike every reader who comes to these stories with a knowledge of what has happened since the First World War. The period from the 1880s to the long-expected outbreak of the war in 1914 saw the emergence of the greatest number of these tales of coming conflicts ever to appear in European fiction. Save for rare exceptions, they are distinguished by a complete failure to foresee the form a modern war would take. The slaughter of the trenches, the use of poison gas, the immense damage caused by submarines, the very scale of a world-wide industrialized war were mercifully hidden from the admirals, generals, politicians, and popular novelists who joined in the great enterprise of predicting what was going to happen.

This was inevitable. It was the result of the now familiar time-lag between the rapid development of technology and the belated abandonment of ideas, mental habits, and social attitudes that the new machines and the new industries had rendered out-of-date. When men thought of war they did not foresee the struggles of great armies and anonymous masses of conscripts that finally came to pass. Instead, drawing on an imagination still burdened by a long tradition, which presented war as an affair of brief battles and heroic deeds by individuals, they underestimated the scale of actual warfare. Further, some were influenced by widespread expectation that the new science would reduce and perhaps even end the danger of wars, others by the equally widespread doctrine that war was a profitable undertaking, or by evolutionary notions about the naturalness of war, and most of all by the characteristic Victorian interest in the novelty and romance to be found in new weapons and new forms of warfare.

As will be seen, a major paradox of the period was the way in which the Victorian sense of human achievement tended to make men regard science as an unmixed blessing. In consequence, the Victorians were as much interested in new weapons as they were in new engineering undertakings. As Macaulay saw science, there were no disadvantages at all:

It has lengthened life; it has mitigated pain; it has extinguished diseases; it has increased the fertility of the soil; it has given new securities to the mariner; it has furnished new arms to the warrior; it has spanned great rivers and estuaries with bridges of form unknown to our fathers; it has guided the thunderbolt innocuously from the heaven to earth; it has lighted up the night with the splendour of the day; it has extended the range of human vision; it has multiplied the power of human muscles; it has accelerated motion; it has annihilated distance; it has facilitated intercourse, correspondence, all friendly offices, all dispatch of business; it has enabled man to descend the depths of the sea, to soar into the air, to penetrate securely into the noxious recesses of the earth, to traverse the land in cars which whirl along without horses, to cross the ocean in ships which run ten knots an hour against the wind. These are but a part of its fruits, and of its first-fruits; for it is a philosophy which never rests, which has never attained, which is never perfect. Its law is progress.[4]

The same gratitude for the wonders of science and the same sense of immense accomplishment ran through the *Lives of the Engineers* as described by Samuel Smiles. He saw them as demigods who had conquered nature for the benefit of mankind. 'Our engineers', Smiles wrote, 'may be regarded in some measure as the makers of modern civilization'; and he declared that his intention in *Lives of the Engineers* was

to give an account of some of the principal men by whom this nation has been made so great and prosperous as it is—the men by whose skill and industry large tracts of fertile land have been won back from the sea, the bog, and the fen, and made available for human habitation and sustenance; who, by their industry, skill, and genius, have made England the busiest of workshops.[5]

Such ideas affected the mood of the nineteenth century; and in spite of occasional moments of anxiety and alarm this unqualified optimism ran its course until 1914.

What Macaulay and Samuel Smiles said in their histories was echoed in the fiction and poetry of the period. Walt Whitman summed up the greatness of nineteenth-century man in phrases that are closely related to the epic fantasies of the new science described by Jules Verne:

His daring foot is on land and sea everywhere;
he colonizes the Pacific, the archipelagos,
With the steamship, the electric telegraph,
the newspaper, the wholesale engines of war,
With these and the world-spreading factories
he interlinks all geography, all lands.

Whitman's verse is a programme for the series of books that Jules Verne poured out between 1863 and his death in 1905. This pious Catholic, who won the commendation of Leo XIII for the purity of his writings, had so perfectly sensed the spirit of his time that he became the first writer to make a fortune by using science as material for fiction. In his stories the machine becomes the object of fiction and the technologist is the Promethean genius who uses science to make the Victorian dream come true by the conquest of the oceans and of the air. His heroes are from the same stock that produced the engineers celebrated by Samuel Smiles; but, where Smiles relates the glories of great achievements in the past, Verne looks to even more glorious achievements still to come. The heroes of the past, as Smiles wrote, were men who were 'strong-minded, resolute, and ingenious, and were impelled to their special pursuits by the force of their constructive instincts'. The heroes of the future are men who have outdistanced the greatest triumphs of the Victorians. Their adventures reveal the prospect of conquests still to come; Captain Nemo has achieved the age-old dream of penetrating the depths of ocean and Robur has anticipated the inventors with his aeronef. 'And now who is this Robur?' wrote Verne. 'Robur is the science of the future. Perhaps the science of tomorrow. Certainly the science that will come.' This was something quite new in fiction. Before Verne the marvels of science had on occasions been incidental to stories of romance; but Verne gained a world-wide success by his ability to make technological achievements a subject for fiction. His heroes are scarcely real in any sense of the word. At best they are manifestations of tremendous energy—men who have learned how to control the great powers of nature. Their adventures are simply occasions for demonstrating man's new-found capacity to shape things to his will.

This delight in the limitless capacities of science was intimately associated with much of the literature of imaginary warfare that appeared after the 1880s. In fact, it seems that only a matter of temperament prevented Jules Verne from following in the steps of predecessors and contemporaries to develop some of the military possibilities implicit in his stories. There is, for instance, an indication of the havoc that could have been caused by the *Nautilus* in Captain Nemo's death-bed story of how he sank one of the hated British frigates. The suggestion that his machines could be used in war becomes explicit in a remarkable episode from the adventures of Robur in *The Clipper of the Clouds*. Verne demonstrates the beneficent result of the white man's inventions by describing how Robur saved the intended victims from the annual sacrifice in Dahomey. The aeronef cruises over the place of sacrifice, and at the right moment 'the little gun shot forth its shrapnel which really did marvels'. It was enough to convince Robur's unwilling passengers of the advantages of his machine, and 'in this way did Uncle Prudent and Phil Evans recognize the power of the aeronef and the services it could render humanity'.

But even clearer than this is the hint of what scientific warfare might achieve as described in *The Begum's Fortune*—the nearest Verne's imagination ever came to contemplating the type of war made possible by specially devised weapons. It is a strange story, a lesson in good and evil, France and Germany, the peaceful and warlike uses of science. Two scientists, one French and the other German, use the wealth they have inherited to build two cities in the United States. Professor Schultz of Jena builds Stahlstadt, a crude anticipation of *Nineteen Eighty-Four*, in which rigid discipline and totalitarian methods contrast effectively with the happy conditions in the ideal city of Franceville. In these circumstances the German scientist plots to destroy the French city. His secret weapon—the first of many successors—is an enormous cannon with a range of thirty miles; its purpose is to fire a single vast shell that holds enough carbonic acid gas to wipe out the 250,000 inhabitants of Franceville in an instant.

Verne is important, both because his work represents the high tide of European delight in the marvels and possibilities of science, and because he stands halfway between the earlier occasional and incidental treatment of future warfare in fiction and the full development of that theme in the last fifteen years of the nineteenth century. It is a telling indication of the speed with which the potential of science had begun to affect the imagination that there is only a century between the sensation caused by the balloon ascents of 1783 and the first large-scale vision of technological warfare in *La Guerre au vingtième siècle*, published in 1883 by the French draughtsman and satirist Albert Robida. His sketches of air bombardments, armoured fighting vehicles, submarine attacks, and gas warfare marked a major stage in the interaction that had been taking place between science and the Western imagination. Since the appearance of Robida's forecast, the gap between what was imagined and what finally came to pass has continued to narrow until in our own day science has at last caught up with fiction. Now, for the first time in the course of these imaginary wars, the general staffs and the politicians agree with the story-tellers that the next great technological war is likely to be over before it can be reported and that the only task left for fiction is to describe the post-warfare state of the world.

This is the present stage in the sequence of scientific discoveries that began with the Renaissance dream of the conquest of nature and the supremacy of

man. The scientific fantasies of Wells, Verne, and Kurd Lasswitz were the
sophisticated nineteenth-century products of a process of development that
went back to a man like Leonardo da Vinci. They described to millions of
interested readers the shape of many things that had not yet appeared, whereas
Leonardo set down his ideas in his notebooks. He bent his restless imagination
to designing giant ballista, a steam gun, bombs, armoured chariots, multi-
barrelled guns, and an under-water craft, of which he wrote in his notebook:
'this I do not publish or divulge on account of the evil nature of men who
would practise assassinations at the bottom of the sea by breaking the ships in
their lower parts and sinking them together with the crews who are in them'.
Similarly, the magnificent ideal states of the nineteenth century—Bellamy's
Looking Backward and Mantegazza's *L'Anno 3000*, for example—belonged to
the tradition inaugurated by Bacon's *New Atlantis*. They prescribed a mixture
of science and centralization as the certain cure for all the problems of their
time; they planned for the whole world the type of highly organized society
Bacon had imagined for the island community of the *New Atlantis*. The technological utopia of the nineteenth century had been designed on the Baconian
principle that 'the end of our foundation is the knowledge of causes, and
secret motions of things; and the enlarging of the bounds of human empire, to
the effecting of all things possible'.[6]

The favourite Victorian dialogue between today and tomorrow, the advance
from the evidence of things accomplished to the vision of the even greater
things still to be done, could only begin from the developments of modern science. Verne and Wells followed in a tradition that went back to the eighteenth
century; for it has already been shown that an immediate result of the success
of the first Montgolfière and Charlière balloons was a flood of prints that
attempted to depict how the invention could be used in warfare. Indeed, the
year of 1783 had not run its course before a twenty-two-page tract had been
published in Amsterdam and Paris, discussing the possibilities of the new
'flying globes' and describing how they might be used to capture Gibraltar.
Again, in 1784 Benjamin Franklin asked: 'And where is the Prince who can
afford so to cover his Country with Troops for its defense, as that ten thousand men descending from the clouds might not in many places do an infinite
deal of mischief before a force could be brought together to repel them?' In
this way, and from this time onwards, fact and prediction began to advance in
parallel with fiction and prophecy. The last decades of the eighteenth century
saw the start of a strangely innocent delight in trying to imagine warlike applications for peaceful inventions. In 1791 the aspiring natural philosopher
Erasmus Darwin celebrated the great success of the new steam engine in
abominable verses that looked forward with complete equanimity to its use
both in peace and war:

> Soon shall thy arm, UNCONQUER'D STEAM ! afar
> Drag the slow barge, or drive the rapid car;
> Or on wide-waving wings expanded bear
> The flying-chariot through the field of air.
> Fair crews triumphant, leaning from above,
> Shall wave their fluttering kerchiefs as they move;
> Or warrior-bands alarm the gaping crowd,
> And armies shrink beneath the shadowy cloud.

The possible application of these discoveries to war seems to have had a peculiar fascination for the early nineteenth century. In 1800 the German writer A. K. Ruh produced a romance of the twentieth century, *Guirlanden um die Urnen der Zukunft*, in which he set a commonplace and sentimental tale against a background of imaginary future changes. This new direction in fiction owed as much to the sense of change born of the great scientific discoveries as it did to the considerable European popularity enjoyed by Sebastian Mercier's account of an ideal state of the future, *L'An 2440*, which had played a great part—especially in Germany—in causing writers to present their hopes in the form of a tale of the future. Most of these early stories were either simple romances or not-too-serious attempts to foresee the pattern of civilized life in time to come.[7] The story by Ruh, for instance, related a long series of adventures that befall the hero while in the service of the Emperor of Germanien. The impression of a different future was established by such devices as an air postal service and a sail-driven balloon squadron used for air reconnaissance.

The same theme of balloons in the service of the military appeared more fully in *Ini*, a story of the twenty-first century published in 1810 by Julius von Voss, a former lieutenant of the Prussian Army. His picture of the new age is striking evidence of the way in which the possibilities of technology had begun to fascinate the imagination half a century before Jules Verne began to write about the marvels to come. The story looks forward to a single European state, ruled by an emperor in Rome. His writ runs from Sicily to Moscow—a reflection of the time when Napoleon was at the height of his power and it was impossible to go from Rome to Hamburg without passing through French-controlled territory. Wars are now fought against the barbarian peoples of Asia; and artillery had become so powerful that cities have deep underground shelters (with all the amenities of shops and churches) to protect their inhabitants in time of war. Once again, the popular fantasy of dirigible balloons appears in the description of the aerial reconnaissance groups:

These had the task of observing the enemy from afar and reporting on the number and disposition of his troops. Since they had ascended high enough, the enlarged field of vision was a considerable help in observation; but the height also meant that they could be seen for twenty miles. But the enemy, eager to conceal his intentions, did not hesitate to send up his own light craft in order to drive back the enemy balloons; and so in the heavens above skirmishes developed between advanced patrols as had once taken place between Hussars and Cossacks centuries before.[8]

Here, then, in the initial exuberance and general innocence with which men welcomed the first scientific advances, one can discern the beginnings of the later European habit of forecasting the course of future wars. The habit was a consequence of regarding war as an affair of small armies, of the exhilaration of living in a period of unprecedented development, and of the assumption that there was no foreseeable calamity in the production of increasingly lethal weapons. Throughout the century there was a widespread belief that, although wars may have been unpleasant and might become horrible, war remained a possible and profitable activity for nations. For instance, the inventor Robert Fulton tried to persuade Congress in 1810 to adopt his torpedoes on the grounds that they would sweep British ships from the seas: 'In all my reflections on this kind of war, I see no chance for their escape other than by retreat; and the moment the English ships of war retreat before torpedo boats, that moment the power of the British marine is for ever lost, and with it the political influence of the nation.'[9]

Few thought of—few were able to think of—the cumulative effects of the constant growth in the size and destructiveness of new instruments of war. Even the brilliant and humane pioneer of the aeroplane, Sir George Cayley, answered Lord Stanhope's fear that men might abuse the power of flight by arguing in 1817 that the discovery of the ship had brought good as well as evil. It was ordained that the aeroplane would or would not succeed:

A new and extended power—commensurate with the still further state of civilization contemplated for our race—now, in my view of the case, presents itself; some evils may possibly be in its train, but let us rest assured either that the subject is *impracticable* and therefore not designed for our use, or *practicable* in which case as a most *powerful* engine it must have been designed for our use. Our business seems to be to put the practicability to the test, and never to hesitate as to the result. Your Lordship seems to think that the means of conveyance will be increased whilst the means of defence remains the same: surely the defendant may use the same instrument as the assailant. I conceive we are looking too far in attempting to unravel all the workings of a power like this. Society may improve commensurably with the improvement of this power and we cannot estimate the moral influence of such improvement.[10]

Since civilized life had demonstrably improved, it was widely felt that war might also moderate its terrors to the point where the possibility of war would have disappeared entirely. Looking at the changes going on about him in 1829, Robert Southey expected that in the matter of warfare 'the chemist and the mechanist will succeed where moralists and divines have failed'. Southey's argument was repeated frequently throughout the rest of the century. He thought that 'the novel powers which, beyond all doubt, will be directed to the purposes of destruction, are so tremendous, and likely to be so efficient, that in their consequences they may reasonably be expected to do more toward the prevention of war than any or all other causes.'[11] On 8 December 1834, when the distinguished French physicist Dominique Arago delivered the *Éloge* in honour of James Watt to the Académie des Sciences, he looked forward to a future full of hope and abundance. He forecast that 'a time will come, when the science of destruction shall bend before the arts of peace'. By the 1870s this view was becoming almost traditional teaching; for one of the more curious results of the Franco-German War was to encourage the belief that, since war had become swifter than ever, it had thereby become more humane than ever before. This was the moment when the nineteenth century had begun to turn in upon itself and contemplate the great progress that had been made since the beginning of the century. It was the time when histories of science began to replace the lives of the engineers, when books about the romance of science were beginning to find an ever-growing demand. These books generally included a chapter on firearms and armaments, which were introduced with enthusiastic remarks on the way the spirit of progress had affected the battlefield. As one writer began, 'Some idea of the marvellous achievements of the inventor on the battle-field—or, rather, in preparing for the battle-field— may be formed by a brief reference to recent statistics on the subject. There are said to be at the present time about 37,000 pieces of cannon in existence in the world.'[12] Another writer proclaimed that 'the man who invents the most rapid and the most effectual means of destruction, as regards war, is the greatest friend to the interests of humanity'. In an exultant chapter on the marvels of 'Gun-powder and Gun-cotton', he told his young readers: 'We are quite sure, however, that if any man could invent a means of destruction, by which two nations going to war with each other would see large armies destroyed, and immense treasure wasted on both sides, in a single campaign, they would both hesitate at entering upon another. We repeat, therefore, that in this sense the greatest destroyer is the greatest philanthropist.'[13]

The historians and the scientists joined with the generals and the novelists in claiming that war had become too terrible to continue, or that it had become so rapid in its results that the modern battle was now far more humane than the dreadful engagements of the bad old days. Behind this confused attitude to war there was a mass of assumption that derived as much from old-fashioned notions as from a general and no doubt unavoidable failure to foresee what might happen when the major industrialized nations went to war. In effect, war was regarded as an international process that resulted in convenient changes for the victor and no markedly unfortunate results for the

loser. War had brought nations to power in Europe; it was extending the territories of European countries across the face of the earth; and, as Ferdinand
Foch told his students at the end of the century, when he was professor of
military history at the École Supérieure de Guerre, 'if war is still national
today, it is for the sake of securing economic benefits and profitable trade
agreements'.

The argument for war had all the answers in its favour: it could no longer
happen; or, if it did happen, then the consequences would not be disastrous.
In this way it came to be accepted that there would be another war, because
there had always been wars, and there could always be more wars. The imagination tolerated the idea, since it lacked the capacity to foresee the devastation,
the immense casualty lists, the chaos and destruction that lay ahead. In 1883
Baron Colmar von der Goltz, the German military writer and later governor of
Belgium, put the case in favour of technological warfare in his book *The
Nation in Arms*. He recognized the force of the complaint that 'all advances
made by modern science and technical art are immediately applied to the
abominable art of annihilating mankind'. His answer was to demonstrate that
the conduct of war had improved almost out of recognition:

The fact that each new invention and each mechanical improvement seems somehow, in these days, to find its way into military service need not, therefore, alarm
us, much less be regarded as a step backward in humanity and civilisation. By
these means, on the contrary, the battle is only the more rapidly decided and the
war brought to an end sooner than in the days of old.

This defence of war was common doctrine throughout Europe; it was not
confined to recruiting speeches by German generals. The English version can
be found in a plain history of science, *Discoveries and Inventions of the
Nineteenth Century*, which put the militarist case at the beginning of a chapter
on firearms:

We often hear people regretting that so much attention and ingenuity as are shown
by the weapons of the present day should have been expended upon implements of
destruction. It would not perhaps be difficult to show that if we must have wars,
the more effective the implements of destruction, the shorter and more decisive
will be the struggles, and the less the total loss of life, though occurring in a
shorter time. Then, again, the exasperated and savage feelings evoked by the hand-
to-hand fighting under the old system have less opportunity for their exercise in
modern warfare, which more resembles a game of skill. But the wise and the good
have in all ages looked forward to a time when sword and spear shall be everywhere finally superseded by the ploughshare and the reaping-hook, and the whole
human race shall dwell together in amity. Until that happy time arrives . . . we
may consider that the more costly and ingenious and complicated the implements
of war become, the more certain will be the extension and the permanence of civilization. The great cost of such appliances as those we are about to describe, the

ingenuity needed for their contrivance, the elaborate machinery required for their production, and the skill implied in their use, are such that these weapons can never be the arms of other than wealthy and intelligent nations. We know that in ancient times opulent and civilized communities could hardly defend themselves against poor and barbarous races. . . . In our day it is the poor and barbarous tribes who are everywhere at the mercy of the wealthy and cultivated nations. The present age has been so remarkably fertile in warlike inventions, that it may truthfully be said that the progress made in fire-arms and war-ships within the last few years surpasses that of the three previous centuries. Englishmen have good reason to be proud of the position taken by their country, and may feel assured that her armaments will enable her to hold her own among the most advanced nations of the world.[14]

This compound of complacency, ignorance, and innocence was the primary condition for the great growth of war fiction during the last quarter of the nineteenth century; and the new genre became so well known that writers and reviewers commented on the latest stories as specimens of *les guerres imaginaires, der Zukunftskrieg*, or the tale of 'the next great war'. There was so little to hold back the imagination from trying to foresee the shape of a future war. In fact, almost everything was a direct encouragement. The singularity of new weapons, the exciting possibilities in the development of the aeroplane and the submarine, the sense of immense achievements past and still to come, the traditional and heroic ideas of warfare—all these factors coincided with the start of the naval arms race and with the growing spirit of nationalism. The result was an entire new fiction of warfare that opened with the strictly political appeal introduced by Chesney and ranged through long stories in aid of new weapons or new ships to tales of 'what it will be like' in destroyers.

The abundance is embarrassing, but not overwhelming; for most of these writers were singleminded enough to turn out stories that kept strictly within their chosen fields of the political, the marvellous, or the romantic. One of the earliest examples of the more serious attempts to examine the pattern of future warfare was a naval application of Chesney's method. It appeared in *The Battle of Port Said*, an anonymous story reputed to be by an admiral, which was first printed in *Engineering*. After causing a considerable stir at home and abroad, it was republished as a pamphlet in 1883 and then translated into French. The technique was still pure Chesney—the argument from defects to disaster. The intention in *The Battle of Port Said*, the author wrote, was, 'to expose certain weaknesses in the construction and management of our warships'. The proof is the outbreak of a war in which Britain and Germany side with Egypt against France, Russia, and Turkey. The result is a resounding defeat for the Royal Navy in which all the weaknesses of machinery and unskilled engineers are made clear.

The reasons behind the story were the many changes then going through at bewildering speed in naval construction. The arms race had begun, and much of the naval expansion that dates from about 1880 was a race between rival nations to keep pace with bigger guns, thicker armour, more effective projectiles, and faster ships. What this meant can be seen from the unending competition between guns and armour. When Britannia's wooden walls had become ironclad warships, the struggle of gun against plate had started. As guns increased in accuracy and effectiveness, the armour had to grow steadily thicker. Thus, the first wrought-iron plates had a thickness of between four and five inches; this increased to twenty-four inches; and then came the new compound armour of iron faced with steel; and finally there was steel alone. It was the same with naval guns: the *Dreadnought* had been launched in 1875 with 12.5-inch muzzle-loaders which could penetrate 18 inches of iron; by 1902 the latest 12-inch breech-loaders fired a projectile that could get through a thickness of 46 inches.

Such a swift see-saw development makes it clear why so many writers sought to describe the shape of wars-to-come. In fact, no one could say with certainty what a war at sea would be like, since the rate of naval development had been so hectic, and had been based on so many theories of offensive and defensive tactics, that even the admirals—to judge from what some of them wrote—were not sure how things would turn out at sea. This is one reason for the sudden burst of predictions in which writers fought out the battle of gun against armour, ram against gun-fire, torpedo against battleship, and speed against defence. And, as had happened with the earlier pamphlets on the dangers of invasion, many of these stories went the rounds of international translations, since the anxiety and fears of one maritime power were of considerable interest to the others.

The process can be seen at work with *The Battle of Port Said*. This had appeared at a time when, in the opinion of a distinguished naval officer like Lord Charles Beresford, the French naval vessels had better guns, better armour, and were generally more efficient than the British. So, when *The Battle of Port Said* had done its best for the Royal Navy, it was next discussed in French service journals and published in book form with a special introduction for French readers. The editor commented on the general interest aroused by the story and noted that the author's intention was 'to make known to his fellow citizens the defects that he finds in the construction of the British ships and in the training of their officers and men'.

Any defect, any reason, any fear provided the starting-point for these completely purposive stories of the disaster that could only be avoided by better ships, better guns, or better treatment for engineers. One long story published in 1896, *The Naval Engineer and the Command of the Sea* by F. G. Burton, began as a serial in *The Practical Engineer* with the sole intention of showing that the growing importance to the Navy of highly trained engineer officers and skilled mechanics has not yet been sufficiently recognised by the Authorities and the result has been a deep feeling of discontent throughout all branches of the engine-room staff. It is in order to direct public attention to this discontent, which threatens serious disaster to us in the event of war, that the following pages have been written.

If the swift advance from wooden walls to steam turbines caused some to look anxiously to the future, there were many others who found it interesting, even exhilarating. There was a large audience throughout the nation for the factual and exciting account of the way in which future wars, especially future naval battles, would be fought. That was the discovery of Arnold-Forster, who pioneered a development of the imaginary war with his account of a ramming action between two warships. His motives explain the intentions of his many successors: 'an attempt has been made to throw into a popular form the teaching of various trials and experiments which have from time to time been made, and to introduce into the story of an actual engagement the results of a long course of careful observations of modern naval progress'. What he wrote, however, was little more than an English adaptation of a famous incident in the Battle of Lissa which had had a considerable influence on the theory of naval warfare in Europe. On 20 July 1866 Admiral Tegetthoff led the Austrian fleet out of Pola in order to engage the Italians. In the action that followed Tegetthoff steered his own ship, *Erzherzog Ferdinand Maximilian*, straight for the Italian *Re d'Italia*, rammed, and sank her. 'Far underneath the water-line,' so ran the account by the narrator in Arnold-Forster's story,

the protruding ram had struck a blow from which no human power could save the victim. For a moment all was still, save for the sound of the stretching and rending of the iron; then suddenly, with a steady but certain heave, the great ship seemed to bow down towards us. I watched her for a moment; long enough to see the surface of the deck as it showed up with the heel of the ship, and then I knew no more.

The style of these new accounts of imaginary battles gives the impression that George Henty had collaborated with Samuel Smiles in describing the conduct of future naval engagements. The most striking qualities of a story like *In a Conning Tower* are a delight in the marvels of the new technology and an eager interest in the seemingly epic nature of a future battle. Arnold-Forster describes the conning tower of a warship of the 1880s in this way:

Here in this spot is concentrated the whole power of the tremendous machine which we call an ironclad ship. Such power was never since the world began concentrated under the direction of man, and all that power, the judgement to direct it, the will to apply it, the knowledge to utilise it, is placed in the hands of one man, and one only. What is this power? Talk of Jove with his thunderbolts, of

Nasmyth with his hammer; the fables of mythology and the facts of latter-day science! where has there ever been anything to compare to it? Here in the Conning Tower stands the captain of the ship, and beneath his feet lie hidden powers which the mind can hardly grasp, but which one and all are made subservient to his will, and his will alone. Picture him as he stands at his post before the battle begins; all is quiet enough, there is scarcely a sound save the lapping of the water against the smooth white sides of the ironclad, and no outward sign of force save the ripple of parted waters falling off on either side of the ram as it sheers through the water.[15]

The same enthusiasm directed the work of the French officer who wrote under the pseudonym of Capitaine Danrit. Between 1889 and 1893 he had started on his career as a patriotic writer by turning out a series of books on the common theme of the next war against Germany. They were all published under the general title of *La Guerre de demain*. Each book was a large two-volume account devoted to one aspect of future warfare as Danrit thought it would develop: *La Guerre en forteresse*, *La Guerre en rase campagne*, and *La Guerre en ballon*. Although Danrit's stories were far more political in aim than Arnold-Forster's *In a Conning Tower*, they gave considerable space to descriptions of new weapons and new machines of war. All the stories in the trilogy of *La Guerre de demain* dealt with the same war between France and Germany; and all were written in the spirit of Danrit's preface to the first of the series:

On every side the nations are arming and preparing for war. By writing this book in the form of an imaginary story I have tried to inspire my French readers with confidence in the outcome of the struggle. With this in mind I reveal to them the resources of our country, and I demonstrate the weapons that will be used in the coming battles: Melinite, the Lebel rifle, and the dirigible balloon.

In describing his imaginary war of the future, Danrit kept his promise to give the reader confidence, to reveal the resources of the country, and to show the new weapons in action. In each book he described the probable conduct of infantry engagements, of fortress troops in the defence of strategic areas, and of the new airmen in their observation balloons and dirigibles. In many ways Danrit's stories were the French military equivalent of the British naval tales about the handling of destroyers and battleships in a future war. But, as will be seen later, his intentions were far more serious. His constant aim in everything he wrote was to prove that French troops and French equipment were always and in all places better than anything on the German or the British side. He continually breaks off the narrative in order to describe how a photographic section operating from a dirigible is able to obtain invaluable information about the size of a German column on the march; or to show how the French rifle is far more efficient than the German model; or to relate how the complicated business of mobilization goes forward rapidly and faultlessly in accordance with long-prepared plans.

While Danrit was busy giving the French his picture of the conduct of the next war, in Britain a complete school of fiction had followed on the success of Arnold-Forster's *In a Conning Tower*. The new writers kept their narratives strictly to accounts of naval battles in which the Whitehead torpedo, the destroyer, and the battleship fought it out according to the theories of the day. They wrote tales like *The Captain of the 'Mary Rose'* by William Laird Clowes in 1892, *The Great War of 1892* by Admiral Colomb and his associates in 1892, the Earl of Mayo's *The Cruise of the 'Aries'* in 1894, F. T. Jane's *Blake of the 'Rattlesnake'* in 1895, and J. Eastwick's *The New Centurion* in 1895. Their simple treatment of future warfare continued until in 1905 it reached its most curious development, when the naval writers William Laird Clowes and Alan Burgoyne joined forces to write *Trafalgar Refought*. The authors combined the taste for novelty with the potent appeal of tradition to produce, as they said 'a vivid picture of the likely happenings at sea had Nelson lived in this present year of grace'.

It was a crowded field in which the authors never hesitated to explain their intentions to their readers. William Laird Clowes set out in *The Captain of the 'Mary Rose'* 'to give a readable tentative answer to the question: "What will the sea-fighting of tomorrow be like?"' Although he cast his story in the form of a war between France and Britain, he was quick to point out that he had 'been animated by no unfriendly and by no unfair feelings towards France'. For James Eastwick the story of *The New Centurion* was meant to answer 'the not unnatural query what fighting with automatic weapons would be like'; and with a sour reference to his competitors he warned the reader that he would have to limit the account, 'otherwise it would be sure to end in describing one of those mythical contests between an unheard-of ironclad and an equally unheard-of enemy, of which we have too many already, and from which nothing ever has been learnt or ever will be'. There was the same declaration of intention and the same desire to apologize in the introduction to F. T. Jane's *Blake of the 'Rattlesnake'*. His aim was 'to work into story-form some of the romance that clings thick around the torpedo service'. And he included a note for the opposition:

I would say one final word to those who object to these "future war yarns" on the grounds that they are likely to set other nations, at present friendly to us, by the ears. Foreign nations are frequently turning out similar stories, describing the utter destruction of the British Navy by their own; yet I have never heard of any of us bearing them ill-will for it. May our Warfare of the Future long be confined to the pages of books; as, indeed, it will be, so long as foreign nations know that we are ready to tackle the lot of them if need be.

This was the idea of progress applied to the future of warfare. It was the product of a European preoccupation with technology and change that could never let the imagination rest. It was part of a general speculation that covered such diverse interests as the strictly professional fiction from members of the armed forces and the more daring conjectures of writers like H. G. Wells and Conan Doyle. While the naval and military writers confined themselves to the immediate and the practicable, others like Albert Robida and H. G. Wells played with the possible and tried to imagine what might happen if the aeroplane, the submarine, even dynamite and Röntgen rays were developed for use in warfare.

The new interest was only the most recent phase in the constant attempt to understand the new circumstances of the epoch, to foresee coming changes, to adjust to a rate of change that had been accelerating steadily ever since technology had begun to transform war as well as peace. In 1660 Robert Boyle had observed that 'the invention of gunpowder hath quite altered the condition of material affairs over the world, both by sea and land'. In fact, the invention of firearms had meant the end of war as an occupation for warriors; it was beginning to be a profession for soldiers. By the end of the seventeenth century the cannon and the musket had brought about changes in tactics and strategy that in their turn demanded a new military discipline. And then, as weapons went on increasing in number and complexity, the soldier had to turn himself into a professional, dedicated to the service of an arm such as the artillery or the engineers. Uniform, drill, regulations, general staffs, conscript armies, balloon observer companies, railway transport battalions, and machine-gun regiments were a consequence of the industrial revolution and of the advice given by Lazare Carnot to the Committee of Public Safety in August 1793—that the nation should organize a *levée en masse*.

The idea of the nation-state coincided with the opportunities of science; and science, being universal and neutral, knowing neither good nor evil, offered its gifts for men to use them as they wished. But once technology had been committed to the conflict between nations, it was inevitable that one day war would become fully automatic. In the half-century after the Franco-German War the general staffs toiled away to perfect techniques for launching great armies like so many offensive missiles. The logic of this union between war and technology—the military physics of speed and mass—has brought us to the point of completely mechanical warfare. The rows of buttons, the winking lights, the brisk ritual of the count-down—everything now waits for the electronic command that will trigger off the first fully automated war.

Today the tale of future warfare has little attraction for the imagination, since fiction cannot say more than is already known about the terror of the hydrogen bomb. But in the half-century before 1914 there was still enough curiosity about the future, and men had enough sense of wonder about technological possibilities, to attempt forecasts of the next war. For the service writers this was often a matter of communication, a desire to tell the civilian what the armed forces were planning; and this has persisted down to our own time in occasional stories like *War—1974* (1958) by the American tank officer Lieutenant-Colonel Robert B. Rigg. The difference is, however, that no military writer before 1914 ever began his story with the warning given to the reader in *War—1974* that, if war is to be prevented, 'people must know, beforehand, the shapes and forms that future conflict could assume. Unless people and governments know and understand the likely proportions of any conflict to come they are ill-equipped to prevent the occurrence of such an event.'

The old world before 1914 was still lost in the dream of constant progress. Warfare too often took on 'the romance that clings thick around the torpedo service' for men to question Treitschke's assertion that 'the mere fact of the existence of many states involves the necessity of war'. So, writers applied themselves to the business of describing what they thought would happen when British and French fleets met in battle, or when the French armies crossed over into Germany to win the great war of revenge. In attempting this they were trying to strike some sort of balance between war as it had been and what they thought it might become as a result of the many changes in artillery, projectiles, and tactics.

In 1887 Prince Kraft zu Hohenlohe, who had commanded the Guard Artillery in 1870, showed the way he thought things might go in the lessons he drew from the Franco-German War: 'The manner in which the campaign was opened on the part of the Germans will, therefore, remain a standard pattern so long as new inventions do not create new strategical means such as aeronautics might do.'[16] Again, in the preface to the 1890 edition of his *Nation in Arms* , Baron von der Goltz wrote that 'military science is at present undergoing revolutionary changes, which may influence the details of the military art, though in essentials it will probably remain unaffected while national armies of huge masses remain in existence'. Who could foresee the battles of the future, when in the 1890s the French were complaining that they had changed the model of their rifle three times since 1870? An even more spectacular development was the discovery in the 1880s of a smokeless powder, the famous 'Poudre B' of the French chemical industry, which was so named out of compliment to the Minister of War, General Boulanger. By ending the usual fog of war, the new powder had totally transformed the conditions of the battlefield. Up to the appearance of 'Poudre B' it had been standing practice for the artillery to engage the infantry over open sights. In 1870 the war correspondents had often reported the dense smoke created by bursting shells and the striking scene when the red trousers of the French infantry suddenly showed through the smoke as battalions advanced at the double in close

column of troops towards the German positions. The simple chemistry of gun-
cotton and the nitration process had in the course of a few brief years done
away with the sense of spectacle that had always surrounded the great set battles; and it had presented a host of problems for the commanders to solve.
Here, for example, is the old-style engagement described by Prince Kraft zu
Hohenlohe in his *Letters on Cavalry*, written just before the introduction of
smokeless powder. Discussing the problem of when to commit the cavalry, he
states that

at a distance of two miles it is exceedingly hard to judge as to the condition of the
enemy, and as to the favourable moment for taking part in the action. Thick clouds
of smoke overspread the locality of the combat, lines are seen swaying backwards
and forwards, hurrahs mingle with the clatter of the infantry fire and with the
thunder of the guns create such a hubbub that the whole seems one long roll of
sound, and it is impossible to judge at all as to the condition of the engagement.[17]

The stories thrown up by these incessant changes in the conditions of warfare began with military and naval writers—British, French, and German.
Most of these stories were at first presented as a fictional version of a staff
exercise; and it was not until the emergence of the mass press in the 1890s
that service writers like Admiral Colomb and the French officer Émile Driant
began to produce full-length stories for serialization in the new dailies and
weekly magazines. While *Black and White* was serializing Admiral Colomb's
Great War of 1892, Capitaine Driant was turning out his trilogy, *La Guerre de
forteresse, La Guerre en rase campagne, La Guerre en ballon*. In all this fiction
there is a correlation between national attitudes and the type of stories these
writers produced. The French were usually concerned with the coming war of
reconquest to be waged against Germany; and, except for the period of dispute
with Britain in the 1880s and 1890s, when some of these stories turned into a
French conquest of Albion, their writers continued to describe the multifarious
forms they imagined for the great task of *la revanche*. The Germans were
markedly different. They produced very little in the field of imaginary warfare
until after 1895, when the expansion of the fleet set them on a collision course
with Britain. In fact, until the appearance of the propaganda for a bigger fleet
in *Wehrlos zur See* in 1900, German writers were far more interested in trans-
lating predictions made in other countries, or turning out very plain pamphlets
that were little more than military appreciations for the general public.

The publications of the military historian Karl Bleibtreu are characteristic of
this aspect of the tale of imaginary warfare in Germany. In the late 1880s he
produced a series of three battle pieces under the general title of *Die
Entscheidungsschlachten des Europäischen Krieges, 18—*. They are exceptionally
tiresome and long-winded. Indeed, the only element of interest is his contempt
for foreign publications of the same kind and his conviction that a future war

would be a fast-moving affair in the manner of 1870. In his account of a war fought by Russia against Germany and Austro-Hungary, he relates in great detail the advance of the cavalry divisions, followed by the engagement of infantry patrols. Then the main forces begin their manoeuvring, and the campaign is swiftly decided by a single major battle. The enemy, it is shown, have been defeated by the superior capacities of the German staff and the greater abilities of the troops. Even the German attempts to describe the next war, Bleibtreu asserted, were better than anything written in other lands. In the introduction to his third story, *Die Schlacht bei Châlons*, Bleibtreu destroyed the reputation of all foreign competitors with his claim that 'the foreign pamphlets about the next war are simply the chatter of the ignorant; the German accounts, both in strategy and in tactics, are workmanlike studies. Moreover, the attempt to describe a future war in such minute detail is completely new.' But Bleibtreu's view, too, was simply the chatter of the ignorant.

The great paradox running through the whole of this production of imaginary wars between 1871 and 1914 was the total failure of army and navy writers to guess what would happen when the major industrial nations decided to fight it out. Even when one takes account of the fact that many of these writers were presenting a special case for changes in equipment or organization by projecting success or disaster into the future, it still remains true that the intense conservatism of the armed forces and years of studying pre-technological battles from Cannae to Waterloo had induced a habit of expecting that wars would continue to be more or less as they had always been. In consequence, the naval and military prophets generally saw war as an affair of adaptation and improvisation. They rarely thought of what their new equipment might do. None of them ever seems to have imagined that technology might be able to create new instruments of war. That was left to the civilian; for in the fifty years before the First World War the only writers who came anywhere near to seeing how science and industry might change the traditional pattern of warfare were Albert Robida, H. G. Wells, and Conan Doyle. One reason is that the imaginative writer, free from the specialist preoccupations of the professional, could allow his mind to move freely over the whole area of the possible.

This comes out clearly in the first major vision of technological warfare ever presented, *La Guerre au vingtième siècle* by Albert Robida, which appeared during 1883 in the French periodical *La Caricature*. The vision of this remarkable engraver, lithographer, caricaturist, architect, and writer represents a distinct phase in the growth of the idea of the future. Robida comes midway in the development that begins with the total optimism of Jules Verne in the 1860s and ends with the first prediction of the universal horror of atomic warfare in *The World Set Free* by H. G. Wells in 1914. The two writers, Robida and Wells, had an unusual awareness of the destructive potential of technology when used for military purposes. As Wells put the matter in 1914, when he described the atomic bombs used in the world war of 1959, science had begun to confront the human race with a choice between total war and total peace:

Certainly it seems now that nothing could have been more obvious to the people of the earlier twentieth century than the rapidity with which war was becoming impossible. And as certainly they did not see it. They did not see it until the atomic bombs burst in their fumbling hands. Yet the broad facts must have glared upon any intelligent mind. All through the nineteenth and twentieth centuries the amount of energy that men were able to command was continually increasing. There was no increase whatever in the ability to escape. Every sort of passive defence, armour, fortifications and so forth was being outmastered by this tremendous increase on the destructive side.[18]

The first stage of this realization appears in the text and drawings of Robida's *La Guerre au vingtième siècle*. They present a picture of future warfare that was very different from what all the admirals and generals had been saying. Unlike Wells, however, Robida is not entirely serious in his forecast of war in the twentieth century. He looks into the possibilities of scientific warfare with all the ironical detachment of a satirist who has no illusions about the readiness with which men would use the most frightful weapons in order to conquer; but the difference between the realities of 1883 and what might happen in the future war of 1945 was still big enough to provoke amusement rather than terror and despair. Robida's position is closer to Verne than to the Wells of *The World Set Free*; he is hardly attacking warfare, but rather the folly of human beings who might one day, if they were so foolish, really develop all the weapons he drew with such admirable ability. He foresaw most of what appeared later on: submarines, underwater troops, mines, torpedoes, smoke-screens, automatic small-arms fire, air bombardments of cities, a chemical corps complete with poisonous shells, a bacteriological warfare company to spray the enemy with microbes, and the *blockhaus roulants*, the forerunners of Wells's land ironclads. If many of the weapons belonged to the future, the world picture of 1945 was still a derisive projection of the anxieties of 1883:

The first half of the year 1945 had been particularly peaceful. Except for the usual goings-on, that is to say a little civil war of three months in the Danubian Empire, an American expedition against our coasts which was driven off by our submarine fleet, and a Chinese expedition smashed to pieces off Corsica—except for these—Europe had enjoyed complete peace.

And then war breaks out. The hero joins the 6th Squadron, 18th Territorial Aeronautics, and is forthwith committed to the swift war of electrically powered aircraft, tanks, and cyclist troops. Outside one town an enemy chemical battalion takes up its position. Four bombs describe a brief parabola through the air:

a sentry who had seen suspicious shadows was about to raise the alarm, when the first projectile exploded in a greenish cloud. A loud cry, a puff of smoke . . . Three more shells followed. And then there was a great silence. The camp fires were extinguished and everything went dead, even the miserable inhabitants remaining in the town who had been suddenly asphyxiated in their homes. But these are the accidents of war to which we have all grown accustomed as a result of the recent advances of science.

However, it is only on rare occasions that so serious a note sounds through the text. For the most part the story proceeds at breakneck speed as the hero moves from one unit to another, in turn air gunner, infantryman, second-lieutenant of a machine-gun company, torpedo engineer in a submarine fleet, and finally commander of the *Voltigeur aérien No. 39* in which he accomplishes great deeds against the enemy air fleets.

As a writer, however, Robida is a lightweight in comparison with his con-temporary H. G. Wells; and any final judgement has to recognize that only the exceptional imagination shown in the drawings makes it possible to contrast *La Guerre au vingtième siècle* with the several Wellsian visions of the wars-to-come. Nevertheless, the two men had a number of things in common: they were fascinated by the immense potential of science; they both had an intuitive awareness of the ways in which the conduct of war might be changed; and they both had an interest in violence and destruction that was characteristic of so much European writing during the last two decades of the nineteenth cen-tury. All these qualities, however, appeared more strongly in Wells and were all given much freer rein in his fiction before 1914. In fact, a sense of groups divided and in conflict seems to have been central to Wells's imagination from the start. He began in *The Time Machine* in 1895 by looking into the far-off future world of 802701, and there he found that humanity had degenerated into two different species, the effete Eloi and the obscene subterranean Morlocks, who were engaged in a fearful Darwinian struggle to survive. This idea of a war to the finish between races had appeared earlier in Bulwer Lytton's *Coming Race* and more spectacularly in W. D. Hay's account of the all-victorious white race in *Three Hundred Years Hence*. But Wells's handling of the theme was very different; it was far more pessimistic. The Time Traveller discovered there was no glorious future ahead for the human race. He grieved 'to think how brief the dream of the human intellect had been' after he made the terrible discovery that 'these Eloi were mere fatted cattle, which the ant-like Morlocks preserved and preyed upon—probably saw to the breeding of'. The law of unending progress had clashed with the greater law of nature—'that intellectual versatility is the compensation for change, danger, and trouble'. In consequence, the human race had split into the divergent species of the Eloi and the Morlocks; and out of that split came the great war of nature.

Three years later the war of nature assumed cosmic proportions. Wells returned to the theme of conflict, and in the best of all his scientific romances, *The War of the Worlds*, he took the Darwinian struggle for survival, combined it with contemporary ideas of a war between peoples, and projected the results upon a planetary scale. This most forceful tale of the Martian invasion of earth is still better than any of the tales of interplanetary warfare that have derived from the great success of the prototype. In fact, *The War of the Worlds* is the perfect nineteenth-century myth of the imaginary war; it says many things about war in many different ways.

At first sight *The War of the Worlds* is all that it claims to be: the invasion of earth by a warrior force from the more highly advanced civilization on Mars. At this level the story keeps close to the original idea, which was suggested to Wells by his brother Frank during a walk in the peaceful Surrey countryside. ' "Suppose some beings from another planet were to drop out of the sky suddenly," said Frank, "and begin laying about them here!" Perhaps we had been talking of the discovery of Tasmania by the Europeans—a very frightful disaster for the native Tasmanians! I forget. But that was the point of departure.'[19] From that the story grew into a true fantasy of the subconscious. In addition to handling the central theme of adventure and horror, Wells's imagination sought to work out three principal ideas: the violence of colonial warfare, the Darwinian idea of a struggle between competing groups, and the devastating potentialities of an advanced military technology. That is to say, his ideas derived from: warfare as the Europeans—especially the British—had experienced it during the great imperial expansion in the last twenty years of the century; warfare as the biologists declared it to be experienced in the universal world of nature; and warfare as it might be experienced if science were turned to the task of producing the most efficient possible weapons.

The first of these themes, although the least important, decided the shape of the story. In fact, it was present from the very beginning in the thought of what had happened to the Tasmanians when the superior technology of the West had 'opened up' their lands. Wells stood colonial expansion on its head, presented Britain as a backward area, and gave the Martians a degree of technological achievement that made the miserable defenders of imperial Britain look rather like the unhappy Tasmanians. The theme of an interplanetary war was an ironical inversion of nineteenth-century imperialism. It was a retort on behalf of the Tasmanians to the lament of Cecil Rhodes: 'The world is nearly all parcelled out, and what there is left of it is being divided up, conquered and colonised. To think of these stars that you see overhead at night, these vast worlds which we cannot reach. I would annex the planets if I could; I often think of that. It makes me sad to see them so clear and yet so far.'[20] This imperialist point of view, when raised to an interplanetary level and combined with the principle of the universal struggle to survive, explains the purpose of the Martian descent on our planet:

And we men, the creatures who inhabit this earth, must be to them at least as alien and lowly as are the monkeys and lemurs to us. The intellectual side of man already admits that life is an incessant struggle for existence, and it would seem that this too is the belief of the minds upon Mars. Their world is far gone in its cooling, and this world is still crowded with life, but crowded only with what they regard as inferior animals. To carry warfare sunward is indeed their only escape from the destruction that generation after generation creeps upon them. And before we judge of them too harshly, we must remember what ruthless and utter destruction our own species has wrought, not only upon animals, such as the vanished bison and dodo, but upon its own inferior races. The Tasmanians, in spite of their human likeness, were entirely swept out of existence in a war of extermination waged by European immigrants, in the space of fifty years.[21]

The twin themes of colonial and evolutionary warfare run right through the story. It explains the devastating success of the Martian invaders in the language of interplanetary imperialism: 'We men, with our bicycles and road-skates, our Lilienthal soaring-machines, our guns and sticks, and so forth, are just in the beginning of the evolution that the Martians have worked out.' And at the very end it explains the irony of earth's salvation. It was a victory won for mankind by 'the putrefactive and disease bacteria'. The microbes had conquered in the name of Darwin:

These germs of disease have taken toll of humanity since the beginning of things—taken toll of our pre-human ancestors since life began here. But by virtue of this natural selection of our kind we have developed resisting-power . . . But there are no bacteria in Mars, and directly those invaders arrived, directly they drank and fed, our microscopic allies began to work their overthrow.

It was a famous victory for the allies and something more than a highly convenient ending to a story; it was a profound humiliation for man. Men had not conquered. In fact, under the conditions imagined by Wells they could not conquer. The warriors may have come from Mars for the purpose of the fiction; but their terrible weapons and the immense destruction they caused might one day emerge from Western industrialism, if science were to create the most lethal possible armoury. The marvels of the poisonous Black Smoke, the Heat Ray, the remarkable Handling Machines, and the tall war vehicles in which the Martians stalked over southern England, calling *ulla, ulla, ulla* to one another—all came from the immensely fertile imagination of Wells as he thought with a fear (half recognized for what it was) of the destruction that would follow on a full-scale industrialized war. This fear appears from time to time in a rudimentary form in *The War of the Worlds*. 'Never before in the history of warfare', he wrote, 'had destruction been so indiscriminate and so universal.' And again, when all southern England is at the mercy of the invaders, he writes that 'had the Martians aimed only at destruction, they might on Monday have annihilated the entire population of London, as it spread itself slowly through the home counties'. The greatest industrial nation upon the planet Earth was defenceless before the power of science. As the Commander-in-Chief announced in a calamitous dispatch, flight was the only way out:

The Martians are able to discharge enormous clouds of black and poisonous vapour by means of rockets. They have smothered our batteries, destroyed Richmond, Kingston, and Wimbledon, and are advancing slowly towards London, destroying everything on the way. It is impossible to stop them. There is no safety from the Black Smoke but in instant flight.

At this point *The War of the Worlds* parts company with the mass of imaginary war fiction as it had developed since the time of *The Battle of Dorking*; for Wells's story transcends all the limitations of national politics, international disputes, and contemporary armaments that had engaged the attention of most practitioners in this field. A scientific education, a logical mind, an exceptionally rich and original imagination had acted on his intense realization of incessant change to create this prevision of the possible. Behind it there was a two-stage logic, which began with Wells giving the invaders everything any army could hope for in terms of protection, speed, and fire-power. For Britain the consequences were total defeat, roads crowded with terrified refugees, and the abandoned city of London. For these reasons, and because of the high quality of the narrative, *The War of the Worlds* is still the most remarkable fantasy of imaginary warfare that has so far appeared in the history of the genre.

Within a year of its initial publication in *Pearson's Magazine* and the American *Cosmopolitan*, the first of many borrowings began. The editors of the New York *Journal* and the Boston *Post* paid Wells the sincerest compliment by publishing, without the author's permission, a totally Americanized version of *The War of the Worlds*. Wells was neither amused nor flattered to find that the text of his story had been adapted for American readers and that—far worse—the geography of the Martian invasion had suffered an oceanic change: the entire action had moved across the Atlantic. In December 1897 readers of the *Journal* had the pleasure of reading about the destruction of New York by the Martians, and in January 1898 Bostonians could enjoy the same horrors transferred to their own city. The economy of effort was prodigious.[22]

Forty years later there was an even more notorious American application of *The War of the Worlds* when Orson Welles and the actors of the Mercury Theatre terrified millions on Hallowe'en night, 31 October 1938, with a broadcast adaptation of Wells's invasion story. The scriptwriter, Howard Koch, did full justice to the original story, retaining all the more powerful scenes; but, once again, he transposed the original context of London and the southern

English counties to Washington, DC, and the eastern states of the United States. The realistic technique, however, proved disastrous. As the dramatization went out from the New York studio of the Columbia Broadcasting System, and those listening could hear a professor of astronomy and the Secretary of the Interior describing the capabilities of the Martians, terror began to grip listeners. Thousands fled in panic—they hid themselves, they prayed, they took to the mountains and the forests, and some committed suicide. Next day the headlines told Americans what had happened: 'TIDAL WAVE OF TERROR SWEEPS THE NATION'. A week later a social science team from Princeton University set off for the New Jersey area with their clipboards and questionnaires. Their director, Hadley Cantril, knew that he had all the elements for an original and important social investigation on his own academic doorstep; and in 1940 he published the findings of his team as *The Invasion from Mars* with the apt sub-title of *A Study in the Psychology of Panic*. As he said, with total accuracy, it was 'the first panic that has been carefully studied with the research tools now available. A complete description of the panic should, in itself, be of value to anyone interested in social problems.'[23]

The theme of *The War of the Worlds* was scientific warfare taken to the limit. It was the prelude to a sequence of similar stories—*War in the Air, The World Set Free, The Shape of Things to Come*—in which Wells went on to deal with the conflict between outdated but still-with-us institutions and the urgent need to adjust everything (techniques, education, attitudes of mind, social practices) to the new world that science had called into existence. The struggle between the old and new tormented Wells. In one way he saw it as the struggle between traditional practices in education and the new approaches required to prepare the citizens for life in a technological epoch. Another form was the contrast he saw between the old-style close-combat battles of the Victorian school primers and the swift world-wide wars of the future. The one reflected the other. As Wells saw the situation, when he was writing *Anticipations* in 1900, two of the principal factors working to change the course of human life in the twentieth century were 'the steady development of a new and quite unprecedented educated class as a necessary aspect of the expansion of science and mechanism' and 'the absolute revolution in the art of war that science and mechanism are bringing about'. War and science, therefore, demanded a better and more widespread form of education, or else a nation would go under in the new international struggle to survive. Wells's thesis was very simple: we must educate or perish. 'The law that dominates the future', he wrote, 'is glaringly plain. A people must develop and consolidate its educated class or be beaten in war.' The reasons were obvious to him:

The nation that produces in the near future the largest proportional development of educated and intelligent engineers and agriculturists, of doctors, schoolmasters, professional soldiers and intellectually active people of all sorts . . . will certainly be the nation that will be the most powerful in warfare as in peace, will certainly be the ascendant or dominant nation before the year 2000.'[24]

It took the British people fifty years of slow change, two world wars, and half a dozen reports on educational reform before they began to catch up with the Wellsian proposition.

Wells was one of the few writers of his time who had the requisite imagination and technical competence to understand the social changes then taking place as well as the ability to foresee the ways in which science would continue to affect the conduct of human life. Contrast, for example, Wells's ideas about future warfare with these concluding lines from *A History of Our Time*, written by the historian G. P. Gooch in 1911. His verdict was peace in our time: 'We can now look forward with something like confidence to the time when war between civilised nations will be considered as antiquated as the duel, and when the peacemakers shall be called the children of God.' The scientist turned writer was much nearer the mark than the professional historian. In the chapter on 'War' in *Anticipations*, Wells wrote:

All this elaboration of warfare lengthens the scale between theoretical efficiency and absolute unpreparedness. There was a time when any tribe that had men and spears was ready for war, and any tribe that had some cunning or emotion at command might hope to discount any little disparity in numbers between itself and its neighbour. Luck and stubbornness and the incalculable counted for much; it was half the battle not to know you were beaten, and it is so still. Even today, a great nation, it seems, may still make its army the plaything of its gentlefolk, abandon important military appointments to feminine intrigue, and trust cheerfully to the home-sickness and essential modesty of its influential people, and the simpler patriotism of its colonial dependencies when it comes at last to the bloody and wearisome business of 'muddling through'. But these days of the happy-go-lucky optimist are near their end. War is being drawn into the field of the exact sciences. Every additional weapon, every new complication of the art of war, intensifies the need of deliberate preparation, and darkens the outlook of a nation of amateurs. Warfare in the future, on sea or land alike, will be much more one-sided than it has ever been in the past, much more of a foregone conclusion.[25]

Wells was not always so far-sighted. Although he expected that the military would have to create some form of armoured fighting vehicle, a land ironclad as he described it in a famous short story, he could not foresee 'any sort of submarine doing anything but suffocate its crew and founder at sea', and in 1902 he did not expect a successful aeroplane to have flown much before 1950. But by 1907, when he set out to write *The War in the Air*, at a time when the Zeppelin was still an experiment and Blériot had not yet flown the Channel, Wells returned to the prophetic style of his earlier fantasies. His new thesis was that 'with the flying machine war alters its character; it ceases to be an affair of "fronts" and becomes an affair of "areas"; neither side, victor or loser, remains immune from the gravest injuries, and while there is a vast increase in the destructiveness of war, there is also an increased indecisiveness.'

He describes the great air battles that follow on the sudden raid made by the German air fleet on New York; he relates the destruction of the American fleet in the Atlantic, the North Sea battle that ended German hopes of naval glory, the epidemics, diseases, the destruction of great cities, the spread of war to every corner of the globe, the collapse of trade and commerce. He explains why it all happened in a paragraph that is even more relevant to the period since 1918:

The accidental balance on the side of Progress was far slighter and infinitely more delicate and complex in its adjustments than the people of that time suspected; but that did not alter the fact that it was an effective balance. They did not realise that this age of relative good fortune was an age of immense but temporary opportunity for their kind. They complacently assumed a necessary progress towards which they had no moral responsibility. They did not realise that this security of progress was a thing still to be won or lost, and that the time to win it was a time that passed. They went about their affairs energetically enough, and yet with a curious idleness towards those threatening things. No one troubled over the real dangers of mankind. They saw their armies and navies grow larger and more portentous; some of their ironclads at the last cost as much as their whole annual expenditure upon advanced education; they accumulated explosives and the machinery of destruction; they allowed their national traditions and jealousies to accumulate; they contemplated a steady enhancement of race hostility as the races drew closer without concern or understanding.[26]

Wells came back six years later to this favourite thesis of science and the coming world conflict in *The World Set Free*, which was written during 1913 and published early in 1914. In many ways it is his most striking forecast, although by no means one of his best stories of the future. Two things make it stand out: his argument that, 'because of the development of scientific knowledge, separate sovereign states and separate sovereign empires are no longer possible in the world'; and—even more remarkable—his prediction that scientists would have discovered how to use atomic energy by 1953 and that in consequence a world-wide atomic war would break out. The account of the lecture by the professor of physics at the beginning of the story is one of those rare occasions when fiction becomes truly prophetic. The subject is radioactivity. Holding a phial of uranium oxide before the audience, the professor foretells what would happen when men tapped 'a source of power so potent that a man might carry in his hand the energy to light a city for a year, fight a fleet of battleships or drive one of our giant liners across the Atlantic . . . Every scrap of solid matter in the world would become an available reservoir of concentrated force.' Long before the mushroom cloud hung over Hiroshima, one man had guessed what might result from the work of Einstein and Rutherford. A quarter of a century before Einstein wrote his letter to warn President Roosevelt that the discoveries of the nuclear physicists had made possible the development of 'extremely powerful bombs of a new type', Wells had already given the term 'atomic bomb' to the English language.

Unfortunately, the story in *The World Set Free* is much more prosaic than the extraordinary leap of the imagination that described the discovery of atomic energy and the manufacture of atomic bombs. The tendency to preach, so characteristic a feature of much of Wells's writing after the early scientific romances, undoubtedly weakens the story. The nearer he comes to the facts of science and society, the more pedestrian he is. But when one contrasts what he thought might happen to the conduct of war in *The World Set Free* with the old-style engagements described in so many contemporary tales of imaginary warfare, Wells is still the major prophet. Here, for instance, is the description of the first atomic war as he imagined it in 1913:

For the whole world was flaring then into a monstrous phase of destruction. Power after power about the armed globe sought to anticipate attack by aggression. They went to war in a delirium of panic, in order to use their bombs first. China and Japan had assailed Russia and destroyed Moscow, the United States had attacked Japan, India was in anarchistic revolt with Delhi a pit of fire spouting death and flame: the redoubtable King of the Balkans was mobilising. It must have been plain at last to every one in those days that the world was slipping headlong to anarchy. By the spring of 1959 from nearly two hundred centres, and every week added to their number, roared the unquenchable crimson conflagrations of the atomic bombs; the flimsy fabric of the world's credit had vanished, industry was completely disorganised, and every city, every thickly populated area, was starving or trembled on the edge of starvation. Most of the capital cities of the world were burning; millions of people had already perished, and over great areas government was at an end.[27]

But the Wellsian forecast of unheard-of weapons seemed too far-fetched, too far away in the barely discernible future, to attract the attention of the general reader in 1914. A prophecy much more to the point in those days was Sir Arthur Conan Doyle's notorious short story of unrestricted submarine warfare, *Danger*, which won the interest of all Europe and the scorn of most naval experts. The story, which first appeared in the July number of the *Strand Magazine* in 1914, was written about eighteen months before the outbreak of the First World War. Doyle was quite as deliberate as Wells had been. He wrote, he said, in order 'to direct public attention to the great danger which threatened this country'. He went to the nation with a story of the way in which the submarine fleet of one of the smallest powers in Europe defeated the entire might of the British Empire by sinking all vessels approaching UK ports.

The story was propaganda in aid of the Channel Tunnel project; and the form was the familiar Chesney method of showing what ought to be done by demonstrating the consequences of failing to do it. Conan Doyle opens with an arrogant ultimatum from the British government to a small and imaginary European country. Captain John Sirius, commander of submarines, urges his government to oppose the British demands and proposes that his submarines should take up stations off the major British ports. When the ultimatum expires, and the British government is left with an easy war to win, unidentified submarines begin to sink merchant vessels all around the British Isles. The submarine blockade is complete. Food supplies begin to run out and the government has to sue for peace terms from the despised but victorious small power.

Conan Doyle's forecast appeared two months before Kapitän-leutnant Otto Weddigen showed what the U-boats could do when he sent the *Aboukir, Hogue,* and *Cressy* to the bottom, and seven months before Vize-Admiral von Pohl, Chief of the German Admiralty Staff, proved the accuracy of *Danger* by proclaiming a submarine blockade of the British Isles. All waters around Great Britain and Ireland were declared to be a military area in which Allied shipping would be destroyed and neutral vessels would be in danger of a like fate. Three months later the Cunard liner *Lusitania* was torpedoed off the south coast of Ireland with a loss of 1,198 lives. Conan Doyle was right and the admirals were wrong. In part, British naval thinking had expected that the submarine would affect only Fleet actions. As Admiral Penrose Fitzgerald said of *Danger*; 'I do not myself think that any civilised nation will torpedo unarmed and defenceless merchant ships.' For Admiral Sir Algernon de Horsey, the story was 'a very interesting but, as most would say, fantastic account of an imaginary war'. Another admiral, Sir Compton Domvile, had the same opinion: 'I am compelled to say that I think it most improbable, and more like one of Jules Verne's stories than any other author I know.' And Admiral William Hannam Henderson, although agreeing that the submarine had modified aspects of naval warfare, rejected the opinion 'that territorial waters will be violated, or neutral vessels sunk. Such will be absolutely prohibited, and will only recoil on the heads of the perpetrators. No nation would permit it, and the officer who did it would be shot.'[28]

Three weeks after these views had appeared in the *Strand Magazine* the fateful ultimatum had been sent to Serbia. And out of that came the first world-wide conflict which most of the authors of these imaginary wars had failed to foresee. On 4 August 1914 the long European peace ended. The Germans set the Schlieffen Plan in operation, and along the whole line of the French frontier seven German armies moved forward. One and a half million men were up on their start lines or in support positions. Opposite them some seventy French divisions were engaged in the task of defeating the enemy according to the scheme laid down in Plan XVII. What followed is a matter of

history, of military strategy, and of national legend. By 23 August the situation
on the French left had become most critical as two German armies sought to
roll up the Fifth Army. At the same time, in the Mons area German troops
had made contact for the first time with the British Expeditionary Force. A
full-scale engagement developed. It opened with a bombardment by six hundred guns, the prelude to a frontal attack by German infantry who advanced
in mass formation. The British troops, all highly trained marksmen, used their
rifles to such effect that their fire halted the frontal attacks.

From this incident came the first great legend of the war; for it is a curious
commentary on the mentality of the British people at that time that their
favourite myth was the story of the Angels at Mons. It began in a commonplace manner as *The Bowmen*, a short story written by Arthur Machen which
appeared in the *Evening News* of 29 September 1914. Thereafter, the myth
grew in size and detail; the bowmen became angels, and the clouds shone with
the glory of the great host of heavenly warriors who fought on the side of the
British soldiers. And with this story, which became a popular legend, half a
century of imaginary wars came to an end. Never again would so many writers
describe the shape of wars to come with so much eagerness and ignorance.
After all the predictions, the final paradox is that the last tale of imaginary
warfare to be published in 1914 was Machen's account of the visionary English
archers. The ultimate irony is that in their moment of greatest anxiety, and at
the start of the first great technological war in history, the people of a highly
industrialized world power should find comfort and hope in a legend of angels
who fought upon the clouds. So, the whole sequence of these stories—from
Chesney to Wells and Conan Doyle—ends with the cry of '*Adsit Anglis Sanctus
Georgius*' and the strange appearance of the bowmen. According to the narrator
in Machen's story, 'the roar of the battle died down in his ears to a gentle
murmur; instead of it, he says, he heard a great voice and a shout louder than
a thunder-peal crying, "Array, array, array!"'

His heart grew hot as a burning coal, it grew cold as ice within him, as it seemed
to him that a tumult of voices answered to his summons. He heard, or seemed to
hear, thousands shouting:

'St. George! St. George!'
'Ha! messire; ha! sweet Saint, grant us good deliverance!'
'St. George for merry England!'
'Harow! Harow! Monseigneur St. George succour us.'
'Ha! St. George! Ha! St. George! a long bow and a strong bow.'
'Heaven's Knight, aid us.'

And as the soldier heard these voices he saw before him, beyond the trench, a long
line of shapes, with a shining about them. They were like men who drew the bow,
and with another shout, their cloud of arrows flew singing and tingling through
the air towards the German hosts.[29]

Chapter Four

Politics and the Pattern of the Next Great War, 1880–1914

MODERN readers seem to find the imaginary wars described by Wells and Robida far more interesting than the many tales of destroyers in action and the even more numerous forecasts of the invasion of Britain that appeared in the thirty years before the outbreak of the First World War. For every person who has read Arnold-Forster's best-seller *In a Conning Tower*, there must be thousands today who have read Wells's *War of the Worlds*. There are obvious differences of quality here, since Wells was a far better writer. Again, there is the added fact that, long after the appearance of *Danger* in July 1914, we are still surprised at the singularity of such an unusually accurate forecast as Conan Doyle's description of unrestricted submarine warfare.

Today, long after the publication in 1914 of *The World Set Free*, readers are still impressed by the way Wells could take abstruse scientific ideas from a paper by Frederick Soddy in 1909 and work them into a forecast about the development of atomic energy in 1933—the very year when Frédéric and Irène Joliot-Curie were concluding important investigations that showed how to achieve artificial nuclear radiation. High narrative qualities and the Leonardo-like capacity of some authors to surprise by describing what could happen are reasons that explain the continued popularity of a few stories like *The War of the Worlds* and *The Riddle of the Sands*, whereas the mass of these imaginary war tales would leave today's readers with strong feelings of the quaint, the almost archaic, and the often unreadable.

When these books were appearing for the first time, however, the interests of the reading public were very different. To judge by the number of editions and the large sales made by some of them, it is clear that, although readers were then interested enough in the Wellsian type of future war story, the themes capable of arousing the greatest excitement were matters affecting the military or naval security of a nation and the dangers to be anticipated from a foreign power or a combination of foreign powers. In the major European countries the golden tribute of the large editions came from stories like Capitaine Danrit's *La Guerre fatale*, August Niemann's *Der Weltkrieg*, and Le Queux's *Invasion of 1910*. All of these dealt in a very factual way with the conduct of a war in the immediate future between France and Britain, or between Germany and Britain.

It is remarkable how much these rival tales had in common. Behind the various slogans of the competing nations, it is difficult to find any great difference in the anxiety or the arrogance that had provoked so many visions of British, French, or German victories. From 1880 to 1914 the progress of the tale of future warfare presents a perfect mirror image of the international situation at the time of writing. The changes that take place in the pattern of European power relationships are indicated by sudden outpourings of these stories. Each moment of international crisis—the French alliance with Russia in 1894, the Fashoda incident in 1898, the Tangier landing in 1905—at once sets off an outburst of propaganda stories and warning visions of the future. These continued for a year or two and then they died down until the next crisis began the process once again. What all this meant in the shape of national attitudes and the scale of book production can be seen from a comparison of publications for the years 1882-8 and for the closing years of the period in 1913-14.

The initial phase coincided with a time of increasing tension between Britain and France which began when Wolseley secured Egypt after the battle of Tel-el-Kebir in 1882. From that date the Anglo-French understanding started to deteriorate, especially after 1887, when the French opposed the British efforts to reach a settlement with the Turks over Egypt; and in 1888 opinion in the United Kingdom was further excited by a naval panic touched off by rumours of the mobilization of the French fleet. The temperature was ideal for a spontaneous patriotic explosion. On both sides of the Channel the propagandists began to open fire in the first great imaginary war to be fought between France and Britain since the fantasies of a French invasion that were turned out during the period of the Great Terror when Napoleon was planning to invade Britain.

The first shot in the new war was fired in France, a ranging round from Camille Debans, who wrote in 1884 a violently chauvinistic tale of the total destruction of British power, *Les Malheurs de John Bull*. The appearance of Debans's story marks the beginning in France of a new development in the literature of imaginary warfare. The language and the sentiments of Camille Debans reflect the mob oratory of men like Paul Déroulède, who founded the Ligue des Patriotes in 1882, one of the many movements that led to the great outburst of patriotism and the nationalistic ideas of Boulangism in the 1880s. The same chauvinism and the same violent language appear in the anonymous *Plus d'Angleterre* (1887). The author opens his story with an incident that must have seemed quite likely to Frenchmen in 1887, for the trouble between Britain and France begins in Egypt when British soldiers attack the French consulate in Cairo. As the narrative unrolls with victory after victory for the French and humiliation upon humiliation for the British, it is evident that the style of *Plus d' Angleterre*, like that of *Les Malheurs de John Bull*, is far more popular and nationalistic than anything that had appeared since the *Battle of Dorking*. These stories, like the fiction of Le Queux in the 1890s, appealed directly to chauvinistic prejudice by presenting an idealized picture of a dedicated nation triumphing at last over the despicable enemy of the moment. Already present in *Plus d'Angleterre* are those elements of violence, hatred of the enemy, and the desire for absolute victory that distinguish so many of these stories right up to the outbreak of the First World War. In general, the authors are so angry and so nationalistic that they lack the humour to see how foolish they are at times. The anonymous author of *Plus d' Angleterre*, like later German and British writers, can only see the wickedness of the enemy; and he writes a book full of French nationalism to attack the evils of British nationalism.

On the British side, feelings had not yet reached this degree of animosity. That was to come after the Franco-Russian agreement of 1894, when the British imaginary wars came to rival the invective of the French ten years earlier. Only after 1894 did stories begin to appear like the *Sack of London in the Great French War of 1901* (1901), which replied in kind by explaining French ill will as a matter of pure envy—'envy of England's great Empire, envy at her freedom, envy of the stability of her Government, of her settled monarchy, and of her beloved Queen'. Before this, however, most of the imaginary wars published in the United Kingdom were concerned with the performance of ships and armaments in a future war, or with political demonstrations in favour of measures to improve the safety of the nation in time of war. Certainly these were the usual types of war fiction that appeared between 1882 and 1894.

The first political differences with France in 1882 coincided with a national debate on the scheme for a Channel Tunnel, which Sir Edward Watkin had put before Parliament in the form of a Private Member's Bill. The uproar that followed provides an interesting lesson on differences in national attitudes. On the part of the French, there were no tales of imaginary invasions by British troops who came suddenly and treacherously into France by way of the Channel Tunnel. The French press looked on the extraordinary commotion then taking place in the United Kingdom as one more example of the eccentric goings-on of a very odd neighbour. One observer, Georges Valbert, remarked with great shrewdness that the panics and protests were not military but psychological in origin. On the day the Channel Tunnel was completed, he wrote, Britain would be no longer an island: 'It will be a prodigious event in the life of an insular people, when they find that they are islanders no more. Nothing is more likely to excite and alarm them, or to affect and upset their preconceived ideas.'[1] How right he was can be seen in the alarm about French intentions shown in the debate on the Channel Tunnel and in the sudden crop of invasion stories during 1882 and 1883.

The typical British reaction to the proposals of the Channel Tunnel Company and the Submarine Continental Railway Company was like that of Palmerston twenty-five years earlier. The Prince Consort had spoken to him with all his usual enthusiasm for great technological enterprises in an attempt to gain his support for Thomé de Gamond's scheme to construct a tunnel. The reports of that famous interview relate that, 'without losing the perfectly courteous tone which was habitual with him', the Prime Minister told the Prince Consort: 'You would think very differently if you had been born in this island.' These sturdy British sentiments explain the reaction against a tunnel, from the thundering of *The Times* and the spate of imaginary invasions by way of the Channel Tunnel to the action of the angry Londoners who smashed the windows in the Westminster offices of the Channel Tunnel Company. The substance of the argument for the opposition was that to build a tunnel would be an act of folly, since it would leave the country open to sudden invasion. The case against the Channel Tunnel was put by a popular ditty sung in 1882:

> By the Great Ruler of the Earth and Heaven
> This Island from a Continent was riven;
> Where mountains could not shield from spoil and slaughter
> He—for a national Bulwark—gave THE WATER!

Opposition to the proposed Channel Tunnel was a popular and national movement that affected every level in society. One of the most striking demonstrations came from that reputable periodical the *Nineteenth Century* during the height of the upheaval in April and May 1882. The editor, James Knowles, took the unusual step of organizing a mass petition against the tunnel—a device considered to be a very great novelty in the magazines and reviews at that time. The petition was signed by many distinguished figures of the day—Browning, Tennyson, Huxley, Cardinal Newman, Spencer, the Archbishop of Canterbury, The Mackintosh of Mackintosh, the editors of the *Spectator*, *Morning Post*, *St James's Gazette*, *Lloyd's Weekly News*, five dukes, ten earls, twenty-six Members of Parliament, seventeen admirals, fifty-nine generals, about two hundred clergymen, and some six hundred other eminent persons. All put their signatures to this protest:

The undersigned, having had their attention called to certain proposals made by commercial companies for joining England to the Continent of Europe by a Railroad under the Channel, and feeling convinced that (notwithstanding any precautions against risk suggested by the projectors) such a Railroad would involve this country in military dangers and liabilities from which, as an island, it has hitherto been happily free—hereby record their emphatic protest against the sanction or execution of any such work.[2]

It was the *Battle of Dorking* panic in another form. Tracts, pamphlets, military forecasts of the consequences of building a tunnel, and tales of imaginary invasions by the French poured off the presses during 1882 and 1883. Letters to newspapers, special articles, and editorials showed that the country was not yet mentally prepared to accept the brutal engineering that would terminate for ever the convenient isolation of 'this fortress built by Nature for herself'. The emotional inheritance, loaded with the magnificent literary tradition inaugurated by Shakespeare's well-remembered lines about 'this scepter'd isle', was far too strong for the less romantic facts of commercial and technological advantage. And yet, when one asks why so many eminent gentlemen should have subscribed to the protest against the Channel Tunnel organized by the *Nineteenth Century*, the only answer can be that they feared the country would be ruined. In this they had the support and example of military and naval opinion. The considered view of the Duke of Cambridge, writing from the Horse Guards in his capacity as the Field-Marshal Commanding-in-Chief, was set down in a memorandum of 23 June 1882. He argued against a tunnel on the grounds that, since the Fenians only a few years before had attacked Chester Castle, it might be possible to take Dover Castle by surprise; that no device could be certain to prevent others using a tunnel, because during the war of 1870 the French had left the splendid Vosges tunnels intact for the Germans to use; that British military forces could not hope to oppose any great Continental power after it had seized the Channel Tunnel; and that, if a tunnel were ever built, then 'we might, despite all our precautions, very possibly some day find an enemy in actual possession of both of its ends, and able at pleasure to pour an army through unopposed'.

The same suggestion of sudden menace and of strange forces moving on Dover at the dead of night came out in another memorandum of June 1882, written by Lord Wolseley in his office as Adjutant-General. One of his arguments against a tunnel gives good cause to claim him as the originator of the fifth-column story that became very popular with writers of imaginary invasion tales. He seems to have fathered the tales of French waiters with rifles packed in their baggage from which grew the stories of German waiters training secretly in London that were a stock feature of the imaginary invasion fiction published before 1914. For the Adjutant-General argued in all seriousness that 'a couple of thousand armed men might easily come through the tunnel in a train at night, avoiding all suspicion by being dressed as ordinary passengers, or passing at express speed through the tunnel with the blinds down, in their uniform and fully armed'. He warned the country that it would be possible for a force of five thousand men to attempt to seize the tunnel installations. Nay, 'half that number, ably led by a daring, dashing young commander, might, I feel, some dark night easily make themselves masters of the works at our end of the tunnel—and then England would be at the mercy of the invader'.

While the chairman of the South-Eastern Railway, Sir Edward Watkin, was arguing the case for his tunnel against the doubters in the scientific committee of inquiry, the railway bookstalls were covered with stories of imaginary invasions written in the great cause of the nation versus the tunnel. The titles carried their message of warning: *The Seizure of the Channel Tunnel*; *The Channel Tunnel, or, England in Danger*; *The Story of the Channel Tunnel*; *Battle of the Channel Tunnel*; *How John Bull Lost London*; *The Surprise of the Channel Tunnel*; *The Battle of Boulogne*. None of them was able to improve in any way on the warnings given by the Duke of Cambridge and Lord Wolseley. They told a tale of sudden attack by French tourists, or by picked groups of Zouaves, or by soldiers disguised as waiters. As the author of *The Surprise of the Channel Tunnel* explained, 'the great increase in size and prosperity that the Tunnel brought to Dover caused a large number of French restauranteurs, waiters, bootmakers, milliners, pastrycooks etc. to settle in that town'. Any patriot could have guessed the results. Those seeming civilians were all trained soldiers, even the milliners; and according to plan they seized their rifles on N-night, rushed from their lodgings, occupied the tunnel installations, and sent the signal that brought the entire French Army pouring into the sleeping land of Britain. In another story, *How John Bull Lost London*, which caused a minor sensation in Britain and provided an occasion for derisive comment in France, a party of French tourists suddenly leaped from their excursion train and opened the way for the invasion forces. According to the author of *The Channel Tunnel*, the invaders would spread terror wherever they went:

The sudden seizure of the tunnel by the French would produce such a panic in England that law and order would probably become impossible, fear and fury would be dominant, and those who had property, or the honour of wives and daughters to save from the French soldiery, would be busy taking speedy measures to escape from London with their valuables.

Propaganda of this kind was completely singleminded in its attempt to influence public opinion against the Channel Tunnel. It is clear from the popular appeal of some of these stories that the authors were in many ways anticipating the methods developed in the mass fiction of the 1890s, since several of them were clearly no longer writing for an exclusively middle-class public, as Chesney had done with *The Battle of Dorking*. These stories show that, in step with the increase in literacy and with the growing importance of the new electors following on the Education Act of 1870 and the various Reform Acts, the conduct of war was ceasing to be a private matter for the higher levels of the nation. It was rapidly becoming a matter for everyone, as the new daily newspapers would demonstrate in the last decade of the century.

An obvious relationship exists between this type of fiction and the political situation at the time of writing; for these stories occupied the attention of the public for a year or two while the anxiety behind them ran its course from panic to prostration, and then they disappeared for ever. This principle is evident in the burst of imaginary invasions caused by the Channel Tunnel controversy in 1882 and 1883. It can be seen at work again in 1887 and 1888, when anxiety at the state of the Royal Navy and anger at the French attitude to British attempts to solve the Egyptian problem produced another crop of imaginary wars between Britain and France: *The Great Naval War of 1887*; *The Battle off Worthing*; *An Omitted Incident in the 'Great Naval War of 1887'*; *The Capture of London*; *The Taking of Dover*; *Plus encore d'Angleterre, or, The Repulse of the French*.

In their different ways, these stories all reflect a general anxiety at the condition of the Royal Navy, which had begun in September 1884 when the astute and influential journalist W. T. Stead published a series of articles in the *Pall Mall Gazette* designed to tell 'The Truth about the Navy'. In the view of Lord Charles Beresford, Stead's articles 'did more than any other Press representations before or since to awaken public opinion to the true condition of our defences'. The articles were certainly effective, since Stead's demands for a more efficient fleet and for more cruisers and improved coaling stations were at once repeated throughout the national press. The First Lord of the Admiralty, Lord Northbrook, was the subject of much criticism; and in 1885 he had the misfortune to inspire a violent attack on himself from the Poet Laureate:

> You—you—*if* you have fail'd to understand
> The Fleet of England is her all in all—
> On you will come the curse of all the land,
> If that Old England fall,
> Which Nelson left so great—

> You—you—who had the ordering of her Fleet,
> *If* you have only compass'd her disgrace
> When all men starve, the wild mob's million feet
> Will kick you from your place—
> But then—too late, too late.

The passion of Tennyson's verse was symptomatic of the public's anger and alarm on discovering that the Navy had fallen behind in the race for technological development and that its direction was often inefficient and inadequate. In 1885, when Britain and Russia were in dispute over Afghanistan, it had taken two months to complete the naval preparations. Again, it was only in 1886, on a suggestion from Lord Charles Beresford, that a Naval Intelligence Department was established to deal with the many problems of the new-style war at sea. The Royal Navy was preparing to meet the challenge of the ironclad and the torpedo. From this point in the 1880s public interest in the past and future achievements of the Navy grew rapidly; and this was matched by a rapid growth of imaginary war stories in which the ships of the Fleet sailed out to glorious triumphs or humiliating defeats according to the intention of the author. At times these were simple yarns about the way in which a future naval engagement might develop, like Arnold-Forster's *In a Conning Tower*. The first of the more purposive stories of naval warfare appeared in 1887, when William Laird Clowes and A. H. Burgoyne wrote a serial for the *St James's Gazette*, a special piece called *The Great Naval War of 1887*, which was intended to show the consequences of an inefficient scheme of mobilization. War breaks out between Britain and France. Mobilization follows, but in the manner of Chesney the authors rub in the bitter lesson that 'the machinery of the Admiralty and War Office collapsed under the strain that was so suddenly thrown upon it, and incredible confusion resulted'. For the rest it is the Chesney formula of brave men and incompetent leadership and the brutal fact that it was all 'the natural result of years of indifference, mismanagement, and parsimony'. The answer soon became a standard item in these naval stories: more funds for the Fleet.

In the eyes of writers like William Laird Clowes, the greatest of all the sins against the Royal Navy was parsimony. As the nation discovered when the Naval Defence Act of 1889 was introduced into Parliament, there had to be more funds. The proposals to build eight first-class battleships and thirty-eight cruisers were essential if the British hoped to maintain their traditional policy of isolation. Until the naval scares of the 1880s, policy had depended on the supremacy of the Navy and on the fact that continental countries could be expected to be so occupied with their own quarrels that they would not think of combining against Britain. But both these cardinal principles were in doubt after 1884. A bigger and better Fleet was the immediate answer to one of the problems; but when the French allied themselves with the Russians in 1894, and so threatened British naval supremacy in the Mediterranean, the only answer to a European combination was to look for allies abroad. In the history of imaginary warfare, these political facts took the shape of future wars fought by the British against the French and their allies until in 1903 the great popularity enjoyed by *The Riddle of the Sands* signalled the beginning of a sudden shift to stories of the coming German invasion of the United Kingdom.

Before the beginning of the Anglo-French Entente in 1904, the *guerres imaginaires* had been almost as much concerned with wars against Britain as against Germany. The one difference was that before the disagreement over Egypt the French stories dealt exclusively with the future war of reconquest to be waged against the Germans: *La Guerre future* in 1875; *La France et l' Allemagne au printemps prochain* in 1876; *La Guerre franco-allemande de 1878* in 1877; *La Guerre prochaine entre la France et l' Allemagne* in 1881. Plans for the sacred task of *la revanche* continued year by year until 1914; but, in parallel with this stream of anti-German tales, a series of triumphant imaginary wars against the British began to appear after the publication of *Les Malheurs de John Bull* in 1884, and these continued down to 1904. They were generally less methodical in their plans of campaign, less concerned with military detail, and much more impassioned in their language than the anti-German stories of this period.

The difference between these two forms of imaginary warfare in France turned on a matter of attitudes. Whenever French writers set about describing the next great war against Britain or Germany, they apparently acted on the principle that, even if the Germans were enemies, the British were undoubtedly their most hated enemies. Anger, resentment, and the desire to destroy utterly were the dominant emotions in most of the tales about the humiliation of proud Albion. This condition was a natural product of the Napoleonic tradition, which seems to have infected most of these writers whenever they turned their attention to a war against the British; and in the political climate of the time it reflected the steady deterioration in the relations between the two countries which reached their lowest level at the time of the Fashoda incident in 1898. To understand the difference between the two styles of imaginary warfare, contrast the plain and matter-of-fact titles given to the anti-German stories with the inflammatory and vindictive style of *Plus d'Angleterre* In 1887; *La Prise de Londres au XXe siècle* In 1891, *Mort aux Anglais* in 1892, and *L'Agonie d'Albion* in 1901. In the last analysis, however, the differences in the two kinds of story reflect a division of interest between the civilians and writers in the armed forces. Most of the narratives about a future war against Germany were produced by army officers. They wrote matter-of-fact accounts in the manner of *La Bataille de Damvillers: récit anticipé de la prochaine campagne* (1888). They repeated the ideas and plans talked over in the mess and the military academy. The description of the war against Britain, on the other hand, was usually left to the civilian writers, no doubt because only those ignorant of naval matters would be rash enough to attempt an account of a successful invasion of the British Isles. There can be no better illustration of this dual attitude than in the numerous publications of Capitaine Émile Danrit—or, as he really was, Capitaine Driant:

DRIANT, Émile Auguste Cyprien. Son of Joseph Driant and Adélaide-Virginie de Fäy. Born 11 September, 1855. Educated at the Lycée de Reims; entered St Cyr in 1875; and in 1877 commissioned as second-lieutenant in the 54th Infantry Regiment. Promoted lieutenant in 1882; in 1886 transferred to the 4th Regiment of Zouaves. In 1888 appointed adjutant to General Boulanger at the Ministry of War. On 29 October, 1888, married Marcelle, younger daughter of General Boulanger. From 1892 to 1896 served as instructor at St Cyr. Recalled to regimental service and in 1898 appointed to command the 1st Battalion Chasseurs à Pied. In 1906 resigned his commission and took part in the elections of that year but without success. In 1910 was elected a deputy for Nancy. In 1914 recalled to command a battalion. Protested against failure to make adequate preparations for the defence of Verdun. Killed in action at the Bois des Caures whilst directing heroic defence against mass of the German XVIII Corps.

As might be expected from a man who was adjutant to General Boulanger at the time of his greatest triumphs and had married the general's daughter, everything Driant wrote was filled with the glories of military service and with a spirit of intense nationalism. His many stories about future wars against the Germans or the British belong to the great body of *revanchiste* literature that sprang up rapidly in the 1880s. What he wrote was only a demonstration of the ideals and intentions to be found in such popular songs of the day as *Réveil de la France*, *La Marseillaise de la Revanche*, *À la frontière*, *Notre Général bien-aimé*, as well as in the poetry of Paul Déroulède. One of the closing stanzas of Déroulède's poem, 'Vive la France', reveals the spirit of reconquest that shaped the French literature of imaginary warfare:

> Et la revanche doit venir, lente peut-être,
> Mais en tout cas fatale, et terrible à coup sûr;
> La haine est déja née, et la force va nâitre:
> C'est au faucheur à voir si le champ n'est pas mûr.

An English variant of these sentiments can be found in the aggressive imperialism of W. E. Henley, who wrote frequently of the 'iron beneficence' of war. In 1892, for instance, he published in the *National Observer* a poem by one of his young writers. It began:

> Give us, O Lord,
> For England's sake,
> War righteous and true,
> Our hearts to shake.

'On every side', Capitaine Danrit wrote in the preface to *La Guerre de demain*, 'the nations are arming and preparing for war.' Danrit was at once the William Le Queux and the Admiral Colomb of France. His books are filled with the arrogant nationalism of stories like *England's Peril* and they make the same use of expert military knowledge that can be seen in *The Great War of 1892*. Running through his stories and through many similar stories by other writers, there is a sense of anger at past defeat, of military honour cast down in 1870. To compensate for past humiliation, the army had to be the symbol of the nation's pride and the guarantee of future revenge. At a time when respect for the military uniform, for the officer, and for the tricolour was greater than in any previous period, it was to be expected that Danrit's stories should turn out to be one sustained glorification of France, the Army, and the great business of *la revanche*. This, no doubt, was the reason why the French Academy crowned *La Guerre de demain* and gave Danrit the Prix Montyon.

The political background of Danrit's three stories of the campaign against Germany was the international situation of the period about 1890. Like Admiral Colomb in *The Great War of 1892*, he thought in terms of a war between France and Germany in which the Russians would come in on the side of the French. The style of the writing recalls the demonstrations before the veiled statue of Strasburg in the Place de la Concorde which in those days was still covered up with the prophetic slogan, *Qui vive? La France, 1870–18–*, and with the initials of the Ligue des Patriotes. For a soldier and a patriot the picture of the future was a vision of French troops driving the enemy out of occupied France. With this in mind Danrit dedicated *La Guerre en rase campagne* to the men of his own 4ᵉ Régiment de Zouaves:

It has been my hope to have gone off with you to the Great War which we are all expecting and which is still delayed. But, if there is a god of battles and if he hears me, I still hope to take part in the war under your banner. To pass the time whilst waiting, I have dreamed of this Holy War in which we will conquer, and this book is my dream.

The same sentiments, enlarged to national proportions, inspire the proclamation of war and the appeal to the French as Danrit describes the moment when the Germans make their sudden and undeclared onslaught on France:

Francais!
In violation of the law of nations our country has been invaded without a declaration of war. German troops are advancing towards the Meuse. The hour of our revenge has struck. The holy war has begun. Frenchmen, young and old, conscripts, soldiers, territorials—to arms!

To arms in the supreme struggle that will restore to us our lost provinces and our place in Europe! To arms for the defence of our homes! Let all the powers of France rise up to punish the barbarians who want to remove our name from contemporary history and our country from the map of the world. The French Army will not be surprised. Every day it has been expecting to do battle, ready to defend or to attack. Our troops will march against the enemy as their fore-fathers did in the heroic past. They will carry on their banners the old words—Victory or Death!

Behind them and by their side stand all those of you who love your country but for reasons of age have not been called to the colours—children, old men, even the infirm. Start now on this war to the death! Answer this treacherous invasion by a war of extermination. Burn your villages before the Germans enter them. With your own hands destroy anything that could help the enemy. Let the East of France become the tomb of our ancient enemy.

Be of good heart! This German empire, a thing of bits and pieces, will collapse at the first reverse! Be of good heart! A powerful ally is about to join forces with us! Frenchmen, have confidence! From today all quarrels among ourselves have disappeared—buried beneath an ardent love for France![3]

The actions Danrit relates have for their tonic and dominant the ideal of national supremacy and the desire for total victory over the ancient enemy. A certain utopian element appears in the selection and projection of all that he considers is best and most admirable in French life. Indeed, his stories, like so many of the contemporary imaginary wars in English and later in German, are perfect para-utopias for an epoch of exaggerated nationalism. Politics and self-persuasion work together to create a vision of the nation imposing its will upon the enemy of the moment. Any comparison of these stories in English, French, or German will show how the nationalistic emotions of the period found their natural outlet in a new mythology of imaginary wars which were no more than a picture of the world rearranged to suit a nation's desires. So, Danrit concludes *La Guerre de demain* on the comforting thought that 'France united with Russia is today the arbiter of Europe and the world.' The same demand that the world should be a reification of national ambitions can be seen in *The Final War* by Louis Tracy. His theme is a variant on the French nationalism of Danrit: 'The Saxon race will absorb all and embrace all, re-animating old civilizations and giving new vigour to exhausted nations.'

On the surface Danrit's stories, like the stories of George Griffith, Louis Tracy, and August Niemann, were all concerned with a likely political situation in the near future; but in reality, Danrit and his contemporaries were creating wish-fulfilment fantasies of a noble people, united in true brotherhood, engaged in the great task of winning for the nation its rightful place in the world. In Danrit's dream—and he called it a dream—all sections of society are joined in the work of *la revanche*. Simple peasants fight as partisans, officers die with conspicuous heroism at the head of their troops, and even the village curé (*le vieux bon homme*) is ready to leave his flock and take up a rifle against the enemies of the sacred soil of France. It is no different in Tracy's account of the Franco-German attack on Britain in *The Final War*. Everything is quite perfect: 'The splendid calm of the House of Commons, amid all the varying fortunes of the war, and its phlegmatic pride, its stern attitude of quiet resolution, formed a striking example of the indomitable character of the English people.' Overnight all political quarrels are forgotten, as in Danrit's stories, and the rich help the poor, with the result that within a few weeks from the outbreak of war 'there was more practical Socialism to be seen in the internal economy of London and other important centres of population than had been dreamed of or spoken of by philosophical reformers in as many centuries'.

At this stage the narratives begin to move away from the realities of the contemporary political situation. The element of fantasy increases and the stories turn into a species of nationalistic utopia in which the superior virtues, intelligence, and vigour of the fatherland, defeat an enemy without honour, without honesty, and without intelligence. The central principle in all of them is that the whole world conspires against the enemy. In Tracy's tale of *The Final War* the American Navy intervenes on the British side, Russian revolutionaries capture the Tsar, the Indian Army storms across Persia to attack Russia, and the new Thomson Electric Rifle gives the British troops a devastating secret weapon. Similarly, in Danrit's account of the Franco-German war, the threat of an Italian invasion from the south is conveniently removed by the action of the Pope, who puts the Italian government under an interdict and then leaves for Spain. A two-day revolution follows in Rome; the Italian government falls, and the war with France ends almost before it had really begun.

It is an understatement to call such extravagance a wish-fulfilment fantasy. Danrit and his contemporaries were projecting an idealized image of the nation in arms. Their stories have all the force and the directness of popular and purposive fiction. The events and the characters are seen in black and white; everything is presented in the form of the polar opposites of the unspeakable enemy and the glorious nation. Since the nation is an object of worship in these stories, the enemy must equally be an object of detestation. This is the other side to the utopian tale of national triumph: complete virtue faces total wickedness. In fact, it would seem that war guilt had been apportioned long before 1914, since some of the British reactions to the Germans in the First World War appear to be stereotyped behaviour patterns carried over from the literature of the imaginary wars. This is especially true of the enemy agent. In all these tales the spy is the supreme symbol of enemy evil, the antithesis of the nationalist thesis of unity, courage, and victory.

One of the major ironies in the literature of future wars is that all European countries expect the worst of the enemy. Espionage represents the depths of villainy on the other side, for the spy always appears where he can do a country the greatest harm. In *The Great Naval War of 1887*, the authors relate that 'it was well known that the whole south of England was full of French spies'. The enemy could always be expected to take the meanest advantage of a hospitable nation, even to the point of employing renegades and traitors against their own country. The plot in Max Pemberton's very popular *Pro Patria* of 1901 turns on the treachery of Robert Jeffrey, a one-time candidate for the Royal Artillery, who directs the French plan to invade Britain by a tunnel secretly constructed under the Channel. What happened and how it all ended can be seen in the last paragraphs, which show how these stories flourished on the ill-feeling between countries:

That France attempted to build a tunnel under the Channel to England is no longer denied. That her engineers had been engaged upon the work for many years is equally well known. Her prospects of success, should such an attempt be repeated, are variously esteemed. We have seen that the more daring capitalists and fanatics of Paris, having compelled the French government to thrust out a tunnel from Calais, sought to open that tunnel here by taking a farmhouse in an Englishman's name. . . . The vigilance of one man defeated this great scheme; he shut the gate, as he says, in the face of France. But the tube of steel still lies below the sea. No living man, outside the purlieus of the secret, can say how far that tunnel is carried, or where the last tube of it is riveted. It may come even to Dover's cliffs; it may lie many miles from them.

During this period it was a convention with writers of imaginary wars to describe in detail the despicable behaviour of enemy spies. Even the Italians, whose tales of future wars were the rarest and mildest of them all, did not fail to dwell on the ill doings of the enemy. In a tale of 1899, *La Guerra del 190–*, the narrative describes how a patrol of Alpini arrested two French officers 'who were caught red-handed in the act of spying, complete with plans and sketches in their baggage'. This attitude to espionage is one of the bigger hypocrisies of the literature before 1914. Civilization, truth, and justice are for the purpose of the story identified with Britain, France, Germany, or Italy; and in this situation the spy has a special role to play, since he can be used to point a moral and reinforce the sense of national virtuousness in the reader.

In support of this attitude, there was the unquestioned fact that espionage had been increasing since the war of 1870, and could be expected to go on increasing as long as new weapons were devised, fortifications built, and strategic plans prepared for the defence of frontiers. If espionage was a condition of the new epoch of industrialized warfare, it was also a fact in the new popular mythology of the imaginary wars. Most of Danrit's stories, for example, make great play with the activities of the spy who, unlike the dignified and humane French officers, is decidedly unchivalrous. He is even devious and conveniently stupid into the bargain. The first rule for the use of enemy agents is that they are always found out in time. The second is that our own agents are always successful. Both rules can be seen in operation in William Le Queux's notorious tale of 1899, *England's Peril*. The French Embassy in London is a nest of spies:

Attached to the Embassy were many spies, for of recent years the French Secret Service had grown almost as formidable in its proportions as that of Russia, and their constant reports from political and official centres in London would have surprised the Admiralty and War Office. Officially they were unrecognized, being controlled by one man, a renegade Englishman.

There is, however, no real cause for alarm, since our own agents know what is going on:

The British Secret Service, although never so prominently before the public as those unscrupulous *agents provocateurs* of France and Russia, is nevertheless equally active. It works in silence and secrecy, yet many are its successful counterplots against the machinations of England's enemies.

Change the names and Danrit could have written those lines, for he was as certain as Le Queux that enemy agents were at work in many places. And he was right in so far as, unknown to him, Colonel Schwartzkoppen had started to operate from the German Embassy in 1891 and was beginning to collect French military documents, the famous *bordereau* that led to the Dreyfus Affair in 1894. In his *Guerre de forteresse* Danrit maintained that 'out of the

25,000 officers who appear in the German Army List, 15,000 volunteered of their own free will for espionage duties. They honour that sort of work with the name of secret mission.' And as *La Guerre de demain* unrolls, the spies and *saboteurs* appear in a variety of cunning disguises. Two Alsatian refugees turn out to be enemy agents and are caught only minutes before they would have passed on vital information to the enemy. An amiable young priest, who claims to be the curé of Bazoilles, is proved to be no priest at all but a member of the German intelligence network. And there is the ridiculous Englishman, Sir John Byde, a pantomime spy with long teeth, side-whiskers, an impossible French accent, and immense arrogance, who operates in the German interest with a comical lack of success.

This black-and-white characterization is part of the implicit contract between the writer and his readers that they will be able to join in the greatest actions of which a nation is capable—war and the reconstruction of the world. The subject-matter of these stories is not the behaviour of recognizable individuals, as it is in the novel; it is the nation, the enemies of the nation, the new instruments of war, and the future greatness of the fatherland. What characters exist in the narrative are there to play chorus and interlude to epic dramas in which the principals are some or all of the great powers.

The process of idealization begins with the way writers describe their wars in the language of gallantry and glory, and not in terms of the courage and endurance needed in real warfare. They are, of course, describing war as they would like it to be right down to the last victorious battle and the future that will be for ever British, or French, or German. This can be seen in the many stories turned out by journalists like George Griffith, Robert Cromie, and Louis Tracy. In 1899 Griffith produced *The Great Pirate Syndicate*, a prodigious tale of imperialistic politics and of secret weapons that give instant victory to the Anglo-Saxon powers; by the end of the story the whole world has been subdued and the happy victors find that 'foreign sea-borne trade had practically disappeared, for no competition with the enormously wealthy firms of Anglo-Saxondom was possible'. An Anglo-Saxon peace in our time completes the happiness of all: 'as no other nation could hope to cope with the colossal forces at the disposal of the Anglo-Saxon Federation, there was every reason to believe that the world was entering upon an era of profound peace as well as unexampled prosperity'.

The French version of this optimistic nationalism can be seen in Danrit's account of the invasion and conquest of the British Isles, *La Guerre fatale: France–Angleterre*, which was first published in 1901. Like so many of these stories written at the beginning of the twentieth century, Danrit's fantasy goes to the limit in describing the swift and merciless destruction of the enemy. The Russians sweep through Afghanistan and conquer India. The new submarines of the French Fleet convoy an invasion force across the Channel in full view of an impotent Royal Navy. And the British troops prove to be as second-rate and incompetent as any enemy general could hope. The French storm up the beaches to pealing trumpets and shouts of victory, for 'the British Army had little importance in the eyes of our soldiers since it had been shown to be so weak in South Africa'. The fortunate invaders find that 'the worst faults of Lord Methuen and Sir Redwers Bulwer [*sic*] in the Transvaal' have been repeated on their home ground.

In this way, the story of the nation's next great war changes into a vulgar utopian vision of total triumph written according to the political specifications of the international situation. For the first time in the course of history, the epic tale of great national achievements had ceased to be told only in retrospect. During the last two decades of the nineteenth century the epic had moved out of the legendary past; it became a popular and prospective myth projected into the near and seemingly realizable future. In the hands of writers like Louis Tracy, Capitaine Danrit, and August Niemann, the tale of future warfare developed into an attractive and spectacular demonstration of how a nation could satisfy its every desire. Victory is, therefore, always absolute, even to the detailed and exultant description of the entry into the enemy capital and the final symbolic act of surrender before the massed battalions of the invader. Danrit closes *La Guerre fatale* with the reading of the peace terms in the shattered ruins of the House of Commons. Similarly, in Niemann's story published in 1904, *Der Weltkrieg*, the Germans land at Leith and rapidly overrun the United Kingdom. The German author ends on the happy thought that 'His Majesty the Emperor will enter London at the head of the allied armies. Peace is assured. God grant that it may be the last war which we shall have to wage for the future happiness of the German nation.'

In their own strange way, these writers were trying to create a Beowulf myth for an industrial civilization of ironclads and high-speed turbines, a new and violent *chanson de geste* for an age of imperialism, told in the inflammatory language of the mass press. They were popular epics for a period of universal literacy, the counterpart of the many tales about the deeds that won the Empire, all written to the glory of the nation-state; for in the closing years of the nineteenth century the aggressive nation-states of Europe had everything on their side except common sense. They were supported by a steady growth in the power of central governments, and especially by the immensely powerful association of the national flag, anthems, magnificent uniforms, and traditional ceremonies. Most of all in the nineteenth century the nation-state meant the glories of war. From the moment when Kellermann called for cheers for the nation as he rode along the line of raw recruits at the Battle of Valmy, war had become the maker of nations. That was the moment when, in the words of Foch, 'a new era had begun, the era of national wars that are fought under no restraint whatever'. And since the cardinal virtues of the nation-state were

love and hate—ourselves against the rest—it followed that any prospective
vision of the nation triumphing in war would be set in terms of life and death,
of total victory and total defeat. So, the tale of imaginary warfare could start
from some incident or possibility in international politics; it could then grow
into a species of nationalistic rhetoric by means of which a writer was able to
demonstrate national values and objectives at one and the same time. This is
one reason why in so many of these stories, although the weapons were the
very latest instruments of destruction, the language and the attitudes recall the
epic moments of Austerlitz and Waterloo.

And here it is necessary to point out that a difference runs through this literature. Although writers may all be agreed on the immediate end, the defeat
of the enemy, it must be emphasized that their motives and purposes vary
considerably. Guy du Maurier's play, *An Englishman's Home* (1909), displays
an effulgent patriotism. Very different is the unquestioned opportunism shown
by Harmsworth when he commissioned an invasion story as part of his scheme
for the general election of 1895. In that year Harmsworth stood as one of the
two Conservative candidates for Portsmouth. To further his campaign, he
bought the *Portsmouth Mail* and obtained the services of William Laird
Clowes, who collaborated with one of Harmsworth's young men, Beccles
Wilson, in concocting a shocking tale of what might happen if the Navy could
not prevent an enemy fleet from approaching the coast. The story, *The Siege
of Portsmouth*, began on 17 June and continued every day for three weeks. The
nasty compound of commercialism and electioneering that caused the story to
be written is admirably illustrated from the announcement advertising the first
issue. The following text appeared under a drawing of the tower of
Portsmouth Town Hall collapsing beneath a rain of shells:

On Monday next the 'Mail' will commence a startling new 'forecast' of the Great
War of 189–. Day by day we shall print a stirring narrative, written by distinguished naval and military authorities, dealing with the story of the Siege of
Portsmouth, and how our country was invaded by the French and Russians. The
names of prominent townsmen will be introduced in this remarkable work, and all
those who do not wish to be left behind in the rush for the 'Mail' should go to
their newsagents today and give an order for the paper to be delivered at their
house regularly.

On Monday next the guaranteed issue of the 'Mail' will exceed 40,000 copies,
and advertisers who wish for publicity in the paper should bring their advertisements to the office at once.

One of the incidents of the Siege, the blowing up of the Town Hall, is depicted
in the above illustration, which will also be found on a larger scale on most of the
hoardings in the neighbourhood.

The story was well calculated to play upon current anxieties in the
Conservative interest. It started from the then obvious fact of British isolation

in 1895, when 'the enhanced hereditary hatred between France and ourselves was unfortunately coincident with a growing coolness between ourselves and Germany'. Here it is possible to detect the hand of William Laird Clowes himself in the account of the war that follows on the visit to Brest by the Russian Baltic Fleet. The episode was a clear reference to the naval scare that blew up over the visit of a Russian squadron to Toulon in 1893. Clowes was largely responsible for the scare, since he went to Toulon as *The Times* special correspondent and sent back a highly alarming report in which he declared that the days of British naval supremacy in the Mediterranean were ended. In his *Siege of Portsmouth* he repeats this technique of exaggerated and alarmist prophecy; he adds fact to fantasy in a deliberate attempt to excite and startle the reader. The story is presented in the usual contrasting terms of the noble and unsuspecting nation surprised by brutal and treacherous enemies. On the British side, there is Rudyard Kipling, Poet Laureate by this time, who composes a song to Old England's glory which was sung by seventy thousand men on Hampstead Heath. On the enemy side, the French display all the meanness and treachery that Capitaine Danrit attributed to the British. Our ambassador leaves Paris and then the mob do their worst:

The mob which remained behind at the Embassy were not slow to take advantage of the opportunity, and before nightfall a blackened heap of ruins represented what had been for many decades the proud official residence of Her Majesty's Plenipotentiary at the French capital.

The Embassy had been stormed at and execrated during many crucial epochs; but the French government had always afforded it protection until then . . . Anglophobia was at its height. The journalists of the Boulevards heaped scorn and contumely upon the English. The French spat upon our countrymen in the streets. The gallant defence made by a party of belated tourists at Rouen gave the signal for a cowardly massacre, the details of which caused a thrill of horror throughout England when it became known.

The enemy employ the meanest and most despicable ruses, because they have to be as vile as election propaganda would have them. The French land at Eastbourne—'whose streets ran blood and whose walls echoed the shrieks of the dying and defenceless'. The miserable citizens endure the agony of seeing 'their sons, their wives, and their daughters at the mercy of a foe who, reared on carnage, hate, and oppression, knew no mercy'. Portsmouth, however, manages to hold out against incessant attacks; the Channel Fleet steams back from the Azores, and the Franco-Russian squadrons are decisively defeated in a tremendous naval engagement off Spithead.

But why had it happened? The reason was to be found in the Conservative case against the Liberals in the election of 1895: not enough money had been spent on the Royal Navy, and no one had learnt the lesson of the 1894 naval manœuvres which revealed that the Fleet was seriously undermanned.[4] As Clowes asked:

And why had Portsmouth been thus pressed, and England thus imperilled? Because men had not sufficiently remembered that 'England's Navy is her All in All'. Because, while creating a big fleet, they had been remiss in the equally important matters of manning and organisation. Because they had allowed the Fleet Reserve to be nominal rather than real. Because they had been so blind as to accept the annual partial mobilisations, at dates known long beforehand, as evidence that the Navy was fit at any and every moment to do all that might be required of it. Because, in one word, they were NOT READY.

The events in *The Siege of Portsmouth* provide a most instructive case-study of the tale of imaginary warfare in all its varieties and applications. It illustrates every device and attitude to be found in this form of fiction: the projection of contemporary anxieties into a specially contrived future, hatred of the enemy, the horror figure of the spy, brutal and violent incidents, fierce nationalistic sentiments, appeals to tradition and to prejudice, the dread picture of the nation alone in adversity and on the edge of defeat, the final swift and facile destruction of the enemy fleet. But more important than these was the attitude of mind to be seen in the unquestioning acceptance of war as a customary exercise between nations, and in the applied art of a story that had been designed to play on mood and sentiment for political and commercial ends. War, as Harmsworth knew, was good for business; but the war described by Clowes and so many others, in spite of the apparent modernity of fleet actions, was still presented in terms of the old-world pattern of Trafalgar and the Crimea. The Western attitude to war was still determined by what might be called the Othello Syndrome:

> . . . the neighing steed and the shrill trump,
> The spirit-stirring drum, the ear-piercing fife,
> The royal banner, and all quality,
> Pride, pomp, and circumstance of glorious war!

The constant and permissive fact behind the development of these imaginary wars from 1871 to 1914 was the customary consideration of war as normal and romantic. The few Europeans who campaigned in the cause of world peace, like Bertha von Suttner and Norman Angell, knew very well that the great arguments in favour of war were the traditional heroics of literature—'the heroic poems and heroic histories by means of which our schools bring us up to be warriors'—and the worship of success that turns war-leaders into national heroes, so that 'when any one comes out of a war as conqueror the guild of historical scribblers fall in the dust before him, and praise him as the fulfiller of his mission of educative culture'.[5] With these ideas in mind, Bertha von Suttner published *Die Waffen Nieder!* in 1889 with the intention of bringing

war down from the level of epic history and romantic literature to the real
world of human suffering and misery. She knew that in the usual literary treatment of war the deed of courage was always the main act in the great drama of
the nation in arms; but it was generally presented in isolation, separated by its
own grandeur and dedication from the real boredom and terror of war. In
describing the experiences of her characters in the wars from 1859 to 1870,
Bertha von Suttner concentrated on what the historians and the novelists so
often omitted: death and disease, the sorrow of wives and parents, the blood
and vomit of the casualty clearing station. It was shock treatment for a society
that could accept Prince Kraft zu Hohenlohe's idealization of the officer as a
man 'influenced only by his desire for fame and glory, and by the high position
which the spotlessness of his true honour wins for him in the society of all
men'.[6]

The many tales of future warfare and the occasional anti-war story show
that until 1914 most Europeans believed that they could have their wars and
enjoy them. The error lay both in fact and in fiction. The first mistake was the
widespread failure to anticipate the scale and duration of the next great war.[7]
It was generally expected that it would be a swift affair—over by Christmas, as
the press announced in 1914. The second mistake was in the continuation of a
romantic attitude to war beyond the point when it had ceased to be an affair of
the thin red line, of cavalry charges and hand-to-hand encounters. This was
the target-area for Shaw's anti-romantic comedy of 1894, *Arms and the Man*.
Shaw turned glory upside down and made very effective fun of the stage soldier with the matter-of-fact behaviour of Bluntschli, the professional, and the
high comedy of Sergius, who saved the day by winning the battle the wrong
way after two Cossack colonels had lost their regiments according to the best
tactical principles.

But Shaw's attack was a forlorn hope at that time and in that climate of
opinion. In face of the combined forces of tradition, jingoism, and the nationalistic press, the advocates of peace had little hope of success. It is evident
from a reading of the few anti-war stories of this period, like *Das
Menschenschlachthaus* (1912) by Wilhelm Lamszus and *War* (1914) by Douglas
Newton, that the authors knew their most difficult task was to demonstrate the
gap between the imagined glories and the bitter realities of war. As Norman
Angell put the matter in *The Great Illusion* (1910), the idea of war had everything in its favour except death and destruction. That book, first published in
1909, had a telling subtitle: *The Relation of Military Power to National
Advantage*. It lived up to its promise, since Angell developed a cool, rational
examination of war and peace that obliged his contemporaries to think carefully about the consequences of the next great war. The book sold by tens of
thousands; it was discussed throughout the world press; the German
Ambassador to the United Kingdom used it for a diplomatic announcement;

and the King presented copies to Cabinet ministers. Angell was clear-sighted enough to accept the fact that 'a sedentary, urbanized people find the spectacle of war even more attractive than the spectacle of football. Indeed, our Press treats it as a sort of glorified football match.'

The language of sport was often the language of war. Captain Guggisberg, for instance, in his *Modern Warfare, or How our Soldiers Fight* (1903), found the perfect analogy in the game of football. He saw nothing incongruous in stressing what for him were the obvious similarities between the great games of peace and war:

An army, in fact, tries to *work together* in a battle or a large manoeuvre in much the same way as a football team *plays together* in a match; and you need scarcely be told what an important thing that is if you want to win. The army *fights* for the good of its country as the team *plays* for the honour of its school. Regiments *assist* each other as players do when they *shove together* or *pass the ball* from one to another; exceptionally gallant *charges* and heroic *defences* correspond to brilliant *runs* and fine *tackling*. All work with one common impulse, given to the army by its general, to the team by its captain.[8]

The subject-matter of the imaginary war supports Angell in his claim that before 1914 war seemed to be regarded as a natural activity of nations. So many forces and ideas worked in its favour. The economic advantage of new markets and the success-story of Great Power Status, the Darwinian doctrine of the struggle for existence and the political fact of imperialist expansion, the immensely powerful influences of tradition, the new press and the jingoistic sentiments it inspired—these were some of the factors working to demonstrate Karl Pearson's contention that 'the path of progress is strewn with the wreck of nations'.[9] Nature's first law seemed to corroborate the facts of international politics—kill or be killed. Translated into military language, and put in the words of Kaiser Wilhelm II to the German troops embarking for action against the Boxers in China, the idea became the simple command: 'No quarter will be granted, no prisoners taken.'

And yet, after everything has been said about the forces of Darwinism, tradition, and imperialistic ambition that played upon the mind in those days, there still remained the hard facts of real antagonism between European countries. They are to be found in any history of the period, from the start of the great change in the European power system after the German victory of 1870 to the Franco-Russian Alliance of 1894. The chapter headings give the sequence of events that led to the great world war so long foretold in fiction: the German Navy Bill of 1900; the entry of the United Kingdom into an alliance with Japan in 1902; French reconciliation with Britain and the beginning of the *Entente* in 1904; the Moroccan crisis of 1905; then the arrival of the *Panther* at Agadir on 1 July 1911; and so it runs from alarm to alarm until the record begins to reach its end with the assassination of Francis Ferdinand on 28 June 1914, which was followed by the ultimatums and finally by the proclamations of war to cheering crowds in the capital cities of Europe.

Nowadays it is a commonplace remark in the history books that the crowds were cheering for a war that never came. All but a very few expected a swift campaign on land and the destruction of the German Fleet in a North Sea engagement. No one could have foreseen that there would be four years of killing and the end of the European domination of the world. The ease and celerity with which most authors of imaginary wars had conducted their fictitious operations reflected the general view, based on the experiences of 1870 and the Balkan wars, that a decisive battle or two would quickly end hostilities. This attitude of mind had much to do with the many social and traditional factors examined earlier in this chapter. And when they combined with the wrong deductions made by the general staffs of the European powers, they could not fail to carry over the ideas of 1870 into the new age of machine-guns and submarines. No one seems to have planned or thought in terms of the extraordinary forecast first made by Ivan S. Bloch that 'everybody will be entrenched in the next war. It will be a great war of entrenchments. The spade will be as indispensable to a soldier as his rifle.'

When he said that in 1897, Bloch had just completed twelve years of work on a statistical and practical examination of the nature of modern warfare, and he had come to conclusions very different from those of the military experts. Bloch had grasped the central fact that the destructiveness of the new armaments and the intricate organization of contemporary society had entirely altered the scale of warfare. His forecast was an epitaph written in full anticipation of the millions who would fall in the next great war. It looked forward to that clash between expectation and event out of which would later come the anger and sense of profound shock that characterized European thinking after 1918:

At first there will be increased slaughter—increased slaughter on so terrible a scale as to render it impossible to get troops to push the battle to a decisive issue. They will try to, thinking that they are fighting under the old conditions, and they will learn such a lesson that they will abandon the attempt for ever. Then, instead of a war fought out to the bitter end in a series of decisive battles, we shall have as a substitute a long period of continually increasing strain upon the resources of the combatants. The war, instead of being a hand-to-hand contest in which the combatants measure their physical and moral superiority, will become a kind of stalemate, in which, neither army being able to get at the other, both armies will be maintained in opposition to each other, threatening each other, but never able to deliver a final and decisive attack.[10]

This was a remarkable prediction of what came to pass in the winter of 1914. What Bloch forecast was not what the generals had expected, as Marshal Joffre related in his memoirs:

Being unable to do anything better, the Germans dug themselves into the earth, erecting a defensive system which grew stronger every day. It was our task to attack this immense fortress, drive the enemy from it, defeat him in open country, and impose our will upon him. Out of this situation grew a terrible form of war to which we had to adapt ourselves as rapidly as possible. The first thing to be done was to create a powerful artillery, provided with a quantity of ammunition which literally staggered the imagination.[11]

In contrast to the imaginary wars with their constant visions of fleet encounters and swift land campaigns, there were no decisive victories. Both the French on the Marne and the Germans at Tannenberg won famous battles, but they did not finish the war. It dragged on. Instead of the expected sequence of great battles, the armies stopped moving; and after the French and British general staffs had, so Haldane reports, reduced their quota of heavy artillery and machine-guns because they believed that speed of manœuvre would determine the outcome, the allied armies found that they had been entrapped in a new and quite unexpected form of siege warfare in which the machine-gun proved to be the king of battle. The figures for French weapons in 1914 and 1918 make this only too clear: although the number of men under arms remained the same, the total of heavy machine-guns increased by a factor of five and the numbers of light machine-guns rose from zero to fifty thousand.

That was the last devastating comment on all that had been written about the shape of future warfare since 1870. Machine-gun fire and massive artillery concentrations along the Western Front suddenly terminated the long argument for more ships, better equipment, and universal compulsory conscription that had run its course from Chesney's *Battle of Dorking* in 1871 to Saki's account of the German conquest of Britain, *When William Came*, in 1913. The armies had obtained all they had asked for, but they could not win the swift victory they had anticipated.

There can be no doubt that the authors of many tales of future warfare shared in the responsibility for the catastrophe that overtook Europe. Men like Danrit, Le Queux, and August Niemann helped to raise the temperature of international disputes. And many others played their part in helping to sustain and foment the self-deception, misunderstanding, and downright ill will that often infected relations between the peoples of Europe. During the forty-three years from 1871 to the outbreak of the First World War, the device of the imaginary war had become an established means of teaching every kind of aggressive doctrine from the duty of revenge to the need for a bigger fleet. It flourished on considerable ignorance and on the constant animosity that encouraged hundreds of writers at every level of ability and intelligence to relate what would happen in the next war. The best that can be said of them is that they often stood for high patriotic ideals at a time when few had realized how technological innovations would totally transform the nature of modern warfare. Their stories represent the last stage in the brief honeymoon between science and humanity, before the military technologies of poison gas, barbed wire, and tanks had shown what could be done with war, given the science to do it. At their worst, they perpetuated an archaic attitude to war by helping to maintain the belief that another war would not cause any profound changes in the state of the world. The most effective proof of this can be seen in the stories of the coming conflict between Britain and Germany that were turned out during the peak period of this literature from 1900 to 1914. It is particularly instructive to note how during this period all the varieties, techniques, and extravagances of the tale of the war-to-come can be seen at work in the mass of literature that grew out of the increasingly bad relations between Britain and Germany. When Guy du Maurier's *An Englishman's Home* could play to packed houses in London and the German press could make fun of British invasion scares, it is clear that the device of the imaginary war had begun to affect international relations in a way never known before.

It is important to recognize that during the first few years of the twentieth century a change began to appear in the pattern predicted for the wars of the future. Although the French continued for a time to pursue the struggle against Britain in stories like *La Guerre avec l'Angleterre* and Danrit's *La Guerre fatale*, the beginning of the Anglo-French *Entente* in 1904 left Germany as the only enemy of France. This had a curious result. There was an immediate decline in the numbers of the more aggressive fictions of the type produced by Capitaine Danrit. The French production returned to less spectacular and more professional forecasts of a future conflict, all devoted to a detailed account of the coming defeat of Germany: *Le Débâcle de l'Allemagne dans la prochaine guerre*; *Une Guerre franco-allemande*; *La France victorieuse dans la guerre de demain*; *L'Offensive contre l'Allemagne*; *La Fin de la Prusse et le démembrement de l'Allemagne*. The ending of the disagreement between Britain and France had at once cut off the source of the hectic fantasies about the invasion and conquest of Albion that had been appearing since the 1880s. The *Entente* left French writers with only the traditional task of *la revanche*; and since this was a straightforward military affair, without any opportunity for exciting but improbable stories about the destruction of a great enemy fleet, their production of future war-stories became for the most part a humdrum business of adding realistic details to what were little more than staff appreciations.

The difference in attitude between two stories of this period, one published in 1900 and the other in 1913, will serve to illustrate the change that took place. The first, *La Guerre avec l'Angleterre*, was the work of an anonymous French naval officer; and it was considered to be so representative of French thinking that the Admiralty Intelligence Department had it translated 'For the use of Her Majesty's Officers Only'. The anonymous author, Lieutenant X, put the French position somewhat more cautiously than Danrit had done in *La Guerre fatale*:

As regards France, there can be but one such war to be considered, and that is against England. It must not, however, be inferred from this that France ought to make this war, or that she has greater interests in bringing it about than in preserving peace. Still less is it to be imagined that she desires war. On the contrary the condition of our Navy makes it advisable that France should so dread making such a war as to persistently avoid it.

The *Entente* quickly put an end to this type of French prediction. The new expectations can be seen in a story of 1913, *La Fin de la Prusse et le démembrement de l'Allemagne*. The book lives up to its title. War breaks out as a result of a dispute between France and Germany. Three hundred thousand British troops speed through the newly constructed Channel Tunnel to take up their positions on the French left; the Russians attack in the east; the Royal Navy wipes out the whole German Fleet in a single great encounter in the North Sea. Germany is invaded; Kaiser Wilhelm II is taken prisoner; the Reich is divided into petty kingdoms; and Poland is restored.

The same change from one enemy to another can be discovered in English fiction. Between the outburst of pamphlets about the dangers of the Channel Tunnel in 1882 and the *Entente* in 1904, France had always figured as the chief enemy, usually in combination with Russia. While the French were turning out their last stories of a successful invasion of the British Isles during the first four years of the twentieth century, writers on this side of the Channel were still describing the menace from France and in particular from a Franco-Russian alliance. In 1900 Colonel Maude, as the anonymous author of *The New Battle of Dorking*, described a French invasion attempt with the customary announcement of his intention of 'calling the public attention to this vitally serious danger'. His proposition was no more than the old case against the French:

There are three months in every year—July, August, September—during which the French Army is fit for immediate warfare. And every year during these months there is a constantly recurrent probability of a surprise raid on London by the 120,000 men whom they could without difficulty put on board ship, land in England, and march to within a dozen miles of London in less than three days from receipt of the order to move.[12]

Propaganda of this kind continued into a series of anti-French stories between 1900 and 1904: *The Sack of London in the Great French War of 1901*; *The Coming Waterloo*; *A New Trafalgar*; *Pro Patria*; *The Invaders*; *Seaward for the Foe*; *Starved into Surrender*; *Black Fortnight*. All of them presented variations on the single theme that, as one author put the issue, 'Great Britain stood face to face with allied France and Russia for the death-grip.'

And then, with the appearance of *The Riddle of the Sands* in 1903 and the translation of Niemann's *Der Weltkrieg* in 1904 as *The Coming Conquest of England*, the great war between Britain and Germany began. For the first time in the course of this literature, the Germans started on the large-scale production of stories like *Der deutsch–englische Krieg*; *Die 'Offensiv-Invasion' gegen England*; *Die Engländer kommen*; *Mit deutschen Waffen über Paris nach London*. Crisis by crisis, they mirrored the state of relations between the two countries, as British writers in their turn described a future conflict with Germany in which every device from the use of spies to a successful invasion was employed to argue the case for conscription or for more dreadnoughts. The brief interlude of simple interest in the new ships and the romance of the torpedo fleet ended abruptly. During the ten years before the First World War, the growing antagonism between Britain and Germany was responsible for the largest and most sustained development of the most alarmist and aggressive stories of future warfare ever seen in European history.

In both countries the new phase in the tale of imaginary warfare turned on the question of naval supremacy. As a result of the construction programmes of 1898 and 1900, the German Fleet had entered on a period of rapid expansion, and already some had begun to suspect that the real intention was not to protect German commerce, as Prince Hohenlohe had told the Reichstag, but to challenge the Royal Navy. After the serious deterioration in relations between the two countries caused by the German attitude during the Boer War, the new and very real dislike of Germany grew into a widespread belief that the great menace of the future was the German fleet. At the beginning of 1901 the editor of *Black and White* wrote on the subject of 'The German Navy' in a way that was typical of the press at that time:

Nothing speaks more strongly of the growth of Germany's power than the rapid strides her navy has made in recent times. It is only quite a few years ago that the idea of an important German navy would have seemed as incongruous as would the notion of a great Swiss fleet. Then suddenly one day the world awoke to the fact that Germany was a great maritime power, and from that day to this, through the tireless exertions of the energetic and far-sighted Kaiser, she had gone steadily forward towards the fulfilment of her dream as the premier naval Power of the world.[13]

There was much to feed the suspicion that Germany had hostile intentions. In 1900 the first German fantasies in support of the naval construction programme had appeared. The author of *Wehrlos zur See* described the coming destruction of Germany in order to demonstrate the case for a continued expansion of the Fleet; and in *Die Abrechnung mit England* of 1900 the same argument was presented in the more encouraging form of a successful war against Britain. Enemy cruisers inflict immense damage on British shipping, and after a humiliating defeat Britain has to surrender Gibraltar and all her African territories. At the same time, some German service writers were beginning to discuss the possibility of using the German fleet to invade Britain. In the many editions of *Das Volk in Waffen* that tedious militarist, Baron Colmar von der Goltz, had never tired of proclaiming the urgent need to prepare against the day when the nation would have to face 'a final struggle for the existence and greatness of Germany'. His solution was a plan for war:

Bearing this constantly in mind, we must work incessantly, by example, by word, and by our writings towards this end, that loyalty towards the Emperor, passionate love for the Fatherland, determination not to shrink from hard trials, self-denial, and cheerful sacrifice may wax ever stronger in our hearts and in those of our children. Then will the German army, which must be and shall ever remain the German nation in arms, enter upon the coming conflict with full assurance of ultimate victory.[14]

In 1900 von der Goltz had begun to argue that an invasion of Britain was possible on the grounds that 'the distance is short and can easily be traversed by an enterprising admiral who succeeds, by the excellence of his fleet and by his audacity, in obtaining for a short time the command of the sea'. In 1901 similar views of other German service writers began to receive considerable attention from the British press. One of them, Freiherr von Edelsheim, discussed plans for a descent on the British Isles in his *Operationen zur See*. His conclusions were, in effect, advance notice of a naval war; for Edelsheim declared that 'it is necessary to have our battle fleet so strong that it will be in a position to assist materially in any undertaking of our troops'. When arguments of this nature coincided with news of the construction of new docks at Emden and of plans for still more warships, the British government came to agree with the press that the Kaiser might really intend to live up to his new title of Admiral of the Atlantic. An immediate consequence of the growing anxieties about the nature of German naval intentions was the demand early in 1903 for a naval base on the east coast and for the establishment of a North Sea squadron.

The contrived nightmare of *The Battle of Dorking* now seemed far closer to realization than ever it had been in 1871 when Chesney had argued the case for military improvements. In fact, the circumstances of 1871 were in many ways repeated in the excitement caused by the appearance of *The Riddle of the Sands* in 1903. Like Chesney before him, that brave and chivalrous yachtsman Erskine Childers had devised the perfect myth in which to convey the anxieties and anticipations of a people beginning to be alarmed at the new menace from overseas. The exciting detective work in the stage-by-stage account of the unravelling of the German invasion plan was admirably calculated to express contemporary fears for the future. The rapid narrative, the constant mystery and adventure, the excellent sailing episodes, and the appearance of the All-Highest himself combined the advantages of realism and romance. The story seemed as if it ought to be true; and for this reason it caused a sensation when it came out. Several hundred thousand copies of the cheap edition were sold, and the Germans ordered the book to be confiscated.

The Riddle of the Sands was undoubtedly the best story of its kind since *The Battle of Dorking*. It inaugurated a new and even more sensational fiction about German intentions which was developed in many later works, especially in Le Queux's notorious *Invasion of 1910*, Guy de Maurier's *An Englishman's Home*, and Saki's *When William Came*. Erskine Childers presented the first stage of a legend that was taken up and enlarged by his successors. This started from the final chapters of *The Riddle of the Sands*, after the hero had hidden himself on the German tug and so had discovered the secret of the mysterious operations off the East Friesland coast:

The course he had set was about west, with Norderney light a couple of points off the port bow. The course for Memmert? Possibly; but I cared not, for my mind was far from Memmert tonight. *It was the course for England too.* Yes, I understood at last. I was assisting at an experimental rehearsal of a great scene, to be enacted, perhaps, in the near future—a scene when multitudes of sea-going lighters, carrying full loads of soldiers, not half loads of coal, should issue simultaneously, in seven ordered fleets, from seven shallow outlets, and under escort of the Imperial Navy traverse the North Sea and throw themselves bodily upon English shores.

Here, then, was a renewal of the ancient anxiety for the survival of an island people in the face of an attempt at invasion by a great overseas military power. For those who wanted evidence of Germany's aggressive intentions, there were the new stories of a future war in which the Germans inflicted a swift and humiliating defeat upon the British. One of the earliest was August Niemann's *Der Weltkrieg* of 1904, a highly optimistic and amateurish attempt to rearrange the world to suit German pretensions. The book was immediately translated into English as a warning of what the Germans had in mind. Niemann's ideas were somewhat over-optimistic, since among other things they called for a combination of France, Russia, and Germany against Britain. Nevertheless, the attitude he revealed in his preface was enough to convince many readers that the Germans meant what he said:

Almost all wars have, for centuries past, been waged in the interests of England, and almost all have been incited by England. Only when Bismarck's genius presided over Germany did the German Michael become conscious of his own strength and wage his own wars. Are things come to this pass that Germany is to crave of England's bounty—her air and light, and her very daily bread? . . . My dreams, the dreams of a German, show me the war that is to be, and the victory of the three great allied nations—Germany, France and Russia—and a new division of the possessions of the earth as the final aim and object of this gigantic universal war.

After Niemann's declaration of the war-to-come between Britain and Germany, stories of the future conflict appeared every year in the two countries until a real war put an end to this literature. For the first time in the history of international politics, as a direct result of universal literacy and mass journalism, the writing of popular fiction had begun to have a recognizable effect on the relations between countries, since these tales of the war-to-come encouraged British and Germans to see themselves as inevitable enemies. Most of these stories were written by earnest men with the best of patriotic motives. One of the more striking examples of this general high seriousness can be seen in the work of Charles Doughty, the author of the classic *Travels in Arabia Deserta*, who wrote two verse plays to warn his countrymen of the German peril. In the first play, *The Cliffs* (1909), he outlined what he considered were the German plans for an invasion of the British Isles:

> . . . given a clear Coast,
> And half-a-week before them, they'd cut off
> Scotland, and raid Newcastle and the Forth:
> And landing in poor disaffected Ireland,
> Promise her irrevocable Home Rule;
> And a Protectorate over her proclaim.
> Tardy or quickly, the Admiralty might enclose
> Both Portland and wide Plymouth Sound with booms.
> But such then might an Enemy's diving ships
> Stoop under; and with contact-mines by night-
> Time sow the field. Some even might, stealing forth,
> Torpedo at their anchorage drowsing Dreadnoughts.
> Moreo'er, they'll seize our great commercial ports,
> Burn British shipping in them and destroy
> All coaling stores.

The first major increase in the production of such propaganda took place in 1906, a bumper year which saw the appearance of several notorious books: *Völker Europas*; *Hamburg und Bremen in Gefahr*; *1906: der Zusammenbruch der alten Welt*; *The Shock of Battle*; *The Enemy in our Midst*; *The North Sea Bubble*; *The Writing on the Wall*; *The Invasion of 1910*. They were all written at a time when international relations had deteriorated perceptibly after Bülow had staged the Tangier incident in March 1905 in the hope of detaching France from her new relationship with Britain. Again in 1905, both the Admiralty and the War Office had begun to consider the possibility of a war between Germany and the Anglo-French powers; and in 1906 the new thinking in

Britain became more obvious when the first of the dreadnoughts was launched and a start was made with the establishment of a Home Fleet.

In March 1906 the *Daily Mail* declared war on Germany in a serial story which proved to be the most sensational of all the pre-1914 imaginary wars. It was written by Queen Alexandra's favourite novelist, William Le Queux; and his account of the German descent on Britain, *The Invasion of 1910*, aroused such intense interest throughout the world that it was translated into twenty-seven languages, including Arabic, Japanese, and Chinese. The story sold over a million copies throughout the world when it was published as a book. It was immediately translated into German, given a different ending, and sold in a special edition for boys under the title of *Der Einfall der Deutschen in England*. The cover of this edition carried a magnificent drawing of the German troops entering the smoking ruins of a thoroughly demolished London.

The story began in 1905 as another of Harmsworth's ideas for the *Daily Mail*. He commissioned Le Queux to do the writing, and, after four months spent in touring the invasion area of south-east England, Le Queux started on the serial, in which he had help from H. W. Wilson, the naval writer, and from that untiring champion of Army expansion, Field-Marshal Lord Roberts. The civilian and the soldier worked out the most likely plan for a German invasion, but when the scheme was presented to Harmsworth they were told that, although the strategy might be faultless, it would be bad for circulation. 'Bobs' or no 'Bobs', the Germans had to pass through every sizeable town, 'not keep to remote one-eyed country villages where there was no possibility of large *Daily Mail* sales'.[15] In the interests of circulation, the invasion plan was altered to allow ferocious Uhlans to gallop into every town from Sheffield to Chelmsford. And, still with an eye to the sale of the *Daily Mail*, Harmsworth placed special advertisements in the London dailies and many of the provincial newspapers. These carried a map showing the district the Germans would be invading next morning in the *Daily Mail*. Another publicity trick was to send sandwich-men, dressed as German soldiers, to parade through London with notices of the revelations to be read in the *Daily Mail*. An eye-witness has described the scene when 'the startling portent was seen of a long file of veterans in spiked helmets and Prussian-blue uniforms parading moodily down Oxford Street . . . They carried sandwich boards to inform all whom it might concern that the great William Le Queux, already famous as the historian (in 1894) of *The Great War in England* (in alliance with Germany against France and Russia) in 1897, was now about to add to his laurels by reporting day by day in the columns of England's most wide-awake newspaper the progress of her great Invasion (by Germany) in 1910. And didn't he just.'[16]

But Le Queux had little to reveal. The German forces assembled for the invasion behind the Frisian Islands, where Erskine Childers had described the first experiments for the descent upon Britain. Thereafter, as Le Queux wrote, the whole campaign went with the regularity of a clockwork machine. Cliché by cliché he enlarged on the arguments in Lord Roberts's call for conscription: distressing news—complete bewilderment—hopeless defence—scowling Uhlans—desperate fight—our own dear London—shot without mercy—literally a shambles—sad page of history. And it would never have happened, said Le Queux, if the feckless inhabitants of Great Britain had not closed their ears to Lord Roberts's warning that the country was not prepared for modern warfare; 'for had we adopted his scheme for universal service such dire catastrophes could never have occurred'. And how he rubbed in the disaster: repulsive Prussian troopers shoot down helpless women; terrified Londoners dig their graves under the eyes of German firing squads; brutal proclamations commanded the requisitioning of everything from private possessions to country houses.

The biggest blow, however, was left for the editor of the German translation to arrange. He removed about two hundred pages of the narrative covering the time between the fall of London and the ending of the war, since these described the British counter-attack and the massacre of the Germans in London. The efforts of the French to intervene between the two countries were ascribed to the United States in the German text; and whereas Le Queux ended with a peace treaty that gave Holland and Denmark to Germany, the translator saved his readers any possible embarrassment by reporting that 'in the German peace terms there was no question at all of any surrender of territory or populations whether in Europe or in other parts of the world'.

The great popularity enjoyed by *The Invasion of 1910* and *The Riddle of the Sands* had the double effect of spreading the idea of a German invasion and of presenting a stereotype of German methods and intentions, since the prediction made by Erskine Childers in 1903 was shown to be true by the events of Le Queux's invasion in 1910. The two books and many others of the same kind played a part in increasing national anxieties. Le Queux was particularly active in developing the legend of the ubiquitous German spy. He took over and improved on the old story of the disguised enemy soldiers first reported in the Channel Tunnel pamphlets of 1882. According to Le Queux, 'advance agents' of the German forces played an important part in the successful invasion. For years the Germans had kept a civilian army in Britain:

Most of these men were Germans who, having served in the army, had come over to England and obtained employment as waiters, clerks, bakers, hairdressers, and private servants, and being bound by their oath to the Fatherland had served their country as spies. Each man, when obeying the Imperial command to join the German arms, had placed in the lapel of his coat a button of a peculiar shape, with which he had long ago been provided, and by which he was instantly recognised as a loyal subject of the Kaiser.

The legend was omitted from the German translation, but it had a considerable vogue in Britain. Other writers added to it, and eventually the story became embalmed in the folklore of the First World War. In another invasion story of 1906, *The Enemy in our Midst*, the author described the operation of a 'Committee of Secret Preparations' which directed the work of Germans resident in Britain:

Every registered alien was an authority on the topography and resources of the district in which he dwelt. If there was a *cul-de-sac* into which the enemy could be driven, or trapped and butchered, he knew of it; if there were mews, or garages, he was acquainted with them and their accommodation for horses and vehicles; he knew the resources of every grocer's shop, every public-house, every dairy, every fruiterer's, every butcher's, and every telephone call office. The capacities of the railways were known to a truck; the tubes were understood throughout every yard of their length, and their possibilities for an appalling sacrifice of English people calculated and put down on paper.

This nonsense was the source of many yarns about the German military bands that spent their time in laying secret concrete foundations for siege guns in the London suburbs, and about the even more sinister characters with telltale sabre cuts on their cheeks who were forever rowing round key ports on the east coast. One indication of the widespread Germanophobia appeared in a letter to *The Times* from the positivist philosopher, Frederick Harrison. He warned his countrymen that the German Army had been 'trained for sudden transmarine descent on a coast; and for this end every road, well, bridge, and smithy in the east of England and Scotland had been docketed in the German War Office'.[17] This was pure William Le Queux and it was widely believed. At this time, for instance, questions were asked in the Commons about the existence of enemy agents in the London area. Sir John Barlow asked Haldane, the Secretary of State for War, for information on the 66,000 German reservists reputed to be living in the Home Counties. Did they maintain a secret arms dump near Charing Cross? Another Member of Parliament, Colonel Lockwood, acting on information from Le Queux, asked the sorely tried Haldane about 'the military men from a foreign nation who had been resident for the last two years on and off in the neighbourhood of Epping, and who had been sketching and photographing the whole district and communicating their information directly to their own country'. Haldane replied that he thought the spies could find all the information they wanted in an Ordnance Survey map.

In fact, Haldane was very worried at the extent of the spy mania. And he had good reason, for after Le Queux had done his work in the *Daily Mail* in 1906 anxious citizens began to discover enemy agents in every part of the country. What they feared was explained in a letter to *The Times* by a Colonel Lonsdale: '. . . there exists in the country at the present moment what some people would call a "spy scare" . . . I hold, as many do, that the cause is very serious and the alarm well grounded.'[18] Reports poured into the War Office of German plans to seize dockyards and put the Fleet out of action in preparation for an invasion. Robert Blatchford, the socialist writer, used to lie awake at night thinking of the coming invasion and saying to himself: 'My God! This horror is marching steadily upon us and our people will not believe it.' And, according to Wilfred Scawen Blunt's diary for August 1908, even the King was talking of Kaiser Wilhelm's plan to throw 'a *corps d'armée* or two into England, making proclamation that he has come, not as an enemy to the King, but as the grandson of Queen Victoria, to deliver him from the Socialistic gang which is ruining the country'.[19] Behind all these anxieties was the one dominant fear that, in the words of a *Quarterly Review* article on the German peril, 'what the Spanish danger was to the Elizabethans, what the Gallic danger was to their posterity, that and nothing less nor other is the German danger to this generation'.[20]

There can be no doubt, therefore, that by 1906, and certainly by 1908, these anxieties and forecasts about German intentions had become a recognizable and potentially dangerous element in the European situation. The propaganda of one country attracted attention in another. One side blamed the other. The English writer P. A. Hislam, in his *Admiralty of the Atlantic*, complained that 'the adolescent maritime instinct and ambitions of Germany have been fed by innumerable books in which the main theme has been a war with England. These works range from the wholly fanciful and impossible stories of the type of *Die Abrechnung mit England*, in which the German Navy successively destroys the fleets of Japan, England, and the United States. . . . '[21]

On the German side, in 1906 Carl Siwinna gave a survey of the major errors perpetrated by British and German authors of imaginary wars in his book *Vademecum für Phantasiestrategen*. In 1908—and this was more serious— the important German naval journal, *Marine Rundschau*, had a special article on the invasion literature then appearing in Britain.[22] One of the points made for the attention of German naval officers reflects on the damage done by William Le Queux and others like him:

Invasion is still a word that today fills the average Englishman with a more or less vague sense of terror. Is it really possible? Or is it only a tale of terror like the *Invasion of 1910*—read by hundreds of thousands in the *Daily Mail*—a horror story like so many similar stories of recent years?

There can be no doubt at all that just now in England they are once more troubled by the idea of invasion—naturally by German armies only. German espionage is almost a standard feature of one section of the press. Never before has hatred of Germany generated such widespread alarm in Britain. The German fleet, which is less than one-third of the British in tonnage, is supposed to be able to clear the way across the North Sea for the unconquered German Army; and this fleet is being built with the express intention of seizing the mastery of the world for ever from the island kingdom! In the English press and in personal contacts with earnest and thoughtful men this idea of invasion is forever emerging, in spite of the fact that in the German press and by word of mouth assurance is constantly being given that a German invasion of Britain is a chimera; that such an invasion would be contrary to the elementary principles of the efficient use of military power; and that it would be made void by the doubtlessly permanent and marked preponderance of the British Fleet.

The German author was right. Fears of an invasion were widespread. During the summer of 1908, for example, national anxieties came close to panic when the Navy began extensive manœuvres in the Channel and the North Sea with the evident intention of practising methods for dealing with an attempt at invasion.[23] When a German torpedo boat on fishery protection duties appeared off the Tyne in the middle of local manœuvres, there was a flood of letters and articles in the press on the single topic of German intentions. And out of this and the Bosnian crisis of 1908 came another crop of invasion stories: *The Swoop of the Vulture*; *When England Slept*; *The Invasion That Did Not Come Off*; *An Englishman's Home*; *The Great Raid*; *The Swoop*.

On 23 November 1908 Lord Roberts returned to the theme of the invasion and asked the House of Lords to consider the case for conscription. Two months later he had dramatic support in the sensational success of *An Englishman's Home*, which opened at Wyndham's Theatre on 27 January 1909. The play was by Guy du Maurier, then second-in-command 3rd Battalion the Royal Fusiliers, and it sprang from a deep anxiety in him that Germany meant to make war. His brother, Gerald du Maurier, produced the play without the knowledge of the author, who was then in South Africa. The plot dealt with a thinly disguised invasion by the forces of 'the Emperor of the North'; and it so caught the public mood that a special recruiting office was set up in the theatre to deal with the rush of volunteers to join the newly formed Territorial Force. Photographs from scenes in the play and excerpts from the dialogue appeared throughout the press; letters from Lord Roberts, Haldane, and others congratulated the author on the finest piece of propaganda they had seen; a gramophone company turned out special recordings from the more important episodes in the play; and, as a result of the uproar it caused about the state of the nation's defences, there was a considerable rise in recruiting for the Territorials.

Throughout 1909 and into 1910 the flood of invasion stories continued. Some began as serials like *The Great Raid*, which started in *Black and White* in February 1909 and continued every week until 15 May, complete with illustrations of enemy troops in Britain. One double-page drawing showed artillery, cavalry, and infantry marching through central London as the Union Jack was lowered on public buildings. The text below carried the message that 'nearly all the chief authorities, including Mr. Haldane, the Minister of War, agree that our present means of home defence are inadequate, and it is hoped that the present outburst of public interest in the subject will lead to the general filling up of the ranks of the Territorial Army'.

One promising young writer was at that time taking an unusual interest in the matter. He seized on the stock device of the German attack on Britain and turned it upside down for his own tale of the great invasion, *The Swoop! or, How Clarence Saved England*. The young writer was P. G. Wodehouse. Wodehouse had set out to make fun of the invasion scare. He opened after the fashion of the propagandists by addressing a letter to his readers from The Bomb-proof Shelter, London W:

It is necessary that England should be roused to a sense of her peril, and only by setting down without flinching the probable results of an invasion can this be done. This story, I may mention, has been written and published purely from a feeling of patriotism and duty. Mr Alston Rivers' sensitive soul will be jarred to its foundations if it is a financial success. So will mine.

The story mocks the invasion legend by a process of inversion and comic inflation. In the first chapter Wodehouse converts Guy du Maurier's theme into the comedy of 'An English Boy's Home'. The patriot who warns an indifferent and bored family of the nation's peril is the hateful boy, Clarence MacAndrew Chugwater, one of General Baden-Powell's Boy Scouts. The news of the German landing reaches an equally indifferent public in the small print of the Stop Press; 'Fry not out, 104. Surrey 147 for 8. A German army landed in Essex this afternoon. Loamshire Handicap: Spring Chicken, 1; Salome, 2; Yip-i-addy, 3. Seven ran.' The rest of the tale deserves its mention in any history of imaginary wars, if only for the solitary element of comedy it brings into such a solemn form of fiction. In the manner of the later master, Wodehouse crams the plot with a great variety of incidents. The invasion is no simple affair of a single German army. Everybody joins in: 'No fewer than eight other hostile armies had, by some remarkable coincidence, hit on that identical moment for launching their long-prepared blow.' The invaders advance in their thousands across the golf courses of southern England. As the bored inhabitants play on, hordes of Germans, Russians, Swiss, Chinese, Young Turks, and Moroccan brigands advance in company with the forces of the Mad Mullah and the Prince of Monaco. And so it went on, but to no effect. The book was not a success. After such a heavy diet of war stories and appeals to join the Territorials, the public was not likely to be amused by such frivolity.

The excessive nervousness revealed in the many tales of invasion had become the object of inquiry at home and abroad. In January 1910 Charles

Lowe had a long article on the subject of these stories in the *Contemporary Review*. His views give an indication of the scale of publishing in this field:

Among all the causes contributing to the continuance of a state of bad blood between England and Germany, perhaps the most potent is the baneful industry of those unscrupulous writers who are for ever asserting that the Germans are only awaiting for a fitting opportunity to attack us in our island home and burst us up. . . . Thus it is that one of the most remarkable signs of the times is the number of works of fiction dealing with the invasion of England—works in which pen and pencil vie with each other in the production of luridly life-like pictures of aggression from across the German Ocean. . . . Such pernicious works of fiction have been positively pouring from the press for the last few years.[24]

Part of the attack was directed against William Le Queux, who had described the German espionage organization, but had not produced 'one tittle of evidence in support of his allegation'. At the end the author demonstrates the basic contradictions in the various accounts of German espionage activities by listing the different totals given by persons who claimed to know the numbers of German spies and agents at work in the United Kingdom:

GERMANS IN ENGLAND

Major Reed's spies	6,500
Sir John Barlow's 'trained soldiers'	66,000
Lord Roberts's 'trained soldiers'	80,000
Colonel Driscoll's 'trained soldiers'	350,000

These extraordinary figures underline the state of widespread alarm that produced the tale of invasion. The mixture of patriotism, political opportunism, militarism, and derivative writing behind this outburst of fiction gives emphasis to the complaint by another writer in the *Contemporary Review* that 'in no country in the world is more heard of the invasion peril than in England at this moment'.[25] But in many ways the most telling indication of the extent of this nervousness about invasion is to be seen in the verdict from abroad. In 1910 there appeared in Paris a book on the subject of the *Fictions guerrières anglaises*, in which the author reviewed the course of imaginary wars from Chesney's day down to the alarms of 1909. His verdict was that:

this fear of invasion, which is endemic in England, shows itself at times in the form of crises the most recent of which, during last Spring, was exceptionally severe. And if one had listened to the alarmists, one would have concluded that the inviolability of Britain had never been so seriously endangered as during the first months of 1909, in the course of which they reported dangers in every direction—at sea, in the air, and even in the bowels of the earth.[26]

According to the Frenchman, beneath the apparently phlegmatic British attitude there was a deep-seated and permanent anxiety which had been exploited 'by many writers who had described the feared invasion usually in the darkest colours'.

Another indication of French interest—or was it compassion?—appeared in *Black and White* exactly eleven months after the magazine had started one more alarmist tale of invasion on its way. On this occasion the editor showed a full-page drawing of the British lion with shield and trident stretched in symbolic fashion across a view of the countryside. Above were the words of an editor who had conveniently forgotten that he had published *The Great Raid*: 'Paul Thiriat's view of the situation. He has profound confidence in the British Lion.' And beneath the drawing by the French artist were the words:

From his studio in Seine-et-Marne, M. Paul Thiriat, the well-known French artist has sent this sketch to 'Black and White' as an expression of his own independent opinion upon the situation. In an accompanying letter he says: 'Everything looks calm; England is at peace; her factories in full work, her trade prosperous, her beloved soil breathing fertility. Suddenly the alarmists conjure up the Invasion spectre. But the British Lion is calm and proud. He seems to say to all the subjects of King Edward, "Don't trouble yourselves. Live in peace. I am here to guard you."'

After that there is little left to say about the progress of these stories of imaginary warfare before 1914. In Germany they continued, not so numerous but just as outrageous as many of the British productions. In the *Weltkrieg in den Lüften* (1909), for example, Britain is defeated by fleets of airships because she had been foolish enough to ally herself with the French. Again, in Adolf Sommerfeld's notorious account of France defeated by Germany, *Frankreichs Ende in Jahr 19??* (1912), there is the savage forecast that 'all clemency, it must be understood, was entirely out of the question, and this not only because of Germany who might be excused since self-preservation had long been admitted as the first law of existence, but because it was necessary to crush for ever the sole disturber of the peace of Europe'.

And finally, in the early months of 1915, the history of these tales of war and invasion came to a full stop with Paul Georg Münch's account of the conquest of Britain in *Hindenburgs Einmarsch in London*. This was in its own way as complete a fantasy as Machen's legend of the English bowmen; and, as in so many of the British invasion stories, the exaggerated sense of absolute right that shapes Münch's denunciation of enemy wickedness is a clear sign of repudiated feelings of guilt. For here one can see how the entire literature of imaginary warfare is in the last analysis a myth-world created out of animosities and anxieties, and the whole projected into a fantasy of the future where only the worst or the best can come to pass. Hence, the last of the old-style German forecasts closed with Hindenburg's address to his victorious troops in London. He told them to go back to Germany and tell their children of the great events they had seen, so that in the years to come their grandsons could say that 'a grandfather of mine camped in front of Buckingham Palace after he had helped to clear the world of our enemies'.

The optimistic account of *Hindenburgs Einmarsch in London* was the last of the many tales of war between Britain and Germany that had derived from the political situation. Stage by stage, the nations moved towards the war so many writers had tried to describe. As Austria became ever more deeply entangled in the Balkan situation, it seemed to be only a matter of time before the alliance with Germany would lead to a great conflict. And then war came, in the words of the *Spectator*, 'exactly as all sensible people knew it would come— very suddenly, without apparent reason, or, at any rate, without apparent reason in the least proportionate to the event'.[27] Somewhere in the Balkans an archduke had been assassinated, and out of that came war, unprecedented killing, and the end of European supremacy in the world. But at first few realized that Gavrilo Prinćip had touched off the long-anticipated explosion. Sarajevo seemed yet another episode in the constant upheavals in the Balkans. Hilaire Belloc has related how he was one of the many who had no idea that war would come. And then, as he sailed down the Channel in the *Nona*, he found the answer to what was happening when he saw that away across the water,

like ghosts, like things themselves made of mist, there passed before me and the newly risen sun, a procession of great forms, all in line, hastening east-wards. It was the Fleet, recalled. The slight haze along that distant water had thickened, perhaps, imperceptibly; or perhaps the great speed of the men-of-war buried them too quickly in the distance. But, from whatever cause, this marvel was of short duration. It was seen for a moment, and in a moment it was gone. Then I knew that war would come, and my mind was changed.[28]

Chapter Five

From the Somme and Verdun to Hiroshima and Nagasaki

SOON after the fighting came to an end in 1918, the literature of future warfare made an abrupt change of direction. The post-war writers turned from the nationalistic ready-for-anything style that had been characteristic of the many tales of 'The Next Great War'. Moreover, the new fiction rejected the old doctrine of inevitable conflict; and ever since the 1920s tales of the war-to-come have for the most part maintained a common front against the dangers of war and, in particular, against the immense destructiveness of modern weapons.

This change followed out of the feelings of stupefaction and horror affecting all who had discovered that trench warfare was not the swift and glorious campaign they had expected. 'For a year after the war had begun,' Winston Churchill wrote, 'hardly anyone understood how terrific, how almost inexhaustible were the resources in force, in substance, in virtue, behind every one of the combatants.'[1] The many post-war autobiographies and accounts of life in the trenches testify that the men who volunteered in 1914 thought they were enlisting for an old-style war of rapid movement. 'It must be remembered', Herbert Read noted by way of explanation, 'that in 1914 our conception of war was completely unreal. We had vague, childish memories of the Boer War, and from these and from a general diffusion of Kiplingesque sentiments, we managed to infuse into war a decided element of adventurous romance. War still appealed to the imagination.'[2] They went in ignorance to battle, so R. H. Mottram recalled in *The Spanish Farm*, because they looked on war 'with an ingrained romanticism possible only to those who live in comfortable leisure, with enough to eat and drink, no frontiers, and plenty of novels'.

This romanticism had begun during the adolescence of the young men who died in tens of thousands on the Somme. From the many books about 'The Deeds that Won The Empire' and from publications like the eight volumes in the popular *Romance of Empire Series*, the young had learnt about heroic actions, imperial destiny, and the certain triumph of the nation. The indoctrination became more sustained and persuasive with the steady output of boys' books from George Alfred Henty. Beginning with *Under Drake's Flag* in 1883,

Henty went on to produce more than fifty books, the last of which, bearing
the appropriate title of *Conduct and Courage*, appeared posthumously in 1905.
The Henty books sold by the hundred thousand, and in his lifetime the total
sales were put at some 25 million. Most of them were tales of personal
endeavour, manly behaviour, straight living, and courageous actions. Parents
and schoolteachers admired them. Henty books were favoured as class prizes
and were often rewards for good attendance at Sunday Schools, a fact well
known to all who have browsed in second-hand bookshops. His biographer
wrote no more than the truth in his claim that 'There was scarcely a book
from his pen, which did not serve to impress some important period of
fighting or diplomatic action upon the mind of the reader.'[3]

Story by story, Henty would work through one of the more reputable
periods of British history. His stock hero was a young boy, of good middle-
class family, who had his way to make in the world. The lad was highly
adventurous, always courageous, and usually a good athlete. He could take a
beating without a murmur and was more than a match for boys of his own
age. According to Henty's biographer, the young hero was above all 'a good
specimen of the class by which Britain has been built up, her colonies formed
and her battle-fields won—a class in point of energy, fearlessness, the spirit of
adventure, and a readiness to face and overcome all difficulties unmatched in
the world.'

George Henty gave the young an image of war as a succession of battles and
campaigns which took place far away in distant lands. The Henty war was a
close-combat affair of small numbers and minimal casualties; it was above all a
commendable activity for patriots. In this he was handing on a belief in the
virtue of war that runs through literature up to 1914. Wordsworth, for
instance, celebrated the Battle of Waterloo with an ode to victory. He assumed
that, just as 'the God of peace and love' made use of pestilence, drought, and
earthquakes to achieve his ends, so war was a divine means of improving
mankind:

> But Thy most dreaded instrument,
> In working out a pure intent,
> Is Man—arrayed for mutual slaughter,
> —Yea, Carnage is thy daughter!

Although Wordsworth had second thoughts about those lines, they became a
standard reference in support of war. In 1854, for example, that mild and amiable writer Thomas De Quincey repeated the Wordsworthian doctrine in an
essay 'On War', in which he presented the argument against the Peace
Societies. The agreed opinion held that war 'is a *positive* good; not relative
merely, or negative, but positive'. War settled disputes between nations, and
by way of a bonus it improved the quality of the combatants. It never seems

to have struck De Quincey that his belief was a judgement that only victors could make. Everything was improving, he thought, and warfare was certain to become less frequent and less bloody. A future war would be shorter, and 'what there is will, by expanding civilisation, and indirectly, through science continually more exquisite applied to its administration, be indefinitely human-ised and refined'. Heartily and with profoundest sympathy, De Quincey wrote, he 'went along with Wordsworth in his grand lyrical proclamation of a truth not less divine than it is mysterious: viz. that amongst God's holiest instru-ments for the elevation of human nature is "mutual slaughter" amongst men'.

Those were the sentiments of John Ruskin when he gave a notorious lecture on 'War' to the Royal Military Academy in 1865. Ruskin began mildly enough, suggesting that his audience had come 'in merely contemptuous curiosity to hear what a writer on painting could possibly say, or would ven-ture to say, respecting your great art of war'. But he warmed rapidly to his subject, and within minutes was arguing that 'war is the foundation of all the arts. I mean also that it is the foundation of all the high virtues and faculties of men.' He went on in his grandiloquent oration to call on the Muse of History. From her lips he heard that 'all great nations learned their truth of word, and strength of thought in war; that they were nourished in war, and wasted in peace . . . in a word, that they were born in war, and expired in peace'. The Ruskin doctrine on war must have struck the Woolwich cadets as an echo of Henty:

The historical facts are that, broadly speaking, none but soldiers, or persons with a soldierly faculty, have ever yet shown themselves fit to be kings; and that no other men are so gentle, so just, or so clear-sighted. Wordsworth's character of the happy warrior cannot be reached in the height of it *but by* a warrior.

This comfortable toleration of war did wonders for the circulation figures of the illustrated magazines. Go back through the bound volumes of publications as different as the *Illustrated London News* and the *Scientific American*, and it will be evident that, month by month, year after year, editors saw to it that their readers had the latest information about new weapons. On 28 July 1866, for instance, the *Illustrated London News* gave a full page, complete with detailed drawings, to the new needle-gun then under consideration for the Army. These reports were constants in the magazine, as they were in the *Scientific American*. The issue in that journal for 13 July 1889, for example, had a striking frontispiece which showed an artist's impression of the Sims–Edison Electric Torpedo on its first trials. And so it went on throughout the illustrated press in Europe and the United States—from engravings of the first ironclads to handsome photogravure illustrations of the latest airships and flying machines in the last years before 1914.

The same painstaking attention to detail sought to give the appearance of

prophetic truth to the serial stories of the next war that were a recurring feature in the illustrated press between 1890 and 1914. Their images of future
wars sustained the set themes of short campaigns, rapid manœuvres, and small
casualty lists. The eye adjusted easily to the expected: cavalry charges, infantry
formed in square or advancing in open order, ship-to-ship exchanges, and carefully staged scenes of conspicuous courage. It was quite exceptional for readers
to see the double-page spread of a torpedoed liner that made a novel point
about submarine warfare in Conan Doyle's short story 'Danger', in the *Strand
Magazine* for July 1914. That could never happen, they said. War would go on
in the same old way, although on rare occasions a writer might have his doubts
about the scale or the duration of a future war. In fact, it was most unusual to
find journalists who ever raised any questions about the new instruments of
war. For instance, an exceptional crack in the ironclad complacency of those
days appeared at the end of a well-informed and fully illustrated article on the
new German zeppelins in *McClure's Magazine* for August 1909:

That the new machine of war will cause great changes in the history of nations
cannot be doubted—if aerial warfare is permitted to exist. But will it be permitted?
War a mile above the earth, between corps of artillery firing into huge bodies of
inflammable gas, where the defeated plunge down to the ground a mass of charred
pulp, will become a thing too spectacularly horrible for conception. Will civilization permit it to exist? Or does this new machine mean the end of war?

The answers to that question were beyond all but the most exceptional of
people, such as Ivan Bloch and Norman Angell. The failure in anticipation
began with the young who had absorbed the military values of their society in
their reading of George Henty. They grew up to find that Drake's spirit still
animated the sailors in the imaginary naval engagements of the tales of 'The
Next Great War'; and they could see the compelling illustrations that showed
how very little would change in the conduct of warfare. After a century of
rhetoric about the romance of war and about the marvels of technological
development, how could there be a ready answer to the question: Does the
areoplane mean the end of war? Although the intellect had readily compre-
hended the enormous powers of the applied sciences, the imagination could
only conceive of their application within the known system of warfare. Then,
in April 1915, there came a last word from the old world before the Somme
and Verdun. Although the scale of warfare had already altered in ways few had
foreseen, a gentle and sensitive scholar, Edmund Gosse, found nothing
unusual in beginning an essay on 'War and Literature' in the manner of De
Quincey: 'War is the great scavenger of thought. It is the sovereign disinfec-
tant, and its red stream of blood is the Condy's Fluid that cleans out the stag-
nant pools and clotted channels of the intellect.' What did they make of that at
Gallipoli?

The world vocabularies were out of date. They lacked words to prepare the mind for casualties on an unheard-of scale and battles of unprecedented ferocity and duration, for a front from the Alps to the Channel and a landscape that would be filled with graves and dominated by the great Ossuary of Douaumont, the last resting place of 300,000 French soldiers.

This failure in language shows most clearly in the poetry written before the Somme. The poetic response to the opening battles came in a form of words that had not changed since the times of Wordsworth and Tennyson. Rupert Brooke's famous sonnet 'The Soldier' was the last manifestation of a literary tradition that had lost all relevance in the entirely new conditions of trench warfare. Because the early months of the war seemed to confirm the expectations of heroic encounters and noble deeds, the poetry remained fixed in the concrete of a traditional vocabulary and set responses. When Robert Graves thought back to his first impressions of active service in 'Recalling War', he remembered a time of romantic happiness; it was an experience of languorous enchantment which had a natural affinity with Keats enthralled by the vision of beauty:

> Never was such antiqueness of romance
> Such tasty honey oozing from the heart.

The raptures of the antique also affected the early poetry of Siegfried Sassoon; but he soon came to see that his verse was filled with 'too nobly worded lines', as he called them. In fact, it was only after he had actually been in the trenches that he finally broke with the habit of writing in the conventional and heroic style about 'the woeful crimson of men slain'. After the dreadful casualty lists of the Somme, everything changed. The accepted ideas of the old hurrah-literature were forgotten as the front-line combatants learnt for themselves that the war, in the words of Ernest Hemingway, 'was the most colossal, murderous, mismanaged butchery that has ever taken place on earth'. After all the forecasts and the many jubilant descriptions of future victories, the new message to the nations came from the front, from the men who had endured a misery and degradation that had not been foreseen in the anticipations of *Der nächste Krieg*, *La Guerre de demain*, and *The Next Great War*. The new authors—British, French, German—were for the most part unable to write in the traditional manner about war as the supreme manifestation of a nation's will. Their concern was with war as an affliction of mankind.

For the first time in a hundred years, a generation of writers had appeared who could speak with full knowledge and experience of war. One of the first was Henri Barbusse, who completed *Le Feu* while in a military hospital recovering from service in the trenches of Artois and Picardy. He wrote with veneration for the dead and with pity for his still-living comrades:

They are not soldiers, they are men. They are not adventurers, or warriors, or made for human slaughter, neither butchers nor cattle. They are labourers and artisans whom one recognises in their uniforms. They are civilians uprooted, and they are ready. They await the signal for death or murder; but you may see, looking at their faces between the vertical gleams of their bayonets, that they are simply men.[4]

The contrast between the war-as-expected and the atrocious experiences of millions in the trenches was so painful and profound that it proved inconceivable for any writer ever again to dwell on 'the pride, pomp, and circumstance of glorious war'. The heroic tone and traditional language disappeared from poetry. The range of themes narrowed down to the elemental conditions of trench warfare, to the pity and suffering of war, to the brotherhood of the front-line fighter which separated the men in the trenches from the rest of their society. Many wrote about their own self-deception, surprised and dismayed that they had ever been taken in by the talk of glorious war. Feelings of disenchantment and dismay run through much of the new poetry. Some turned angrily on the literary tradition that had been guilty, they thought, of hiding the bestiality of war under a cloud of senseless rhetoric. 'Who is the happy Warrior?' Wordsworth had asked in a famous poem; and, in a deliberate, resentful protest against 'all the glory camouflage', Herbert Read gave his answer from the Somme:

> His wild heart beats with painful sobs,
> His strain'd hands clench an ice-cold rifle,
> His aching jaws grip a hot parch'd tongue,
> His wide eyes search unconsciously
> He cannot shriek.
> Bloody saliva
> Dribbles down his shapeless jacket.
> I saw him stab
> And stab again
> A well-killed Boche.
> This is the happy warrior,
> This is he . . .

That revolt against a long-established literary tradition had comparable effects within the fiction of future warfare. After 1918 it was no longer possible to say that war was merely the extension of policy by other means; and so a new race of propagandists converted the traditional tale of the war-to-come into a straightforward plea for peace by demonstrating the horrors, the uselessness, and the fearful consequences of technological warfare. Although the device of projecting contemporary possibilities into an imagined future remained unaltered, the code was largely rewritten.

This radical change in the tale of the war-to-come has developed through two principal phases; and these are no more than stages in the dialogue about the conduct of international affairs and the increasing menace of armed conflict that has been going on ever since the end of the First World War. In the opening period, before 1939, the central theme was the argument for peace by the revelation of the terrors to be expected from gas and air attacks on cities. The second stage began with the explosion of the first atomic bombs; and, as might be expected, the main purpose of the post-1945 stories has been to display the post-warfare condition of mankind in such warning visions as *Ape and Essence*, *On the Beach*, *Le Diable l'emporte*. What they all say can be best conveyed in the concluding sentences of Hans Kirst's *Keiner kommt davon*. After describing the first and last nuclear war upon the planet Earth, the narrator ends his account with the brief statement: 'Germany no longer existed. And so ended the sixth day. Europe did not survive the seventh day. The last hours of the human race were running out.'

Fact and fiction are at last in almost complete agreement. The brief history of imaginary warfare and the even briefer history of the swift advance from high explosives to atomic bombs now teach the one lesson: the deliberate application of technology to the waging of war will undoubtedly achieve the final logic of absolute success by causing the destruction of mankind. This conviction, expressed in hundreds of books and many international conferences, marks the final stage in the century-long discussion about armaments that began in 1862 when Ericcson's *Monitor* started off the arms race. In the words of an editorial in the *Illustrated London News* for 5 April 1862, 'We may depend upon it that we are now entering upon a race in which success will no longer be achieved by wealth or material resources, under merely ordinary conditions of skilful development, but that skill, science, and individual energy will need only moderate means to obtain the greatest triumphs.' The editor was wrong about the cheapness of the new ironclads, but he was unhappily accurate about the effectiveness of calling in science to adjust the balance of war. His views were a paraphrase of what John Ericcson had told Lincoln: 'The time has come, Mr. President, when our cause will have to be sustained not by numbers, but by superior weapons . . . if you apply our mechanical resources to the fullest extent you can destroy the enemy without enlisting another man.'[5]

Ericcson's views seemed tenable enough one hundred years ago, when war was still a continental affair, a confrontation between relatively small groups. But, ever since the episode of the *Monitor* and the *Merrimac*, the constant development of new military technologies and of completely new weapons has more and more threatened to involve the entire world in war. The Korean War, the Cuban Crisis of 1962, and the response of the United Nations to the Iraqi invasion of Kuwait have made it clear beyond all questioning that the scale of conflict on the planet Earth is no longer continental but world-wide.

And in this swift change that has come upon the world since the construction of the *Monitor*, the year 1914 marks the great divide between the old

Tennysonian delight in 'all the wonder that would be' and the realization that war can no longer be considered either natural or inevitable. For this reason, the tales of future wars that have appeared during the past half-century serve as epigraphs on the social consequences of scientific advance. They reflect the many problems thrown up by the almost catastrophic increase in population throughout the world, by the rapid development of terrestrial communications which have made the world one small place, and above all by the urgent need to create a new attitude of mind in place of the traditional belief that war is a satisfactory means of solving differences between nations.

All these changes had an immediate and decisive effect on the tales of future warfare. Before 1914 these projections had started from the known base of an established and assured way of life; and behind most of them there was the unquestioned assumption of a common European civilization which would return to the old world as it used to be before the projected wars began. Once the lessons of the First World War had been understood, however, the fiction of future warfare went through a series of instant changes that have persisted to this day. Most of its practitioners are no longer the captains, colonels, admirals, and military correspondents who once played so large a part in preaching the need for national preparedness; and most of the post-war projections have moved into new territory. From the 1920s to the present day, save for occasional fiction from the military, the tales of the war-to-come have been written by civilians for civilians. Although the context of their stories has been the next war, the authors rejected the hallowed conventions of the nation-in-arms and chose instead to concentrate on the disasters that would affect all humankind. The revised formula has for the most part avoided all detailed accounts of the campaigns and the great battles that were once the chief glory of the tales of 'The Next Great War'. One sign of this transformation is that, for the first time in the history of these projections, women take to writing about the dangers of modern warfare. The most striking changes of all, however, are the sudden disappearance of the serial stories of 'The Next Great War' from the illustrated magazines, and the simultaneous termination of the patriotic alliance that had long united civilians and the military in service to their nations. Thus, the market responded to the revised view of war by acknowledging a fundamental division of interests. The military have continued to address a limited audience on the strategy and probable use of the new weaponry in a future war, and the civilians have written their very different tales of the catastrophe-to-come for the general public.

The two groups rarely join forces in a common action, because the propaganda of the anti-war stories has to go well beyond the logistics of possible military actions. The parables turned from the probable so that for the sake of peace readers could contemplate the worst possible scenario—the swift destruction of capital cities by vast air fleets, instant death for millions in clouds of poison gas, famine and pestilence for the survivors, and in the last forty years the sudden ending of all life on our planet.

The military, for their part and for most of the time, kept to the facts and took a cool look at the possibilities as they saw them. The first off from the start-line was Friedrich von Bernhardi, a veteran of the Zukunftskrieg, who had caused great alarm with his notorious *Deutschland und der nächste Krieg* in 1912. He returned to his favourite subject in the last months of the war and in 1920 published *Vom Krieg der Zukunft*, yet another call from an old trumpeter who summoned all good Germans to fall in for the great mechanized war that was sure to come. Thereafter, year by year, the experts brought out their professional studies on the future of modern warfare. In particular, they aimed to explain the new dispositions and strategies brought about by tanks, aeroplanes, poison gas, and submarines: Colonel Fuller, *Tanks in Future Warfare* (1921); Général Maitrôt, *La Prochaine guerre* (1921); General Schwarte, *Die Technik im Zukunftskrieg* (1923); Lt.-Col. Velpry, *L'Avenir des chars de combat* (1923); Hauptmann Ritter, *Der Zukunftskrieg und seine Waffen* (1924); Captain Liddell Hart, *The Future of War* (1925).

Only one work of fiction, however, stands out as a worthy survivor from the old projections of future warfare: *The Great Pacific War* (1925) by the British naval writer Hector Bywater. He argued against Franklin D. Roosevelt's belief that distances in the Pacific made a Japanese–American war impossible; for he showed in his book how the Japanese could successfully employ a strategy of surprise attacks against US naval forces at the same time as they captured Guam and the Philippines. The Japanese naval attaché in Washington read the book with great interest, and in 1934 he called on Bywater in London to discuss strategic questions in the Pacific. In 1939 Isoroku Yamamoto was promoted to be commander-in-chief of the Japanese imperial navy, and according to Bywater's biographer he began to plan a Pacific campaign against the Americans on the lines the British analyst had suggested.[6]

Nevertheless, the old-style tale of the war-to-come remained in terminal decline. In fact, there is little more than a period interest in most of the fiction that continued with the old model. The Germans began by looking forward to their own great war to restore the Fatherland: Major Solf, *1934: Deutschlands Auferstehung* (1921); Wilhem Grassegger, *Der Zweite Weltkrieg* (1922); Gen.-Maj. Schoenaich, *Der Krieg im Jahre 1930* (1925). On rare occasions a writer would break with the stereotype of rapid German victories to produce a more interesting variant on the stock theme of Germany at war. Johann von Leers, for example, opens his story *Bomben auf Hamburg* (1932) with an account of mass unemployment and economic decline. The French demand the repayment of war reparations; and when Germany pleads poverty and refuses, the French fleet sails into Hamburg and troops storm ashore to seize the port. Where is the German navy? The German readers know that, although it lies at the bottom of Scapa Flow, the nation is not defenceless. All citizens unite beneath the Swastika; the Nazis form a national government; and the world blames the French for the war.

The French are again to blame for the war of 1934, as Hans Gobsch relates in *Wahneuropa* (1931), which the author intended to be 'a vision and not a shocker'. In the Europe of 1932 he perceived the shapes of coming events; and he aimed, therefore, 'at personifying various points of view, political trends and spiritual tendencies which, while mutually antagonistic, are seeking to determine the form and destiny of present-day Europe'. In 1934 a war breaks out between the French and the Italians. Mass air attacks follow. The Italians destroy Paris; and with equal facility the French destroy Milan, Turin, Florence, Genoa, and Rome. As the disastrous war ends, the author gives his last warning: Russian armies are on the move, moving westward through Poland and central Europe.

There is a melancholy interest in observing the fading-away of a propaganda device which in its day had alarmed nations and filled newspapers with ominous accounts of coming wars. For the few French writers who continued in the tradition of *La Guerre qui vient*, the enemy of the future could only be Germany. Their warnings came at intervals. In 1921 Raymond Boschmans gave his account of the coming air war in *Les Ailes repoussent*; and in 1924 he returned to the theme of the German plan for air attacks on France in *La Guerre nécessaire*. More French answers to the expected German threat appeared in *1935*, an account of the next Franco-German war by C. Meillac in 1924. A more original story was *Paix sur la terre* (1931), by Louis Artus. He dedicated the book to Adolf Hitler in the name of peace; and he warned him that the misuse of science would be the end of mankind, unless . . . His proof is the near-catastrophe of the next Franco-German war. A toxic powder proves so destructive that wisdom prevails; international reconciliation follows as the French and German armies work together to rescue the survivors. As the 1930s advanced, the anticipations in these stories came closer to the true history of events. In 1936, in his *Le 'Redoutable': journal d'un commandant de vedette*, Pierre Louis Deverdun expected the next war to break out on 5 June 1939, when the Germans would attack Dantzig. The British would join with the French against the Germans; and as both sides become exhausted the Russians move into Europe in March 1940.

The turbulent history of these imaginary wars ended with a chain explosion in the five-part series which Commandant Cazal, otherwise Jean de la Hire, began with *La Guerre! La Guerre!* in 1939. He started writing on 1 February, the month when Germany announced plans for a greatly enlarged submarine fleet and for the reorganization of the air force; and as the fateful months went by—the Axis a military alliance, the non-aggression agreement with Stalin, the demand for Dantzig—the imagined war raged on in story after story. On

25 June 1939 the Germans and Italians make a sudden attack on France: there are mass air attacks by Junkers in formations of hundreds; the United Kingdom sends 2,000 fighters and 1,000 bombers; and wish-fulfilment arranges for twenty British divisions to arrive in France with the most formidable celerity within days of the first engagements. The Maginot Line proves impregnable to all frontal attack; the allied fleets inflict severe losses on the Italians in the Mediterranean; and in consequence the Italians decide to make a separate peace. Then, officers of the German OKW seize Hitler and order an immediate cease-fire. The peace treaty divides the Reich into a number of small states. The imaginary war was over by 28 July 1939, and Jean de la Hire finished writing on 10 August, three weeks before the Germans invaded Poland. He could congratulate himself on one of the more remarkable performances in the often exciting and at times explosive chronicles of *les guerres imaginaires*.

Across the Channel they were writing very different accounts of the next war. There was a far-fetched story about the Channel Tunnel, or How Britain was saved in the great war against America, Russia, and India; an even more improbable tale about the operations of the Bolshevists and the Freemasons in destroying the British Empire; a romantic yarn about a war with Russia fought out on the Northwest Frontier; and even an alarming vision of the end of the world which was to be expected after the German Bolshevists have overrun Europe.[7] Although these stories were more banal than the contemporary war fiction in French and German, they were unusual in so far as they showed a common determination to use all possible means of carrying on the tradition of the war-to-come. They were early signs of a renewed delight in war for the pleasure of the fighting; and that desire for war at any cost went on to encourage the post-catastrophe serials that became the most popular form of American fantasy in the 1980s. The total improbability of the plots, then and now, give the authors what they want most: the free play of the imagination which makes it all too easy to follow fancy into the most extravagant of make-believe worlds and alternative histories. The limitless range of the context is the necessary sanction for the tale of what-you-will. Moreover, the absolute separation between the evident dangers and anxieties of the contemporary world and the ceaseless fighting and many disasters in this kind of fiction is more than a simple narrative device. These recent survivalist fantasies are the darker shadow of reality. They depend upon the total distancing of the mind which allows an author to transform the unquestionable violence of life in the twentieth century into the unconventional and often casual mayhem that is the principal formula in these epic tales of the future.

After the First World War, the centre of anxiety within the tale of the war-to-come shifted. All the absolute convictions and political expectations of the self-righteous nation vanished; and since then very few writers have attempted to create up-to-date versions of tales like *Blake of the 'Rattlesnake'* and *Trafalgar Refought*. The first phase in this transformation appears in the publications of the 1920s; for the handful of stories that continued to put forward arguments for new equipment were survivals from an earlier and more innocent age. This appears most clearly in the propaganda of three stories published in 1926 and 1927: *The Broken Trident*, *The Naviators*, and *The Harbour of Death*. The author, E. F. Spanner of the Royal Corps of Naval Constructors (Retired), had taken to print in order to demonstrate that 'the Navy, as it is at present, is entirely useless to prevent this Country from being defeated by a Continental Power possessing a strong Air Force'.

But this use of futuristic fiction was most unusual during the inter-war years. From 1918 to 1939, the mood shaping most of these tales of the war-to-come was a profound sense of anxiety and doubt about the future, which came out in many stories describing the end of civilization and in frightening visions of the terrible disasters that awaited humankind. Since 1918 the tale of future warfare has moved steadily from bad to worse as the means of destruction have advanced from the Gotha and Handley–Page bombing planes to the hydrogen bomb and the ingenious devices of the Strategic Defence Initiative. And whatever the anxieties of the day may have been, readers could always be sure of finding their worst fears realized in fiction. No sooner had the fighting ended in 1918 than the alarms began to sound again; but the dangers were not what they used to be.

The night flares go up to illuminate a landscape that has changed in every way. In the unstable post-war world the old steady-state certainties of king and country have vanished. The new menace to national security is the enemy within, who represents any of the forces believed to endanger social stability at any time. As the pre-war device of the war-to-come had found shape and substance in the contemporary discussion of German intentions, so the new stories of the coming revolution and the servile state have followed out of the warnings and the forecasts of national disruption. These have maintained a consistent pattern, from the first tales of the tyranny-to-come to the long-running yarns about the holy war against the KGB and the Soviet occupation of Great Britain.

Such tales go back to 1919, when there began to appear a series of stories devoted to the horrors of revolution. The titles indicate the intentions of their authors: *London Under the Bolshevists*, *The Red Fury*, *The Battle of London*, *The Red Tomorrow*, *Against the Red Sky*, *Revolution*. Their forecasts of a mass rising by the workers show clearly how this kind of story is parasitic upon the contemporary mood. For the fear of insurrection owed as much to the dread example of the Russian Revolution as it did to the wave of post-war strikes and to the growing strength of the Labour Party. To the more timorous in 1919, it seemed that the country was on the verge of a Bolshevist uprising. According to the authors of the new tales of a future civil war, this danger was the immediate consequence of a widespread sense of disillusionment. Men had expected too much, wrote the author of *Anymoon* (1919). During the war 'the minds of all mankind had been seeking new ideals, searching frantically for some universal panacea that would bring security and happiness . . . All confidently expected a new heaven and a new earth to rise almost spontaneously, with the aid of a little coaxing by mortal hands, directly the war had ended.' This view was common ground with the authors of imaginary revolutions of the future. They all traced the origins of the disaster to the anger of the masses when they found that there was to be no perfect world for them after the long agony of trench warfare. There is an example of this in J. D. Beresford's *Revolution* (1921), when the embittered ex-serviceman, a stock character in these stories, explains the resentment that made him take up arms against the government of the day: 'Some of us over there thought we were coming back to a wonderful fine place after it was all over. We believed it was all going to be different, sort of Utopia, short hours, and good pay, and everybody pals with everybody else.' The contrast between the promise and the fulfilment had made the ex-servicemen angry. After the slogans about 'the War to end War' and 'the war to make the World safe for Democracy', they had returned to find that their country was certainly not 'a place fit for heroes to live in'. This fact coincided with the spread of revolutions throughout Europe. It made some think that Britain might go the way of Russia if the middle classes did not act in time.

This was the simple philosophy presented by the author of *The Battle of London* (1923). He explained the purpose of his story in a foreword:

The Battle of London was written with the frank intention of shocking what the friends of Red Russia call the *bourgeoisie* into a realisation of the only means of meeting revolution if and when it should arise. It is to be hoped, and is indeed most likely, that a Liberty League, or something like it, will never be called upon to save England as the Fascists saved Italy. But nobody can say to-day that all danger is absolutely over, so that a consideration of how to meet it is not merely academic. Should the catastrophe of a Labour Government ever arrive—and futile dissension between the main body of the middle classes may some day bring it about—we know in advance what is the minimum tyranny the milder Labour Leaders would inflict upon us, and may be certain that the wilder spirits would soon be clamouring for more. Fortunately we now have the example of the Fascists—and the Liberty League—to show us what to do in a real crisis.

That was tomorrow's terror—the first in a new series of desperate images of disorder, imminent collapse, and the final disintegration of civilized society. They have their place in the new literature of foreboding that grew out of the anxieties of the 1920s. Many of them were the fictional counterpart of the anxieties of T. S. Eliot, who contemplated the spiritual wasteland of a world perishing for want of moral order and right purpose:

> What are the roots that clutch, what branches grow
> Out of this stony rubbish? Son of man,
> You cannot say, or guess, for you know only
> A heap of broken images, where the sun beats,
> And the dead tree gives no shelter, the cricket no relief,
> And the dry stone no sound of water.

Like T. S. Eliot in 'The Waste Land', another great poet looked past the tumultuous upheavals of the post-war period to the dreadful evils still to come; and in his poem on 'The Second Coming' William Butler Yeats foresaw the beginning of a savage and merciless age:

> Things fall apart; the centre cannot hold;
> Mere anarchy is loosed upon the world,
> The blood-dimmed tide is loosed, and everywhere
> The ceremony of innocence is drowned;
> The best lack all conviction, while the worst
> Are full of passionate intensity.

The poetry provides most apt texts for the new fiction of civil disruption and fearful calamities that begins in the 1920s. For the first time since the eighteenth century, when the earliest tales of the future began to appear, there was a succession of stories devoted to a single theme: the coming destruction of civilization. The old, unquestioning delight in change and technological innovation vanished. In response to the great fears of the twentieth century, writers everywhere helped to develop a form of futuristic fiction that concentrates exclusively on the last days of the human race and the experiences of the Last Man. The stereotype was established in 1920 with the publication of *The People of the Ruins* by Edward Shanks; and after 1945 it reached the point where the world-wide reception of stories like Aldous Huxley's *Ape and Essence* and Arno Schmidt's *Die Gelehrtenrepublik* made the survivor's tale a means of salutary instruction for the epoch of the atomic bomb.

Since 1918 most of these tales of the catastrophe-to-come have presented the history of an obsession engendered by a loss of faith in the grand old doctrine of inevitable progress. They range through all the emotions—from anxiety and anger to the most violent, anarchic desire to obliterate all the causes of pain. Most of these stories are apprehensive. They reflect a general fear that men have unleashed forces beyond their control, a fear that—as Freud observed—'men have brought their powers of subduing nature to such a pitch that by using them they could very easily exterminate one another to the last man'.[8] This theme runs through many tales of the future, from the first statement by Edward Shanks in *The People of the Ruins* in 1920 to the moral lesson in Alfred Noyes' story of *The Last Man* in 1940. Stories like *Theodore Savage, The Collapse of Homo Sapiens, Last of my Race, Ragnarok, At the End of the*

World, *Day of Wrath*, *The World Ends*, and others all condemn a civilization that has not yet learnt how to make wise use of its powers over nature. This judgement follows on the test to destruction. In the 1920s these new stories introduced the highly effective strategy of working through episodes of unrestrained violence—burning cities, widespread destruction, starving populations—as they took the reader to the end of civilized life and on to the ominous appearance of the Last Man. The Germans, for example, coined the term *Weltuntergangsroman* to describe stories like *Der Bazillenkrieg*, *Der Pestkrieg*, and *Gletscher über Europa*. In the French stories of this period— *La Guerre microbienne* (1923), for instance—the feckless inhabitants of Earth have been destroyed by their own folly, and the wild beasts—superior to *Homo sapiens* in every way—are the only survivors on the planet.

Given the entire future of our world as the subject of their stories, the authors took inventiveness as far as imagination could go. Victor Méric, for example, chose the dangers of chemical weapons and air warfare as the theme of his *La 'Der des Der'* (1929); and in exemplary fashion he showed in detail how a chronic moral failure to control the instruments of war must lead to the extermination of all mankind. His last and hardest word for the reader is that the rats alone will survive in the desolate world of the future. Ernest Pérochon went much further in *Les Hommes frénétiques* (1925), to the thirtieth century in our time and the golden age of world community of prodigious scientific advances. In the Century of Avérine, named for the greatest of future scientists, our fortunate descendants are shown to enjoy every conceivable technological advantage, but the homily requires that they fail to control the human passions. Great wars follow and radiation systems succeed in sterilizing all human beings—save for a young couple destined to regenerate the race of man by reconciling the dangerous opposites of technological progress and social morality.

These variations on the theme of world's-end were as numerous as the authors who were eager to play surgeon to the future and apply the knife to the malefic cancer of human self-interest. In France, for instance, the limitless scope of *le cataclysme du futur* attracted some distinguished writers. There was the case of Léon Daudet, grandson of Victor Hugo, a fiery and greatly feared polemicist in the royalist interest, and an inventive writer of fiction. In 1927 Daudet published one of his best stories, *Le Napus: fléau de l'an 2227*, wherein, with his characteristic sense of irony, he selected a simple, unexplained accident to set the action going in his cataclysmic story. This occurs one day when, without warning and without any apparent reason, the first incident of *napusification* causes the immediate annihilation of the first *napusifié* in human history. Soon the mysterious process of instant annihilation is at work throughout the world. War has to follow, and Daudet records with apparent ironic pleasure that the German attack on France leads to the volatilization of the enemy armies. And so on, even to the final logic of the *napusification* of the narrator.

The Daudet story was a rare and ironic variation on a subject of undoubted seriousness for the British, French, and German authors who wanted to have their say on the great issues of science and society. Their theme was novel enough in the 1920s, but nowadays it is immediately recognizable as a commonplace of the late twentieth century. Their fiction carried the now familiar message of 'Act today: tomorrow is too late.' The human race must find a way of adapting itself to the new environment created by the applied sciences or it will suffer the most terrible catastrophes: it may vanish entirely, perishing as surely as the last inhabitants of earth meet their end in these tales of the final times.

To this end Edward Shanks described a desolate England of the year 2074, a land in ruins, split into small barbarian principalities, where the few brutalized inhabitants scratch a wretched existence in the shadows of their ruined factories. The folly of men in waging war has brought about the cataclysm; for the moral Shanks reveals is that the disaster was the immediate consequence of man's inability to put an end to war. And so, he writes, 'it kept on breaking out again, first in one country and then in another. For fifty years there was always war in some part of the world.' This view is typical of post-1918 stories. Like the author of *The Collapse of Homo sapiens* (1923), the new writers look forward to 'a succession of bloody, ruthless, annihilating wars'. The details might vary, but the result described is generally the same. Britain, Europe, and sometimes most of the human race have been destroyed. The familiar world of the twentieth century is obliterated; and the time-traveller to the London of the future can only report that St Paul's is a heap of rubble, the bridges over the Thames have vanished, the great crowds have shrunk to the few stunted half-animal inhabitants of 'a little settlement containing all that was left of the civilisation of the British Empire'.

The theme of the Last Man was, however, but one of several reactions to the First World War that found expression within the tale of the future. While these after-the-disaster stories were moving forward to their natural conclusion in the apocalyptic end-of-the-world theme described by Alfred Noyes in *The Last Man*, another series of quite different stories began in the 1920s. Although the point of origin for these is not some imaginary future war, their common theme of the Arcadian blessedness reserved for a surviving few is so closely related to the anger and dismay behind the future war stories that they call for some comment. Where the imaginary war stories find the source of disaster in man's failure to limit the destructiveness of modern weapons, these parallel visions of the simple Arcadian life take the argument one stage farther. They represent in its most extreme form the sense of frustration and discontent caused by the complexities and difficulties of an urban and technological

The first balloons prompted visions of air warfare in the 1780s.

AN ACCURATE REPRESENTATION of the FLOATING MACHINE Invented by the FRENCH for INVADING ENGLAND. and Acts on the principals of both Wind & Water Mills. carries 60 000 Men & 600 Cannon

A floating fortress said to be waiting in Boulogne for Napoleon's invasion of the United Kingdom.

British Patent no.747, 1855, was an early, but unsuccessful, attempt to develop a steam-propelled war vehicle.

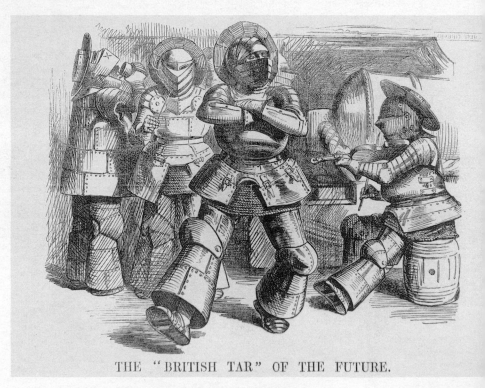

THE "BRITISH TAR" OF THE FUTURE.

Punch took an amused look at the new ironclads in the 1860s.

Scientific American.

A SUBMARINE TORPEDO BOAT.

The accompanying engravings represent a submarine
torpedo boat, designed by Mr. J. L. Tuck, and built at

Fig 1.—THE TORPEDO LEAVING THE VESSEL.

By the 1880s technological warfare attracted great interest.

A. ROBIDA
RÉDACTEUR EN CHEF

La Caricature

JOURNAL
HEBDOMADAIRE

Abonnements d'un an, Paris et départements : 20 francs. — Union postale : 24 francs. — Trois mois : 7 francs. — Bureaux : 7, rue du Croissant.

LA GUERRE AU VINGTIÈME SIÈGLE

LA GUERRE DE RAILWAY
PRISE D'UNE BIFURCATION IMPORTANTE PAR LES TROUPES DE RAILWAY D'AVANT-GARDE

Les locomotives-forteresses blindées des Australiens, lancées avec toute la vitesse que les capitaines-ingénieurs ont pu obtenir de leur propulseurs électriques, ont surpris et bousculé les premiers blockhaus roulants rencontrés après la frontière, et, soutenues par une division aérienne, se sont emparées des lignes, malgré les efforts désespérés d'une division de railway mozambiquoise et de quelques ballonnets blindés.

The possibilities of new weapons were a source of innocent merriment for gifted artists.

The remarkable drawings of Albert Robida made a comedy out of technological warfare . . .

OPÉRATIONS SOUS-MARINES

Les flottes sous-marines australiennes et mozambiquoises s'abordent à 50 mètres de profondeur. Les éperons des cuirassés australiens lancés à toute vitesse par les propulseurs électriques pénètrent à travers les plaques de blindage et coulent 12 navires ; mais les braves torpilleurs sous-marins du Mozambique réussissent, par d'habiles manœuvres, à faire sauter une partie de la flotte ennemie.

. . . to the point of anticipating an attack by *les blockhaus roulants* on a position held by the Women's Territorial Army.

blockhaus étaient déjà détruits, d'autres se défendaient plus mollement, mais deux aéronefs gisaient à terre sur les débris fumants.

Atteinte par des avaries graves, l'aéronef l'Épervier se laissa tomber à pic sur un groupe de blockhaus dont l'équipage décimé dut mettre bas les armes.

Tout est fini : seuls quelques blockhaus ont pu s'échapper et trouver un refuge dans une forêt où les aéronefs sont bien forcées de les laisser. Les équipages de l'Épervier et des quelques aéronefs hors de combat furent répartis sur les blockhaus pris, et lancés en avant. Fablus ayant pour sa belle conduite été nommé sous-ingénieur, reçut le commandement du blockhaus d'avant-garde.

A toute vitesse ! Vers 9 heures du matin le blockhaus lancé comme s'il était poursuivi, pénétra sans difficulté dans les ouvrages d'une place forte gardée par une brigade de territoriale féminine ennemie convoquée pour relever l'armée de 1re et de 2e ligne comprenant tous les hommes de 17 à 50 ans. Terrible surprise pour ces guerrières inexpérimentées. En un clin d'œil elles furent désarmées et la ville prise.

Although the warriors come from Mars in Wells's *War of the Worlds*, their weapons demonstrated what science could do for warfare.

Opposite: from the beginning of the 20th century, anticipations of future warfare became a feature of the illustrated magazines.

"*The airy navies grappling in central blue*"
The war of the future—from a German point of view

There were accounts of German invasions . . .

. . . that sometimes ended with the enemy marching on London.

SUBMARINES ATTACKING A WAR VESSEL.

Cribb

The *London Magazine* in 1909 gave its readers a forecast of possible submarine warfare.

A Vision of the Future: A Trafalgar of the Air

'An army of airships is attacking a fleet lying off a fortified port . . .'

Rocket-powered fighting planes in their pens waiting for the order to attack.

Sometimes books warned of the consequences of air warfare.

V. GERMAN TROOPS, DISGUISED AS BRITISH EXCURSIONISTS, CROSSING THE NORTH SEA.

However, the celebrated and ingenious artist Heath Robinson found it was possible to make fun of the German invasion scare.

Victory and world power go to the robots in Čapek's *R.U.R.*

The daily parade in the perpetual warfare state in Orwell's *Nineteen Eighty-Four*.

By the 1960s the US Army had begun to experiment with jet-packs for infantry reconnaissance units.

The airborne cavalry of the future go into action.

Heads bent in prayer as the end of the world draws near in Kubrik's *Dr Strangelove*.

The eternal struggle between good and evil continues in *Star Wars*

civilization. Since science alone is to blame for the unhappy state of the world, the simple solution is to destroy the machine and return to a state of nature. So, the terrors of modern society are released by the vision of the primitive and peaceful life of the future. In *The Secret of the Desert* (1923), for example, urbanized man's feeling of helplessness in a dangerous and difficult world is exorcized by a return to the simple, self-explanatory cycle of an agricultural society. The contrivance that brings about this desirable state is always some natural disaster—a great wind, a flood, a plague—that destroys all but a chosen few of the human race.

It is indicative of the mood and the intention in these stories that the survivors show no desire to play heir to all the ages. For them the industrial world is well lost. The complex society of the twentieth century is reduced to the scale of the individual. The human termites of the great cities find a personal significance and a sense of individual value in the close relationships described in future Arcadias like *Tomorrow, And a New Earth, Unborn Tomorrow, Deluge, Dawn, The Machine Stops, Three Men Make A World, Gay Hunter*. Here at last in an archaic world of the future the human mind can once again comprehend its environment. The multiplex becomes simple, understandable, manageable; and society is now a community in which all men have their recognized and respected functions.

One example can speak for all these stories. In *Three Men Make a World* (1939), Andrew Marvell describes how a scientist's discovery of petrol-destroying bacteria is the means of freeing the world from the Old Man of Industrialism. Mechanical transport breaks down everywhere, and after a period of famine and disease Britain becomes a land of small kingdoms. The machine is the symbol and the cause of evil, according to the author:

It has added little to knowledge, and the application of that knowledge has been most damnable. It's given us a new range of brutality, but little happiness. We grow more miserable as the machine grows more perfect, for it is supplanting us. It has killed the craftsman, the man who moulded things with his own hand and brain. The individual, the man long tempered by his work, is gone, the man with a shop of his own, the worker with a lathe or a plough or a shovel. He's dead. That is the one thing the machine has done for us.

The argument belongs to the great debate of the 1930s on the place of man in a highly organized society which reached its most sophisticated form in Huxley's *Brave New World*. The conflict between the Savage and the world of Our Ford, between individual values and the advantages of a planned economy, produced the characteristic anti-Utopia of the period. The paradox was that, although *Brave New World* had all the signs of the ideal state as it had been described by Bellamy, Wells, and scores of other optimists, it could not find a place for a man who wanted what Utopia could not provide.

The initial violence in these anarchic begin-again Arcadias is the first collective response to the grand secular aberration that began with Turgot, Priestley, Condorcet, and Herbert Spencer. Their belief was that, as knowledge increased, so society would advance towards universal concord, and at the same time the ever-greater control of nature would enlarge the sum of human happiness. However, for the author of *Three Men Make a World* progress of that kind could only lead to disaster: 'We grow more miserable as the machine grows more perfect.' That protest runs through the futuristic literature of the inter-war years: it animates the drama of mankind versus the robots in Čapek's *R.U.R.*; it is the primary consideration in the tales of mass warfare; and it is the prime mover in all those angry dystopias of the twentieth century that present mechanism as the means of maintaining the straitjacket control of human freedom and individual spontaneity.

Although the immediate focus for these protests is the menace of the new war machines or the coming conflict between the individual and industrial society, they are truly lamentations for a hope that failed. The generation of the First World War had experienced a double betrayal. The entirely unexpected conditions of trench warfare had given the lie to the popular scenario of a story-book war that would be over by Christmas; and the unforeseen scale of the fighting was a brutal denial of the countless optimistic forecasts of the more peaceful centuries to come. For a century before the First World War—from Condorcet to H. G. Wells—a succession of prophets had contributed to a vast new literature dedicated to the description of coming things. As more and more writers looked into the future, they iterated a number of simple but powerful assumptions about industrial society and mechanism, and these looked forward to an expanding universe of steady material improvement.

For so long as the hectic love affair between science and society lasted, the greatest ambitions for the betterment of humanity were concentrated on images of future power. The balloon fantasies of aerial navigation in the late eighteenth century, the spectacular achievements of Verne's heroes in their victories over the forces of nature, and the perfection of human power in the Wellsian journeys through space and time—these were signs that, in the Wellsian phrase, one day men would be like gods. That happy thought was the leitmotiv in the many utopian symphonies of world peace and continuous progress that appeared at frequent intervals between 1871 and the outbreak of the First World War. In 1871, for example, the Dutch writer and social commentator, Pieter Harting, looked into the future and in *Anno Domini 2071* revealed how universal happiness would be sure to follow upon the turn of a wheel or a touch of a switch. There would be the most desirable improvements in mechanism: new energy systems, solar-light devices, highly efficient airships, a Channel Bridge, express trains from Peking to Europe—and an end to all wars, thanks to the deterrent effect of advanced weapons.

These anticipations were the common coinage of nineteenth-century optimism; they found their validation in a dogma of scientific progress that was both licence and incentive for the serious forecasts in *Glimpses of the Future* by the American journalist David Goodman Croly. Croly was the first self-styled 'Sir Oracle' in the then new business of predicting the advances to be expected in industrial societies; and for more than a decade he entertained the readers of the *Record and Guide* with his encouraging accounts of the better things-to-come. The keystone of his confident expectations for the future of mankind was scientific knowledge joined with technological invention:

It is hard to put any limitations to what man may do in the way of inventions and new discoveries. He is undoubtedly the god of this planet, and he will in time dominate the entire surface of the globe. Aerial navigation will solve the mystery of the poles, and eventually there will be no 'dark region' on any of the continents. Waste places will be reclaimed, deserts made productive by irrigation, forest regrown where needed, and waters dyked out in districts where the same conditions obtain as in Holland. These changes will modify the rigors of the various climates of the world.[9]

The alluring prospect of a peaceful and progressive world was certainly not the private domain of journalists and writers of science fiction. There was the eminent physiologist and winner of the Nobel Prize, Charles Richet, a man who in his time had led the way in immunization research. In 1892 Richet published *Dans Cent Ans*, in which he set out his impressions of life as it would be at the beginning of the twenty-first century: food for all, faster trains, better health, and the applied sciences labouring ceaselessly in the service of mankind. The heart of the forecast was a great hope for the future. Richet repeated with reverence the common belief: 'The idea of perpetual peace is not utopian; it is a certainty. What is perhaps utopian is to believe that the coming of world peace is close at hand.'[10] This blessed state would follow from the growing equality between peoples and the steady rise in civilized behaviour. Even better than that, said Richet, the development of new and more destructive weapons would prove the ultimate deterrent: 'By dint of making warfare more effective, they will end by making it impossible.'

Although these sanguine expectations represented the received wisdom of industrial society before the First World War, there had been a committed opposition of most imaginative writers who had apprehended intuitively the inherent dangers of run-away technological progress. The earliest manifestation of this fear for the future appears in Mary Shelley's *Frankenstein; or, A Modern Prometheus*, where the tragic story opens at the centre of the new sciences, in the laboratory. The fatal discovery that destroys the world of Mary Shelley's story is not the fire from heaven of ancient mytholgy: it is 'the cause of generation and life', the creative power that makes gods of mortal men. The new creature brought into existence by reason of 'the improvement which every day takes place in science and mechanics' turns out to be a destructive monster. Daedalus, it seems, had released the Minotaur from the labyrinth.

The point was made in much greater detail by Samuel Butler half a century after Byron and the Shelleys had thought of passing the time by writing ghost stories during that rainy summer in Switzerland. Surveying the extraordinary advances of the nineteenth century, Butler was able to state more comprehensively what had been simply hinted at by Mary Shelley. In an essay for a Christchurch newspaper in 1863, 'Darwin among the Machines', he dealt both earnestly and playfully with the idea of a gradual evolution of increasingly complex machines. These, he imagined, might one day develop a consciousness of their own, as the higher animals had done, and in consequence they might come to dominate their creators. Butler returned to this theme when he started to write *Erewhon*, and he made it one of the central points in his attack on Victorian values. After the narrator had crossed over the range into Butler's imaginary 'Nowhere', he set about the usual business of his kind by investigating the state of man in the new-found commonwealth. He came upon a museum in which cylinders, pistons, and fragments of advanced contrivances were preserved. The Erewhonians had experienced and had, therefore, rejected all the marvels of Victorian technology four hundred years before the industrial revolution had begun in Europe. They had discovered that the machines were destined to supplant the race of man. Butler had helped to start the now familiar debate about the effects of science on humanity; and that debate gained in clarity during the half-century before the First World War as other able writers followed Butler's precedent with the Luddite visions in W. H. Hudson's *A Crystal Age*, William Morris's *News from Nowhere*, E. M. Forster's *The Machine Stops*, and with the successful war for Merry England in G. K. Chesterton's *The Napoleon of Notting Hill*.

Later on, soon after the First World War, another and more important extension of this argument developed in a number of even more famous representations of the inescapable conflict between man and modern technological society. These began with two classics of the 1920s, Zamyatin's *We* and Karel Čapek's *R.U.R.* They continued through Huxley's *Brave New World* and Orwell's *Nineteen Eighty-Four*. Thereafter American dystopias took their turn at developing the theme of the potential conflict between the citizen and the authoritarian state in a New World setting. Again, there were some classic stories, especially Vonnegut's *Player Piano* and Bradbury's *Fahrenheit 451* in the 1950s; and this transatlantic exercise in dystopian writing continued into the 1980s with the most recent variations in *Eclipse* and *Fort Privilege*.

All these authors—from Zamyatin to Vonnegut—place the action in a future period, for they seek to analyse a social malady that must be shown fully formed so that the danger may be realized before it is too late. All of them function on a system of total reversal: for freedom, they say, read the absolute control of all citizens; for symbols of the new society there are the Thought Police, the Mechanical Hound, and the World Controller. That is, they all follow the example of Zamyatin and Čapek who took their themes to the limit— the perfection of a helot society in the One State and the triumph of mechanism in a world served by obedient robots. These were the conditions that would lead to an inevitable conflict between mankind and the immense, inhuman powers of technology. Thus, the action of the story in the Zamyatin dystopia develops within the highly organized and rigidly controlled society of The One State. There technology is the faithful servant of political authority and the numbered citizens have their appointed roles as these are laid down in The Tables of Hourly Commandments. Zamyatin is careful to make the parallel between the fault-free operations of the old-time railway systems and the even more efficient functioning of the perfect social machine:

We all (and perhaps all of you also) have read as schoolchildren that greatest of all monuments of ancient literature which have come down to us: *Time-Tables of All the Railroads*. But place even that classic side by side with The Tables of Hourly Commandments and you will see, side by side, graphite and diamond. Both contain the one and the same element—C, carbon: yet how eternal, how transparent the diamond, and how refulgent! Who can help but catch his breath as he thunders and races headlong through the pages of the *Time-Tables*? The Tables of Hourly Commandments, however, really does transform each one of us into the six-wheeled hero of a great poem. Each morning, with six-wheeled precision, at the very same minute and the very same second we, in our millions arise as one. At the very same hour we mono-millionedly begin work and, when we finish it, we do so mono-millionedly. And, merging into one body with multi-millioned hands, at the very second designated by The Tables of Hourly Commandments we bring our spoons up to our mouths; at the very same second, likewise, we set out for a walk, or go to an auditorium, or the Hall of Taylor Exercises, or retire to sleep.[11]

There will be war in heaven, however, for there is only one way of escaping from the oppressive routine of life within the retaining barrier of the Green Wall. Inner conflict can only end in open rebellion. So, D-503 chooses selfhood and becomes the first in a famous line of dystopian refuseniks—The Savage, Winston Smith, Dr Proteus. All of them are given to speaking at length on their reasons for rebellion. Some of them have made statements that are keynote speeches in the sacred book of liberty. 'I wanted to turn the whole of mankind into the aristocracy of the world', says the General Manager for Rossum's Universal Robots; and he goes on to speak his apologia for the labours of the scientists. 'An aristocracy nourished by millions of mechanical slaves. Unrestricted, free, and perfect men.' In the most ingenious and original play of *R.U.R.*, the Czech dramatist seized on a noble ambition—'to shatter the servitude of labour'—and pushed that obsession to the inescapable conclusion of the play: the robots will take over from their creators, and the products of human inventiveness will prove more than a match for the human brain. The parable calls for the triumph of mechanism: 'The power of man has fallen,' says the robot commander. 'By gaining possession of the factory we have become masters of everything. The period of mankind has passed away. A new world has arisen. The world of the Robots.'

Čapek worried away at the dilemma of scientific inventiveness and social organization, as Aldous Huxley and Kurt Vonnegut would do in their time. As early as the 1920s the Czech had seen what has become a truism of late twentieth-century thinking: that the powers of science are universal, but the choice between good and evil rests with mankind. That was the theme of Čapek's first novel, *The Absolute at Large* (1922), where the action opens with an engineer who has developed a process for the industrial application of atomic energy. The results have to be catastrophic. The indiscriminate use of the Carburator leads to the collapse of the world economy; and then the Carburator takes over with disastrous consequences. Wars break out everywhere: the Japanese invade the west coast of the United States; Asiatic hordes storm into central Europe; and religious wars break out in Europe. The solution is quite simple: destroy the Carburators, repudiate all absolutist dogmas, and have faith in mankind alone. Two years later, in *Krakatit: an Atomic Fantasy*, Čapek produced a variation on his favourite theme of technology and moral responsibility. Again the plot opens with a young engineer who invents a most powerful explosive, and once again the safety of the world is endangered; but in fear and sorrow the inventor realizes his duty to humanity, and in symbolic fashion forgets how to make Krakatit.

Zamyatin and Čapek were the first to devise the modern choreography for the struggle of the individual against the all-powerful state and for the great drama of man against the machine. Others followed where they had first shown the way; for their original arguments contributed to the debate of the 1930s on the place of the citizen in any highly organized society, which reached its most sophisticated form in Huxley's *Brave New World*. The conflict between the Savage and the world of Our Ford, between personal values and the advantages of a planned economy, produced the characteristic anti-Utopia of the period. The seeming paradox was that, although *Brave New World* had all the signs of the ideal state as foretold by Bellamy, Wells, and scores of other optimists, Mustapha Mond could not find a place for a man who wanted God, poetry, freedom, danger, and sin. To recover his lost liberties the rebel would have to choose: either destroy the complex society that caused so much pain, or retreat from it entirely; either build an Arcadia in the blank spaces of the future, or find a Shangri-La in the remotest corner of the earth. This dilemma explains why the characteristic ideal state of the 1930s was Hilton's sentimental *Lost Horizon*. The great success of the book, and of the film of the book, depended to a great extent on the way Hilton succeeded in reducing the vast problem of war and peace to the comfortable but cloudy philosophizing of Father Perrault. The only point in the story was that Shangri-La would be a sanctuary for the things of the spirit that could not hope to survive in 'a time when men, exultant in the technique of homicide, would rage so hotly over the world'. Father Perrault's belief that 'the Dark Ages that are to come will cover the whole world in a single pall' was also the dominant fear in the many tales of future wars that came out during the 1930s.

One source for the fear haunting Europe was the recollection that before 1914 the general staffs had all failed to foresee how the new military technologies would change the conduct of warfare. To repeat that failure was to invite certain defeat, perhaps even total extinction if the worst were to happen. It was, therefore, axiomatic with the post-war writers that accurate anticipation was the first law of survival. One eminent military theorist, Captain Liddell Hart, argued that it was essential to look backward in order to find the right way forward. He pointed to the accuracy of I. S. Bloch's prediction of a great war of entrenchments. Bloch was right, said Liddell Hart, 'only to be ridiculed by the General Staffs of Europe'. The stalemate he had foreseen came true— 'with the sole difference that he underestimated the blind obstinacy of the leaders and the passivity of the led in continuing for four more years to run their heads against a brick wall'. There was a lesson in that for the next time: Think carefully about every possible application of every new weapon.

As early as 1921, one of the most influential of the new theorists, Giulio Douhet, had produced the first major study of air warfare in *Il Dominio dell'aria*; and, with an eye to the ominous lessons of the First World War, he opened his arguments in favour of the air arm with great emphasis on the need to avoid repeating the errors of the past. All thinking about the use of the aeroplane in any future war, he insisted, had to begin from the fact that 'the inability during the period just before the war to answer the question of what the war would be like in the near future, jeopardized the successful outcome of it, lengthened the war, and made victory more costly'. That recollection served to concentrate the general attention on the many possibilities of the bombing plane, so that 'the threat from the air' became a topic of great interest in the popular press. War was no longer an affair of 'over there': the new thinking held that the aeroplane had made it possible for nations to wage war against the civil populations of their enemies. No one questioned the statement made by the Secretary of State for Air on 10 November 1927, when he told a meeting of the League of Nations Union that the target of the bombers would be 'the whole body of the population, men, women and children. I shudder to think of the devastation that will be created by the development of the air arm upon our civil population, and particularly upon the civil population of

London and the south-east of England.' The great danger, reflected in the disaster stories of the 1930s was not the high explosive bomb: it was 'the rain of death' or 'the dew of death', as the newspapers called the poison gas that would be discharged from low-flying aircraft. The experts calculated that forty-two tons of Lewisite or mustard gas would be enough to wipe out all living things in an area the size of metropolitan London. That dreadful possibility and the other great anxieties about the new war technologies explain the marked falling away in the numbers of the fictional projections that continued with the old practice of relating the most likely conduct of a future war.

The glory had departed from the tale of the war-to-come. For the first time in the history of this literature, the eager predictors had to take account of instant annihilation and total destruction. In consequence, the new weapons did not lead to any great revival of the once popular account of 'what it will be like in the next war'; and the few projections of this kind that appeared in the 1930s are yet another indication of the transformation that had overtaken the tale of future warfare.

It may not come as a surprise that Guilio Douhet kept the old tradition alive with his anticipatory account of *La Guerra del 19—*, which first appeared in the *Rivista Aeronautica* for March 1930. The elementary fiction of this future war—fought by Germany against the French and Belgians—was no more than a convenient means of presenting a simple operational appreciation. That was as far as the fiction went, since Douhet clearly saw no advantage in giving his tale an acceptable starting-point in the international situation of the day. The war came about for trifling reasons, because Douhet had set himself the limited objective of demonstrating the truth of his beliefs: that the air arm is a means of offensive action; that it must be an independent force, free to operate in mass; and that it has the overriding task of securing the command of the air. So, the French deserve to lose the war because their system of 'three independent ministries for the armed forces and three separate Chiefs of Staff of the three General Staffs was the least suitable system for bringing about the harmonious proportion which can be attained only from an integrated consideration of the war problem'. Victory comes for the Germans, because they had developed the right doctrine of air warfare. They planned to keep to the defensive by land while maintaining the most vigorous air offensive possible to them. The German General Staff repeated the Douhet doctrine in their directives: 'Aerial action enjoys the advantage of unrestricted choice of objective . . . aerial action can be exercised against the objectives which best suit one's purpose—that is, against the enemy's land armed forces, his maritime resources, his aerial resources, or his country itself . . . ':

By integrating the aerial arm with poison gas, it is possible today to employ very effective actions against the most vital and vulnerable spots of the enemy—that is, against his most important political, industrial, commercial, and other centres—in order to create among his population a lowering of moral resistance so deep as to destroy the determination of the people to continue the war.

These principles of action were repeated in the solitary full-scale piece of fiction that attempted to foresee the operations of an air war. This was *Luftkrieg-1936: Die Zertrümmung von Paris* which appeared in 1932 and immediately went into French and English translations. The author was Robert Knauss, who affected military rank with the style of Major von Helders, and in the book he had given himself the congenial task of describing the rapid defeat of the French in a war with the United Kingdom. Further, his story presents the other side of contemporary expectations, since the bombardments of his air fleets have a spectacular success in paralysing the enemy but do not bring on the end of civilization. As in the Douhet story, the origin of the future war is entirely contrived to suit the projected demonstration of air power. Indeed, Helders wrote with such ingenious malice about the French that the victorious squadrons of the British Air Fleet appear like stand-ins for a Luftwaffe that had not yet been created. The occasion of the war was the lamest of inventions: a French intervention in Egyptian affairs, followed by the landing of French troops at Alexandria and haughty notes from the French about Egyptian sovereignty. The press told the story in banner headlines:

AGGRAVATION OF THE CONFLICT. A WARNING TO FRANCE. FALL OF EGYPTIAN GOVERNMENT. NATIONALISTS FORM PROVISIONAL GOVERNMENT AND PROCLAIM REPUBLIC. EGYPTIAN NATIONALISTS INVOKE THE ASSISTANCE OF FRANCE.

Once Helders had established the cause of his future war, he devoted the rest of the book to a sustained demonstration of the effects of air power. Members of the Cabinet hear the classic doctrine of concentration and independent action from Air Commodore Brackley, officer commanding the Air Fleet:

The British Air Fleet is ready for immediate action. Its task, gentlemen, is to break France's will to continue the war by carrying the offensive into the enemy's country, by destroying his bases of operation and by terrorizing his population. I am convinced that this is possible because the British Air Fleet is a strong and homogeneous instrument of war, which has been called into existence for one sole purpose, namely to wage independent aerial warfare. Within a few days the Air Fleet can, and will, decide the war in Britain's favour.

The expectations of 1932 called for daylight bombing by mass formations of aircraft. At five in the morning of 6 July 1936, ten squadrons form into two columns eight miles apart over the Isle of Wight, and all 180 planes make for the French coast and their designated targets in Paris. These are the formidable G-planes, powered by the latest diesel engines which enable them to fly at 20,000 feet, well beyond the effective range of anti-aircraft fire. They complete their missions with the faultless accuracy of a tactical exercise. Seven hundred tons of high explosive bombs, 3,000 incendiary bombs, and ten tons of mustard gas are enough to obliterate all the major industrial and communication centres in Paris. The Eiffel Tower collapses across the Seine, the Gare du Nord disappears, and all services—gas, water, electricity, telephones, and the Métro—cease to function. All this was the prophetic demonstration of a theory of air warfare. The fiction anticipated what would become reality ten years later, for the bombers bring the war to the inhabitants of Paris:

The truth was then brought home with unpleasant clarity that this raid was the outcome of a plan for the systematic destruction of the capital's nerve centres. In the inner part of the city all the streets between the Rue de Rivoli and the boulevards, in fact, an area bounded by the Admiralty, the Halles, and the Banque de France were one mass of ruins. On the left bank of the Seine the districts between the Gare Quai d'Orsay and the Military School up to the Seine islands were in flames; and among the buildings thus destroyed were the Palais de Justice, the Ministry of Foreign Affairs, the Chamber of Deputies and the Prefecture of Police.

Although the German author arranged the engagements in his demonstration of air warfare to the point of making the French defensive measures absurdly ineffectual, his prevision of massed aerial bombing was accurate enough for the 1930s. The great novelty, however, was the careful attention to technicalities that brought a frightening authenticity to the imagined air attacks on the population of a great city. It was one more sign of a growing toleration of the new methods of warfare, of a readiness to contemplate actions that would once have been condemned as outwith the articles of war. And yet, only eighteen years before the publication of *Luftkrieg-1936*, the account of unrestricted submarine warfare in Conan Doyle's *Danger* had so shocked Admiral Henderson that he exclaimed against the fiction of torpedoed merchant ships: 'No nation would permit it, and the officer who did it would be shot.'

The admiral did not live long enough to discover a fact of life in the twentieth century: if weapons are invented, they will be used. That certainty was the hidden regulator that controlled the production of imaginary wars throughout the 1920s and 1930s. It worked in favour of all the disaster stories that dealt with the devastation-to-come; and it operated with equal effectiveness to damp down any desire writers may have had to do for the inter-war period what Capitaine Danrit, William Laird Clowes, and Admiral Colomb had done for the 1890s. How could any writer hope to turn out a roaring, patriotic version of *Trafalgar Refought* in order to give 'a vivid picture of likely happenings at sea had Nelson lived in this present year of grace'? How could any sane writer consider the possibility of an atomic bomb save as a means of raising crucial questions about the morality of modern warfare? So, the Bomb existed as a subliminal terror for almost thirty years—from the first use of the term 'atomic bomb' in Wells's story of *The World Set Free* in 1913 to that morning in August 1945 when the *Enola Gay* came up south-west by west over Hiroshima.

The atomic bomb story begins around the year 1900, when Ernest Rutherford and Frederick Soddy started on the research project that led to their theory of radioactivity. Soddy later published an intelligent person's guide to the atom in his *Interpretation of Radium*, and from that book Wells gathered his information about atomic energy. In fact, in the first chapter of *The World Set Free* Soddy appears as Rufus, a professor of physics in the University of Edinburgh, where he lectures on radium and radium activity. As Rufus talks about the reservoir of immense energy within the atom, he holds up a bottle which contains fourteen ounces of uranium and pauses before he makes one of the most prophetic statements in the history of science fiction: 'If at a word, in one instant, I could suddenly release that energy here and now, it would blow us and everything about us to fragments.' From that came the first atomic war in fiction. And there the fearful secret remained, hidden in a book that all could read, until Leo Szilard came upon a German translation of *The World Set Free* in 1932 when working at the Institute of Theoretical Physics in Berlin. The work of fiction set the physicist thinking about the means of developing a nuclear chain reaction. From that came the letter composed by Szilard and sent by Einstein to warn President Roosevelt of the possibility that the Germans could make an atomic bomb. When they started work on the Manhattan Project, Szilard ordered two works of fiction for the library: *The World Set Free* by Wells and another atomic bomb story, *Public Faces*, by Harold Nicolson, English diplomat, biographer, and joint-creator with Vita Sackville-West of the great garden at Sissinghurst.

The Nicolson story appeared in 1932, the year when Adolf Hitler was preparing to become chancellor, the year after another German had written the obituary notice for industrial civilization. Oswald Spengler had introduced his prophecies of disaster in *The Decline of the West*, and in his *Man and Technics* of 1931 he found philosophic reasons to support the thesis Čapek had put forward in the play of *R.U.R.* A machine civilization was the contradiction of the natural and spontaneous; and the catastrophe of mechanization must inevitably lead to the collapse of Western society—'our railways and steamships will be as dead as the Roman roads and the Chinese wall, our giant cities and skyscrapers in ruins like old Memphis and Babylon'. There would be no second chance, nothing like the fresh start that Wells had offered in *The World Set Free*; for industrial society was beyond hope, well beyond the last warning Nicolson gave in *Public Faces*.

Where Spengler talked of machine-technics, Wells and Nicolson had science in mind, especially the rational and measured use of the applied sciences. For both of them, the greatest danger for the future, and the worst abuse of science, would be the manufacture of the ultimate weapon, the atomic bomb.

In his favourite role as the scourge of God, Wells had already described the consequences as he had imagined them before the First World War. Two decades later Nicolson went back to the beginning of the problem: the manufacture of atomic bombs and the moral responsibility of the politicians who will have to decide on the day and the target. Nicolson arranges his warning tale around two projections: that the British government has atomic bombs, and that some powerful members of the Cabinet are most eager to secure the British hold on the island of Abu Saad in the Persian Gulf, the source of material for the bombs. As the politicans argue among themselves—right versus wrong, vanity and ambition against prudence and concern for others, diplomacy versus instant action—the dangers for the rest of the world approach the point of the ultimate catastrophe. The principal devil in this morality is the Minister for Air, as arrogant and reckless a careerist as a one-time diplomat can present him. He causes an atomic bomb to be detonated in the Atlantic in order to demonstrate the fearsome might of Great Britain. And then the unforeseen comes into play: a US cruiser is sunk by accident, and a great tidal wave drowns tens of thousands in South Carolina. The British recoil from the disaster and, as the morality requires, they write their *never again* into the historical record. Their communiqué is an admirable confession of sin, and the fifth article carries a promise of amendment which is a message to the world and to the future:

The British Government, moreover, recognising that these new and potent engines of destruction are inimical to existing civilisation, are prepared (subject to the condition outlined below) to pledge themselves to destroy within a period of six months their existing stock of atomic bombs and to manufacture no further bombs in the future.

Nicolson had been most careful to separate his theme of the atomic bomb from all connection with the political situation of the 1930s, because his target was the dangers of technological warfare. He wrote at that time when recent advances in tanks and aeroplanes had led to many speculations about the scale of fighting in any future war. Indeed, that most successful politician and one-time Lord Chancellor, the Earl of Birkenhead, had a chapter on future warfare in his book of forecasts, *The World in 2030 AD*. Looking at the world in 1930, he was quite certain that, 'in the future as in the past, victory in warfare will fall to those who command the most efficient weapons'. Television, wireless communications, giant tanks, amphibious fighting machines, the mechanization of all arms—these would come before long. Those expectations, however, could find a place in fiction only when they provided material for making the case against the development of military technology, as in *Public Faces*, or on those rare occasions when a writer like Robert Knauss in *Luftkrieg-1936* was eager to share his vision of war in the air. Indeed, it is noteworthy that the large-scale production of tales of future wars had to wait until the beginning of the 1930s. Moreover, the new stories confirmed the continued decline of the traditional tale of the war-to-come. Although as time went on many authors came to expect that Germany would start another great European war, the social and human consequences of modern warfare engaged their attention far more than the political dangers of a resurgent Germany. For example, in *The Gas War of 1940*, published in 1931, the author put forward a thesis that was common to most of these stories: 'Man has created a peril which he must at all costs avoid. That peril is the perfection of instruments of destruction. If man cannot so adapt himself, shall I say re-make himself, so that he can live in amity with man, he is lost.' The author's message is delivered by means of a world conflict which breaks out on 3 September 1940. He describes a German blitzkrieg:

Poland was attacked from the air, and its bloody ruins occupied by tanks. Alsace and Lorraine were invaded after punishment from a German air-fleet that left alive a mere handful of their people. The great forts, the network of trenches and gun-emplacements on which France had spent labour and treasure so lavishly, were battered and pulverised into tumbled heaps of earth and steel and concrete.

All the great cities of the world experience the terrors of poison gas and high explosive. Governments collapse and fearful pestilences afflict the wretched survivors of the shattered cities. London is smashed by a succession of air raids:

And then, in a moment, the lights of London vanished, as if blotted out by a gigantic extinguisher. And in the dark streets the burned and wounded, bewildered and panic-stricken, fought and struggled like beasts, scrambling over the dead and dying alike, until they fell and were in turn trodden underfoot by the ever-increasing multitudes about them. . . . In a dozen parts of London that night people died in their homes with the familiar walls crashing about them in flames; thousands rushed into the streets to be met by blasts of flame and explosion and were blown to rags; they came pouring out of suddenly darkened theatres, picture-houses, concert and dance halls, into the dark congested streets to be crushed or burnt or trodden to death.

This vision of a desolate city and its mutilated inhabitants was the image of a contemporary fear. Peace and not politics was the aim of stories like *The Poison War*, *The Black Death*, *Menace*, *Empty Victory*, *Invasion from the Air*, *War upon Women*, *Chaos*, *Air Reprisal*, *What Happened to the Corbetts*. The authors all described war in order to preach peace. For example, Moray Dalton begins the narrative in *The Black Death* (1934) with an account of poison-gas clouds that kill off the entire population of the United Kingdom except for a holiday group stranded in the Cheddar Caves at the time of the air raids. Their experiences on returning to the surface are used to bring out the devastation of modern warfare. An enemy airman delivers the author's message to the reader:

Your factories made poison gas, too, but you shilly-shallied. You would and you would not. Compromise. The middle way. You thought there might be something between our will to power and the Sermon on the Mount. Well, you have found the road between. You must not blame us.

How, then, shall civilization be saved? According to a story published in 1934, *North Sea Monster*, salvation can only come from closer international relationships. For the purposes of the demonstration, it is imagined that an earthquake has created a new island, Aphroditeland, in the North Sea. Since it is unusually rich in minerals, it becomes the object of ferocious international disputes. In this there is a lesson for the time:

To think that the appearance of a spot of land in the North Sea had aroused the old national rivalries and seemed about to plunge Europe into the vortex of war! And why so, when the average citizen in the countries concerned would affirm that he did not want to go to war over a coalfield? Was it not due to the fact that states still strove to maintain their isolation; that they had not learned the lesson of the last war and its aftermath? Instead of tackling fundamental problems which were crying out for solution they spent the intervening period in bickering over trivialities and trying to run a modern state by antique political methods. What could be more obvious than that the complex economic life of today demanded the closest co-operation between nations and governments?

But *how* shall civilization be saved? The solution seems to vary in direct proportion to the strength of a writer's desires. The majority favour the method outlined in the preface to *Invasion from the Air*: they write books which are of set purpose 'neither anti-German, nor pro-French, but anti-war'. Their hope is that a vision of the horrors-to-come will make readers ponder the consequences before it is too late. Others create extraordinary wish-fulfilment fantasies in which some danger to the world causes all the nations to unite, or in which some form of international police force prevents the outbreak of war. The most interesting, however, are stories like *The Woman who Stopped War* by Cornwallis-West and *The Impregnable Women* by Eric Linkater, in which the completely new figure of a redemptive Aphrodite appears to save men from their own folly. For the first time in the fiction of future warfare, the realization of the terrors at man's disposal touches off an attack on man himself. In these stories the warrior, the central figure of innumerable imaginary battles, has ceased to count. Indeed, man himself no longer matters. In *The Woman who Stopped War* (1935) the masculine world is shown to be morally bankrupt; in the face of male destructiveness, the women are everywhere constructive, positive, and hopeful. While the women of Europe and the world work together to prevent the outbreak of war, the men bumble on in the old way, and in every capital city politicians work day and night to extricate themselves from a situation for which they alone were responsible. The heroine preaches the same lesson everywhere: 'It is the men and only men who make war, and they will continue to make it until women use the weapon men put into their hands when they made the greatest war of all.' Their secret weapon is a world-wide strike; and they use it to give peace to a world dominated by man-made instruments of destruction.

These ideas reveal the great change in attitude that has affected European thinking since the brave days at the end of the last century when Lord Wolseley, the conqueror of the Ashanti and the Egyptians, could say that 'all other pleasures pale before the intense, the maddening delight of leading men into the midst of an enemy, or to the assault of some well-defended place'. But now that the majesty and glory have gone out of war, only the misery and horror remain to give point and purpose to the tale of imaginary warfare in its newfound task of compelling men to take an unblinkered look at their world.

For some writers, like Eric Linklater in *The Impregnable Women* (1938), the true enemy was the folly of Political Man:

In the second decade of the century there had been created a huge nexus of treaties and covenants, by which everyone agreed to abjure and renounce war as an instrument of policy, and protect his neighbours from unwarranted aggression. But this admirable machinery had never been given engineers to work it. As often as the signatories were called on to implement their pledges—in plainer language, to keep a promise—they declined to do so, but dressed their refusal in such a way as to make it seem they were activated by some higher motive than self-interest. A breach of contract, thus ingeniously phrased, was known in diplomatic cant as a formula, and by so-called democratic governments the formula was much esteemed.

After this prelude to a twentieth-century version of *Lysistrata*, a war breaks out in Europe. The comedy develops when a group of women—the wives of Cabinet ministers and distinguished soldiers—decide with admirable common sense that they must end the fighting in order to bring their men home. Their reasons for stopping the war are an attack on the validity of the wholly male world of politics and warfare:

Politics are a male invention. When men have interests which must be defended, they contrive a screen of words which they call a policy, and if they can persuade a few simple people that their screen is of general value, then they are ranked as politicians. But we are women, and our concern is not the defence of any clique or faction or vested interest. It is the defence and happiness of all humanity.

The date of that was 1938, close to the end of an anxious and terrible decade. What followed is too familiar for repetition. It is enough to say that the tale of imaginary warfare kept pace with the mood of the period; and as Europe drew nearer to the Second World War, the new stories became more fearful. In 1939 R. C. Sherriff brought out *The Hopkins Manuscript*, which looked forward to a time when the nations of western Europe have been wiped out and the world is ruled by coloured peoples. Then in 1940, in *The Twenty-Fifth Hour*, the tale relates the almost total destruction of the human race and the rebirth—for man must always have hope—of civilization in the Nile Valley. And finally, just before the full terror of total war had burst upon Europe, Alfred Noyes produced the last commentary on the period in *The Last Man*. He began the book in 1939 with the intention of showing how the complicated modern world had hampered the true development of the human being. Noyes has the doubtful distinction of having written the first account of instant warfare in the history of this literature, for he begins with the invention of an 'all pervasive ethereal wave' that can stop the beating of the human heart. Of course, the lunatic governments use the invention and in the space of half an hour they kill every human being on earth, save for one couple. After this the story becomes a moral tale, as the new Adam and Eve journey through Italy to Rome. In contrast to the many solutions put forward by authors of imaginary wars, in Noyes's view there can be no easy solution to the spiritual problem at the heart of war and political folly. A ban on bombing planes, the control of machinery, even a return to a state of nature have nothing to do with the problem. Man has to reform himself from within according to the ideal pattern of Christianity. 'The most tragic thing of all', he writes, 'was that the complete answer to all those tragic disputations and conflicts was there, all the time, in the *philosophia perennia* of Christendom.'

Shortly afterwards the realities of the blitzkrieg in France and the Low Countries abruptly ended the practice of predicting the shape of the war-to-come. What happened after the panzers and the dive-bombers began their work was often far worse than anything forecast in fiction. In the abominations of modern warfare, in the inhumanity of Dachau, Buchenwald, and Oswiecim, in the mass extermination of millions of Jews, and in all the brutalities of a new iron age, men were forced to recognize a capacity for evil that had, so it was thought, vanished for ever from the earth. As the war spread across the continents until almost the entire human race had been drawn into the conflict, a feeling of the unprecedented and the unpredictable grew out of the events of a war that was everywhere destroying long-accepted ideas and revealing more and more opportunities for destruction. The speed of development from aeroplanes to ballistic missiles, and the immense range of operations from the Don to North Africa, from the Arctic Circle to the South Pacific, demonstrated the lethal capacities of applied science.

And then, after all the changes and disasters of the first really world-wide war in human history had had their effect upon the mind, the imagination had somehow to find a place and an explanation for the last news of all. In May 1945 Colonel Paul W. Tibbetts began the organization of the 509th Composite Group of the US Air Force, the first formation to receive the new B-29 high-altitude pressurized bombers. He named his own plane in memory of his mother, Enola Gay Haggard of Glidden, Iowa; and for weeks he exercised the crew of the *Enola Gay* in simulating the exact sequences of a new bombing run. They began by descending rapidly from a cruising height of 30,000 feet. Next, they had to align themselves on the practice target and then make their bombing run at the required height. After they had released their bomb load, the pilot made a sharp 155-degree diving turn to ensure that their aircraft would be not less than 10 miles away from the explosion.

These procedures proved successful on the morning of 6 August 1945, when the *Enola Gay* began an operational bombing run at about 0800 hours Japanese time. The plane came in across the Inland Sea on a bearing of 5 degrees south of due west. The bombardier located the aiming point as he had done during many earlier rehearsals, but on this occasion the target was the Aioi Bridge. The fiction of Wells and Nicolson became fact at 0816.02 hours, when the Little Boy atomic bomb exploded over Hiroshima, 550 feet south of the aiming point, with a yield equivalent to 12,500 tons of TNT.

The Lord President of the Council, Sir John Anderson, found the exact words for what had happened at Hiroshima when he said: 'This is not a mere development of something already known. It is something quite outside all human experience; and this is only the beginning.' The mushroom cloud above Hiroshima was at once a symbol and a cause. It started off a new dialogue of the Western mind with itself and its achievements that is still going on today. For those who had known the golden epoch before 1914, this took the form of endless lamentations for the fate of Europe and its sad fall from the mastery of the world. The atomic bomb, then the hydrogen bomb and the development of the intercontinental missile, added to the anxieties caused by the division of world power between Russia and the United States, and the rapid abandonment of great colonial empires.

To the old, the years after Hiroshima seemed a decadent, perverted, desperate time. Looking at the post-war world, through the memory of what he believed to be a happier age, Lord Vansittart had said that 'it almost breaks my heart when I think that I started life in a world inhabited by hope and am ending it in one inhibited by doubts of its own duration'.[12] In like manner, as H. G. Wells saw how the war had smashed his hopes for the future, and had given the lie to all his predictions of limitless progress and happiness for all, the last years of the ageing visionary grew increasingly gloomy. After so many years spent in promising new worlds for old, the end of his life was embittered by a sense of frustration and by doubts about the future of mankind. After so many prophetic tales of the paradise just ahead for all men, it is ironic that his last book, *Mind at the End of its Tether*, should carry the despairing message that 'this world is at the end of its tether. The end of everything we call life is close at hand and cannot be evaded.'

Chapter Six

From the Flame Deluge to the Bad Time

WHEN the atomic bombs burst over Hiroshima and Nagasaki, they ended the first truly world-wide war ever fought; they realized the worst anticipations of future war fiction; and they marked the beginning of a universal debate about the conduct of technological warfare which has gone on ever since. Long before there was any talk of the greenhouse effect, acid rain, and the hazards of pollution, the mushroom cloud above Hiroshima was the first unmistakable sign that the ever-accelerating rate of advance in the applied sciences could have the most serious consequences. The Bomb had raised the gravest questions about the future of all human beings. In a single devastating release of energy, the 20-kiloton explosion terminated the old belief in the uniformly benign progress of the technologies. The most spectacular display of controlled power ever seen on Earth up to that time spoke to all humanity of sudden endings and violent new beginnings. When man became lord of the thunderbolt, with powers of life and death over the whole world, it seemed in those early years after Hiroshima and Nagasaki that our planet and all living things had reached the point of no return. What did the future hold for mankind? The way ahead would be dark and dangerous, as W. H. Auden wrote in 1947:

> Both professor and prophet depress,
> For vision and longer view
> Agree in predicting a day
> Of vast convulsion and vast evil,
> When the Cold Societies clash
> Or the mosses are set in motion
> To overrun the earth,
> And the great brain which began
> With lucid dialectics
> Ends in a horrid madness.[1]

It was the Age of Anxiety according to Wystan Auden, and the Age of Longing according to Arthur Koestler. The deliberate choice of special titles with which to mark the immediate post-war period was the writers' shorthand way of saying that they were living in a time of troubles. The past had taken on the appearance of a foreign land. The present offered little joy for a most uncertain future. So many of the old ideas and habits of mind could no longer fit the new age of a Europe then facing, some said, the greatest changes since the Napoleonic wars. Western Europe had to look on as communist governments took control in the East and the consequent political allegiances began to decide the geography of the Cold War. The communist coup in Czechoslovakia in February 1948 and the so-called suicide of Jan Masaryk, the beginning of the Berlin Blockade, and then the Korean War in 1950—these were signs that there might be worse to come.

Everything was changing. There were new political alignments, new weapons of warfare, and new-made vocabularies as language followed on events in the greatest burst of words and acronyms since the days of the first ironclads and breech-loaders. The new lexicons recorded the start of the Cold War in March 1946 when Winston Churchill borrowed a phrase from *The Food of the Gods* by H. G. Wells in a famous speech at Westminster College, Fulton: 'From Stettin, in the Baltic, to Trieste, in the Adriatic, an *Iron Curtain* has descended across the Continent.' The new language of confrontation went on growing from one crisis to another: to the *Strategic Defense Initiative* (SDI) which President Reagan gave the world in 1983, and to those most recent entries in the military dictionary—*frequency agility*, *smart bombs*, *collateral damage*. There have been so many innovations, and there is so much to know, that the uninitiated have need of a glossary to understand the great range of armaments that have come into service since 1945. Indeed, some authors soon began to follow the kindly practice of including a glossary to guide their readers round the new arsenals and the new military theories. These checklists run through an alphabet which begins with A-4, A-6, A-7, A-10, AAA, AAM, ABM, AEW, AGM-88, ANG, APC, ARM, ATFS, ATGW, AWAC, BALTAP, BATES, B-52, BMP, BT, and continues through scores of entries to UKAD, ULMS, USAFE, VC-10, VDV, V/STOL., WTO, ZSU-23-4.

All these terms have their designated roles within the operational strategies laid down in the new grammar of decision and control, and this has its own prescribed timetable of operations. In an orderly fashion, the established procedures start from theories of *first-strike strategy*; they go on through considerations of *escalation* to the possibility of *multi-stable deterrence* and *de-escalation dominance*; and they conclude with the prospect of *radiation sickness*, the *nuclear winter*, and *mutually assured destruction*. The precise terms spell out the worst of all possible futures for all mankind. They have told the world what the editors of the *Bulletin of the Atomic Scientists* have continued to show the world for more than forty years. On the cover of their issue for July 1947 they placed the first Doomsday Clock:

The new cover of the BULLETIN bears the design of a clock, its hand approaching twelve. This symbol of urgency well represents the state of mind of those whose closeness to the development of atomic energy does not permit them to forget that their lives and those of their children, the security of their country and the survival of civilization, all hang in the balance as long as the specter of atomic war has not been exorcised.

The image remains a final warning from science that time is running out for rash, imprudent *Homo technologicus*. In fact, the symbol of the Doomsday Clock was one of the early alarm signals that pointed to the perilous conjunction of knowledge and power: the search for the laws of nature which leads to the making of atomic weapons; the political theories that have sanctioned the use of force and in our times have laid the foundations of many police states. It serves as the Last Day prelude to the many tales of the catastrophe-to-come which have confronted the unthinkable in order to pass judgement on the terminal folly of nuclear warfare.

After Hiroshima, the tales of future warfare returned to the business of anticipation, and by the 1950s they were appearing by the dozen in most years and on both sides of the Atlantic. There were, however, striking differences in the distribution of the new stories—very few in Germany and the USSR, some more in France, still more in the United Kingdom, and the largest output of all in the United States. The worse the experience of war, it seems, the less the eagerness to contemplate another one. The Americans knew nothing of air bombardments, invasion and occupation by the enemy, hunger, and concentration camps. They came out of the war knowing that the United States was the major world power and that, for as long as they had sole rights in the atomic bomb, they could look forward to maintaining their dominant role throughout the globe. That difference between the Old World and the New had a decisive effect on the American tales of the war-to-come. Although most of these American projections have followed common practice in describing the disasters of a nuclear war, some have revealed very different perceptions of the future. The more confident and self-reliant mood of the Americans in the early post-war period—their conviction of assured success, for example—encouraged some writers to set down their anticipations of the next great conflict in the blow-by-blow style of the old accounts of future warfare.

Thus, three months after the end of hostilities in 1945, the editors of *Life* magazine obtained an official report on missile technology which General Henry Harley Arnold, Commanding General of the US Army Air Force, had prepared for the Secretary of War.[2] They used the information for a nine-page article with many illustrations, 'The 36-Hour War', which described a first strike by an unknown enemy. Their projection was the uncovenanted end-product of a policy decision Arnold had made in November 1944. He had then directed his principal scientific adviser, the Hungarian refugee Theodore von

Karman, to investigate all conceivable future developments in warfare; and von Karman delivered his findings in a series of documents, *Toward New Horizons*, in which he reported on the many promising military applications for recent discoveries in electronics, nuclear physics, and aerodynamics. Those reports were the source for the *Life* article on 'The 36-Hour War', which gave a spectacular demonstration of the new theory of *push-button warfare*: rockets with nuclear warheads destroy thirteen American cities and enemy airborne troops attack major centres, but the Americans strike back with atomic weapons and win the war.

The readiness of some Americans to examine the circumstances of a third world war revealed a remarkable intellectual fortitude—the fearless in pursuit of the frightful, as it were. It was the same in many of their fictional projections of nuclear warfare, which carried a singular transatlantic signature very different from the contemporary disaster stories in Europe. For example, Captain Walter Karig of the US Naval Reserve published his account of *War in the Atomic Age?* in 1946 in order to convince his compatriots that the nation had need of atomic weapons and a large navy. His demonstration opens in the year 2076, when a confederation of nations attacks the United States. In the fashion of *Astounding Science Fiction* stories, an electronic force field detonates the incoming enemy missiles, and other scientific marvels enable the American forces to overcome all opposition and annihilate the enemy. A more realistic projection of 1946 was *The Murder of the USA* by Will F. Jenkins, a science fiction writer of talent, who presented a clever anticipation of calculated vulnerability, deterrence theory, and massive retaliation a decade before these phrases went the rounds of the Pentagon. An unknown enemy launches nuclear missiles in a surprise attack, and then, when the enemy has been identified, the survivors dispatch their atomic missiles in an annihilating counter-strike.

American readers in the late 1940s seem to have been willing to endure long accounts of the worst imaginable destruction. In 1947 they had five years of warfare—atomic, biological, gas—from Leonard Engel and Emanuel S. Piller in the *World Aflame: The Russian American War of 1950*, and the war was still going on in 1955 when the narrative ended. In 1951 there was a far more exhilarating report from the editors of *Collier's*, who must have imagined that they were giving their American readers the best possible news from the future:

COLLIER'S
October 27, 1951

RUSSIA'S DEFEAT
and OCCUPATION
1952-1960

PREVIEW OF THE WAR WE DO NOT WANT
Principal Events of World War III
1952

Assassination attempt on Marshal Tito's life, May 10th, precipitates Cominform-
planned uprising in Yugoslavia. Troops from satellite nations of Bulgaria, Romania
and Hungary, backed by Red Army, cross borders. Truman terms aggression
'Kremlin inspired'; Reds call it 'an internal matter'.

Third World War begins when Moscow, still insisting that uprising is 'the will of
the Yugoslav people', refuses to withdraw Red Army units. Stalin miscalculates
risk: had believed US would neither back Tito nor fight alone. US is joined by
principal UN nations in declaration of war.

Neutrals include Sweden, Ireland, Switzerland, Egypt, India, and Pakistan.

SATURATION A-Bombing of USSR begins. Avoiding completely population centres,
West concentrates on legitimate military targets only. Principal objectives: industrial installations; oil, steel, and A-bomb plants.

The editors sought to achieve the maximum realism by presenting the nar-
rative as a series of reports from the near future by well-known writers.
Edward R. Murrow, the man who went everywhere, set the style with his
account in 'A-Bomb Mission to Moscow'. He opened with words from a
latter-day apocalypse: 'At long last we were ready to retaliate for Washington,
Detroit, New York, London – all those places which had been indiscriminately
A-bombed by the Reds.' The date was 22 July 1953. In 1954 Beria replaced
Stalin; the Red Army began to retreat from Europe; and UN armoured troops
seized Warsaw and pushed on into the Ukraine. In 1955 the war was over, the
USSR was in a state of chaos, and the UN Temporary Occupation Command
had taken over in Moscow. Arthur Koestler reported on the disappearance of
communism in Russia, 'Freedom—At Long Last'; J. B. Priestley had good
news about the rebirth of the arts in 'The Curtain Rises'; and Stuart Chase
had his say about the economic future of the new Russia in 'Out of the
Rubble—A New Russia'.

There were, however, some notable omissions in the narratives. Had the
editors thought of consulting military experts, they would not have given their
readers such an absurd account of atomic bombardments that lasted for
months; and they would never have described leaflet raids that persuaded the
Russians to rise up against their rulers. No doubt it was a calculated exercise
in wish-fulfilment—the profitable patriotism that supplies media fodder for the
unreflecting. The absolute division between the Reds and the Rest of the
World, between the Bad Russians and the Good Russians, has the appearance
of a war fought to the finish between stereotypes.

In total contrast to the unquestioning confidence of the *Collier's* projection,
contemporary fiction in Europe had nothing good to report about another
world war. Those British, French, and German writers who chose to write on
the matter were certain that a future war would be the most dreadful of all
possible catastrophes. It would be the disaster-to-come described in the unrelenting narratives of *Ape and Essence* (1949), *Death of a World* (1948), *The*

Purple Twilight (1948), *Le Diable l'emporte* (1948), *Der achte Tag* (1950), *Late Final* (1951), *Die drei grossen Weltkriege der Endzeit der christlichen Aera* (1952), *Ce pourrait se passer comme ça* (1950), and *Keiner kommt davon* (1957).

In fact, in 1949 three most original British writers had already established the new models for telling the tale of the war-to-come: George Orwell demonstrated the structure and the operations of the perpetual-warfare state in *Nineteen Eighty-Four*; Aldous Huxley created the classic admonitory account of the hateful post-warfare state in his *Ape and Essence*; and in *Seven Days in New Crete* Robert Graves went forward into the third millennium through disastrous wars and the wasting of Europe, China, and Japan. Far away in the distant future, the remnants of humankind will have learnt from the follies of the past. The intent in the new fiction was corrective. The three forms dealt with the whole world and all human beings—with their responsibility for the final disaster as taught by Huxley, or with their helplessness and degradation in the iron grip of the police state according to Orwell, or with the hope of the resurrection-to-come in the remote future as revealed by Robert Graves.

In their different ways, these three authors summoned the world and especially Western civilization to reflect on the failings that could lead to the disasters they described. Orwell's satire gave formal shape to one of the familiar terrors of the twentieth century: the means that technology provides for achieving the complete domination of human beings. The logic of the desire for absolute power could only lead to the conquest of the world. Consequently the three super-states of Eurasia, Oceania, and Eastasia must be organized to wage a war without end; for the great advantage of war is that, by using up the products of technology, it most effectively keeps down the standard of living so that the totalitarian state can maintain an unshakeable hold on its helot subjects. Here is the iron future of the new iron age:

In one combination or another, these three super-states are permanently at war, and have been so for the past twenty-five years. War, however, is no longer the desperate, annihilating struggle that it was in the early decades of the twentieth century. It is a warfare of limited means between combatants who are unable to destroy one another, have no material cause for fighting and are not divided by any genuine ideological difference. This is not to say that either the conduct of war, or the prevailing attitude towards it, has become less bloodthirsty or more chivalrous. On the contrary war hysteria is continuous and universal in all countries, and such acts as raping, looting, the slaughter of children, the reduction of whole populations to slavery, and reprisals against prisoners which extend even to boiling and burying alive, are looked on as normal, and when they are committed by one's own side and not by the enemy, meritorious.

In a mood of black and bitter idealism, Orwell had set out to show the evils as yet only latent in the admired world of democracy and technology. His method was to invert contemporary values and give the lie to all former hopes of continuous improvement in the condition of humanity. He was one of the first of the postwar writers to look backwards at the errors and false beliefs that were the source of contemporary evil. He pointed to the deceptive mirage of the early twentieth century, when 'the vision of a future society unbelievably rich, leisured, orderly, and efficient—a glittering antiseptic world of glass and steel and snow-white concrete—was part of the consciousness of nearly every literate person'. Orwell had Wells in mind, and in particular the Wellsian Utopias which carried the false promise of an ever-improving world in the future. Thus, the narrative gains much of its effect from the painful disparity between hope frustrated and fear completely realized, between the heaven that might have been and the hell that is sure to come.

In *Nineteen Eighty-Four* Orwell created a myth for the epoch of Himmler and Beria. It is the story of a secular fall and the consequent expulsion from the paradise of everlasting progress. By means of memorable slogans—'progress in our world will be progress towards more pain'—and by his ability to convey meaning through symbolic situations—Winston in the Ministry of Love—Orwell was able to present the world with the images of its worst fears. The final terror in the story, however, is that Orwell does not offer any hope of a redeemer. Man is completely and irrevocably a fallen creature. Orwell's projection of the seemingly inevitable into a certain future was an unconditional and, in the last analysis, a nihilistic and despairing vision. When the book burst upon the reading public in the United States as the American Book-of-the-Month choice for July 1949, it was at once proclaimed the complete commentary on the morbid anatomy of modern technological society. In a review of the book, *Time* declared that Orwell had no need for anyone to explain or interpret his story—'for the simple reason that any reader in 1949 can uneasily see his own shattered features in Winston Smith, can scent in the world of 1984 a stench that is already familiar'. The stench lasted at full strength for close on three decades. By 1984, however, the scent could not be distinguished from the odour of sanctity that hung about the many meetings during the Holy Year of recalling Orwell and his story. Indeed, the Council of Europe arranged a secular canonization for the English St George, when the Secretary-General called an international three-day conference 'to celebrate the year given symbolic significance by George Orwell's famous novel'. The topics for discussion were: '*1984*: Myths and Realities—Man, the State, and Society in Question'.

The anger and anxiety of Orwell and Huxley had issued into visions of the future that were immediately accepted as symbolic of the dilemma facing the contemporary world. For the two writers the dangers were equal and opposite —either the tyrant state, or no state at all; either Big Brother, or the Thing. Like Orwell, Huxley spoke to all men under the universal shadow of a potentially destructive technology. His message was that, in his own phrase, we all get precisely what we ask for; and in *Ape and Essence* he composed a homily on the danger of confusing ends and means. The entirely logical lunacy of total warfare would be the final triumph of scientific method and political opportunism. His text came straight from Pascal: 'We make an idol of truth; for truth without charity is not God, but his image and idol, which we must neither love nor worship.' The proof comes from the everyday facts of science and politics. There are the scientists in their government institutes all over the world—biologists, pathologists, physicists, physiologists. They are kindly men, good fathers and devoted husbands, who come home of an evening for a quiet dinner followed by chamber music and intelligent talk with friends. And then, in the morning, 'after orange juice and Grape-nuts, off they go again to their job of discovering how yet greater numbers of families precisely like their own can be infected with a yet deadlier strain of *bacillus mallei*'. Again, there are the politicians and the political theorists who represent the collective madness of the modern world. So, Gandhi stood for the eternal opposite of the political creeds, but his tragedy was that 'this man who believed only in people had got himself involved in the subhuman mass-madness of nationalism, in the would-be superhuman, but actually diabolic, institutions of the nation-state. He got himself involved in these things, imagining that he could mitigate the madness and convert what was satanic in the state to something like humanity'. But nationalism and politics, said Huxley, proved too much for Gandhi; and they would be too much for our world, so the lesson ran in *Ape and Essence*, if men did not mend their ways.

By the device of a film-script, Huxley introduces the reader to the broken world of AD 2108 some time after the atomic bombs and the man-made plagues of the third world war have destroyed most of the human race. In southern California, and in what used to be the City of the Angels, Huxley seeks to prove Pascal right by describing an unbelievably degraded community in which the pursuit of truth without charity has ended in the religion of Moloch. The survivors worship Belial, the Lord of the Flies, to whom they sacrifice the children deformed by gamma radiation. The script cuts from one horrifying scene to another; young voices in chorus repeat the new catechism answer that 'the chief end of Man is to propitiate Belial, deprecate his enmity and avoid destruction for as long as possible'; and in the interior of the Los Angeles Coliseum by the intermittent light of torches a massed congregation of the faithful chants monotonously: 'Glory to Belial, to Belial in the lowest'. In the usual manner of major characters in imaginary future worlds, the Arch-Vicar of Belial talks freely of all that has happened. He explains how Belial works in the world, and he conveys to the reader Huxley's own *argumentum ad mundum*:

Progress and Nationalism—those were the two great ideas he put into their heads. Progress—the theory that you can get something for nothing; the theory that you can gain in one field without paying for your gain in another; the theory that you alone understand the meaning of history; the theory that you know what's going to happen fifty years from now; the theory that, in the teeth of all experience, you can foresee all the consequences of your present actions; the theory that Utopia lies just ahead and that, since ideal ends justify the most abominable means, it is your privilege and duty to rob, swindle, torture, enslave and murder all those who, in your opinion (which is, by definition, infallible), obstruct the onward march to the earthly paradise. Remember that phrase of Karl Marx's: 'Force is the midwife of Progress'? He might have added—but, of course, Belial didn't want him to let the cat out of the bag at that early stage of the proceedings—that Progress is the midwife of Force. Doubly the midwife, for the fact of technological progress provides people with the instruments of ever more indiscriminate destruction, while the myth of political and moral progress serves as the excuse for using those means to the very limit.

Huxley's warning vision of a catastrophic future is very much a period piece. It derived from the immediate post-war feeling that the world was facing the end of things, that Western civilization had come perilously close to dissolution. It is an unhappy book, the product of contradictory moods. Huxley alternates between indicating the path of salvation and attacking humanity for its failures with a bitterness he had not previously shown. Indeed, *Brave New World* is almost idyllic in comparison with the often unrestrained savageness of *Ape and Essence*. But then, the difference between the two satires is far more than a mere hardening of mood: it is the measure of a civilization's advance in the self-conscious realization of its own defects and past failings. It belongs to the contemporary revision and rethinking of inherited ideas which were the point of departure for W. H. Auden's *New Year Letter* and William Golding's *The Inheritors*. Huxley deals with the heart of the matter, as he saw it, by telling his tale of the consequences that are to come. Here, for example, is the Arch-Vicar summing up the case against the modern world, as he describes how the success of the first industrial revolution caused Western man to lose all sense of right order:

'And remember this,' he adds, 'even without synthetic glanders, even without the atomic bomb, Belial could have achieved all His purposes. A little more slowly, perhaps, but just as surely, men would have destroyed themselves by destroying the world they lived in. . . . From the beginning of the industrial revolution He foresaw that men would be made so overwhelmingly bumptious by the miracles of their own technology that they would soon lose all sense of reality. And that's precisely what happened. These wretched slaves of wheels and ledgers began to congratulate themselves on being the Conquerors of Nature. Conquerors of Nature, indeed! In actual fact, of course, they had merely upset the equilibrium of Nature and were about to suffer the consequences. Just consider what they were up to during the century and a half before the Thing. Fouling the rivers, killing off the wild animals, destroying the forests, washing the topsoil into the sea, burning up an ocean of petroleum, squandering the minerals it had taken the whole of geological time to deposit. An orgy of criminal imbecility. And they called it Progress.'

These ideas have been familiar patter in innumerable lay sermons from Hiroshima to Chernobyl. The malady of our age, so the charges run, is that Western technological man has been too greedy, too witless, too lacking in self-control, or simply not farsighted enough to anticipate the consequences of unregulated advances in the applied sciences. These are the main themes in the familiar and long-running debate about the impact of science on society. In the Babel of our times the loudest voices cry out—the Bomb, Ecology, World Population, Future Shock, and so on. They say that knowledge may give too much power to mankind. That conviction is certainly the motive force in many tales of the disaster-to-come, and it is a source of hope in the utopian fantasies of the good society that will one day follow out of the calamity of a destroyed world.

The prototype for these tales of paradise regained was the elegant parable of *Seven Days in New Crete* by Robert Graves. The British edition came out in the September of 1949,[3] and was the last in the new trialogue about the Bomb and the future. Time has moved on, from 1984 and from the Huxleyan setting of AD 2108 to some time in the third millennium long after the devastating wars that wiped out most of the human race. In New Crete the time-traveller from the twentieth century finds a regenerate community which has learnt from the bitter history of past disasters that 'we must retrace our steps, or perish'. The new beginning had started from an analysis of some seventy of the most famous literary Utopias, and from that came the scheme for an experiment in living—anthropological enclaves which reproduced the social and physical conditions of life in prehistoric and early historical times. The model new-world community emerged on Crete; and everything about it is apparently an ambiguous lesson for the twentieth century. The one hundred books in the Golden Archives contain all necessary knowledge; and Graves is careful to note that there is no information whatever about philosophy, advanced mathematics, physics, or chemistry. The amiable, co-operative inhabitants of New Crete are seen to enjoy their very simple, rural life: travelling is on foot, or on asses, or by ass-cart for the elderly; agriculture is late Iron Age; and there are no machines, not even a printing press. Graves dwells on the tranquillity of New Crete. Their wars are ritual occasions, fought only on Tuesdays, for the taking of life is forbidden. When the account arrives at that point, Graves deliberately goes back in his persona as narrator to the very different experiences of the twentieth century:

I thought of the strewn corpses on Monte Cassino, where I had been almost the only unwounded survivor of my company; and of the flying-bomb raid on London, when I had held a sack open for an air-raid warden to shovel the bloody fragments of a child into it; and finally of Paschendaele where, in the late summer of 1917, my elder brother had been killed in the bloodiest, foulest and most useless battle in history—as a boy I had visited his grave soon after that war ended, and the terror of the ghastly, waterlogged countryside with its enormous over-lapping shell-craters had haunted me for years.

Some eight pages later, and two pages from the end of the book, it suddenly becomes clear that New Crete is not quite the ideal state it seems. Because the carefree inhabitants have never known adversity, they lack fortitude. That is the lesson Graves would have us learn. The narrator reveals that he is 'a seed of trouble' brought by the Mother Goddess to restore the balance in human affairs. So, he calls up the whirlwind that will blow away security and set the madmen free. The Cretans were wrong in thinking that they could retrace their steps and begin at the beginning. There is no going back, says Graves. We go forward from one danger to another. We have to manage as best we can. Endurance is all.

The prophetic writings of Orwell, Huxley and Graves made absolute the petition for divorce—first entered in 1918—between the old epics of 'The Next Great War' and the new fiction of the day when history would come to an end. After 1918 war could no longer be the whole story and nothing but that story, as it had once been in so many projections like *The Great War of 1892*. After Hiroshima the new tales of future warfare—with a few notable exceptions—have confirmed that the description of the war-to-come, inaugurated by Chesney in his *Battle of Dorking*, is now a tale of terror. As the conduct and the scale of warfare have gone on changing throughout the twentieth century, new formulations have transformed this singular form of fiction. Up to 1914 the tales of the next war had marked similarities, and their drill-order campaigns invariably took place at some time in the near future; that is, they were written according to the long-established specifications of an international brief that laid down the rules of engagement with the enemy of the day, the intentions and the objectives of the enemy, the relative size of fleets and armies, and the limitation of the conflict to the principal antagonists and their allies. The rest of the world was to look on undisturbed. Since 1918, however, tales of the war-to-come have for the most part repudiated the self-sufficient values of the nation-state. When the bombing plane and then the atomic bomb put civilians in the front line, without any regard for age or sex, the common fellowship of death made nonsense of the once popular tales of triumphant nations in arms.

From 1945 onwards, then, the evolutionary development of the new fiction has followed the turns and twists in the Forty-Year Confrontation between East and West. These established the context for the many projections that traded in the hopes and the fears for future relations between the two power blocs. They now read like chapters in the history of some ancient world—a tale of much sound and frequent fury. Their history opens with the Russian blockade of Berlin in 1948; it goes forward through the worst moments—Hungary, Czechoslovakia, the Berlin Wall, Cuba—to the Hotline Agreement in 1963 and to the beginning of better relations after Gorbachev came to power in 1985. The main stages have followed upon the introduction of ever more powerful and more accurate weapons. The Russians got their A-bomb in 1950 and the Americans produced their H-bomb in 1952. Then, on 4 October 1957, an SS-6 put the first Sputnik into space and the 'missile gap' became a menacing new term in the American vocabulary. By 1962 that master of bluff, Nikita Khruschev, was boasting of the new Soviet missile, so accurate that 'it could hit a fly in space'. The *space race*, as they called the leapfrog development of new systems, went on for three decades—from the IRBMs and ICBMs of the 1960s to the Trident and Cruise missiles of the 1980s to the recent and now happily half-forgotten Star Wars talk about energy beam weapons.

Most fortunately for the future of humanity, there has been the parallel movement towards the limitation and control of armaments—the Partial Test Ban and Non-Proliferation Treaty, the Strategic Arms Limitation Talks, the 1990 Treaty on Conventional Armed Forces in Europe, and the 1992 UN proposals for the creation of a global security system. As the prospects for permanent peace between the two groups continued to improve, in keeping with the astonishing political changes in Eastern Europe and the Soviet Union, it became more and more difficult to carry on with the imagined war of the future between East and West. Once again the context had changed. The rigid attitudes, the instant suspicion, the assumption of permanent ill-will and hostility, the frontier guards, the border crossings, the defectors, and the spy satellites—an entire psychology of regulated aggressiveness—rapidly lost the power it once had to inspire and to energize the tale of the war-to-come. One early sign of this change came in a brief report from Sarny in the western Ukraine. There, on 8 August 1990, a delegation of American military and government officials watched as Russian engineers destroyed eighteen of their SS20 medium-range nuclear missiles. It was good news for the world, and bad news for would-be authors of future war stories.

Before that, however, the conflict-to-come between East and West raged on unchecked for more than forty years in the greatest outpouring of fiction in the history of the genre. Every stage in the projected third world war—from initial manoeuvres to final annihilation—has its appropriate place in the sequence of specific modes that compose the modern literature of imaginary warfare. During the preliminary phase the world is still at peace, save for the ceaseless activity of the intelligence agencies; and these tales of espionage and counter-espionage increase in violence to the point when covert actions—attempted assassinations, clandestine operations, and the like—develop into a more open struggle with the other side. After that the second phase begins

with tales of the expected war between East and West and with the swift
Russian victories that lead to the Soviet domination of the United Kingdom or
the United States; and these conquests are the starting-point for tales of great
oppression or of heroic uprisings against the occupying forces. Phase Three
demonstrates how agreed strategies for defensive and counter-offensive operations are decisive in the few but important accounts of the probable NATO
response to a Warsaw Pact offensive. The fourth and final phase presents
many anticipations of the final catastrophe awaiting all mankind. That fearful
possibility has generated the greatest volume of disaster stories in the history
of futuristic fiction, as Paul Brians has demonstrated with admirable scholar-
ship in his authoritative analysis of these stories, *Nuclear Holocausts*.[4]

For the first time in the course of this literature, writers throughout the
world—American, Canadian, European, Japanese, Russian—have found a common objective and a rare unity in their accounts of the final disaster. In many
languages and in many ways, they express the universal fear of extinction in
their versions of *La Nuit des temps* (1968), *Quatre Montrélais en l'an 3000*
(1963), *America RIP* (1965), *Efter Floden* (1982), *Lo Smeraldo* (1974), *Die letzten Kinder von Schewenborn* (1983). Finally, and most varied of them all, are
the survivors' tales which refuse to acknowledge that history can have an end.
Instead, the authors make full use of the opportunity to play Moses for the
chosen few who live on in the wilderness after The Thing. Like so many
latter-day Lincolns, they face the final dissolution and announce that mankind
shall not perish from the face of the earth. And so, in the distant age of the
after-time, a renewed and chastened society will restore the world; or survivors
from Old Terra will find new homes in space; or the barbarian warriors of a
remote future epoch will fight out their everlasting, limited wars in extravagant
survivalist fantasies.

Technology and politics have literally changed the world for the tale of
future warfare. In 1763 the author of *The Reign of George VI* expected that
the weaponry and the tactics of his time would carry on unchanged into the
twentieth century. He was confident that in 1920 the American colonists
would still be loyal subjects of a British king, and that events in Europe
would decide whatever was to happen in the rest of the world. In 1963 cinema audiences had their first viewing of Stanley Kubrick's famous film, *Dr
Strangelove*, a most telling end-of-the-world lesson which spoke directly and
with great effect about the immense dangers of nuclear weapons. Indirectly,
the sequences showed the Americans, their colonial days long forgotten, in
their familiar role as a great nation and dominant world power. At the same
time, the images demonstrated the prodigious capacity of the motion picture
to display every conceivable kind of future possibility. These changed circumstances have had much to do with the marked increase in American tales of
the war-to-come and with the rapid growth of the many American films that

run through all the variations on the theme of future warfare—from the fearful possibilities so ably presented in Stanley Kramer's production of *On the Beach* to the heroic adventures in *Star Wars* and the rest of the George Lucas productions.

After the end of the Second World War the future took on many different shapes throughout the world; and these differences in expectation carried over into the futuristic fiction of the 1950s and 1960s. In this Atlantic period, when the political will and military power of the United States were changing the destiny of nations from Japan to Germany, the tale of the future followed wherever technology or politics led. For the Europeans, the signs were not auspicious—divided between East and West, their great empires in dissolution, dependent on the massive subventions of the Marshall Plan. Those melancholy facts provided material for the uniformly pessimistic anticipations of the late 1940s which appeared at their most uncompromising in *Nineteen Eighty-Four* and *Ape and Essence*. It was very different for the Americans. They looked out on a world where, for a time, they could expect to have their way. There was General MacArthur ruling as Supreme Commander in Japan; the President of the United States inventing the Truman Doctrine to sanction the transfer of former British commitments to the United States; and General Eisenhower working on the initiatives for the defence of the West which led to the signing of the North Atlantic Treaty in 1949. The achievements of American technology were no less remarkable; for they led the world in the second industrial revolution—computers, credit cards, microwave ovens, nuclear submarines, lasers, transistors, word processors, and the spectacular launchings and lunar landings of the space programme.

All these changes, political and technological, raised many questions about the future; and, here again, the Americans were well prepared for the business of finding rapid answers. Historical experience had long accustomed them to dealing with the problems of growth and expansion. Twenty years before there were any associations or commissions for investigating the future, the President of the United States, Herbert Hoover, had established the National Resources Committee. His instructions called for a report upon recent social trends; it was to be 'such a review as might supply a basis for the formulation of large national policies looking to the next phase in the nation's development'. That was the start of several initiatives—sociological and technological appraisals—that came together as a distinct technique at the end of the Second World War. The name of the method was *Futurology*, a bastard word coined by a German refugee professor in an American college. Nevertheless, it proved a convenient way of describing the sundry forecasting and analytical procedures that began to spread like a forest fire across the United States at the end of the 1940s. That was the time when the von Karman report to the US Army Air Force, *Toward New Horizons*, had started the American think-tanks that were to have great influence on military thinking in the Pentagon and would provide abundant material for the new tales of the nuclear war-to-come.

The information passed to General Arnold in 1945 had added to the general satisfaction with the proven success of the Operational Research techniques that the US Army Air Force had learnt from the British. The logic of the new analytical and forecasting procedures, as von Karman recommended, called for the establishment of a scientific research centre which would serve the interests of the military. The new centre began to operate on 1 December 1945, when General Curtis Le May took up his appointment as the first Deputy Chief of Air Staff for Research and Development. His directorate was the first of the American think-tanks and a first step in the then new practices of futurology. It had the special task of overseeing and assisting in the development of Project RAND: 'a continuing program of scientific study and research on the broad subject of air warfare with the object of recommending to the Air Force preferred methods, techniques and instrumentalities for this purpose'. In 1948 the staff of Project RAND were encouraged to establish themselves as an independent, non-profit organization; and, with the help of a substantial grant from the Ford Foundation, they went into business as the RAND Corporation under contract to the US Air Force. Their calculations and recommendations were to have an immense influence on military planning and on presidential decisions about the manufacture and the use of nuclear weapons. For three decades the RAND Corporation 'would be considered the nation's leading center for intellectuals who based their careers on thinking about the bomb—how to deter nuclear war, how to fight nuclear war if it could not be deterred'.[5] One of the new futurologists was Herman Kahn, a physicist and a senior member of the Hudson Institute. His books gave the general reader a precise, unblinking assessment of the terror-to-come. Their titles told the world what the future might have in store for humankind: *On Thermonuclear War* (1960), *Thinking about the Unthinkable* (1963), *On Escalation* (1964).

As many Americans took to the new futurological practices and as knowledge of them spread, there was a corresponding rise in both the numbers and the quality of American tales of the future. Up to 1939 all the chief begetters and most of the major writers in this field had been Europeans. Since 1945, however, the originality and considerable output of so many excellent writers in the United States have proved more than sufficient reason for calling the second half of the twentieth century the 'American epoch' in the history of this literature. Many able and imaginative writers have widened the scope of modern futuristic writing. Any list of their principal achievements would have to include the many innovations that have advanced the genre beyond the European tradition: the robots and imperial histories of Isaac Asimov, the flying cities of James Blish, the non-stop struggles between good and evil in the hallucinatory fiction of Philip K. Dick, the exuberant space adventure tales of Harry Harrison, the giant sandworms and desert-dwellers in the *Dune* stories of Frank Herbert, the marvellous self-contained worlds of Ursula Le Guin, and the mordant fantasies of Kurt Vonnegut. All these writers have dealt with the theme of warfare in one way or another. In fact, a count of titles will show that the Europeans now come second to the Americans in writing stories about the war of the future. There is, for example, no longer any European equivalent of the exaltation of military roles and close-combat fighting that appears in Robert Heinlein's *Starship Troopers* (1959). No European writer has attempted anything on the scale of the twelve-volume series of Gordon Dickson's *Dorsai* stories, which celebrate the exemplary virtues and evolutionary role of the professional warriors dedicated to the great advance through space. Again, the few British survivalist fantasies cannot hope to compare with the non-stop production of American serials about the strange new wars of the post-holocaust epoch: Robert Adams's *The Horseclans*; Jerry Ahern's *The Survivalist*; Piers Anthony's *Battle Circle*; Suzy McKee Charnas's *Motherlines*; Patrick Tilley's *The Amtrak Wars*; Paul O. Williams's *The Pelbar Cycle*; and so on to the most recent arrival, *The Burning Land* series by Barbara and Scott Siegel, an entertainment for adolescents set in the devastated world after the third world war where two young people go from one adventure to another.

There are other typical features that distinguish these American tales of future warfare. One notable difference—not surprising, in a nation of poker players—is a tendency of American writers to take their plots as far as they can go at every stage, from the espionage preliminaries to the final catastrophe. Only American authors advance beyond the no-man's-time of this fiction, when the counter-intelligence struggle ends and the expected war could break out. Indeed, some Americans are ready to cross that imagined brink—the final frontier, no doubt—in order to describe activities that have no regard for normal international practices and can become acts of open warfare. One form of this shadow confrontation appears in Tom Clancy's most popular tale, *The Hunt for Red October* (1984). It is a pursuit story, a sequence of actions and counter-actions, as the US Navy with the support of the Royal Navy helps Captain First Rank Marko Ramius of the Soviet Navy to bring his submarine into safe harbourage in the Eight-Ten Dock at Norfolk, Virginia. That was war without the shooting, and it counted as a major defeat for the Russians. For the Americans the first fruits of victory are reported on the last page: 'The *Red October* sat alone with the dry dock draining around her . . . Already a select group of engineers and technicians was inspecting her. The first items taken off were her cipher books and machines.'

There have been other ingenious stories that turned the Cold War into sudden incandescence. Because the Russians develop a laser weapon that will neutralize all SDI technology, an old B-52 sets off on a special mission to destroy the laser installation. Because the Russians have launched a vast space station, with twelve thousand inhabitants and an arsenal of secret weapons, two heroic Americans take off to wrest their secret from the Russians.[6] And then there are the recent Rambo stories and the Rambo films, which show the all-competent and all-American hero forever in action against the Reds and their comrades.

The immense outpouring of these books that relate every imaginable phase in the predicted third world war, the innumerable paperback editions, the films, and the television serials—these have given the tale of the war-to-come a specialized vocabulary and a singular imagery that isolate and characterize each stage in the anticipated struggle for world domination. This is especially apparent in the secret warfare of the espionage agencies that began with the extraordinary success of the James Bond stories in the 1950s and the films of those stories which started with *From Russia with Love* in 1963.[7] After that, the spy stories advanced to the operations of the Soviet mole, Smiley, and the Circus in John Le Carré's *Tinker, Tailor, Soldier, Spy* in 1974 and to the celebrated BBC television serial of that tale in 1980. And they have now arrived at what seems to be a possible end-of-play in the recent Russian television serial of Julian Semyonov's story about CIA agents at work on the subversion of an African state. The plot in *TASS is authorized to Announce . . .* was undoubtedly relevant in the Cold War conditions when the book was first published in 1979. By 1990, however, the elaborate account of 'Operation Torch' and of the CIA mole in Moscow had almost reached the stage of historical drama, especially in the final set-piece confrontation between the Soviet Minister of Foreign Affairs and the US Ambassador:

What we have here, Mr Ambassador, are photocopies of questions which the CIA put to its agents. These questions show that in the very next few days an act of aggression is planned to begin in Nagonia. If we give the press the information that the CIA has been passing poison to its agents, and if we release the CIA's list of questions relating to Nagonia, then . . .

A far better indication of the recent climatic change was the television serial *Sleepers*, which was made by Cinema Verity. It had a first showing with the BBC and the episodes ended most appropriately on May Day 1991. The ingenious scriptwriters, John Flanagan and Andrew McCulloch, had discovered that the dead can come back to life in a different form. Their charming comedy turns on two KGB officers, Vladimir and Sergei, posted to England in 1966 as sleepers and forgotten by Moscow. They live happily ever after, more English than the English, until someone comes upon a dusty file in Moscow, and then the fun begins.[8]

New techniques, remarkable new modes of communication, a level of professionalism not seen before, chains of command from the KGB, or the CIA, or testy old M in his Whitehall office—these innovations point to the changes that have promoted the spy story from the haphazard tale of chance encounters to a planned operational role in the holy war against Smersh. Once convention held that our man was an amateur and a gentleman. His mission was not given. It came out of the blue and imposed itself—for example on Richard Hannay in *The Thirty-Nine Steps*, and on the two dedicated yachtsmen who uncover the German plan for the invasion of Great Britain in Erskine Childers's *Riddle of the Sands*. By the 1950s, however, the scale of operations had shifted from a solitary man on the run in the Scottish Highlands to the command centres that control the operatives of the major intelligence agencies. Every one of these new men is a highly trained warrior, licensed to kill; and they are all directed at their targets like so many guided missiles. They exist in a world created out of the many sensational reports of spy and counter-spy activities between East and West. These have provided ample material and convincing models for all those lurid tales of minders and dead-letterboxes, moles and sleepers, station chiefs and field operators, double agents and double-cross operations. From the days of Igor Gouzenko and Klaus Fuchs, of Colonel Oleg Penkovsky and Greville Wynne, the truth seemed to bear out all that fiction has had to tell. Were there foreign agents at work in the United Kingdom? The Czech defector Josef Frolik stated: 'We had our agents in Parliament, the trade unions, the police, the Treasury, government research and private business.' Did the KGB employ trained killers? Another defector, Peter Deriabin, testified to the US Senate Subcommittee on state security that 'murder is an instrument of Soviet policy. Spetsburo No 1, or Department 13 of the Foreign Intelligence Directorate of Soviet State Security, is responsible for kidnapping and assassination.'

These revelations of a clandestine order of battle established the operational conditions for the fictional counter-offensive. They were, in fact, a gift to writers of spy fiction. Any reference to the known workings of the Russian intelligence system seemed to confirm the authenticity of their stories. So, Frederick Nolan made his play for realism in *Red Centre* (1987) with the omniscient statement that introduced his tale of thwarting the Russians: 'The Chief Intelligence Directorate of the Soviet General Staff—*Glavnoye Razvedyvatelnoye Upravleniye*—is smaller and less well-known than its sister organization. GRU does not advertise itself.' In these stories every episode fitted into the legendary strategies of the secret war—there was nothing the Russians would not attempt—and every story confirmed the established dogmas of the Cold War. Thus, the activities of James Bond and his successors represent the reconnaissance phase in the modern tale of future warfare. They compose a gladiatorial display that comes as a sportive prelude to the far more alarming accounts of the violent conflict-to-come. In fact, they are their authors' collective tribute to a profitable patriotism; they belong to a category of popular fiction that in the 1960s had grown into a minor publishing industry and a most attractive source of plots for films. The often frantic adventures of their heroes are constant reminders of the enemy without, and their successes are the promise of final victory when the Hot War begins.

At times, the secret struggle of the few against the many erupts into clandestine skirmishes when the future of the nation or of the world is seen to depend on the outcome of a desperate search for the source of some fearful danger. These are occasions of extreme anxiety that make for the most exciting reading. One favourite plot turns on a fact of the Cold War—the sleeper, or the enemy within. The wicked Russians place their agent in the White House, but no one can find a face for the unknown enemy. That was a recurring American nightmare, well related in Richard Condon's story of *The Manchurian Candidate* in 1959 and then most effectively presented in the 1962 film version: a brainwashed Korean War veteran is turned into a Soviet sleeper, waiting for the day when he will be activated and sent out to kill the presidential candidate. This hidden enemy is the writer's best friend. All things are possible to these unknown and as yet undiscovered agents, even the bomb-in-a-suitcase that waits to be detonated somewhere in England. The Russians take three nuclear scientists to a secret location where they see the cobalt bomb that could prove the end of everything in *Doomsday England* (1967). The scientists tell Whitehall that the Russian bomb is a true secret weapon: 'It has the capacity to vaporize, or roast, three-quarters of our entire population . . . a vast hurricane of fire would be released. A cube of destruction roughly three hundred and twenty-five miles in length, breadth and altitude . . .'

That was a plot that could be repeated in many ways. A recent British variation on that theme appears in *The Fourth Protocol* (1985), where Frederick Forsyth's story of many alarms and panics turns on a Russian agent sent to detonate a nuclear device in Britain and so ensure an election victory for the left. The account of Plan Aurora is a most perfect example of the well-calculated realism that gives a semblance of possibility to these fantasies of the secret war between East and West. Mrs Thatcher is in Downing Street, and in the Kremlin a new General Secretary has succeeded Brezhnev. He calls on Comrade Colonel Philby to work out the programme of the covert operation that is designed to wreck NATO. There are whole chapters on the great traitor, and interludes about his home life, as Kim Philby plans the surest means of driving the British electorate into voting for unilateral disarmament.

Anything can happen in this waiting time before the ICBMs arrive. In Crawford Kilian's *Ice Quake* (1979) a man is killed in Washington, and suddenly it becomes evident that the Russians have a scheme to melt the Arctic ice caps and flood the decadent West. The counter-action begins far away in the Russian north, when a small group sets out for a research station on North Island, Novaya Zemlya. Their mission is to locate and rescue the scientist who had sent the cryptic message about the Russian intentions. Mission accomplished after great excitement. There were dangers everywhere, and the closer to home, the worse they were. Take a venal British diplomat, a fanatical Welsh nationalist, and an Irish-American linked to the IRA; add the dangerous fact that Moscow has had news of a powerful new British rocket, capable of orbital flight; and it is clear that this is a matter for the head of the Special Task Force, an autonomous subdivision of the Second Chief Directorate of the KGB. So, the operation begins in John Denis's *The Moscow Horse* (1978) when Dublin nominees purchase an oil rig in the Irish Sea for a reputable company which is a front for the Russians. They intend to use the rig as a base for a submarine which is to transfer men and equipment for an attack on the British rocket research centre. Their plans go well until our woman, the Hon. Victoria Emmaline Cristal, appears.

In this way, stage by stage, these tales move ever closer to open warfare. There is the sudden threat that starts things off with a bang in William Craig's *The Tashkent Crisis* (1971). The world seems to be at peace, and suddenly the teletype machine in the White House spews out a message from Russia without love to the President. It begins:

TO THE PRESIDENT OF THE UNITED STATES OF AMERICA FROM THE SECRE-TARY OF THE PRESIDIUM, UNION OF THE SOVIET SOCIALIST REPUBLICS: WE HEREBYE INFORM YOU THAT WE DEMAND THE UNCONDITIONAL SURRENDER OF YOUR COUNTRY EFFECTIVE SIXTY-TWO HOURS FROM THIS TRANSMISSION. RESISTANCE TO THIS ULTIMATUUM WOULD BE FOOLHARDY SINCE WE POS-SESS A WEAPON OF UNUSUALLY DESTRUCTIVE FORCE WHICH CANNOT BE CHALLENGED. . . .

The next stage in this schedule of graded actions is the sudden offensive which gives the Russians the immediate victory that is their proper reward for infinite cunning and thorough preparation. Their agents penetrate the White House in *American Surrender* (1979) and the First Lady is forced to broadcast the Russian ultimatum: 'On the stroke of midnight we shall saturate your country with nuclear bombs. Over one million of you will die.' A variant on this theme of secret preparations appears in *Silent Night: The Defeat of Nato* (1980), where spearhead groups and assault regiments capture all NATO air bases, take heads-of-state prisoner, and secure all objectives according to plan.

But that was a long time ago, in the days before the astonishing changes that followed after *glasnost* had begun to work in Eastern Europe and the former Soviet Union. When the KGB was disbanded, the operations of Moscow Centre had perforce to end in the counter-espionage stories. And now that the Soviet Union has gone the way of all great empires, writers can only tell the tale of things as they used to be. The time has come for the burial service; and the first to appear at the graveside is Oleg Gordievsky, the most famous of all the defectors from Moscow Centre. His book, which he wrote with Christopher Andrew, has the appropriate title of *Instructions from the Centre* (1991). It reveals all that is still worth knowing about Moscow Rules and about the methods and the operations of the agents who once gave authors so much to write about. RIP KGB.[9]

Although these tales of terror vary greatly from author to author, there is general agreement about the origination of the final war and about the immediate effects of the expected nuclear exchange. The war could begin by accident—a misreading of radar signals, a shower of meteorites, a failure in communications, an accidental launching, the malign actions of religious or political fanatics, the decision of some deranged military commander to initiate the first strike—even a mouse in a missile silo or a flight of vultures. Again, the war could begin according to plan and in keeping with contemporary expectations of a surprise attack, usually by the Russians or sometimes by the Chinese. Although the choice of models is immense, an initial paradox affects all thinking about the outbreak of the first nuclear war. The would-be chroniclers of the Last Days do not lack information. The annual bibliographies offer them hundreds of books under the subject headings of modern weapons, military planning, missile systems, nuclear conflict, space warfare, World War III. And yet, very few of their stories concentrate on what would seem to be the obvious themes of life, death, and destruction on the day the earth shook and the cities were obliterated. One reason is the problem of scale. In the old days before the Bomb there was no difficulty in convincing readers that the future of the nation depended on some distant set-piece battle, or on the results of a campaign overseas, or on a great fleet engagement. Once atomic weapons entered into the equation of victory and defeat, however, all proportion vanished both in fact and in fiction. The entire national territory would be the battlefield. To talk of combatants and non-combatants would be meaningless, and destruction would be so widespread that a writer could only guess at the number and the state of those who survived. In the long-considered view of an eminent biologist, the possibility of survivors indicated an Orwellian world of the future:

Suppose that one of the contending groups in a nuclear war is victorious in the sense that half its population and an organized government survive; this government would inevitably attempt to conquer the rest of the world to prevent future nuclear wars, and might well succeed. A few centuries of Stalinism or technocracy might be a cheap price to pay for the unification of mankind. Such a government would perhaps take extreme precautions against the outbreak of war, revolution, or any other organized quarrels. It might be thought necessary to destroy all records of such events; and the successors of Lenin or Washington, as the case might be, would not be permitted to learn of the deeds of these great men. Most of litera-ture, art, and religion would be scrapped.[10]

Once a writer had chosen his set of probabilities, there was still the narra-tor's problem of finding the right point of view for a tale of sudden death, when so much would happen to so many in so brief a space of time. In conse-quence, the majority of writers made their pact with the Bomb. They con-verted the old epic of the war-to-come into a tale of before-and-after. They chose to concentrate their attention on one major stage in the well-known pro-gramme which goes from the launching of the missiles to the counting of the dead on the day after. These stages in the final drama read like the ritual unfolding of a dreadful and inevitable tragedy, as the sequences of events moves from the political decisions to the command posts and to the moment when the ICBMs burst upon their targets. Once the worst has happened, and the nuclear strikes have obliterated great cities on both sides of the Atlantic, then the history of the desolation becomes a blank screen on which anyone can project any kind of story. One frequent scenario has a few cities taken out on either side and then an abrupt end to hostilities. Another describes the end of civilization—everything gone within hours and the last, miserable survivors of the human race hoping for a swift death. Thus, the unprecedented has become the stuff of fiction. In consequence, these tales of the first nuclear war on Earth present many different possibilities for the future, because their primary expectations vary from author to author according to knowledge, fertility of imagination, and seriousness of purpose.

The authors are all agreed, however, that a nuclear war will prove the great-est divide in Earth history. In fact, they are in total agreement with the late Field-Marshal Montgomery on the catastrophic effects of a single H-bomb:

We will assume that the weapon has struck the centre of a large city. The explo-sion produces a crater about 350 feet deep, and 3,700 feet in diameter. Beyond this enormous crater a 'lip' of radio-active debris extends outwards for approximately 1,800 feet, and to a height of nearly 100 feet. The resulting fireball is about 4 miles in diameter and temperatures within it are around 8,000 degrees Fahrenheit. All matter within that area, living and inanimate, has been pulverized, and linger-ing radioactivity will make it impossible to rebuild this area—certainly within fifty years. Large buildings within 6 miles from where the bomb hit the centre of the city would be nothing more than shells of rubble and collapsing roofs and walls. In addition to the blast effects which have caused this damage, the terrific heat has started fires; widespread devastation, raging fires, electrical short circuits, and mil-lions of casualties extend to some 18 miles from the centre of the city.[11]

There is ample contemplation here for a modern Hamlet, matter enough for brooding by the hour on the infinitude of the imagination. Which is the more extraordinary—the catastrophe of a nuclear war or the compulsion to find a place for that catastrophe in the imagined history of the after-time? The self-appointed doom-sayers of these future war stories write their obituaries for the still living who, they believe, could well depart this world in a moment, in the twinkling of an eye. No trumpets shall sound for them—no sound at all, only the instant incinerating heat of the fireball. Language becomes a crutch to help the walking wounded on their last journey into the never-before. Today they find words for the disasters of tomorrow. They signal the coming of the dark age by naming The Great Disaster with code-words that mark the absolute disruption between the old days and the far from brave new world of the future. Disaster comes too swiftly for the historians to note more than a few details in what they knew as The Destruction, The Ten-Minute-War, The Twenty-Five-Minute-War, The Half-Hour War, The Forty-Five Minute War, The Three-Hour War, The Six-Hour War, The Five-Days War, The Nine-Days Tranquillizer.

Every stage in the well-known procedure of intercontinental warfare has been the focus for classic accounts that are now eloquent legends in the new mythology of the war-to-come. For example, one famous narrative of the first stage opens in the underground command posts that Mordecai Roshwald describes so well in *Level Seven*. Roshwald was born in Poland, studied at the Hebrew University in Jerusalem, and has held teaching posts in British and American universities. He wrote his story for Everyman, and he dedicated it most appropriately to the two men who could have made it come true: 'To Dwight and Nikita'. Roshwald has the apposite mode for his tale of push-button preparedness and unquestioning obedience. His debt to Zamyatin's *We* is apparent in the busy clockwork routine of a monstrous hive dedicated to the service of the military machine. A narrator with the official name of X-127 communes with his diary about his daily life in an enclosed environment 400 feet underground, sealed off from the world outside, the temperature set for an eternal summer of 68 degrees. All communications come by loudspeakers, and from them X-127 receives his first instructions: 'Attention please, attention! This message is addressed to all underground forces on Level 7:'

You have been brought here today to serve as the advance guard of our country, our creed, our way of life. To you men and women on Level 7 is entrusted the operation of the offensive branch of the military machine of our country and its allies. . . . From here you will be able to defend our country without the slightest chance of danger to yourselves. From here you will be able to attack without being attacked. To the world above you you are invisible, but you hold the destiny of the world beneath the tips of your fingers. A day may come soon when some of you will be commanded to push a button, and your fingers will annihilate the enemy and make the victory ours.

The grotesque tale has a cipher for narrator and a command system that is both centre and circumference for an existence regulated by the timetable and the loudspeaker. The language artfully reproduces the tone of infantile enthusiasm and of total subservience to a military regime. So, the beginning of the end comes on 10 June, as the diary records:

So the war is over. It started yesterday at 09.12 hours, as far as our offensive action was concerned, and it ended when our last missiles exploded in enemy territory at 12.10 hours.
  The whole war lasted two hours and fifty-eight minutes—the shortest war in history. And the most devastating one. For both these reasons it is very easy to write its history: no complicated and lengthy campaigns, no battlefields to remember—the globe was one battlefield.

In the new canon of this disaster fiction, the final war often begins by a simple mischance so that the readers will undersand how they live on the edge of possible extinction. Imagine the US Sixth Fleet on patrol in the eastern Mediterranean, as normal an occasion as any in the days of the Cold War. Between Cyprus and Lebanon four planes from Fighter Squadron 44 catapult off the carrier *Saratoga*. Sunflower Four takes up station to the east of Haifa. Order from fighter control: 'We have a bogy. Your intercept course is thirty degrees. Go get him!' Ensign James Cobb alters course, arms his rockets for manual fire, goes down to nine thousand feet, and then makes the mistake that starts the third world war. Instead of ending the chase when he sees the port of Latakia, as standing orders require, he holds on for five seconds and fires his Sidewinder. The missile wavers away from the target and makes straight for the dock area of Latakia. Within hours Damascus radio is reporting a mass raid, many civilian casualties, and heavy damage. Soon after that Moscow radio goes off the air. Has the count-down begun?
  That is the scenario with which Pat Frank chose to open the action in his celebrated account of the third world war in *Alas, Babylon* (1959). Frank was the pseudonym of the American writer Harry Hart, a government official who had served with the Allied Political Warfare Council and with the UN Mission in Korea. His intention, as he explained in a foreword, was to make Americans comprehend the scale and the consequences of a nuclear war: 'To someone who has never felt a bomb, bomb is only a word. An H-bomb's fireball is something you see on television. It is not something that incinerates you to a cinder in a thousandth of a second.' So, Hart chose to recount events at one remove through the experiences of the inhabitants of a small town in Florida. They escape the holocaust and they live to tell the fearful tale of the war that reduced the United States to the level of a third-class nation, dependent on Thailand, Indonesia, and the South American countries for food. The war begins for the Americans with a broadcast message from the President:

Fellow countrymen. As all of you know by now, at dawn this morning this country, and our allies in the free world, were attacked without warning with thermonuclear and atomic weapons. Many of our great cities have been destroyed. Others have been contaminated and their evacuation ordered . . . Our reprisal was swift, and from the reports that have reached this command post, most effective. The enemy has received terrible punishment. Several hundred of his missile and air bases, from Chukchi Peninsula to the Baltic, and from Vladivostok to the Black Sea, have certainly been destroyed . . . The United States has been badly hurt, but is by no means defeated. The battle goes on. Our reprisals continue.

The Hart story, placed firmly within the parameters of the possible, looked into the immediate future in order to terrify readers into agreeing that the military systems of the day could be the death of tomorrow's world. A more distant and more comprehensive perspective on the future opened up when another and more famous American writer pushed fantasy to the limit in two most original stories of technology and warfare. In 1950 Ray Bradbury gained a world audience with his accomplished history of *The Martian Chronicles*,[12] a series of short stories moulded into a single narrative with the addition of new episodes. Bradbury took the stock devices of contemporary science fiction— space travel, space colonies, telepathy, atomic weapons, the Last People—and used them with great effect in his meditation on the inhumanity of *Homo astronauticus*. In 1999 the Earthmen arrive on Mars, the home of the most artistic and peaceful of creatures. By 2001 the Martians are dead, killed by chickenpox and by the appalling stupidity of the beings from the other planet. In their death they are an object lesson for the inhabitants of Terra. The captain of the space-ship speaks their epitaph:

From the look of their cities they were a graceful, beautiful, and philosophical people. They accepted what came to them. They acceded to racial death, that much we know, and without a last-moment war of frustration to tumble down their cities. Every town we've seen so far has been flawlessly intact. They probably don't mind us being here any more than they'd mind children playing on the lawn, knowing and understanding children for what they are. And, anyway, perhaps all this will change us for the better.

Alas, the colonists are set in their ways, convinced they know best, incapable of learning anything from another civilization but ever ready to ruin whatever is alien to their experience. 'Anything that's strange is no good to the average American. If it doesn't have Chicago plumbing, it's nonsense.' So, Bradbury adds incident to incident in a sustained condemnation of a greedy, unreflecting society which has the technological capacity to send colonists to Mars but lacks the wisdom and humanity to deal justly with the Martians and with themselves. Their doom is written into world history. The colonists go on as their kind have always done, building their atomic plants and atomic bomb depots on Mars, while the peoples of Earth prepare for another war. The telescopes reveal the end in the brilliant flashes that tell the universe—'No more

Minneapolis, no more rockets, no more Earth.' Amen, says Bradbury, so be it.
And he concludes with the epitaph that is customary in these tales: 'Life on
Earth never settled down to anything very good. Science ran too far ahead of
us too quickly, and the people got lost in a mechanical wilderness, like children making over pretty things, gadgets, helicopters, rockets; emphasizing the
wrong items, emphasizing machines instead of how to run the machines. Wars
got bigger and bigger and finally killed Earth.'

Bradbury returned to his urgent theme of 'how to run the machines' in
Fahrenheit 451 (1953), a famous variant on the Orwellian perpetual-warfare
state. His future world is an All-American nightmare, conceived in servitude
and dedicated to the proposition that the citizen exists to serve the state.
Conflict is universal. There is the enemy without—two atomic wars since 1960
and another about to break out—and there is the enemy within—the dissident
citizen who has to be hunted down. Bradbury concentrates on the one fact
that the state claims the minds and bodies of the citizens; and he makes the
abstractions of tyranny come alive with two brilliant inventions. The Fireman
is not the admirable saviour of lives and the dedicated protector of homes: he
is the destroyer of imaginative life and the principal agent of oppression; he
burns books, any of the one million forbidden books. And the Mechanical
Hound is no plaything: it is the pursuing will of the state—mechanized, infallible, unnatural, untiring in the hunt for transgressors.

Will this new iron age last for ever? There can be no end to tyranny until
the individual, like Montag the Fireman, asks questions, reads the forbidden
books, and blasts the Hound with his flame-thrower. That is the first lesson in
'how to run the machines'. The second lesson comes with the bombs that
obliterate the city and hundreds of other cities throughout the world. The survivors are the readers of books, and they know about 'a silly damn bird called
a Phoenix . . . He must have been first cousin to Man'. So, Bradbury ends his
lesson on the humane uses of technology with the hope that mankind will one
day recognize 'all the damn silly things we've done for a thousand years, and
as long as we know that and always have it around where we can see it, some
day we'll stop making the goddam funeral pyres and jumping into the middle
of them'.

Since 1945 these stories about the final catastrophe and the tyranny-to-come
have given specific answers to urgent questions about science and society, the
citizen and state, power and violence, the present and the future. They are
part of a general rethinking of beliefs, of accepted values and inherited ideas,
that still continues. What could explain Adolf Hitler and Heinrich Himmler,
the gas chambers and the millions who died in the concentration camps? What
kind of knowledge and what train of decisions led to the first atomic bomb?
Before Hiroshima there had been the Manhattan Project and before that the
well-known letter, written by Leo Szilard and signed by Albert Einstein,

which was sent to Alexander Sachs for the information of President Roosevelt: the most recent atomic research had caused Einstein 'to expect that the element uranium may be turned into a new and important source of energy in the immediate future', and the danger was that 'extremely powerful bombs of a new type may thus be constructed'. This warning of August 1939 followed out of famous research programmes—those of Edward Teller, Leo Szilard, Irène and Frédéric Joliot-Curie, Edward Rutherford, and Frederick Soddy. They were all dedicated in the most admirable way to investigating the unknown, pursuing knowledge for the sake of knowledge. Their brilliant intellectual discoveries had led to the unravelling of the secrets of the atom and—more dangerously—to unexpected decisions that would change the conduct of warfare.

In consequence, the search for adequate explanations has centred on the question of violence—between nations and within the nation. In 1962, on the occasion of the Ciba Foundation symposium, 'Man and his Future', the former director of the World Health Organization, Dr G. B. Chisholm, put that issue very clearly. We can no longer subscribe to the old doctrine that the power and prosperity of our group are 'more important than the welfare, prosperity, power, or even the lives of the members of any or all other groups. . . .:

The whole method of survival by groups in competition to the death with other groups has broken down. The survival group, for the first time in human experience, has become the human race itself. From now on we will survive as members of the human race or not at all, but we have no previous experience of this situation and no traditional concern or education for survival of the human race. The occasion for such concern had not arisen until about fifteen years ago and was not foreseen or provided for by our parents or ancestors. Now we are all threatened with extinction by our own traditional survival patterns, a position which most of us still find impossible to accept as real, because we have been taught in infancy to depend on our 'conscience' values, and even to consider changes in them is commonly felt to be immoral and disloyal.[13]

'The situation of our time', W. H. Auden wrote in 1940, 'surrounds us like a baffling crime.' And in the *New Year Letter* he went on to give his own extensive explanation of the moral failings and political falsehoods that had made the world safe for tyrants:

> The flood of tyranny and force
> Arises at a double source:
> In PLATO's lie of intellect
> That all are weak but the Elect
> Philosophers who must be strong,
> For, knowing Good, they will no Wrong,
> United in the abstract Word

> Above the low anarchic herd;
> Or ROUSSEAU's falsehood of the flesh
> That stimulates our pride afresh
> To think all men identical
> And strong in the Irrational.

That going back to the source of contemporary anxieties, the search for the primal aberration, the safari through the hinterland of wrong choices and wrong decisions—these have been the controlling strategies in the campaign to discover the original sins of technological civilization. The fault-finders return from the dark backward of history to pass judgement on the nation, or on technological civilization, or on that chief of sinners and conspicuous failure, the Eternal Adam in the heart of everyone.

From this chase after the great white whale of moral truth has come a new and powerful literature that sees the world as a battlefield between knowledge and ignorance, good and evil, the old and the new. For example, Anthony Burgess projected the violence and the moral chaos of the 1950s into the even more violent future of *A Clockwork Orange*; and our age has taken the Burgess message to heart by turning it into a tract for the times—first in the Kubrick film version of 1971, and then in Ron Daniel's forceful stage adaptation of *A Clockwork Orange 2004* of 1990. The cult-language of the young in the 1950s becomes the invented language of Nadsat, a corrupt and brutal lingo which delimits and confirms the identity of the delinquent young. They wage a perpetual guerrilla war against the rest of their society, as the 15-year-old Alex and his three droogs make very clear from the first paragraphs—always ready to use their britvas on the creeching bugatty in order to crast some pretty polly. Burgess describes the unrelenting war of the state against the deviants—the aversion therapy of Ludovico's Technique that destroys personality. 'Kill the criminal reflex!' That is the slogan of the penal system. 'This vicious young hoodlum will be transformed out of all recognition.'

Doris Lessing has pursued similar themes of disorder and disruption through the five volumes of her *Children of Violence* series. She has looked into manifestations of violence from colonial Africa in the 1930s to the recollections of the survivors from Destroyed Area II (British Isles) described at the end of *The Four-Gated City* (1969). From that she moved on to the most original and imaginative explorations of barbarism and civilization, good and evil, empires and colonies which run through the books of the *Canopus in Argos* series.

Again, there are the comparable journeys through space and time that take William Golding to the source of all evil. In *The Lord of the Flies* (1954) he followed the trail of guilt to a wrong turning in the high Victorian period. The island in his story is a little world of great violence set in the far greater violence of a future war. The narrative is an ambush of skilful deceptions. It opens, like any Crusoe story, by a lagoon bright with coral and tropical fish,

with palm trees along the shore, and hills in the distance. Golding emphasizes
the links with *The Coral Island*, that nineteenth-century classic of improving
literature for the young. The boys Ralph and Jack are named after their forerunners in the Victorian story, and Piggy recalls the resourceful Peterkin who
was the third member of the original trio. Golding would have us remember
that their adventures in *The Coral Island* were an energetic demonstration of
the most admired Victorian values. The unfailing ingenuity and determination
of the original trio made for a faultless tale of triumphant survival; and their
boundless self-confidence took them from one heroic episode to another as
they fought their way out of many dangers. Like good Victorian adolescents,
they knew they belonged to a dominant race. 'Here is the island,' says Peterkin
after they have come ashore: 'We'll take possession of it in the name of the
king; we'll go and enter the service of its black inhabitants. Of course, we'll
rise, naturally, to the top of affairs. White men always do.' This target-rich
environment is the ideal stalking ground for Golding. The actors in his
tragedy are schoolboys, stranded on another coral island during the third
world war. There the similarities end, for the story develops into a long and
painful denial of Victorian assumptions about the natural virtue of Western
man. The boys are no better than their elders. They follow their instincts and
rapidly slip into savagery and murder. At the end, the island scorched up like
dead wood, Simon and Piggy dead, 'Ralph wept for the end of innocence, the
darkness of man's heart, and the fall through the air of the true, wise friend
called Piggy.'

After that journey from the recent past to the near future, Golding went
back to the remote beginnings and to another kind of conflict in *The Inheritors*
(1955). Again, he rejected the fashionable certainties of the past: with a calculated gesture of repudiation, he chose for the epigraph a passage from Wells's
Outline of History, that great juggernaut of the idea of progress. The little we
know about Neanderthal man, Wells had written, suggests 'a repulsive
strangeness in his appearance over and above his low forehead, his beetle
brows, his ape neck, and his inferior stature'. That was a starting-point, both
in the Wellsian history of constant moral and social improvement and in the
very different version of human origins from Golding. His story opens with
one of the most subtle and imaginative accounts in modern fiction. Bare, elementary language invites participation in the life of a primitive people. In that
ancient, mythic time of the lost paradise the Neanderthals live in a close, intuitive, and harmonious association. They have no concepts; they can barely
communicate. Were they one of nature's failures, marked for disappearance
before the higher and the better? What is higher and better? And the history
books answer: *Homo sapiens*. For Golding, however, very conscious of what
Homo sapiens has been doing in the twentieth century, the old Wellsian doctrine of progress is void of meaning. He leads on to the fatal climax, when the

innocent primitives meet their killers—rational, organized, inventive tribesmen with clothes, weapons, canoes, and a code of social behaviour. These, says Golding, are your true men, the destroyers of the future for other peoples. The final episodes resonate against the recollected experiences of modern times—lethal technologies, senseless slaughter, triumphant imperialisms.

Jean-Paul Sartre expressed similar views after he had attended a performance of *The Trojan Women* during the Algerian War. The play by Euripides, he said, 'had a precise political significance when it was first produced. It was an explicit condemnation of war in general, and of imperial expeditions in particular. We know today that war would trigger off an atomic war in which there would be neither victor nor vanquished.'[14] Sartre's response was to make his own adaptation of *The Trojan Women*, and British audiences heard the English version for the first time during the Edinburgh Festival of 1966. In the last lines the god Poseidon has the same message for the Greece of 440BC and the France of AD 1965:

> You stupid bestial mortals
> Making war, burning cities,
>
> > violating tombs and temples,
> > torturing your enemies,
> > bringing suffering on yourselves.
>
> Can't you see
> War
> Will kill you:
> All of you?

The sentiments are most familiar—the matter of countless homilies, the cause of innumerable demonstrations and peace-marches throughout the world, the objective of some successful arms reduction treaties, and the primary source of ideas for most of the future catastrophe stories that have appeared since Hiroshima. Unfortunately, sentiments do not of themselves create policies. Sentiment did not hold back Saddam Hussein from the war against Iran and the invasion of Kuwait. 'War cannot abolish itself': that was the conclusion of the late Field-Marshal Montgomery at the end of his long *History of Warfare*. The peculiar problem of modern war, he wrote, is that 'nuclear weapons have given mankind a choice between either abolishing war or being abolished by it'; and he went on to say with great emphasis: '*What has got to be achieved is a resolution of the political and ideological differences which divide the world*; unless this is first done, nuclear disarmament is likely to increase the likelihood of "conventional" war.'[15]

The Montgomery proposition marks the most recent stage in the long debate between the proponents of the military technologies and the self-appointed guardians of the future which began with the first prodigious advances of the industrial revolution. Two hundred years ago, when the British kept watch along the Channel coast for an expected French invasion of the United Kingdom, the worst fears of the defenders did not get beyond fantasies of landing craft propelled by windmills. The inventors, however, had a clearer view of coming things. In 1810 Robert Fulton published *Torpedo War and Submarine Explosions*, in which he set out his proposals for a new weapon and a new kind of warfare. His torpedoes would have the immediate advantage of removing the ships of the Royal Navy from the oceans of the world. There would be an even greater advantage, Fulton maintained; and he made the first statement of the first strategic defence initiative: the introduction of the new weapon would lead to a Pax Americana and the end of wars. Seven years later, Sir George Cayley was happily experimenting with an early model of the flying machine. He knew very well that success would lead to the use of the aeroplane in war, yet he was confident that everything would work out for the best. His reasons have proved to be a major argument in the war-and-peace debate. Cayley said in 1817, and a distinguished general wrote in 1968, that any major advance in the military technologies would compel society to reconsider the use of destructive weapons. That sanguine belief was a climactic point in Tennyson's 'Locksley Hall' of 1842, where the poet looked forward with delight to 'all the wonder that would be'. The coming conquest of the air would bring peace to the world; for one day the last battle in world history would be fought in the skies:

> Heard the heavens fill with shouting, and there rain'd a ghastly dew
> From the nations' airy navies grappling in the central blue;
> Far along the world-wide whisper of the south-wind rushing warm,
> With the standards of the people plunging thro' the thunder-storm,
> Till the war-drum throbb'd no longer, and the battle-flags were furl'd
> In the Parliament of Man, the Federation of the world.

Forty-four years later, after many wars and after the new-style War of 1870, Tennyson returned to thoughts of his younger days. The old man reconsidered his ardent hopes for the future of mankind in 'Locksley Hall: Sixty Years After'; and the experience of a lifetime made him reject out of hand the belief in inevitable progress that resounds throughout the earlier poem. Technology had not lived up to his expectations. The sense of the marvellous had vanished from those first 'triumphs over time and space'. There were no signs of the moral and social improvements he had anticipated; and world peace was still a dream. As the interrogator of his age, Tennyson put the question: 'Earth at last a warless world, a single race, a single tongue?' And he was moved to answer in dismay:

> Warless? when her tens are thousands, and her thousands millions, then—
> All her harvest all too narrow—who can fancy warless men?

Warless? war will die out late then. Will it ever? late or soon?
Can it, till this outworn earth be dead as yon dead world the moon?

The angry verse of 1886 exemplifies a fundamental ambivalence in our attitudes to the dangers of war and the problems of peace. The most prolific and
most popular English poet of the nineteenth century dreamed of peace but
wrote about war in poems that were favourite entries in Victorian books of
recitation. Tennyson had helped to form national opinion on the issues of
peace and war: on military preparedness in 'Riflemen Form!', on the vital role
of the Royal Navy in 'The Fleet', on imperialism in 'The Defence of
Lucknow'. His most famous piece on death and duty, 'The Charge of the
Light Brigade', still has a place in the anthologies and the curricula of British
schools. Tennyson took his duties as Poet Laureate seriously. In the twelve
books of *The Idylls of the King* he gave the Victorians an instructive narrative
of high romance, noble endeavour, and courageous achievements. The spirit of
the master lives on today in the heroic episodes of the *Star Trek* series and
especially in the epic struggle between good and evil that the scriptwriters
have made the principal theme of *Star Wars, The Empire Strikes Back*, and *The
Return of the Jedi*.

This evident distancing of warfare is not a subtle argument for peace. It is
the best that can be done nowadays to accommodate an obsessive interest in
human conflict at a time when the enormity of modern weapons has altered
the scale of destruction and has thereby abolished the traditional associations
between war and individual heroism. And yet, the business of war is still the
greatest single enterprise on our planet: everywhere there are ministries for the
armed forces, tens of millions in the fighting services, annual manoeuvres to
assess their readiness for combat, vast and most profitable industries dedicated
to the manufacture of new weapons and better machines, and a non-stop flood
of books about the wars that have been and the wars that will be. The annual
bibliographies record the hundreds of volumes that pour out every year on
bygone campaigns and past wars, on successful commanders and their battles,
and on famous engagements from Marathon to the Falklands and the Gulf
War. Everywhere the paperback sections of the bookshops confirm this abiding
interest in warfare. Nelson still takes the *Victory* through the enemy line to
engage the *Bucentaure* at Trafalgar; the US Marine divisions storm ashore at
Iwo Jima; and by June 1991 the first accounts of Operation Desert Storm were
going through the press.

A surprise awaits those readers who scan the shelves in search of forecasts
and projections about a third world war. They will not find many titles. In
another stack, however, there will be rows of books under 'Galactic warfare'—
yarns of every kind of encounter with the enemy in deep space and serial stories of planetary adventures. Most of these are American in origin, like the

Retief cycle by Keith Laumer, the heroic *Dorsai* tales by Gordon Dickson, and the most recent addition to this fiction, the *Biowarriors* trilogy by Robert E. Vardeman.

These tales of interplanetary warfare, like the parallel battle fantasies of survivalist fiction that began in the 1980s, mark yet another shift of direction in the literature of future warfare. The further these stories move away from their traditional task of immediate admonition and earnest warning, the less they have to do with the most probable shape of a future war. Although the old delight in technological marvels and the taste for aggressive adventure stories continue, there is no place left for them in the world we know. Before 1914 it had been general practice in this type of fiction for writers to project the military possibilities of their day into the following year or the next decade; but ever since Hiroshima, the work of the old-time tales of destroyers and airships in action has for the most part been carried on in totally changed circumstances. The modern jargon of blaster guns, power fields, atomic weapons, and space-ships is the martial language of a future that has no more than an occasional and allegorical connection with the condition of our times. Here, at this point where purposive fiction gives way to far-fetched tales of heroic adventures, the wars of the future reach their most fantastic development. In the remote epoch of galactic civilization, when the inhabitants of Terra have penetrated to the farthest regions of the universe, the old tale of future warfare becomes a ritual game in which it cannot possibly matter to the reader how many millions are snuffed out. Thus, the realities of our world— nuclear weapons, the Cold War, the cauldron of the Near East—dissolve into reassuring patterns of a new age of discovery. Vast machines voyage through infinite space and the White Man—especially *Homo americanus*—is forever triumphant, for ever dominant in a future that knows no insurmountable problems.

These are tales of the heart's desire. In the remote future and far away in the galaxies, the happy readers can enjoy a holiday of the mind: peace, prosperity, highly advanced technologies, uncomplicated adventures, and wars so distant in time that they have no menace in them. Most of them read like stories written by Zane Grey and Edgar Rice Burroughs. The cowboys of the western frontier have moved out to the interstellar ranges of the galaxies. What happens out there has little to do with science, although their fantastic wars are often presented with careful attention to an absurd pseudo-scientific jargon.

The book stacks have another surprise for readers, especially for that familiar angel-demon of contemporary mythology, the space-traveller who has come to investigate the bizarre activities of the Terrans. The planetary visitor will find that, although there are not many stories like *Fail Safe* (1962), and *Two Hours to Doom* (1958), which describe how the world came close to disaster, there are whole shelves of books about life in the after-time. The diverse stories in this catalogue of the coming catastrophe—*Earthwreck* (1974), *Dark December* (1960), *The Last Continent* (1970), *The Chrysalids* (1955), *The Fallen Sky* (1954), *Twilight World* (1961), *The Long Voyage Back* (1983), and *Regenesis* (1983), for example—run through all the possibilites. They go from the promise of total extinction and the most desperate of futures to the subdued hope that civilized life will continue somewhere on earth or in the solar system.

And here the sharp-eyed planetary investigator on a first reconnaissance mission to Terra would notice the small section of books dedicated to fore-telling the most likely course of a third world war. These reveal an instructive imbalance. There are the projections—the majority—that find reasons to expect an encouraging conclusion to any confrontation between East and West; and there are the few well-informed accounts that describe the real terrors of a nuclear war. That is the most astonishing fact of all in this literature. For some forty years, these tales of the war-to-come have poured from the presses—everything from the initial drama of the count-down to the last days of humankind—and yet there are no more than half-a-dozen stories that describe The Day when the cities are obliterated. In one of these rare projec-tions, *Ende* (1983), the German author takes his readers through the thirty-four days of the third world war and makes them experience the total destruction of familiar places:

The grotesque sight of the place where Mainz and Wiesbaden once were. . . . A single, ashen-grey wasteland, a flattened, vast bed of dust, as if it had been levelled off by some huge roller. Here and there black smudges, still smoke, fire storms! Biebrick and the western parts of Mainz have disappeared under a lake.

It is not surprising that the best of these nuclear horror stories are the work of women. Judith Merril in *Shadow on the Hearth* (1950) and Helen Clarkson in *The Last Day* (1959) set their stories in the one place where the nuclear weapons will have the worst imaginable effect—in the family and in close human relationships. One day the external forces of politics and military power explode within the dedicated centre of the home and of familial affections. Thus, two women writers apply the only valid human measure to the abom-inable consequences of a monstrous technology; they centre everything on the fear, suffering, agony, and painful death of friends, children, parents, wives, and husbands, and on the appalling problems of trying to maintain the home and live as normal a life as they can during the great disruption.

Only one book can compare with these two stories as a different but equally well-informed account of a nuclear exchange, and that is *Warday, and the Journey Onwards* (1984) by the American journalists Whitley Strieber and James Kunteka. These authors take a man's-eye view of the great catastrophe;

they are factual and analytical in all the major details of their projection. The scale changes from the microcosm of the family to the macrocosm of the nation. The tone shifts from the familiar and friendly to the impersonal and measured statements of the historian. The chosen form is the documentary report, for that allows the authors to introduce every device from casualty statistics and interviews with government officials to newspaper reports. Their war begins with a Soviet nuclear attack at 4.20 pm on 28 October 1988, within minutes of which the American response follows. Thirty-six minutes later the war is over. Six million Americans are dead, and the cities of New York, San Antonio, and Washington DC are little more than craters and radioactive rubble. Five years after that, two friends set off on a journey across America to see and to record the last days of a great world power. This projection of the apparently inevitable disaster, like those of Judith Merril and Helen Clarkson, had followed from the initial assumption that any East-West conflict must end with the swift destruction of the warring nations. But that could not be the whole future, since there remained the still unanswered questions: Would contemporary military thinking on the deterrent effect of nuclear weapons prove to be correct? Would the Atlantic Alliance survive in any full-scale war with the Warsaw Pact countries?

The answer came in the best military manner—sudden, unexpected, and exceptionally well prepared—in the *The Third World War: A Future History*. The book first appeared in 1978 and it immediately seized the high ground in the modern literature of future warfare. The co-ordinator of this collective work was General Sir John Hackett, undoubtedly the most senior officer to secure a commanding position for himself in the turbulent history of this fiction. The response to *The Third World War* proved even greater than the excitement that Admiral Colomb and his associates had caused close on a century before with their account of *The Great War of 1892*. Moreover, the book has enjoyed a national and international success on the same scale as the legendary triumph of William Le Queux's *Invasion of 1910*, with sales of more than two million copies, translations into ten languages, and a pirated edition from Taiwan; it provided summer reading for Mrs Thatcher, and there were reports that it had been seen next to the Bible on the desk of President Reagan. What Chesney did for nineteenth-century warfare and the politics of defence in his *Battle of Dorking*, the contributors to *The Third World War* have done for the armaments and alliances of modern times. Sir John Hackett brought great knowledge and exceptional experience to his task as writer-in-chief for *The Third World War*. He is an Honorary Fellow of New College, Oxford, and he was Principal of King's College in the University of London from 1968 to 1975. His military career has been the record of constant advance: commissioned into the cavalry, transferred to the Parachute Regiment, wounded at Arnhem, Commandant of the Royal Military College of

Science, GOC in C Northern Ireland, Deputy Chief Imperial General Staff, and finally Commander-in-Chief British Army of the Rhine.

The history of *The Third World War*, however, did not start from a military initiative. It began as a thought that came to the managing director of the publishers Sidgwick and Jackson when he perceived that the market lacked a serious study of a possible war between NATO and the Warsaw Pact countries. William Armstrong found the ideal author for the military projection he had in mind when he attended the annual Waterloo Lecture at Sandhurst and heard Sir John Hackett speak on Napoleon and Wellington. He commissioned the book during a meeting at a London club. The general then assembled the team of experts; and there were three plenary sessions to agree on the main lines of the projected campaign. The collaborators wrote their narratives, and Sir John Hackett worked these into the projected history of *The Third World War*. In the Author's Note at the end of the book, the co-ordinator made two important points: that the contributors did not seek 'to suggest that a war is bound to happen, or even that it is likely'; and that to reduce expenditure on defence was to increase the possibility of war:

We who have put this book together know very well that the only forecast that can be made with any confidence of the course and outcome of another world war, should there be one, is that nothing will happen exactly as we have shown here. There is the possibility, however, that it could. There is also the very high probability that, unless the West does a great deal within the next few years to improve its defences, a war with the Warsaw Pact could end in early disaster.

The account in *The Third World War* is the most detailed and well-informed projection in the history of these imaginary wars. The self-evident authority of the narrative follows from the exceptionally wide range of knowledge the collaborators brought to their work. Their team of all-the-talents included an air chief marshal, a NATO commander North Atlantic, the deputy editor of *The Economist*, and a former British ambassador to Turkey. Their scenario for the War of 1985 has, however, shown early signs of a benign ageing. It came from the dark age of the Cold War, when Iran was a close and powerful ally of the United States, and it was still prudent to assume that the Soviet Union would take the greatest risks—even go to war—in order to maintain its interests in Eastern Europe.

The book's political brief was the work of Viktor Suvorov, who had commanded a motor rifle company in the invasion of Czechoslovakia; and he forecast that strikes in Poland would make the Russians act in order to maintain their hold on the Warsaw Pact countries. The fiction begins when the Politburo decides to implement the Ryabukhin Plan, a scheme that started from the proposition that: 'The position in Poland makes it important that we should put the Americans in a position of weakness somewhere else, and *ensure*

that some humiliating retreats have to be undertaken by the Americans.'
Operations commence in November 1984, and all goes well with the main
stages of the plan. The Russians encourage the Egyptians to take control of
the Saudi and Iraqi oil fields; they promote guerrilla activities against South
Africa; and they serve notice on all would-be dissident members of the
Warsaw Pact by an overnight occupation of Yugoslavia. The United States
calls for a meeting of the Security Council and sends a unit of Marines to
Ljubljana airfield. In this most up-to-date of projections, television is seen to
be a potent element in modern warfare. An Italian cameraman records—and
the world sees—the first encounter when the US Marines destroy three
Russian tanks on the outskirts of Kostanjevica. It was the beginning of the
third world war.

From the start of hostilities at 0400 hours on 4 August 1985, the detailed
narratives combine command appraisals of the main engagements—air, sea,
land—with episodes that recount the actions of the combat units as the
Russian divisions advance westwards. The critical day is 15 August, when
reinforcements make possible a counter-offensive. And here the narrative
pauses for a comment about the defence of the West. The day would be 'a
major turning point in the whole battle for Europe . . .':

What would have happened if the Alliance had done as little for its defences in the
past quinquennium as in the wasted years before is, as we look back today,
painfully evident. The Russians would by this time have been secure on their stop-
line on the Rhine, the Western Alliance would have lain in ruins, and the brutal
obliteration of the Federal Republic of Germany would already have begun.

As the Russian offensive comes to a halt and the hard men in the Kremlin face
the possibility of defeat, they seek to rescue what they can by a nuclear strike
on one city: Birmingham. Within the hour two submarines, one British and
the other American, had launched their nuclear missiles and the town of
Minsk had been obliterated—end of the war, and the beginning of the end for
the Soviet Union. The final chapter on 'The Beginning of the Future' is more
of an exhortation than a prediction. It looks forward to closer ties between the
European nations, the admission of Eastern Germany to the EC, and the
extension of the Community so that there will be one Europe from the
Atlantic to the Urals.

That was not the end of the matter. Within four years sudden political
tremors had altered the political landscape of 1978. Question marks began to
appear about the balance of the equations in *The Third World War*. The situation was no longer what it had been in Poland, Iran, and Egypt. And so the
collaborators felt that the new set of circumstances obliged them 'to take a further look at the events we imagined then and to amplify and explore them a
little further'. The result appeared in 1982 with the title of *The Third World*

War: The Untold Story. The new version bears witness to the rate of change—that Great Satan of twentieth-century stability—for it is the first reconsideration and rewriting of a future war story in the history of the genre. Although circumstances might have changed, Sir John Hackett took care to point out that the message remained the same:

the scene here and there has changed. The Shah has gone. Egypt is no longer dependent on the Soviet Union. The story we now offer takes account of these events. Our purpose, however, has remained the same. It is to tell a cautionary tale (with such adjustment as the passage of time suggests) in an attempt to persuade the public that if, in a dangerous and unstable world, we wish to avoid a nuclear war we must be prepared for a conventional one.

The great success of *The Third World War* suggests that Sir John Hackett and his associates did the world a service in 1978 by offering readers their collective and carefully considered last word on the probable conduct of a war between East and West. The calm language, the total absence of rant and triumphalism, the wealth of detail, and the abundant evidence of great professional experience—these were positive encouragements to take a cool look at modern warfare. Indeed, the success of the *Third World War* broke the dead man's grip of the nuclear disaster stories. Suddenly writers felt free to present their own variants on the subject of future warfare; and in consequence, the 1980s saw a modest revival of the old tradition of describing 'The Next Great War'. In 1980 the former British naval officer, John Wingate, led the way with the first of three stories in which he described the typical operations of frigates, carriers, and submarines in the modern war at sea. Again in 1980, another British writer began a series of five stories that described small-unit fighting in Germany during a conventional war between East and West.[16] And then in 1982, an expert on Russian politics, John Bradley, produced another Russian attack on the West in the *Illustrated History of World War Three*, a conflict that ends when the French destroy Kiev with nuclear missiles and the Russians do the same to Lyons: an immediate armistice follows, and all parties agree on a world disarmament conference.

The new writers had the future before them and the whole world for their battlefields. One warning story, *August 1988* (1984) by General Sir David Fraser, opens with a British decision to begin unilateral disarmament and to withdraw from NATO; a Russian air division lands on Shetland, and the British have to accept the most humiliating Russian demands. Another warning story on the dangers of nuclear proliferation opens in the Middle East, which would be, according to the American authors of *The First Nuclear War* (1983), the centre of world tension in 1985. Iran and Iraq exchange nuclear missiles—Teheran, Baghdad, Kharg Island, Bandar Abbas—and the United States then threatens military action against any country that tries to intervene.

The Soviet Union concurs. Iran and Iraq agree to accept an international peace-keeping force.

The range of these stories went from world projections, like William Jackson's *The Alternative Third World War, 1985–2035* (1987), to Kenneth Macksey's small-scale study of anti-tank fighting in *First Clash: Combat Close-Up In World War Three* (1985). This was a training aid, 'an illustrated narrative of battle scenarios dealing in chronological order with the successive phases of a Battle Group's approach to and involvement in mobile defence against a Soviet Tank Division in the European setting, the summer circa 1984'.

These two stories seem to have been the last cannonade in the great war between Russia and the NATO alliance. As the prospects for permanent peace between the two groups continued to improve, in keeping with the astonishing political changes in Russia and Eastern Europe, it became more and more difficult to carry on with the imagined war of the future between East and West. In consequence, signs of strain show in *Red Thrust* (1989), where the American writer on Russian military technology, Stephen Zaloga, clearly felt it necessary to explain his failure to discuss the origins of a possible future war. His book 'tries to avoid directly addressing this issue. The decision to go to war is more in the realm of grand diplomacy and military strategy than the muddy world of small unit tactics, which is the focus of this book'. Zaloga goes on to sound what may yet prove to be the Last Post in the Forty Years War between East and West:

Indeed, as this book was being written, Mikhail Gorbachev announced unprecedented, unilateral cuts in Soviet conventional forces. After over forty years of armed tension, the Cold War seems to be finally abating. This book attempts to show how internal pressures in the Soviet armed forces helped to promote these unilateral cuts.

These accounts of the third world war were all careful projections from experts who concentrated on the application of modern weapons, on the most probable main points of engagement, and on the manoeuvres to be expected during any Russian move against the West. It was very different with the writers of conventional fiction. Although they accepted the initial proposition of a sudden and unprovoked Russian attack, they did not make an idol of probability. They preferred to follow wherever fantasy led. One version of the shooting war appears in Charles D. Taylor's *Show of Force* (1980), where US Task Force 58 takes on a Soviet battle group in the Indian Ocean in an operation dedicated to preserving the American base of Islas Piedras. Although both sides remain at peace in the sense that they do not declare war on each other, their naval forces engage in three fleet actions. Missiles take out cruisers, submarines make for the carriers, destroyers hunt and attack submarines. Peace follows—or, rather, hostilities end—when both sides can no longer sustain the action.

Another writer who told an exciting tale was Dennis Jones in *Barbarossa Red* (1985), where he had the West German Chancellor recruited by the KGB in preparation for a Russian assault on the West. A small-scale account of unit action occupies the whole of *Team Yankee* (1987), and there Howard Coyle borrows—with grateful acknowledgements—his scenario for the fighting man's experience of tank warfare from the books of Sir John Hackett.

Again, Robert Lawrence Holt drew on the accounts of Russian airborne troops in Afghanistan for his tale of the Soviet assault on Saudi Arabia in *Good Friday* (1987). In this story the Iranians seize Kuwait and then deploy an army of 300,000 on the Saudi border. That is the signal for the Russians (still the expected enemy in 1988) to send a large force of troop-carriers and fighter planes to seize the Saudi oilfields. The President of the United States tells reporters in the White House: 'Military units of the United States have intervened in Saudi Arabia . . . The oil reserves of Saudi Arabia area are vital not only to the United States, but also to our allies in Western Europe and the Far East.' The Marines land and the F-18s take on the enemy. The rest is rapid victory.

Although a swift and total victory over the Soviet Union was the desired end in these anticipations of the third world war, such endings belong to the smallest category of the future war stories. One good reason was that the prospect of defeat and destruction offered far more possibilities and much greater dramatic opportunities. Writers were free to place their stories at any point within the agreed schedule of coming disasters. They could begin at the beginning with their histories of conquest and occupation; or they could describe the desolation of the after-time; or they could tell the tale of rebirth and regeneration in the far-off future. Minor publishing industries have appeared, prospered, and declined these last forty years, as the categories of this disaster fiction enjoyed their brief moments of notoriety.

The first to fall on hard times was the tale of oppression and humiliation under an enemy occupation. Authentic and frightening echoes from the worst years of the Cold War sounded through stories that carried out the threats in their titles: *Born in Captivity* (1952), *The Conquered Place* (1954), *The Iron Hoop* (1949), *Two Rubles to Times Square* (1956), *Last Post for a Partisan* (1971), *Not This August* (1955), *Russian Hide and Seek* (1980). They reveal a hateful future when subject peoples learn to obey their masters. For example, C. M. Kornbluth records the beginning of bad times for all Americans in *Not This August*, when the Secretary of State announces the defeat of the nation:

Fellow citizens, I have been ordered to communicate to you the Articles of Surrender which were signed in Washington, DC, today by the President on behalf of the United States, by Marshal Ilya Novikov on behalf of the Union of Soviet Socialist Republics, and by Marshall Feng Chu-tsai on behalf of the Chinese People's Republic.

Although these stories are set in the time of enemy occupation, they often have little connection with the theme of foreign domination. At times they are so extravagant in their conjectures that they read like accounts of surrealistic nightmares in which nations clash with one another in the dark. At one extreme there is Russian occupation of the United Kingdom which Ted Allbeury relates in *All Our Tomorrows* (1982). All ends satisfactorily when the Chinese—Den Xiaoping in person—combine with the United States against the Soviet Union to impose an agreement upon the Russians:

The Soviet Union will withdraw its forces from all territory outside the Soviet Union including the UK, Afghanistan and the Warsaw Pact countries. It will also instruct its Cuban and South-east Asian mercenaries to cease operations wherever they might be. A separate disarmament treaty will be negotiated based not only on a reduction in arms but on a mutual defence treaty between the Soviet Union, the USA, and China.

At the other extreme there is *Russian Hide and Seek*, in which Kingsley Amis transforms the theme of a Russian occupation of the United Kingdom into an arcadian fantasy. By the year 2060, time will have erased all the worst memories of the Cold War. The Old Russia of nineteenth-century fiction is recreated in an English country setting—old families, old customs, old regiments, and old forms of address, but with the difference that a few subservient natives replace the servile Russian peasants. There is, of course, an underground movement to restore Britain to the British; but the plotters are romantic, highly inefficient young Russians.

A Russian occupation, however, could never be the greatest disaster in the revised canon of imaginary warfare. The most frightening histories of the future begin with the sudden destruction of twentieth-century civilization. After the worst has happened, when life of a sort starts again for the survivors, the scribes have to relate the event that blasted their world into a new and terrible epoch. The accounts vary from obscure folk memories of the Bad Time to fragmentary recollections of the Flame Deluge:

And the prince smote the cities of his enemies with the new fire, and for three days and nights did his great catapults and metal birds rain wrath upon them. Over each city a sun appeared and was brighter than the sun of heaven, and immediately that city withered and melted as wax under the torch, and the people therof did stop in the streets and their skins smoked and they became as fagots thrown on the coals. And when the fury of the sun had faded, the city was in flames; and a great thunder came out of the sky, like the great battering ram *PIK-A-DON*, to crush it utterly. Poisonous fumes fell over all the land, and the land was aglow by night with the afterfire and the curse of the afterfire which caused a scurf on the skin and made the hair to fall and the blood to die in the veins.[17]

Here begins the chronicle of The Atomic Disaster, The Closing, The Collapse, The Death of Cities, The Destruction, The Devastation, The Doom,

The Doom War, The Downfall, The Falling, The Flame Deluge, The Great Blast, The Great Blow Up, The Great Disaster, The Great Fire, The Great Holocaust, The Happening, The Last War, The Levelling, The Rat Bomb Wars, The Suicide War, The Thing, The Third World War to end all Wars, The Time of Destruction, The Time of Fire, The Upheaval, The War of Judgment, The War of a Thousand Suns, World War Terminus, Zero Day. The narratives go on to describe the terrors of the new time: the famous towns buried under the rubble, everywhere the stench of death in the survival areas, the deserts of fused glass where the radioactive wastelands glow at night, the roads and highways jammed with rusting vehicles, the savage packs of ferocious animals, the roving bands of rapers and looters, the cruel Bikers out for a killing, the People of the Darkness and the New People, the Contaminated Persons and the Normals, the Crazies and the Warriors, the Free Fems and the Riding Women, the Pioneer Zones and the Dark Places, the matriarchies and the patriarchies, the grotesque mutants—giant fleas, pygmies, winged men, cat people, centaurs, the seven-toes, and the two-heads.

Even these terrors do not make for the worst of all conceivable futures. The truly final disaster is the end of this world and of all human beings. That point of absolute zero has a name in *Adam and Eve 2020 AD* (1974), *After Doomsday* (1963), *Death of a World* (1948), *Earthwreck* (1974), *The Last Adam* (1952), *World in Eclipse* (1954), *Savage Tomorrow* (1983), *The Last Day* (1959), *43,000 Years Later* (1958), *The End of it All* (1962), and *On the Beach* (1957). It is not surprising that Stanley Kramer's well-known film version of *On the Beach* by Nevil Shute had considerable effect throughout the world when it first appeared in 1959. The radioactive cloud moving south towards Melbourne and the submarine voyaging the seas in search of survivors from the universal disaster—these told the story of the last days in images that required no interpretation. They were the visual counterpart of the 103 cantos in the gloomy allegory, *Aniara*, by the Swedish poet and Nobel Laureate Harry Martinson. His long poem describes an incident in the far-off future when the goldonda *Aniara* is engaged in the routine business of ferrying passengers to Mars from radiation-poisoned Earth. An accident sends the spacecraft off-course, speeding for ever towards the distant constellation of Lyra. In the last two cantos the narrator speaks for the dead and the dying. The message is for our world and our time:

> I had coveted a Paradise for this race
> but since we left the one we had destroyed
> the Zodiac's lonely night became our only home,
> a gaping chasm in which no god could hear us.
>
> The eternal mystery of Heaven's stars,
> the miracle of the celestial mechanism,

is the law but not the Gospel.
Mercy can only thrive where there is life.

We failed to grasp the true meaning of the Law,
and found an empty death in Mima's hall.
The god on whom we fixed our final hopes
lay wounded on the plains of Douris.

The unmistakable parallels with Eden and the Fall are background scenery in the contemporary morality play of the Bomb—a form of consensus fiction that acts out the final struggle between good and evil in a desolate and terrible future time. This tale of the last days begins with the knowledge that brought death into the world, and these sad projections end with recollections of the old world now lost and gone for ever. Some narratives open long after the Death Time when astronauts return from a space mission to discover, and reflect upon, an empty world, or when the barbarians of the third millennium find the ancient texts that reveal the past.[18] Other survivors live through the swift end of things: American and Russian crews in their space stations watch as nuclear missiles and biological weapons destroy all life on earth. Again, an American and a Russian submarine traverse the oceans in search of uncontaminated air, and their perilous journeys finish with the mariners' truly happy ending when the crews discover an all-female community in Southwest Ireland. They embrace their opportunities. And in like manner, far away in Antarctica the crew of an American airship survive the nuclear exchange only to find that they have been left to share an empty world with the crew of a Russian ship. The last human beings on our planet continue the war of nations until the Americans approach the Russians with a show of peace; 'and soon all of the Russian troops were walking rapidly toward the Americans. The Russian soldiers had their arms out, and they had already tossed their weapons far behind them.'

A very different morality informs the violent post-disaster stories that came to dominate the field in the 1980s. At least twenty-one of these serials have appeared so far; all but two of them are American, and all of them describe the most brutal actions with the closest attention.[19] Ryder Stacy, for example, charges through the eighteen books of his *Doomsday Warrior* stories: heroic American resistance fighters engage in a ceaseless struggle against the vile, torturing, depraved Russian occupation forces. In a more distant and even more depraved future time, six centuries after the great disaster, the barbarian survivors of the *Horseclans* series slaughter their captives, rape at will, and generally behave in the most savage manner possible. In the scribal histories of the new age, the great disaster is the half-forgotten far-off event that destroyed the towns and returned the North Americans to a state of barbarism. These serials are little more than ingenious versions of the man-to-man cowboy stories, as the titles of some make clear—*Freedom's Rangers*, *The Last Ranger*, *Turbo Cowboys*, *The Outrider*. All concentrate on the novelty of changed land-scapes, strange new warrior groups, tribal practices never recorded in any anthropological survey, and constant fighting.

Here, for instance, is a typical setting from the cycle of *The Amtrak Wars*. In the land of the feudal Ne-Issan between the Appalachians and the Eastern Sea, the principal domains are held by the descendants of the Seventh Wave: the Yama-Shita, the Yama-Ha, the Matsu-Shita, the Toh-Yota. All their sub-jects are forbidden on pain of death to attempt the reintroduction of the Dark Light, for 'the creation of the Dark Light—electricity—had corrupted mankind and led the gods to destroy The World Before with a tidal wave of golden fire'. There is, however, another world beyond the mountains . . .

beyond the Western Hills, inhabited by grass-monkeys and long-dogs: Plainfolk Mutes and Trackers—the soldier-citizens of the Amtrak Federation. The Mutes were hairy savages, semi-nomad hunters with no craft skills beyond those needed to supply their simple mode of life. All their edge-weapons, crossbows and metal implements were supplied by the Iron Masters. But the Trackers were warriors who had no fear of the Dark Light. It was the life force of their underground soci-ety. It enabled them to send images and voices through the air, it powered their weapons, their giant, caterpillar-like land-cruisers and their sky chariots.

These survivalist stories do not merit more than a brief note. In spite of the incessant and most bloody fighting, they are peripheral to, and parasitic upon, the main body of future war fiction. That is to say, the sequence of the post-disaster fiction opens in the unchanging present of the adventure story. It remains there, for ever confined within the novelty of terror, until authors find the means of giving their readers a most serious summons to accept the whole burden of humanity and face the consequences. Only then can the disaster story become a tract for our times in the revelatory manner of *The Long Tomorrow*, *A Canticle for Leibowitz*, and *Riddley Walker*. These three outstand-ing American parables for the nuclear age seek to involve readers in a long meditation on the self-ignorance and moral blindness that drive humankind to work against the best interests of all living things. They show that, although their future worlds have changed disastrously, human beings remain bound everlastingly to the cruel wheel of wrong thinking and wrong doing. Their narratives are future journeys of discovery—in person and in spirit—that reveal the failures and wrong turnings of the twentieth century. Archetypal patterns and apt parallels with the contemporary world reinforce both the timelessness of moral experience and the continuity of human history.

So, Leigh Brackett places her account of *The Long Tomorrow* (1955) within the still-living memory of the near future. The recent past is a dream of the old American paradise before The Destruction, which only the elderly can recollect. 'I can remember,' says Gran, 'on the teevee they talked about it a lot, and they showed pictures of the bombs that made clouds just like a tremendous mushroom, and each one could wipe out a city, all by itself.' The present is a life-long purgatory of repression, of strict prohibitions that forbid the use of machines, and of a conformist existence in small communities that may not contain more than one thousand inhabitants and two hundred buildings. This is the setting for a journey of discovery in which the young cousins Len and Esau Coulter, seekers after the forbidden knowledge, set off on their Promethean quest to find Bartorstown. The town exists in the Eden of the American myth, far away in the remote West, 'pieced together out of Gran's stories, and bits of sermons and descriptions of heaven. It had high buildings that went high up in the air . . . and in it there was every kind of thing that Gran had told about, machines and luxuries and pleasures.' But that image of old America would prove to be the never-never-land of an impossible dream.[20]

Leigh Brackett emphasizes the challenge of, and response to, this sad new America by relating the quest of the travellers with telling references to the glorious story of the heroic past. Their journey follows the historic trail of American expansion along the Ohio River, the chosen land for the first wave of settlers who once came westwards out of Pennsylvania and Virginia; and there are echoes of the pursuit and flight theme in *Huckleberry Finn*. Then, as they move westwards towards their own promised land, they advance along the *via sacra* of American history. From the Ohio they go by barge north into the Mississippi, then north again to join the wide Missouri—'Roll on thou mighty river'—and finally they reach the Platte River, where the wagon trains once assembled for the westward journey across the Great Plains. They leave the barge and set off like their forefathers. 'The long whips cracked and the drivers shouted. The mules leaned their necks into the collars and the wagons rolled slowly over the prairie grass, with a heavy creaking and complaint of axles.' They reach their rendezvous at the South Fork of the Platte 'in a meadow faded and sun-scorched'. It was the point where Francis Parkman recorded his own arrival in *The Oregon Trail* on 8 June 1846, at eleven o'clock in the morning. He noted that 'the hills were dotted with little tufts of shrivelled grass, but betwixt these the white sand was glaring in the sun'. *Incipit vita nova*.

As it was in the beginning, when Americans first sought their future beyond the Great Plains, so is it now in the desolation of The Destruction. Although all signs of the old America have passed away, these pioneers of time-to-come are called to repeat in their own way the national epic of the frontier. The reader is led to ask: Will the new generation use their second chance to recreate the old America? The answer begins with the discovery that Bartorstown is not what the two travellers expected. The secret nuclear installation may be the worst imaginable evil in that new world, but it is also a serious call to pass judgement on the dilemmas of good science and evil applications. Young Len comes to maturity when he accepts the primacy of the moral will. 'Time goes on without any of us. Only a belief, a state of mind, endures, and even that changes constantly; but underneath there are two main kinds—the one that says, Here you must stop knowing, and the other which says, Learn.'

The future for Walter Miller in his *Canticle for Leibowitz* (1959) has to be a long history of challenge and response. He requires millennia so that he can use the events of the sixth century AD to throw light on his projected cycle of destruction and restoration. Long ago, in the dark times after the Roman Empire, the Benedictine monks saved what they could of the old learning; and in time-to-come after a devastating nuclear war the monks of the Albertian Order of Saint Leibowitz will once again preserve the books that contain the ancient knowledge. The cultural parallel is both occasion and context for Miller's sustained moral colloquy on God and Mammon. The monks in his story repeat through the centuries the Christian rejection of secular values. Their monastery is the City of God—the stability of the moral order in a shifting, dangerous epoch. So, in the course of time there is another renaissance; science is rediscovered, the secrets of the atom are tracked down, and once more in the thirty-eighth century the world comes to the brink of destruction. Miller puts the question of questions in the mouth of Abbot Zerchi:

Are we doomed to do it again and again? Have we no choice but to play the Phoenix in an unending sequence of rise and fall? Assyria, Babylon, Egypt, Greece, Carthage, Rome, the Empires of Charlemagne and the Turk. Ground to dust and plowed with salt. Spain, France, Britain, America—burned into the oblivion of the centuries. And again and again and again.

As a nuclear war begins, a space-ship takes off for the planets with a party of children in accordance with the papal instructions contained in *Quo peregrinatur grex*. Whatever may happen to our world, the race of man must not die out. *Resurgemus*.

Learn or perish: that is the common text for these tales of the nuclear catastrophe. Indeed, learning is the beginning and the end of *Riddley Walker* (1980), for Russell Hoban opens his story with a puzzle for the reader: 'On my naming day when I come 12 I gone front spear and kilt a wyld boar he parbly ben the las wyld pig on the Bundel Downs . . .' The eye takes in the changed orthography—*agen, noatis, smoak, girzly, tremmering*—and the language confirms that young Riddley writes in a form of Post Modern English which reflects perfectly the spear-and-bow culture of a primitive society. Russell Hoban, an American writer long domiciled in England, tells a riddling tale which is undoubtedly the most subtle and original of all the post-disaster stories. The book is a marvel of lexical inventiveness. Hoban exploits the resources of historical linguistics to create a language that nobody has ever spoken and yet every word adds to the impression of social degradation and vernacular corruption. The medium is in part the message, for Hoban maintains a rigorous control of his language so that he can employ words to establish the social geography of his future Inland. Elementary spelling, primitive punctuation, folk etymologies, a simple and often crude vocabulary—these sketch the psychic background of the future people and they reveal the determination and honesty of that seeker-after-truth, Riddley Walker. In a seemingly artless way, young Riddley writes down the brief account of his life. Gradually the map of his future Inland fills with names that locate the action in south-east Kent: Cambry is obviously Canterbury, Do it Over is Dover, Fork Stoan is Folkestone. In the common style of these future histories, young Riddley pieces together his account of the past. Before the Bad Time there are vague recollections of happier days in a better age which ended when knowledge and the desire for power shattered the primal harmony between man and nature. These tribal memories cause Riddley to reflect that by 'the time they done 1997 years they had boats in the air and all them things and here are weve done 2347 years and mor and stil slogging in the mud'. This is the familiar history of the great disaster which opens with the Berstyn Fyr and the destruction of Canterbury:

They had the Nos. of the sun and moon all fractions out and fed to the machines. They said, 'Wewl put all the Nos. in to 1 Big 1 and that wil be the No. of the Master Chaynjis.' They bilt the Power Ring thats where you see the Ring Ditch now. They put in the 1 Big 1 and woosht it roun there come a flash of lite then bigger nor the woal worl and it ternt the nite to day. Then every thing gone black. Nothing only nite for years on end. Playgs kilt people off and naminals nor there went nothing growit in the groun. Man and woman starveling in the blackness looking for the dog to eat it and the dog out looking to eat them the same. Finely there comne day agen then nite and day regler but neer like it ben befor.

Riddley is the centre of the story. He records all he sees, all he experiences, and all that he can discover about the past. And so, when he sets off for Cambry, the narrative becomes a journey of discovery for the reader. As Riddley learns from his experiences, it becomes evident that this future people are caught up in the dangerous triad of knowledge-progress-consequences. They have rediscovered gunpowder, and the first reinvented bomb has caused the first deaths and wiped out the government of Inland. Riddley learns from that crude exercise in power that 'Its not the sturgling for Power thats where the Power is. Its in jus lettin your self be where it is. Its tuning in to the worl its leaving your self behynt . . . ' And so said Len Coulter long before young Riddley, and so Abbot Zerchi would say in his turn.

The line of this disaster fiction runs straight and true, from *Ape and Essence* to *Riddley Walker* and to the most recent variation on the common theme, *Die letzten Kinder von Schewenborn* (1983). As long as nuclear weapons continue to exist, nation will speak to nation in the common language of the fear that unites the peoples of our planet. And yet the terror-to-come can prove to be both the end of things and the start of a better life for the survivors. Thus the Orcadian poet Edwin Muir plucks hope out of fear in his poem 'The Horses', where he employs a symbolist technique to describe the sudden death of the self-sufficient and self-satisfied technological society. The poem appears in the collection *One Foot in Eden*, which Muir began writing in the Orwellian year of 1949 soon after he had taken up his post as director of the British Institute in Rome. The experience of living in the Eternal City reinforced Muir's sense of the timeless, prompting thoughts on creation, time, human survival, and the harmony of Eden. These themes come together in 'The Horses', which opens abruptly and in the apocalyptic manner barely twelve months after 'the seven days war that put the world to sleep'. Death and rebirth, man and nature, good and evil, the mechanical and the spontaneous—these contraries give great power and meaning to the poem. It opens at the zero point of a world in the last days of self-destruction:

> On the second day
> The radios failed; we turned the knobs; no answers.
> On the third day a warship passed us, heading north,
> Dead bodies piled on the deck. On the sixth day
> A plane plunged over us into the sea. Thereafter
> Nothing. The radios dumb;
> And still they stand in corners of our kitchens,
> And stand, perhaps, turned on, in a million rooms
> All over the world. But now if they should speak,
> If on a sudden they should speak again,
> If on the stroke of midnight a voice should speak,
> We would not listen, we would not let it bring
> The bad old world that swallowed its children quick
> At one great gulp.

Muir finds reasons for hope, however, in the broken world where the tractors lie useless and rusting on the fields. A distant tapping along the road, a drumming that changes to hollow thunder, and the horses come in a wild wave. There is a lesson there in the new relationship between the survivors and the animals: 'Our life is changed; their coming our beginning.'[21]

That rejection of the bad old world is the rite of passage to the new and better life on the other side of the great divide between the calamitous past and the more hopeful future. There the pessimistic anticipations of the disaster-to-come receive their joyous contradiction in many tales that begin with the collapse of civilization and end with a happier life in the future. Hope for the sake of hope keeps on breaking in with a vision of the time when a purged and regenerate group, or a nation, or even all humankind, has learnt the lesson the Old People failed to understand in their time. The matter of these stories of rebirth and renewal is the heroic drama of human survival— Crusoe adventures, journeys into the unknown, escapes from repressive societies of the after-time, warrior myths of the fight for freedom. These tales of before-and-after begin with the burial of the dead past, and they develop into initiation rites for the next stage in human evolution. Their histories lead up to the moment of total discontinuity when the survivors learn to reject 'the bad old world that swallowed its children quick'; and then in symbolic fashion they cross the mountain range, or strike out across the ocean, or start on the foundations of the new city.

One of the earliest of these tales was George Borodin's *Spurious Sun* which appeared in 1948. It opened with a world driven mad by devastating wars and great destruction; and then the world's children begin a campaign for peace which opens the way to universal peace and understanding. Another excellent example of this fiction is John Wyndham's *The Chrysalids* (1955), which used the tell-all title of *Rebirth* for the American edition of the same year. In the bad times after The Thing, the human race has a hope of regeneration in a race of benign telepaths who act without violence against their would-be exterminators; they make contact with New Zealand, where civilization has survived, and they leave to play their part in the renewal of mankind. Another variant was Paul MacTyre's *Midge* (1962), a post-holocaust story which carried the hope that the remnants of humanity would learn true brotherhood and wisdom from the swarms of intelligent, telepathic, and highly moral insects that emerged after the great disaster. Although the catastrophic origins of these stories do not promise well for the future of the survivors, somehow, and in ways not explained, a mysterious impulse will transform the feckless blundering Old Adam into a new and better human being. So, as late as 1985 this wilful fantasy of renewal was the subject matter of Louise Lawrence's *Children of the Dust*—from the final war to the time when the purified and regenerate survivors evolve into the new species of *Homo superior*.

These tales of the resurrection-to-come hold the balance of hope between the promised extinction of life on planet Earth, as exemplified in Nevil Shute's tale of the last days in *On the Beach*, and the desperate condition of the survivors in post-warfare stories like *Ape and Essence*. This begin-again fiction may be a collective vote of confidence in the human capacity to learn from past errors, but many of the stories read like a sustained refusal to accept the possibility that humanity could be for the dark. Their titles are statements of survival—*The Long Way Back* (1954), *The Survivors* (1965), *City of the First Time* (1975), *Forty Years On* (1958), *The Last Space Ship* (1952), *Songs from the Stars* (1980), *Utopia 239* (1955). Like the other forms of future war fiction, however, these survival stories have gone into a rapid decline since the late

1980s; and the most recent specimens (Michael Reaves and Steve Perry's *Dome* (1988), for example) have little to say about the origin of the world disaster.

Indeed, the traditional power of the male as saviour and innovator is no longer the primary condition for human survival: in some of the most recent American tales women describe how women have assumed the dominant role as saviours of the human race. In Sheri Tepper's *The Gate to Women's Country* (1988), women keep the peace in the cities while the warrior males go on fighting the good fight outside; and in Joan Slonczewski's *The Wall Around Eden* (1989) the women are again the guardians of the life force.

However, there is justice of a kind for the men in those other stories of the great natural disasters that wipe out most of the human race. Men cannot be held responsible for the virus epidemics and the plagues, the devastating earthquakes, the droughts and the floods, the mutant rats and the killer-bees, the onset of a new ice age, or the other natural catastrophes—all those uncovenanted accidents that put an end to civilization. These stories repeat the pattern that evolved in futuristic fiction after the First World War; and once again the action starts in the recognizable contemporary world. The authors have transposed the anxieties aroused by the Bomb to a setting in which mankind will eventually triumph over the most desperate catastrophes. They describe the worst that could happen and then show how there is every reason to expect that the indomitable human spirit will be equal to the most terrible adversities. And—most important fact of all—this type of fiction is common to modern industrial society.

There have been American, English, French, German, and Japanese versions that all tell the same story of catastrophe and survival. After floods and earthquakes have destroyed the continents in Freder Van Holk's *Weltuntergang* (1954), a new primal pair restores the race of man. Again, in that very successful story *Earth Abides* (1949) by the American writer George Stewart, the few survivors of a world-wide virus epidemic (Americans, of course) go back to their origins and become a tribe of hunters. That story opens in the characteristic end-of-things style with the first sentence: '. . . and the Government of the United States of America is herewith suspended, except in the District of Columbia, as of the emergency.' The survivors, the chosen people of nature, learn to live by the new law. Another Abraham unites the tribe, binding them to their compact with nature; and at the end, as he lies dying, he looks at the young men who will follow after him. 'They will commit me to the earth,' he thinks: and then the story ends with a message for the modern world: 'Yet I also commit them to the earth. There is nothing else by which men live. *Men go and come, but earth abides.*'

All these prophecies of the great renewal have the same theme of casual destruction and determined reconstruction. They are myths of encouragement for a time of troubles. For that reason their authors have been careful to avoid all reference to contemporary anxieties—never a word about the East–West confrontation which has been the source for so many tales of the conflict-to-come. They are the purest of fictions, without any trace of the original sins of technological society; they are utopian epics of the final harmony that will come when the new people enter their promised land. They have their place in the scale of measured responses to contemporary anxieties that opens with the Cold War espionage fantasies, goes on to the third world war and to the destruction of our world or the extinction of humankind, and ends with the painful restoration and hard-won reconstruction after the greatest calamities in future history. They describe disasters as great as any nuclear war. But they are not the end of things, because the earth has not been poisoned, and some human beings are well enough and have supplies enough to make a fresh start. This has the exhilarating effect of returning humankind to the Promethean stage of an empty world and to the solitary group destined to start once more on the whole sequence of development from tribe to nation.

This going back to an aboriginal or an uncomplicated pastoral condition throws up archetypal images of survival and achievement. A new Adam and Eve walk the Earth again. The Aeneas theme of perilous adventures and the foundation of a city had great meaning for the anxious modern world during the worst years of the Cold War. For example, in *The Death of Grass* (1956) the message comes through loud and clear in the last line of all. As the hero goes out to the settlement, he turns to the heroine: 'There's a lot to do. A city to be built.' The same assurance of renewal is the source of power in *The Day of the Triffids*, and it sounds triumphantly through the final lines: '. . . when we, or our children, or their children, will cross the narrow straits in the great crusade to drive the triffids back and back with ceaseless destruction until we have wiped the last one from the face of the land that they have usurped.'

Imagine that the ice fields of Antarctica slide into the sea. The world climate changes overnight, the oceans rise, vast cities vanish, 600 million people perish. In Crawford Kilian's *Ice Quake* (1979) the few indomitable survivors are equal to the universal disaster. 'We're new,' they say. 'If this really is a new Ice Age starting, we're the first people who've had to live in it.' Yesterday and its web of personal associations and political obligations have vanished. They will remake their world as they want it to be: 'If we owe loyalty to anyone, it's to the people who come after us.'

A more recent and most ambitious variant on the theme of mortal peril and hard-won survival is the tale of world's end in Arthur C. Clarke's *The Songs of Distant Earth* (1986). In the year 2008 all the peoples of the world hear the news that around the year 3600, plus or minus 75, the sun will become a nova. In the time remaining, generation after generation, the great seedships set off for the new homes in the region of Alpha Centauri A. Earth may pass away, but the race of man will go on and on, somewhere and somehow. In this new celestial harmony mankind is made immortal with a phrase.

To everything there is a season, said the Preacher; and these prophets of the last days answer that there is also a time to every purpose under the heaven. Indeed, time has been of the essence in these tales of the future, ever since the anonymous author of the *Reign of George VI* (1763) felt it necessary to explain why his history was 'taken up at a what's-to-come period, and begun at an aera that will not begin these hundred years'. The explanations soon vanished, and by the time *The Battle of Dorking* appeared in 1871 the connections between today and tomorrow had become part of the established chronology in tales of future warfare. The historians of coming things have always taken care to set a beginning and an end for their accounts of the wars-to-come. They assign a month and a year for the day of victory or of defeat. They project the consequences of a nuclear exchange into the desolate societies of the third millennium, and they even go forward to the destruction of our planet and the end of time.

The decided historicity of the narratives is the necessary mode for a form of fiction that can only begin to find an appropriate shape after the authors have chosen one item from the register of contemporary possibilities. In this way what is no more than potential in its day seems to become authentic and verifiable in the tale of tomorrow. Thus, the French make their expected landings from across the Channel around the year 1800; the Germans enter London in triumph in 1910; and the third world war begins in 1985. This imagined continuity between today and tomorrow is central to the tale of consequences; for the paradox woven into this most ephemeral of fiction is the authors' belief that, like the Roman augurs, they can open up the future for inspection even to the point of crying *Absit omen!* That belief undoubtedly holds good for the tales of future wars, and authors can go on delivering their messages for as long as the readers agree upon the scale of probabilities; but once the political and military context changes, there is an immediate all-change in the fiction. So, Nelson's victory at Trafalgar removed the French invasion stories from the contemporary book of the future; and after the Entente Cordiale of 1904 the Germans took the place of the French as the future enemy in any tale of 'The Next Great War'. And so it has continued to the 1990s, one set of possibilities after another, until the rapid changes throughout the Warsaw Pact countries and the sudden disappearance of the Soviet Union annulled the licence to describe the great war-to-come.

These recent changes do not allow for any rousing last pages to this history of future wars. The trumpeter now has to sound a Last Post over the hundreds of stories that related every conceivable phase in the Forty-Year Confrontation. For the first time in the course of this fiction, there are reports of vanishing plots, shrinking markets, and authors in search of new material.

The good news for the world is the steady improvement in relations between East and West. The bad news for writers of fiction is that ever since 1985 the tale of the coming conflict has gone into a rapid decline. After the extraordinary events of 1989 in Eastern Europe and the Kohl–Gorbachev Agreement of July 1990, it has been difficult to find sufficient reasons for continuing to write about the old Cold War struggles.

The first casualties were the spy stories. As the powers of the KGB contracted and the Eastern European intelligence agencies were closed down, writers began to search for some means of accommodation with the changed Europe of the late 1980s. There was Len Deighton working through his stories about the British agent, Bernard Samson, when the Berlin Wall came down after he had finished *Spy Line*, the sixth in the series. That opened with a sentence from the distant past: 'Glasnost is trying to escape over the Wall, and getting shot with a *silenced* machine gun!' Other writers have rescued what they could from the old routines of the secret war between the two blocs. One method is to suppose that there are unregenerate intelligence warriors in the Pentagon who plan to engineer a clash between East and West. Another story imagines the KGB and CIA working together against a mysterious organization that causes the assassination of major government officials; and yet another story has the intelligence agencies of East and West united in their operations against the PLO who plot to hold the world to ransom.[22]

This rapid movement away from the alliances and rigid attitudes of the Cold War has had comparable effects upon the once prolific fiction of the third world war and after. When NATO and the Warsaw Pact countries accepted the Treaty on Conventional Armed Forces in Europe on 19 November 1990, they made a formal end to the Cold War. Moreover, their common declaration wiped out all details of the scenario that had long been the source of so many stories about the great conflict between East and West. Only the most determined authors could ignore the declaration: 'The era of confrontation and division in Europe has ended. We declare that henceforth our relations will be founded on respect and cooperation.' That was the signal for the armed forces, from the Urals to the Rockies, to start on operations never foreseen in the fiction of future warfare: filling tanks with concrete, destroying aircraft, blowing up their artillery. Armament factories began to close down, the military revised their budgets, and the minute hand of the Doomsday Clock of the *Bulletin of the Atomic Scientists* was moved back by ten minutes.

These momentous changes have reduced the number of future war stories to a handful, and they have forced authors to stretch invention to the limit. The world is at peace in one story, and then the Americans discover large deposits of rubidium below the Ross Ice Shelf in Antarctica; the Russians, still eager for world power, send in their submarines and aircraft carriers to seize the precious mineral. In another story President Gosnetsov of the Soviet

Union risks a world war in order to destroy the laser weaponry of the American space defence system. Yet another story moves the action to the Far East: Hong Kong has collapsed, there is civil war in China, the North Koreans have invaded South Korea, and Japan awaits the turn of events.[23]

These recent entries in the long list of future wars suggest the terminal condition of a genre which in its time has alarmed nations for the best and the worst of reasons. The prospects of its survival do not seem promising at a time when the Americans propose to eliminate their multiple warhead missiles and to reduce the number of their sea-launched missiles, when the Russians announce that they are to cut their armed forces by half, when the armed forces of the European countries are contracting rapidly.

What, then, are the prospects for the tale of the war-to-come in the last decade of the twentieth century? The cautious answer begins with the fact that this fiction has an almost unbroken record of failing to forecast the true course of future wars. The Germans never invaded the British Isles; and the French did not conquer Germany. When the long-expected war came in 1914, it turned out to be very different from the swift campaigns and decisive naval actions described in the tales of 'The Next Great War'. Between the two world wars the bombers did not destroy the great cities of Europe; after 1945 the Russians did not conquer the West; and there has not been a nuclear war. It is evident that the future is in the main unforeseeable. For that reason, the last word can be left for a distinguished soldier who compiled the one classic account of a possible modern war. At the end of *The Third World War*, Sir John Hackett warned the reader that the unexpected can come between the anticipation and the event: 'We who have put this book together know very well that the only forecast that can be made with any confidence of the course and outcome of another world war, should there be one, is that nothing will happen exactly as we have shown here.'

Notes

Chapter One

1. Professor Oskar Morgenstern, *The Question of National Defense* (1959); quoted by John Strachey, *On the Prevention of War* (1962) 11.
2. François Mallet, *La Conquête de l'air et la paix universelle* (1910), 73.
3. Anon., *The Reign of George VI. 1900–1925* (1763); reprinted with preface and notes by C. Oman (1899), 46–7.
4. The Letters Patent of Nobility to the Montgolfier brothers noted that their invention of the aerostatic machine 'will cause a memorable epoch in physical history; we hope, also, that it will furnish new means to increase the power of man, or at least extend his knowledge'.
5. J. Coriande Mittié, *La Descente en Angleterre: Prophétie en deux actes et en prose; représentée pour la première fois le 4 nivose, an 6, au Théâtre de la Cité-Variétés* (1798), 12–14.
6. William Burke, *The Armed Briton* (1806), 32–4.
7. *The Anti-Gallican* (1804), 132.
8. Robert Southey, *Sir Thomas More; or, Colloquies on the Progress and Prospects of Society* (1829), 2 vols., ii. 77.
9. The Prince de Joinville, *On the State of the Naval Strength of France in Comparison with that of England* (1844), 4.
10. Hansard, 3rd ser., lxxii, 1223–34. One typical reaction of many came from Captain J. Ryden Burton, RN, in *A Letter addressed to the Editor of the 'Morning Herald' on the National Defence*. He began with the notorious first sentence from the Prince de Joinville: 'Avec la marine à vapeur, la guerre d'aggression la plus audacieuse est permise sur mer.'
11. General Sir R. Biddulph, *Lord Cardwell at the War Office* (1904), 47.
12. *Illustrated London News*, 5 April 1862, 328.
13. A. C. Benson (ed.), *The Letters of Queen Victoria* (1907), 3 vols., ii. 86
14. Anon., *A History of the sudden and terrible Invasion of England by the French in the month of May, 1852* (1851), 10–11.
15. David Urqhart, *The Invasion of England* (1860), 11.
16. Captain H. M. Hozier, *The Invasions of England* (1876), 2 vols., ii. 86.
17. Admiral Colomb, *Essays on National Defence* (1896), 138.
18. Hansard, cliv, 623.
19. George W. E. Russell (ed.), *Letters of Matthew Arnold* (1895), 2 vols., i. 96.

Chapter Two

1. For a full discussion see Basil L. Crapster, 'A. B. Richards (1820–76): Journalist in Defence of Britain', *Army Historical Review*, 12 (1963), 94–7.
2. Mrs Harry Coghill, *Autobiography of M. O. W. Oliphant* (1899), 229–30.

3. *All the Year Round* (22 April 1871), 498.
4. *Annual Register* (1871), pt. 1, 2.
5. Anon., *The Fox's Prophecy* (1914), 3.
6. Anon. (Sir George Tomkyns Chesney), *The Battle of Dorking* (1871), 7.
7. Ibid. 34–5.
8. *Annual Register* (1871), pt. 1, 108. On 24 May 1871 Gladstone wrote with feeling on the matter to Col. C. H. W. A'Court-Repington: 'The article is mischievous as well as mad, heaping together a mass of impossible or incredible suppositions, and sending forth to the world the idea that this country is so degraded in intelligence as to bring them within the range of reasonable anticipations.' H. C. G. Matthews (ed.), *The Gladstone Diaries* (1982), 10 vols., vii. 500.
9. *Daily News*, 23 September 1871.
10. Clarendon Macaulay (Walter Marsham Adams), *The Carving of Turkey* (1874), 15.
11. Stochastic (Henry Grattan Donnelly), *The Stricken Nation* (1890), 10. A full account of these early American stories will be found in H. Bruce Franklin, *War Stars; the Super Weapon and the American Imagination* (1988). This most informative and challenging book is the first major study of war fiction in the United States.
12. Quoted by Percy Dunsheath, *A History of Electrical Engineering* (1962), 77.
13. Alexis de Tocqueville, *Democracy in America* (ed. H. S. Commager) (1946), 16.
14. *Saturday Review*, 11 April 1868.
15. Some of the first tales of the future to appear at this time were: J. F. Maguire, *The Next Generation* (1871); Octogenarian (pseud.), *The British Federal Empire* (1872); Edward Maitland, *By and By* (1873); Anon. (A. Blair), *Annals of the Twenty-ninth Century* (1874); Anon., *In the Future* (1875).
16. Viscount Wolseley, *The Story of a Soldier's Life* (1906), 2 vols., ii. 232.
17. Anon., *Plus d'Angleterre* (1887), 11.
18. William Delisle Hay, *Three Hundred Years Hence* (1881), 235–6.

Chapter Three

1. Lieut.-Col. F. Maurice, *Sir Frederick Maurice* (1913), 213–14.
2. Kennedy Jones, *Fleet Street and Downing Street* (1920), 198.
3. There is a full account of Harmsworth's interest in future war stories in Reginald Pound and Geoffrey Harmsworth, *Northcliffe* (1959), 150–1.
4. Lord Macaulay, 'Lord Bacon', in *Literary Essays* (1932), 385.
5. Samuel Smiles, *Lives of the Engineers* (1874), 5 vols., i, p. xxiv.
6. Francis Bacon, *Essays and New Atlantis* (ed. Gordon S. Haight) (1942), 288.
7. Some of the first of these were: Jean-Baptiste Cousin de Grainville, *Le Dernier homme* (1805); Mary Shelley, *The Last Man* (1826); Jane Webb, *The Mummy* (1827); Lord Moresby (pseud.?), *A Hundred Years Hence* (1828); R. F. Williams, *Eureka: A Prophecy of Future Times* (1837).
8. Julius von Voss, *Ini* (1810), 88–9.
9. Robert Fulton, *Torpedo War and Submarine Explosions* (1810), 40.
10. Quoted by Charles H. Gibbs-Smith, *Sir George Cayley's Aeronautics* (1962), 83.
11. Robert Southey, *Colloquies on the Progress of Society* (1829), 244.

12. James Burnley, *The Romance of Invention* (1886), 317.
13. Anon., *A History of Wonderful Inventions* (1862), 37.
14. Robert Routledge, *Discoveries and Inventions of the Nineteenth Century* (1876), 118.
15. H. O. Arnold-Forster, *In a Conning Tower* (1891), 11.
16. General Prince Kraft zu Hohenlohe-Ingelfingen, *Letters on Strategy* (1897), 2 vols., i. 266.
17. General Prince Kraft zu Hohenloge-Ingelfingen, *Letters on Cavalry* (1899), 72.
18. H. G. Wells, *The World Set Free*, Atlantic edn. (1926), 11.
19. Quoted by Bernard Bergonzi, *The Early H. G. Wells* (1961), 124.
20. Quoted by Kenneth Allott, *Jules Verne* (1940), 223.
21. H. G. Wells, *The War of the Worlds* (1926), 11.
22. There is a full and fascinating account of this episode in David Y. Hughes, 'The War of the Worlds in the Yellow Press', *Journalism Quarterly*, 43 (1966), 639–46.
23. Hadley Cantril, *The Invasion from Mars*, Princeton University edn. (1986), 14.
24. H. G. Wells, *Anticipations* (1902), 212.
25. Ibid. 204.
26. H. G. Wells, *The War in the Air* (1926), 246.
27. H. G. Wells, *The World Set Free* (1926), 116.
28. The opinions of many experts were printed at the end of Conan Doyle's short story under the heading of 'What the Naval Experts Think', *Strand Magazine* (July 1914), 20-2.
29. Arthur Machen, *The Bowmen and other Legends of the War* (1915), 34-5.

Chapter Four

1. Georges Valbert, *Hommes et choses* (1833), 303.
2. *The Channel Tunnel and Public Opinion* (1882), 1; reprinted from the *Nineteenth Century*, April 1882.
3. Capitaine Danrit, *La Guerre de forteresse* (1893), 2 vols., ii. 126–7.
4. Arthur J. Marder, *British Naval Policy, 1880–1905* (1940), 233.
5. Bertha von Suttner, *Lay Down Your Arms* (1892), 212.
6. Prince Kraft zu Hohenlohe-Ingelfingen, *Letters on Cavalry* (1892), 93.
7. In 1906 General Bonnal stated in *La Prochaine Guerre*: 'The outcome of the next war will be decided in less than a month after the opening of hostilities.' In 1912 Commandant Mordacq thought that another war might last 'about one year'. He told the politicians that it was their duty—for reasons of national morale—'to prevent the idea spreading that the next war will certainly end after the first great battle' (*La Durée de la prochaine guerre*, 32).
8. Ubique (Captain F. Guggisberg), *Modern Warfare; or, How our Soldiers fight* (1903), 94.
9. Quoted by William L. Langer, *The Diplomacy of Imperialism* (1935), 2 vols., i. 88.
10. Ivan S. Bloch, *Modern Weapons and Modern Warfare* (1900), xvi.
11. *The Memoirs of Marshal Joffre*, trans. Col. T. Bentley Mott (1932), 2 vols., i. 320.

12. Shaw read the book and at once wrote to the publisher, Grant Richards: 'Who wrote the *New Battle of Dorking?* Not Arnold Forster surely? Only a professional soldier could be so ignorant of warfare.' Grant Richards, *Author Hunting* (1934), 156.

13. 'The German Navy', *Black and White*, 19 January 1901.

14. Baron Colmar von der Goltz, *The Nation in Arms* (1887), 391.

15. Bernard Falk, *Bouquets for Fleet Street* (1951), 65.

16. Esmé Wingfield-Stratford, *Before the Lamps Went Out* (1945), 209–10. Two questions were asked in the Commons about this incident on 13 March and 14 May 1906.

17. *The Times*, 17 July 1908.

18. *The Times*, 17 July 1908.

19. William Scawen Blunt, *My Diaries* (1919), 624.

20. *Quarterly Review* (July 1908), 268. In his *Germany and England* (1909), a collection of articles reprinted from the *Daily Mail*, Robert Blatchford stated: 'I write these articles because I believe that Germany is deliberately preparing to destroy the British Empire; and because I know that we are not able or ready to defend ourselves against a sudden and formidable attack.' The book was translated and published in Germany in 1915 with the title of *Englands Furcht und Hasse*; and in the introduction the editor accused Lord Northcliffe, 'who for years had used his newspapers to rouse all classes in Britain against Germany'.

21. P. A. Hislam, *The Admiralty of the Atlantic* (1908), 216. See also this report by the same author: 'Briefly, the British Government, by those means which are always open to the Power ready to pay for information, came into possession of a matured scheme for the invasion of this country which had not only been submitted to the German Government, but had been adopted as a plan of campaign that could be put into operation at almost any moment with the minimum of ostentation and the maximum probability of success. While British naval forces nominally in home waters were at some distance from their stations—at Lagos or Gibraltar, for instance, or even in the western end of the Channel—a military force was to be embarked in the numerous liners and trading steamers that are always to be found in the German North Sea harbours. This invasion flotilla was to make for the Humber, and at the same time the whole German fleet was to seize the Straits of Dover' (75-6).

22. v. R., 'Die Invasion Englands in englischer Beleuchtung', *Marine Rundschau* (November 1908), 1246-58.

23. Élie Halévy, *A History of the English People, 1905-1915* (1934), 387.

24. Charles Lowe, 'About German Spies', *Contemporary Review* (January 1910), 42-56.

25. A. Hurd, 'England's Peril', *Contemporary Review* (April 1910), 679.

26. Louis C., *Fictions guerrières anglaises* (1910), 7.

27. *Spectator* (8 August 1914), 185.

28. Hilaire Belloc, *The Cruise of the Nona* (1925), 150.

Chapter Five

1. Winston Churchill, *The World Crisis, 1911–1914* (1923), 11.
2. Herbert Reed, *Annals of Innocence and Experience* (1946), 118.
3. G. Manville Fenn, *George Alfred Henty* (1907), 305. Publication figures for Henty's books will be found in Robert L. Dartt, *G. A. Henty: A Bibliography* (1971).
4. Henri Barbusse, *Under Fire*, trans. W. Fitzwater Wray (1965), 242–3.
5. Quoted by T. K. Derry and Trevor Williams, *A Short History of Technology* (1960), 706.
6. For the full account, see William Honan, *Visions of Infamy; A Biography of Hector Bywater* (1991).
7. These are, respectively Harry Edmonds, *The Riddle of the Straits* (1932); Julian Sterne, *The Secret of the Zodiac* (1933); D. Christie, *The Striking Force* (1934); Martin Hussingtree, *Konyetz* (1924).
8. Sigmund Freud, *Civilization and its Discontents* (1929), 144.
9. David Goodman Croly, *Glimpses of the Future: Suggestions as to the Drift of Things* (1888). The Dutch author was Dr Dioscorides (Alex, V. W. Bikkers), *Anno Domini 2071* (1871).
10. Charles Richet, *Dans cent ans* (1892), 61.
11. Yevgeny Zamyatin, *We* (1924), trans. Bernard Guilbert Guerney (1970), 36.
12. *The Times*, 11 June 1947.

Chapter Six

1. W. H. Auden, *The Age of Anxiety* (1947), in *Collected Longer Poems* (1968), 349–50.
2. The full story is told in: Fred Kaplan, *The Wizards of Armageddon* (1984), 56–62.
3. Also published in the USA in 1949 with the title of *Watch the North Wind Rise*.
4. Paul Brians, *Nuclear Holocausts: Atomic War in Fiction, 1895–1984* (1987). This invaluable book covers the fiction of nuclear warfare from the earliest science fiction fantasies in the 1890s down to 1984. The introductory survey gives an excellent history of origins and developments; and the main part of the book, a fully annotated bibliography, provides accounts and commentaries on more than 800 titles. This information is kept up to date in *Nuclear Texts and Contexts*, the newsletter of the International Society for the Study of Nuclear Texts and Contexts, Department of English, Washington State University, Pullman, WA 99164–5020, USA.
5. Kaplan, *Wizards of Armageddon*, 288.
6. These were, first, Dale Brown, *Flight of the Old Dog* (*1987*); second, James P. Hogan, *Endgame Enigma* (1987).
7. There is no RIP for 007. After the death of the author, Ian Fleming, in 1964, the holders of the Bond copyright commissioned John Gardner to continue the series. This publisher's life-support system has so far produced: *Licence*

Renewed, For Special Services, Ice Breaker, Role of Honour, Nobody Lives For Ever, No Deals Mr Bond.

8. The producer was Caroline Gold and the director was Geoffrey Sax. There were memorable performances by Nigel Havers (Jeremy Coward, or Sergei Alekseyevich) and Warren Clarke (Albert Robinson, or Vladimir Yefimovich).

9. See the article by John Starnes, 'Why I Write Spy Fiction', in Wesley K. Wark, *Spy Fiction, Spy Films and Real Intelligence* (1991). This study by 12 contributors gives an excellent analysis of recent spy fiction.

10. J. B. S. Haldane, 'Biological Possibilities in the Next Ten Thousand Years', in *Man and his Future* (1963), 319.

11. Field-Marshal Viscount Montgomery of Alamein, *A History of Warfare* (1968), 560.

12. The English edn., published in 1951 had the title *The Silver Locusts*.

13. G. B. Chisholm, 'Future of the Mind', in Gordon Wolstenholme (ed.), *Man and his Future* (1963), 319.

14. Jean-Paul Sartre, *Three Plays* (1969), 288.

15. Montgomery, *History of Warfare*, 561.

16. These were, first, John Wingate, *Frigate* (1980); *Carrier* (1981); *Submarine* (1980); second, James Rouch, *The Zone: Hard Target* (1980) was the first; the rest were *Blind Fire* (1980); *Hunter Killer* (1981); *Sky Strike* (1981); *Overkill* (1982).

17. Walter M. Miller, *A Canticle for Leibowitz* (1960), 198.

18. These are: George Turner, *Beloved Son* (1978); Poul Anderson, *Vault of the Ages* (1952); Alexander Fullerton, *Regenesis* (1983); Thomas Block, *Airship Nine* (1984).

19. The most recent listing of these post-holocaust adventure serials appears in *Nuclear Texts & Contexts*, Spring 1991, no. 6. It gives the titles of the following serials and the books so far published in them: *The Amtrak Wars* (6); *Ashes* (12); *Blade* (13); *C.A.D.S.* (5); *Deathlands* (12); *Doomsday Warrior* (18); *Eagleheart* (3); *Endworld* (27); *Firebrats* (4); *Freedom's Rangers* (5); *The Guardians* (15); *The Last Ranger* (10); *The Marauders* (5); *The Outrider* (5); *Phoenix* (5); *Traveler* (13); *Turbo Cowboys* (10); *Waste-world* (4); *Wingman* (8); *The Zone* (9).

20. There is an excellent study of this in: Diane Parkin-Speer, 'Leigh Brackett's *The Long Tomorrow*: A Quest for the Future America', *Extrapolation*, 26 (1985), 190–200.

21. A full account of Muir's poem will be found in Christopher Wiseman's *Beyond the Labyrinth* (ch. 5: 'One Foot in Eden') (1978).

22. These are: Robert Littell, *An Agent in Place* (1991); Philip Cornford, *Katalyst* (1991); James Adams, *The Final Terror* (1991).

23. These are: Payne Harrison, *Thunder of Erebus* (1991); Robert L. Holt and Frank R. Holt, *Peacemaker* (1990); Simon Winchester, *Pacific Nightmare* (1992).

Checklist of Imaginary Wars, 1763–1990

The following list is arranged in chronological order. It gives the authors, full titles, and place of first publication for all those imaginary wars of the future so far discovered down to the cut-off date of 1990; and it includes entries for the many post-holocaust stories that have appeared since 1945.

1763 ANON., *The Reign of George VI* (London).
1784 ANON., *Aerostation; or, The Templar's Stratagem* (London).
1797 ANON., *Les Prisonniers français en Angleterre* (Paris).
1798 MITTIÉ, J. CORIANDE, *La Descente en Angleterre: Prophétie en deux actes et en prose; représentée pour la première fois le 4 nivose, an 6, au Théâtre de la Cité-Variétés* (Paris).
1803 ANON., *The Invasion of England: A farce in Three Acts* (London).
1806 BURKE, WILLIAM, *The Armed Briton; or, The Invaders Vanquished: A Play in Four Acts* (London).
1836 SYDNEY, EDWARD WILLIAM (TUCKER, NATHANIEL), *The Partisan Leader: A Tale of the Future* (Washington, DC).
1841 GEOFFROY, LOUIS, *Napoléon Apocryphe, 1812–32: Histoire de la conquête du Monde et de la Monarchie universelle* (Paris).
1851 ANON., *The History of the Sudden and Terrible Invasion of England by the French in . . . May, 1852* (London).
1854 COEURDEROY, ERNEST, *Hurrah!!! Ou, La Révolution par les Cosaques* (Paris).
1860 RUFFIN, EDMUND, *Anticipations of the Future to serve as Lessons for the Present Time* (Richmond, Va).
1870 RICHARDS, ALFRED BATES, *The Invasion of England*, privately printed August 1870.
1871 ANON. (CHESNEY, SIR GEORGE TOMKYNS), *The Battle of Dorking: Reminiscences of a Volunteer* (London); first printed in *Blackwood's Magazine*, May 1871, and subsequently republished in numerous special editions. The literature relating to the *Battle of Dorking* episode is listed below:

    1. *Overseas editions in English*

        The Battle of Dorking: being an account of the German invasion of England, and capture of London & Woolwich, etc, as told by a Volunteer to his Grandchildren (Toronto, 1871).
        The Battle of Dorking: Reminiscences of a Volunteer, Reprinted from Blackwood's Magazine for May 1871 (Melbourne, 1871).

The Fall of England? The Battle of Dorking: Reminiscences of a Volunteer (New York, 1871).

The German Conquest of England in 1875, and Battle of Dorking; or Reminiscences of a Volunteer (Philadelphia, 1871). This edition was also published in Toronto in 1871.

Reminiscences of a Volunteer, A.D. 1925. The Battle of Dorking, abridged version published in the *Otago Witness*, Dunedin, 19 August and 26 August 1871.

2. *Foreign translations*

A batalha de Dorking; Episodio do conquista da Inglaterra pela Allemanha em 187– (Rio de Janeiro, 1871). In this edition the authorship was attributed to Disraeli.

La Bataille de Dorking (Paris 1871), preface by Charles Yriarte.

Englands Ende in der Schlacht bei Dorking (Hamburg, 1879).

Engelands Val: 1871–1925 (Deventer, 1871).

Il Racconto di un guardiano di spiaggia (Rome, 1871).

Die Schlacht bei Dorking, in *Grenzboten*, 30 (1871), 870–9; 910–24; 936–47; 786–90.

Slaget vid Dorking (Fahlun, 1872).

Was England erwartet: Voraussagen eines englischen Militärschriftstellers aus dem Jahre 1871 (Berlin, 1940).

3. *Related Works*

ANON., *After the Battle of Dorking; or, What Became of the Invaders?* (London, 1871).

ANON., *The Battle of Dorking: A Myth* (London, 1871).

ANON., *The Battle of Foxhill* (London, 1871).

ANON., *The Battle of the Ironclads; or, England and her Foes in 1879* (London, 1871).

ANON., *Britannia in Council* (London, 1871).

ANON., *The Cruise of the Anti-Torpedo* (London, 1871).

ANON., *The Hens who Tried to Crow* (London, 1871).

ANON., *The Official Despatches and Correspondence relative to the Battle of Dorking, as moved for in the House of Commons, 21st July 1920* (London, 1871).

ANON., *Our Hero; or, Who Wrote 'The Battle of Dorking'* (London, 1871).

ANON. (HAYWARD, ABRAHAM), *The Second Armada* (London, 1871).

ANON., *The Suggested Invasion of England by the Germans* (London, 1871), translation of a facetious German scheme for an invasion of the United Kingdom. See entry under J. M. Trutz-Baumwoll.

ANON. (STONE, CHARLES), *What Happened after the Battle of Dorking; or, The Victory of Tunbridge Wells* (London, 1871).

The Battle of Berlin: Celebrated Medley written by Frank W. Green, Esq. Music composed and arranged by Carl Bernstein (London, 1871).

> *The Battle of Dorking: A Dream of John Bull's. Written by Frank W. Green, Esq. The Music arranged by Carl Bernstein* (London, 1871).

HEMYNG, BRACEBRIDGE, *The Commune in London; or, Thirty Years Hence: A Chapter of Anticipated History* (London, 1871).

HUNTER, LT.-COL. WILLIAM, *Army Speech by an old Harrovian dedicated to those who have been frightened by the Battle of Dorking* (London, 1871).

LEIGHTON, SIR BALDWYN, *The Lull before Dorking* (London, 1871).

M., J. W. *The Coming Cromwell* (London, 1871).

M., J. W., *The Siege of London; Reminiscences of 'Another Volunteer'* (London, 1871).

McCAULEY, MOTLEY RANK (pseud.), *Chapters from Future History: The Battle of Berlin* (London, 1871).

MOLTRUHN, M. (pseud.), *The Other Side at the Battle of Dorking* (London, 1871).

SKETCHLEY, ARTHUR, *Mrs Brown on the Battle of Dorking* (London, 1871).

TRUTZ-BAUMWOLL, J. M. (pseud.), *Sendschreiben des deutsch-englischen Zukunftspolitiker . . . an S. M. den Deutschen Kaiser, in Auserordentliche Beilage zur Allgemeinen Zeitung, no. 154,* 3 June 1871.

1871   DANGIN, ÉDOUARD, *La Bataille de Berlin en 1875* (Paris).

1872   OCTOGENARIAN (pseud.), *The British Federal Empire: How It Was Founded. A Speech . . . in a Certain City of the Empire* (London).

1873   STAMPF, FR., *La Dernière Bataille (Die letzte Schlacht)*, allegedly translated from the German by Edmond Thiaudière (Paris).

1874   MACAULAY, CLARENDON (ADAMS, WALTER MARSHAM), *The Carving of Turkey* (London).

       VOSS, RICHARD, *Visionen eines deutschen Patrioten* (Zürich).

1875   ANON., *The Battle of Pluck* (London).

       ANON., *Europa's Fate* (London).

       ANON., *La Guerre future* (Paris).

1876   ANON., *La France et l'Allemagne au printemps prochain* (Paris).

       ANON., *The Invasion of 1883* (Glasgow).

       ANON., *A Parallel Case; or, The Straits of Dover Question AD 2345* (Darlington).

       CASSANDRA (pseud.), *The Channel Tunnel; or, England's Ruin* (London).

1877   ANON., *Fifty Years Hence: An Old Soldier's Tale of England's Downfall* (London).

       LA MÈCHE, GÉN., *La Guerre franco-allemande de 1878* (Paris).

1878   ANON., *Gortschakoff and Bismarck; or, Europe in 1940* (London).

1879   ANON. (CHESNEY, SIR GEORGE TOMKYNS), *The New Ordeal* (Edinburgh).

       DEKHNEWALLAH, A. (pseud.), *The Great Russian Invasion of India: a Sequel to the Afghanistan Campaign of 1878–9* (London).

       SANTI, LUIGI, *L'Europa nel 1900* (Milan).

1880   DOONER, PIERTON, W., *The Last Days of the Republic* (San Francisco).

1881   BOLAND, HENRI, *La Guerre prochaine entre la France et l'Allemagne* (Paris).
       BUDGE (pseud.), *The Eastern Question Solved* (London).
       LANG-TUNG (pseud.), *The Decline and Fall of the British Empire* (London).
       SPERBER-NIBORSKI, LÉON, *Krieg mit Russland!* (Loeban).

1882   A., F., *The Seizure of the Channel Tunnel* (London).
       ANON., *The Channel Tunnel: A Poem* (London).
       ANON., *Ireland's War! Parnell Victorious* (New York).
       ANON., *1900: Garde à vous: De la Sprée à l'Escaut par la Marne* (Paris).
       ANON., *The Story of the Channel Tunnel* (London).
       ANON. (BUTLER, SIR WILLIAM F.), *The Invasion of England* (London).
       THE DEMURE ONE (pseud.), *The Battle of Boulogne; or, How Calais Became English Again* (London).
       GRIP (pseud.), *How John Bull lost London; or, The Capture of the Channel Tunnel* (London).
       GUTHRIE, T. A., *The Seizure of the Channel Tunnel* (London).
       REED, SAMUEL ROCKWELL, *The War of 1886 between the United States and Great Britain* (Cincinnati).

1883   ANON., *The Battle of the Moy; or, How Ireland gained her independence in 1892–1894* (London).
       ANON., *The Battle of Port Said* (London); also published in Paris (1883) as *La Bataille de Port Said.*
       ANON., *How Glasgow Ceased to Flourish* (Glasgow).
       ANON., *La Guerre de 1884* (Paris).
       ANON., *India in 1983* (Calcutta).
       FORTH, C., *The Surprise of the Channel Tunnel* (London).
       ULIDIA (pseud.), *The Battle of Newry* (London).

1884   DEBANS, CAMILLE, *Les Malheurs de John Bull* (Paris).
       POSTERITAS (pseud.), *The Siege of London* (London); published in Paris (1885) as *La Bataille de Londres en 1881–.*

1885   ANON., *The Battle of Tomorrow* (London).
       ANON., *The Great War and Disastrous Peace of 1885* (London).
       BARILLET-LAGARGOUSSE, *La Guerre finale; histoire fantastique* (Paris).
       COVERDALE, SIR HENRY STANDISH (pseud.), *The Fall of the Great Republic* (Boston, Mass., and London).
       GREER, T., *A Modern Daedalus* (London).
       X., *La Revanche* (Paris).

1886   ANON., *The Great Irish Rebellion of 1886* (London).
       ANON., *Newry Bridge; or, Ireland in 1887* (Edinburgh).
       ANON., *Openings and Proceedings of the Irish Parliament* (London).
       LESTER, EDWARD, *The Siege of Bodike: A Prophecy of Ireland's Future* (London).
       S., H. W., *Wie wir Indien verloren* (Leipzig); translated from the English original published at Allahabad, India.

1887   ANON. (CLOWES, W. L., and BURGOYNE, A. H.), *The Great Naval War of 1887* (London).
       ANON., *Der rache Krieg zwischen Frankreich und Deutschland* (Hanover).

1887   ANON., *Plus d'Angleterre* (Paris); published in London (1888) as *Down with England*.

CAPTAIN OF THE ROYAL NAVY, A, *The Battle off Worthing; or Why the Invaders Never Got to Dorking* (London).

GOPCEVIC, SPIRIDION, *The Conquest of Britain in 1888, and the Sea Fights and Battles That Led to It* (London); translation of *Der grosse Seekrieg im Jahre 1888*, first published in *Internationale Revue über die gesamten Armeen und Flotten* (July–Sept. 1886). Published in Paris (1891) as *Comment la France conquit l'Angleterre en 1888*.

HOPE, LT.-COL. W., *An Omitted Incident in the 'Great Naval War of 1887'* (London).

MONFALCONE, PIERRE, and CASTELIN, ANDRÉ, *La Première bataille Franco-Allemande le 18 Août 18 . . . Réponse à la brochure: Die erste Schlacht im Zukunftskrieg par le Général . . .* (Paris).

PEDDIE, JAMES, *The Capture of London* (London).

ROBIDA, ALBERT, *La Guerre au vingtième siècle* (Paris).

1888   ANON., *La Bataille de Damvillers: récit anticipé de la prochaine campagne par un cavalier du 35e Dragons* (Paris).

ANON., *Der europäische Coalitionskrieg* (Hanover).

ANON., *Der Krieg in Galizien im Frühjahr 1888* (Minden).

ANON., *Plus encore d'Angleterre; or, Repulse of the French* (London).

ANON., *The 'Russia's Hope'; or, Britannia no longer Rules the Waves*, translated from the Russian by C. J. Cooke (London).

BARTON, SAMUEL, *The Battle of the Swash; and The Capture of Canada* (New York).

BLEIBTREU, KARL, *Die Entscheidungsschlachten des europäischen Krieges 18. .* (Leipzig):

1. *Die Schlacht von Bochnia.*
2. *Die Schlacht bei Belfort.*
3. *Die Schlacht bei Châlons.*

LESTER, HORACE FRANCIS, *The Taking of Dover* (London).

MACKAY, DONALD, *The Dynamite Ship* (London and New York).

ROPE, CHARLES, *Opérations sur les côtes de la Mediterranée et de la Baltique au printemps de 1888* (Paris).

1889   ANON., *The Bombardment of Scarbro' by the Russian fleet in 1891* (London).

ANON., *England's Danger; or, Rifts within the Lute: A Russian Plot* (Portsmouth).

ANON., *La Prise de Cherbourg* (Paris).

CROMIE, ROBERT, *For England's Sake* (London).

STOCKTON, F. R., *The Great War Syndicate* (New York and London).

'V', *The Swoop of the Eagles* (London).

WATERLOO, STANLEY, *Armageddon: A Tale of Love, War, and Invention* (Chicago).

1890   ANON. (WATSON, H. C. M.), *Decline and Fall of the British Empire* (London).

STOCHASTIC (DONNELLY, HENRY GRATTAN), *The Stricken Nation* (New York).

WALSH, RUPERT, *The Fate of the Triple Alliance* (London).

1891 ARNOLD-FORSTER, HUGH OAKLEY, *In a Conning Tower; or, How I took H.M.S. Majestic into Action*, (London); reprinted from *Murray's Magazine* (1888).

DANRIT, CAPITAINE (DRIANT, ÉMILE AUGUSTE). *La Guerre en rase campagne* (Paris).

FERRÉOL, PIERRE, *La Prise de Londres au XXe siècle* (Paris).

1892 CLOWES, WILLIAM LAIRD, *The Captain of the 'Mary Rose'* (London).

COLOMB, REAR-ADML. PHILIP and others, *The Great War of 189–: A Forecast* (London), published in Leipzig (1894) as *Der grosse Krieg von 189–*.

DONNELLY, IGNATIUS, *The Golden Bottle* (New York and London).

LE FAURE, GEORGES, *La Guerre sous l'eau* (Paris).

LE FAURE, GEORGES, *Mort aux Anglais!* (Paris).

SEAFORTH (CLARKE, G. S.), *The Last Great Naval War* (London).

SOMNOLENT (pseud.), *Invasion of England in the 19th Century* (Madras).

1893 DONOVAN, REV. A., *The Irish Rebellion of 1898* (London).

EX-REVOLUTIONIST (pseud.), *'England's Downfall'; or, The Last Great Revolution* (London).

FAWCETT, EDWARD DOUGLAS, *Hartmann the Anarchist; or, The Doom of the Great City* (London).

GRIFFITH, GEORGE, *The Angel of the Revolution* (London).

HAYES, F. W., *The Great Revolution of 1905; or, The Story of the Phalanx* (London).

SMITH, J. H. DEVILLIERS, *The Great Southern Revolution* (Cape Town).

1894 ANON., *La France et la Russie contre la Triple Alliance* (Paris).

DANRIT, CAPITAINE (DRIANT, ÉMILE AUGUSTE), *La Guerre de forteresse* (Paris).

DANRIT, CAPITAINE (DRIANT, ÉMILE AUGUSTE), *La Guerre au vingtième siècle* (Paris).

1. *La Mobilisation africaine.*
2. *Grand pélérinage à la Mecque.*
3. *Fin de l'Islam.*

EARDLEY-WILMOT, CAPT. S., *The Next Naval War* (London).

GARÇON, AUGUSTIN, *Un corsaire anglais* (Paris); condensed translation of *The Captain of the 'Mary Rose'* (1893).

GRIFFITH, G., *Olga Romanoff* (London).

LE QUEUX, WILLIAM, *The Great War in England in 1897* (London).

MAYO, EARL OF, *The War Cruise of the Aries* (Dublin).

NIGOTE, CHARLES, *La Bataille de la Vesles* (Paris).

ROSA, SAMUEL ALBERT, *The Coming Terror; or, The Australian Revolution* (Sydney).

1895 ANON. (CLOWES, WILLIAM LAIRD and WILSON, BECCLES), *The Siege of Portsmouth*, in *Portsmouth Mail* (June 1895).

DANRIT, CAPITAINE (DRIANT, ÉMILE AUGUSTE), *L'Invasion noire* (Paris).

DANYERS, GEOFFREY, *Blood is Thicker than Water* (London).

1895 EASTWICK, JAMES, *The New Centurion: A Tale of Automatic Warfare* (London).

GRIFFITH, G., *The Outlaws of the Air* (London).

JANE, FREDERICK THOMAS, *Blake of the 'Rattlesnake'; or, The Man who Saved England: A story of torpedo warfare in 189–* (London).

LERMINA, JULES, *La Bataille de Strasbourg* (Paris).

MACKAY, KENNETH, *The Yellow Wave; A Romance of the Asiatic Invasion of Australia* (London).

X (FAWKES, F. ATTFIELD), *Marmaduke, Emperor of Europe* (London).

1896 ANSON, CAPT. (ed?), *The Great Anglo-American War of 1900* (London).

BURTON, FRANCIS GEORGE, *The Naval Engineer and the Command of the Sea* (London).

CROMIE, ROBERT, *The Next Crusade* (London).

DANRIT, CAPITAINE (DRIANT, ÉMILE AUGUSTE), *Le Journal de guerre du Lieutenant Piefke* (Paris).

TRACY, LOUIS, *The Final War: A Story of the Great Betrayal* (London).

1897 ANON., *The Back Door* (Hong Kong).

BJELOMOR, A., *Der Zukunftskrieg im Jahre 18. . . .* (Dresden).

GLEIG, CHARLES, *When All Men Starve* (London).

GRIFFITH, GEORGE, *Briton or Boer* (London).

PALMER, JOHN HENRY, *The Invasion of New York; or, How Hawaii was Annexed* (New York and London).

THORBURN, SEPTIMUS SMET, *His Majesty's Greatest Subject* (London).

1898 DAVENPORT, BENJAMIN RUSH, *Anglo-Saxons Onward!* (Cleveland, Ohio).

GRAVES, C. L., and LUCAS, E. V., *The War of the Wenuses*, translated from *The Artesian* of H. G. Pozzuoli (Bristol).

MORRIS, JOHN, *What will Japan do?* (London).

MUNDO, OTO, *The Recovered Continent: A Tale of the Chinese Invasion* (Columbus, Ohio).

ODELL, S. W., *The Last War; or, The Triumph of the English Tongue* (Chicago).

OPPENHEIM, E. P., *Mysterious Mr Sabin* (London).

SHIEL, M. P., *The Yellow Danger* (London).

WELLS, H. G., *The War of the Worlds* (London).

WILSON, H. W., and WHITE, A., *When War Breaks Out* (London).

1899 ARGUS (pseud.), *La Guerra del 190– (Spezia)*.

GRIFFITH, GEORGE, *The Great Pirate Syndicate* (London).

HILL, HEADON (GRAINGER, FRANCIS EDWARD), *Spies of the Wight* (London).

JANE, FREDERICK THOMAS, *The Violet Flame: A Story of Armageddon and After* (London).

LE QUEUX, WILLIAM, *England's Peril* (London).

STEVENSON, PHILIP L., *How the Jubilee Fleet Escaped Destruction, and the Battle of Ushant* (London).

1900 ALLAIS, ALPHONSE, *Projet d'attitude inamicale vis-à-vis de l'Angleterre* (Paris).

ALLEN, F. M. (DOWNEY, EDMUND), *London's Peril* (London).

ANON. (MAUDE, COL. FREDERIC NATUSCH), *The New Battle of Dorking* (London).

COLE, R. W., *The Struggle for Empire: A Story of the Year 2236* (London).

DE NOUSANNE, HENRI, *La Guerre Anglo-Franco-Russe*, special number of *Le Monde Illustré* (10 March).

EISENHART, DR KARL, *Die Abrechnung mit England* (Munich).

ERDMANN, GUSTAV ADOLF, *Wehrlos zur See; eine Flottenphantasie an der Jahrhundertwende* (Berlin).

NEWCOMB, SIMON, *His Wisdom the Defender* (New York and London).

OFFIN, T. W., *How the Germans took London* (London).

WHITE, F. M., *The White Battalions* (London).

X, LIEUTENANT, *La Guerre avec l'Angleterre*, (Paris).

1901   ANON., *The Sack of London in the Great French War of 1901* (London).

CAIRNES, CAPT., *The Coming Waterloo* (London).

DANRIT, CAPITAINE (DRIANT, ÉMILE AUGUSTE), *La Guerre fatale* (Paris).

DEMOLDER, EUGENE, *L'Agonie d'Albion* (Paris); later published in Munich (1915) as *Albions Todeskampf.*

FORD, WILLIAM WILBRAHAM, *Psyche, 1902* (London).

NETTERVILLE, LUKE (O'GRADY, JAMES STANDISH), *Queen of the World; or, Under the Tyranny* (London).

PEMBERTON, MAX, *Pro Patria* (London).

SHIEL, M. P., *The Lord of the Sea* (London).

TRACY, LOUIS, *The Invaders* (London).

1902   CURTIS, ALBERT CHARLES, *A New Trafalgar: A Tale of the Torpedo Fleet* (London).

OPPENHEIM, E. P., *The Traitors* (London).

STABLES, W. G., *The Cruise of the 'Vengeful'* (London).

1903   ANON. (JAMES, L.), *The Boy Galloper: By the Intelligence Officer* (Edinburgh).

BACKSIGHT FORETHOUGHT (SWINTON, SIR EDWARD), *The Defence of Duffer's Drift* (London).

CHILDERS, ERSKINE, *The Riddle of the Sands* (London).

HILL, HEADON (GRAINGER, FRANCIS EDWARD), *Seaward for the Foe* (London).

MEHEMED, EMI EFFENDI, *Das neue Weltreich* (Leipzig).

UBIQUE (GUGGISBERG, CAPT. SIR FREDERICK GORDON), *Modern Warfare; or, How Our Soldiers Fight* (London).

1904   CLARKE, A., *Starved into Surrender* (London).

HALL, GEORGE ROME, *Black Fortnight; or, The Invasion of 1915* (London).

HASTINGS, G. G., *The First American King* (New York and London).

NIEMANN, AUGUST, *Der Weltkrieg—Deutsche Träume* (Berlin); also published in London (1904) as *The Coming Conquest of England.*

1905   ANON. (MILLS, ELIOT EVANS), *The Decline and Fall of the British Empire: A Brief Account . . . appointed for use in the National Schools of Japan, Tokio, 2005* (London).

BARNES, JAMES, *The Unpardonable War* (London and New York).

BYATT, HENRY, *Purple and White* (London).

1905   CLOWES, SIR WILLIAM LAIRD, and BURGOYNE, ALAN H., *Trafalgar Refought* (London).

CONDOR (pseud.), *Im Kampf um Südamerika: Ein Zukunftsbild* (Berlin).

IVOI, PAUL, and ROYET, COL., *La Patrie en danger* (Paris).

S., *'Sink, burn, destroy': Der Schlag gegen Deutschland* (Berlin).

STABLES, GEORGE, *The Meteor Flag of England* (London).

1906   ANON., *Une guerre franco-allemande* (Paris); published in London (1907) as *A Second Franco-German War and its Consequences for England.*

ANON., *Völker Europas . . .! Der Krieg der Zukunft* (Berlin).

BEOWULF (pseud.), *Der deutsch-englische Krieg* (Berlin).

CASSANDRE (pseud.), *Une guerre franco-allemande* (Paris).

GENERAL STAFF (pseud.), *The Writing on the Wall* (London); also published in Hanover (1906) as *Mene, mene tekel upharsin! Englands Überwaltigung durch Deutschland: Von einem Englischen Generalstabsoffizier: Autorisierte übersetzung von einem deutschen Stabsoffizier.*

GOY, LUCIEN, *La Bataille de 1915* (Paris).

HANSA (HOEPNER, KAPT. A. D.), *Hamburg und Bremen in Gefahr* (Berlin).

LE QUEUX, WILLIAM, *The Invasion of 1910* (London); published in Berlin (1907) as *Der Einfall der Deutschen in England*; and in Paris (1907) as *L'Invasion de 1910.*

MORITURUS (pseud.), *Mit deutschen Waffen über Paris nach London: Briefe von der Elbe* (Hanau).

OLDMEADOW, ERNEST, *The North Sea Bubble* (London).

SEESTERN (GRAUTOFF, F. H.), *'1906'—der Zusammenbruch der alten Welt* (Leipzig); published in London (1907) as *Armageddon 190-.*

VAUX, PATRICK, *The Shock of Battle* (London).

WOOD, WALTER, *The Enemy in our Midst* (London).

1907   ANON. (BRAMAH, ERNEST), *What Might Have Been: The Story of a Social War* (London).

ANON. (KERCHNAWE, H.), *Unser letzter Kampf* (Vienna and Leipzig).

ASKEW, ALICE, and ASKEW, CLAUDE, *The Sword of Peace* (London).

BLEIBTREU, KARK, *Die 'Offensiv-Invasion' gegen England* (Berlin).

BUNDSCHUH (pseud.), *Die Revolution von 1912* (Leipzig).

COLE, ROBERT WILLIAM, *The Death Trap* (London).

DAWSON, A. J., *The Message* (London).

GRIER, SYDNEY, C. (GREGG, HILDA CAROLINE), *The Power of the Keys* (Edinburgh).

GRIFFITH, GEORGE, *The World Peril of 1910* (London).

HOPPENSTEDT, MAJOR JULIUS, *Die Schlacht der Zukunft* (Berlin).

MACPHERSON, JOHN F., *A Yankee Napoleon* (London).

MARTIN, RUDOLF EMIL, *Berlin-Bagdad: Das deutsche Weltreich im Zeitalter der Luftschiffahrt, 1910–1931* (Stuttgart).

OPPENHEIM, E. P., *The Secret* (London).

SCOTT, H., *The Way of War* (London).

TERANUS, V. E. (ZAPP, ARTHUR), *Der letzte Krieg* (Berlin).

VAUX, PATRICK, and YEXLEY, LIONEL, *When the Eagle Flies Seaward* (London).

1908   AGRICOLA (pseud.), *How England Was Saved: History of the Years 1910–1925* (London).

ANON., *Luftschiff 13: Ein Zukunftsroman* (Leipzig).

ARGUS (pseud.), *Die Engländer kommen! Der Ueberfall Hamburgs durch die englische flotte* (Hamburg).

BURGOYNE, ALAN H., *The War Inevitable* (London).

CRABAPPLE, JOHN (pseud.), *The War of 1908 for the Supremacy of the Pacific* (London).

DANRIT, CAPITAINE (DRIANT, ÉMILE AUGUSTE), *Guerre maritime et sousmarine* (Paris).

GIFFARD, P., *La Guerre infernale* (Paris).

GODFREY, HOLLIS, *The Man Who Ended War* (Boston, Mass.).

GRACE, S., *Dennis Martin, Traitor* (Cardiff).

KERNAHAN, COULSON, *The Red Peril* (London).

KIPLING, A. E., *The New Dominion: A Tale of Tomorrow's Wars* (London).

MAYNE, JOHN DAWSON, *The Triumph of Socialism* (London).

NAVARCHUS (VAUX, PATRICK, and YEXLEY, LIONEL), *The World's Awakening* (London).

NORTON, ROY, *The Vanishing Fleets* (New York and London).

ORIEL, ANTRIM (MOORE, ARTHUR), *The Miracle* (London).

PARABELLUM (GRAUTOFF, F. H.), Banzai! (Leipzig); published in London (1909) as *Banzai!*.

STEVENS, ROWAN (ed.), *The Battle for the Pacific and other Adventures at Sea* (New York).

WAGEBALD, MICHAEL, *Europa in Flammen: Der deutsche Zukunftskrieg von 1909* (Leipzig).

WELLS, H. G., *The War in the Air* (London).

1909   ANDREW, STEPHEN (LAYTON, FRANK GEORGE), *The Serpent and the Cross* (London).

ANON., *Provinz Nordmark* (Berlin).

BERNSTORFF, HANS NIKOLAUS GRAF VON, *Deutschlands Flotte im Kampf* (Berlin).

BLYTH, JAMES, *The Swoop of the Vulture* (London).

CAINE, HALL, *The White Prophet* (London).

CHESTER, LORD, *The Great Red Dragon* (Jacksonville, Fla.).

CURTIES, CAPT. HENRY, *When England Slept* (London).

DOUGHTY, CHARLES MONTAGU, *The Clouds* (London).

FITZPATRICK, ERNEST HUGH, *The Coming Conflict of Nations; or, The Japanese American War* (Springfield, Ill.).

HAWKE, NAPIER, *The Invasion that Did Not Come Off* (London).

HOOKHAM, ALBERT E., *Amid the Strife* (London).

HOPPENSTEDT, JULIUS., *Ein neues Wörth: Ein Schlachtenbild der Zukunft* (Berlin).

1909 KIRMESS, C. H., *The Australian Crisis* (London).

MARTIN, RUDOLF., *Der Weltkrieg in den Lüften* (Leipzig).

MAURUS (pseud.), *Ave Caesar! Deutsche Luftschiffe im Kampfe um Marokko* (Leipzig).

A PATRIOT (DU MAURIER, GUY), *An Englishman's Home: A Play* (London).

SLADEN, DOUGLAS, *The Tragedy of the Pyramids* (London).

TOWNROE, B. S., *A Nation in Arms* (London).

WILLIAMS, LLOYD, *The Great Raid* (London).

WODEHOUSE, P. G., *The Swoop! or, How Clarence saved England: A Tale of the Great Invasion* (London).

1910 ANON., *The German Invasion of England* (London).

ANON., *Nederlands doodsstrijd in 1918* (Utrecht).

BELL, COL. CHARLES PERCIVAL LYNDEN, *How Germany Makes War* (London).

BERESFORD, LESLIE, *The Second Rising* (London).

CUTCLIFFE-HYNE, C. J., *The Empire of the World* (London).

DANRIT, CAPITAINE. (DRIANT, ÉMILE AUGUSTE), *L'Alerte* (Paris).

DUDLEY, CARL HENSON, *And This is War* (New York).

GLENDON, G., *The Emperor of the Air* (London).

HALE, COL. LONSDALE, *The Horrors of War in Great Britain* (London).

KIPLING, ARTHUR WELLESLEY, *The Shadow of Glory, being a History of the Great War of 1910–11* (London).

1911 BOUCHER, COL. ARTHUR, *La France victorieuse dans la guerre de demain* (Paris).

GRIFFITH, GEORGE, *The Lord of Labour* (London).

POLLOCK. LT.-COL. ALSAGER, *Lord Roastem's Campaign in North-Eastern France* (London).

SCHMIDT-KESTNER, HANS, *Die Gelbe Gefahr* (Wiesbaden).

1912 ANON., *Birkenfeld, Und dann . . .?! Fortsetzung der Schlacht auf dem Birkenfelde in Westfalen 191..! Errettung des deutschen Reichs vom Untergang! Von einem aktiven deutschen General* (Leipzig); see entry below under Civrieux.

BLYTH, JAMES, *The Peril of Pines Place* (London).

BOUCHER, COL. ARTHUR, *L'Offensive contre l'Allemagne* (Paris).

BRACCIO DI MONTONE, N. (MAUNI, BARON ROGER DE), *La Bataille de la Woevre (1915)* (Paris).

BREX (TWELLS, JOHN), *The Civil War of 1915* (London).

CAMPBELL, SPENCER, *Under the Red Ensign* (London).

CIVRIEUX, COMMANDANT DE, *La Bataille du 'Champs des Bouleaux' 191..* (Paris).

EXSELSIOR (SCHULZE-GALLERA, DR SIEGMAR), *Michael der Grosse: Eine Kaiserbiographie der Zukunft* (Leipzig).

FAWKES, F. ATTFIELD, *Found—a Man* (London).

GASTINE, LOUIS, *Les Torpilleurs de l'air* (Paris), published in London (1913) as *War in Space: A Grand Romance of Aircraft War between France and Germany*.

JANSON, GUSTAF, *Lognerna: berattelser om Kriget* (Stockholm); also published in London (1912) as *Pride of War*.

LAMSZUS, WILHELM, *Das Menschenschlachthaus* (Leipzig); published in London (1913) as *The Human Slaughter-House*.

MARK TIME (IRWIN, H. C.), *A Derelict Empire* (London).

MOTTA, LUIGI, *La Principessa delle rose* (Milan); published in London (1919) as *The Princess of the Roses*.

NAVAL OFFICER, A, *Great was the Fall* (London).

PALMER, WILLIAM, *Under Home Rule* (London).

ROSNY, J.-H., *Bataille* (Paris).

SEARCHLIGHT (EARDLEY-WILMOT, REAR-ADML.), *The Battle of the North Sea in 1915* (London).

SOMMERFELD, A., *Frankreichs Ende im Jahre 19??* (Leipzig).

WALLACE, EDGAR, *Private Selby* (London).

1913   ANON., *Les Ailes de la victoire* (Paris).

ANON., *Le Partage de l'Allemagne* (Paris); written in answer to Sommerfeld (1912),

AUSTIN, F. BRITTEN, *In Action: Studies in War* (London).

BLEIBTREU, KARL, *Weltbrand* (Berlin).

FRANCS-AVIATEURS, LES, *Comment nous torpillerons Berlin* (Paris).

GAULOIS, FRANC (pseud.), *La Fin de la Prusse et le démembrement de l'Allemagne* (Geneva).

HANSEN, V., *Die vierte Waffe* (Leipzig).

HOPPENSTEDT, JULIUS, *Deutschlands Heer in der Entscheidungsschlacht* (Berlin).

HOPPENSTEDT, JULIUS, *Die Millionenschlacht an der Saar: Ein Beispiel moderner Kriegskunst* (Berlin).

MATTINGLEY, SIDNEY, *The Terror by Night* (London).

POLLOCK, LT.-COL. ALSAGER, *In the Cockpit of Europe* (London).

SAKI (MUNRO, HECTOR HUGH), *When William Came* (London).

SHIEL, M. P., *The Dragon* (London).

1914   ANON. (BUAT, LT.-GÉNÉRAL), *La Concentration allemande: D'après un document trouvé dans un compartiment de chemin de fer* (Paris).

ANON., *Der europäische Krieg* (Berlin).

ANON., *Das Resultat des russisch-österreichischen Krieges, 1918* (Cracow).

ANON. (LEHMANN-RUSSBÜLDT, O.), *Die Schöpfung der Vereinigten Staten von Europa* (Leipzig).

DOYLE, SIR ARTHUR CONAN, *Danger* (London); first published in *Strand Magazine* (July 1914).

GOUVRIEUX, MARC, *Haut les ailes: Carnet de route d'un officier aviateur pendant la guerre de 19. .* (Paris); published in London (1916) as *With Wings Outspread*.

HAINES, DONAL HAMILTON, *The Last Invasion* (New York).

LEONARD, FRANÇOIS, *La Conquête de Londres* (Geneva).

MACHEN, ARTHUR, *The Bowmen* (London); first published in *Evening News* (20 September).

1914   NEWTON, W. D., *The North Afire; A Picture of What May Be* (London).
       NEWTON, W. D., *War* (London).
       PALMER, FREDERICK. *The Last Shot* (New York and London).
       RAUTENBERG, L., *Die Dreibund an die Front* (Dresden).
       WELLS, H. G., *The World Set Free* (London).
       Y, *The German Campaign against France* (Washington, DC); reprinted from
         the *Fortnightly Review* (Sept. 1911).

1915   ANON. (MÜNCH, PAUL GEORG), *Hindenburgs Einmarsch in London* (Leipzig);
         published in London (1916) as *Hindenburg's March into London: Being a
         Translation from the German Original*, edited with a preface by L. G.
         Redmond-Howard.
       BARNEY, J. STEWART, *L.P.M.: The End of the Great War* (New York).
       BERNSTORFF, HANS NIKOLAUS ERNEST GRAF VON, *Ran an den Feind*
         (Leipzig).
       COWEN, LAURENCE, *'Wake Up!' A Dream of Tomorrow* (London).
       GIESY, JOHN ULRICH, *All for His Country* (New York).
       HAINES, DONAL HAMILTON, *Clearing the Seas; or, The Last of the Warships*
         (New York and London).
       LANDSBERGER, ARTHUR, *Hass: Der Roman eines Deutsch-Engländers aus d.j.
         1950* (Munich).
       THORNE, GUY (GULL, CYRIL ARTHUR RANGER), *The Secret Seaplane*
         (London).
       WALLACE, EDGAR, *'1925': The Story of a Fatal Peace* (London).
       WALKER, J. BERNARD, *America Fallen! The Sequel to the European War*
         (New York and London).

1916   ANON., *Der nächste Weltkrieg: Die Prophezeiung eines neutralen Diplomaten*
         (Geneva).
       DIXON, THOMAS, *The Fall of a Nation* (New York and London).
       MOFFETT, CLEVELAND, *The Conquest of America: A Romance of Disaster and
         Victory: USA AD 1921* (New York and London).
       MULLER, JULIUS WASHINGTON, *The Invasion of America* (New York).
       WALKER, ROWLAND, *Buckle of Submarine V2* (London).

1917   ALLEN, ROBERT, *Captain Gardiner of the International Police* (London).
       KARTOFFEL, BARON VON (pseud.), *The Germans in Cork: Being the Letters of
         his Excellency, the . . . Military Governor of Cork in the Year 1918*
         (London).
       STEAD, F. HERBERT, *No More War!* (London).

1918   GREGORY, OWEN, *Meccania: the Super-State* (London).

1919   BLEACKLEY, HORACE, *Anymoon* (London).
       NEWTE, H. W. C., *The Red Fury: Britain under Bolshevism* (London).
       WAGNER, ÉMILE R., *La Troisième guerre punique; la revanche de la kultur*
         (Paris).

1920   COURNOS, JOHN, *London under the Bolsheviks: A Londoner's Dream on
         Returning from Petrograd* (London).
       HAMBROOK, EMERSON C., *The Red Tomorrow* (London).
       SHANKS, EDWARD, *The People of the Ruins* (London).

1921 AUTENRIETH, OTTO, *Bismarck II: Der Roman der deutschen Zukunft* (Munich).

BANNERMAN, SIR ALEXANDER, *Leaders of the Blind* (London).

BERESFORD, J. D., *Revolution* (London).

BOSCHMANS, RAYMOND, *Les Ailes repoussent* (Paris).

DE SAUNIER, BAUDRY, *Comment Paris a été détruit* (Paris).

SOLF, MAJ. F. E., *1934: Deutschlands Auferstehung* (Naumburg).

1922 ABEL-MUSGRAVE, DR KURT, *Der Bazillenkrieg* (Frankfurt).

BARBOR, HUBERT REGINALD, *Against the Red Sky: Silhouettes of Revolution* (London).

ČAPEK, KAREL, *Továrno na Absolutno* (Prague); published in London (1922) as *The Absolute at Large*.

FECHNER, E., *Die Vernichtung der Westmächte durch den erwachenden Orient* (Naumburg).

GRASSEGGER, WILHELM, *Die rächende Stunde: Englands Schicksaltsag; Ein Zukunftsbild; Vom deutschen Aufsteig zu neuer Macht und Grösse* (Naumburg).

GRASSEGGER, WILHELM, *Der Zweite Weltkrieg: Deutschland, die Waffenschmiede; Eine militärische Prophezeiung* (Naumburg).

LIST, MAJOR SINGLE (pseud.), *The Battle of Booby's Bluff* (London).

RABE, C., *Nie wieder Krieg* (Naumburg).

VAN PEDROE-SAVAGE, E., *The Flying Submarine* (London).

1923 ADDISON, H. (OWEN, HARRY COLLINSON), *The Battle of London* (London).

GRAHAM, PETER ANDERSON, *The Collapse of Homo sapiens* (London).

WHARTON, ANTHONY (MCALLISTER, ALISTAIR), *The Man on the Hill* (London).

X, PROFESSEUR, *La Guerre microbienne; la fin du monde* (Paris).

1924 ANON. (FORBES, ALEXANDER), *The Radio Gunner* (Boston, Mass.).

BOSCHMANS, RAYMOND, *La Guerre nécessaire* (Paris).

ČAPEK, KAREL, *Krakatit* (Prague); published in London (1925) as *Krakatit*.

HUSSINGTREE, M. (BALDWIN, OLIVER RIDSDALE), *Konyetz* (London).

MACCLURE, VICTOR, *Ultimatum* (London); also published in New York as *The Ark of the Covenant*.

MEILLAC, CHARLES, *1935: Roman sur la prochaine guerre franco-allemande* (Paris).

THORNE, GUY (GULL, CYRIL ARTHUR RANGER), *When the World Reeled* (London).

1925 BYWATER, HECTOR C., *The Great Pacific War: A History of the American-Japanese Campaign of 1931–33* (London and New York).

CORON, HANNAH, *Ten Years Hence?* (London).

LYNCH, BOHUN, *Menace from the Moon* (London).

OPPENHEIM, E. P., *The Wrath to Come* (London).

PANHANS, ERNST J., *Der schwarzgelbe Weltbund* (Hamburg).

PÉROCHON, ERNEST, *Les Hommes frénétiques* (Paris).

SCHOENAICH, GEN.-MAJ., *Der Krieg im Jahre 1930* (Berlin).

SHAW, STANLEY, *The Locust Horde* (London).

1926   ALEXANDER, HANS, *Der Völkermord im kommenden Giftgaskrieg* (Wiesbaden).

AUSTIN, F. BRITTEN, *The War-God Walks Again* (London).

BAXTER, G. (RESSICH, J. S. M., and DE BANZIE, E.), *Blue Lightning* (London).

BECHER, JOHANNES, R., *(CHCI=CH)3As (Levisite): oder der einzige gerechte Krieg* (Vienna).

DESMOND, HUGH, *Ragnarok* (London).

GRANT, ISABEL FRANCIS, *A Candle in the Hills* (London).

HALSBURY, EARL OF, *1944* (London).

SPANNER, E. F., *The Broken Trident* (London).

SPANNER, E. F., *The Naviators* (London).

TOLSTOI, ALEXEI, *Giperboloid inzhenera Garina* (Moscow), published in London (1936) as *The Deathbox*.

1927   DAUDET, LÉON, *Le Napus* (Paris).

GUGGENBERGER, S., *Eurafasia* (Vienna).

HOFBAUER, L., *Der Pestkrieg* (Regensburg).

MONTAGUE, CHARLES EDWARD, *Right off the Map* (London).

NOYES, PIERREPONT B., *The Pallid Giant* (New York).

OXENHAM, JOHN (DUNKERLEY, WILLIAM ARTHUR), *The Man who Would Save the World* (London).

SPANNER, E. F., *The Harbour of Death* (London).

1928   BENTLEY, NORMAN K., *Drake's Mantle* (London).

LINDSAY, CAPT. CHARLES McDONALD, *Betrayed! or, What Might Come To Pass* (London).

RAXIN, ALEXANDER, *Der nächste Massenmord* (Leipzig).

SADLER, ADAM, *Red Ending* (London).

1929   EDWARDS, G. (PENDRAY, GEORGE EDWARD), *The Earth Tube* (New York and London).

GIBBONS, FLOYD, *The Red Napoleon* (New York and London).

GRAHAM, H. E. (HAMILTON, ERNEST GRAHAM), *The Defence of Bowler Bridge* (London).

HEYCK, HANS, *Deutschland ohne Deutsche* (Leipzig).

MÉRIC, VICTOR, *La 'Der des Der'* (Paris).

PENMARE, WILLIAM (NISOT, MAVIS ELIZABETH), *The Man Who Could Stop War* (London).

SHIEL, M. P., *The Yellow Peril* (London); first published (1913) as *The Dragon*.

1930   ANON., *Revolution 1933* (London).

BLAIR, HAMISH, *1947* (Edinburgh).

GÜNTSCHE, GEORG, *Panropa* (Cologne).

DOUHET, GIULIO, 'La Guerra del 19—', *Rivista Aeronautica* (March 1930).

JERROLD, DOUGLAS, *Storm over Europe* (London).

MILES (SOUTHWOLD, STEPHEN), *The Seventh Bowl* (London).

SUTHERLAND, MORRIS (MORRIS, GWENDOLEN SUTHERLAND), *Second Storm* (London).

1931   ALTER, JUNIUS, *Nie wieder Krieg . . .?! Ein Blick in Deutschlands Zukunft* (Leipzig).

ANON., *La Surprise. Überaschung: Traduction de C. Bernart* (Paris); claims to be the translation of a manuscript written in 1931 by an officer in the German army.

ARTUS, LOUIS, *Paix sur la terre* (Paris).

BARTZ, KARL, *Krieg-1960* (Berlin).

BERKELEY, REGINALD, *Cassandra* (London).

BLAIR, HAMISH (BLAIR, ANDREW JAMES FRASER), *Governor Hardy* (London).

BLAIR, HAMISH (BLAIR, ANDREW JAMES FRASER), *The Great Gesture* (London).

BRAUN, F., *Einfall in London* (Berlin).

GOBSCH, HANS, *Wahn-Europa, 1934* (Berlin); published in London (1932) as *Death Rattle.*

GÖTZ, WILHELM, *Vor neuen Weltkatastrophen: Eine Warnung und ein Ziel* (Leipzig).

GRAHAM, H. E. (HAMILTON, ERNEST GRAHAM), *The Battle of Dora* (London).

LE PRÊTRE, WILLIAM, *The Bolshevik* (London).

MILES (SOUTHWOLD, STEPHEN), *The Gas War of 1940* (London).

NEWMAN, BERNARD, *Armoured Doves* (London).

ROYET, COL., *La Guerre est declarée* (Paris).

1932 EDMONDS, HARRY, *The Riddle of the Straits* (London)..

GODWIN, GEORGE, *Empty Victory* (London).

HELDERS, MAJ. (KNAUSS, ROBERT), *Luftkrieg 1936: Die Zertrümmung von Paris* (Berlin); published in London (1932) as *The War in the Air, 1936.*

IMMANUEL (pseud.), *Der grosse Zukunftskrieg* (Berlin).

KONDOR (pseud.), *Gelb gegen Weiss* (Wiesbaden).

KOSSAK-RAYTENAU, KARL LUDWIG, *Katastrophe 1940: Nieder mit Versailles!* (Oldenburg).

LEERS, JOHANN VON, *Bomben auf Hamburg* (Leipzig).

NICOLSON, HAROLD, *Public Faces* (London).

NITRAM, H. (MARTIN, HANS), *Achtung! Ostmarkenrundfunk! Polnische Truppen haben heute die ostpreussische Grenze überschritten . . .* (Oldenburg).

O'SHEEL, S., *It Never Could Happen; or, The Second American Revolution* (New York).

1933 BLACK, LADBROKE, *The Poison War* (London).

CORDAY, MICHEL, *Ciel rose* (Paris).

EDMONDS, HARRY, *Red Invader* (London).

GROSSER, R. F., *Asakafu mobilisiert den Osten* (Bremen).

HERMANN, FRANZ, *Die Erde in Flammen* (Leipzig).

SIBSON, FRANCIS H., *Unthinkable* (London).

STERNE, JULIAN, *The Secret of the Zodiac* (London).

VIERECK, G. S., and ELDRIDGE, P., *Prince Pax* (London).

WELLS, H. G., *The Shape of Things to Come* (London).

WILLIAMS, CHARLES, *Shadows of Ecstasy* (London).

1934 CHOMTON, WERNER, *Weltbrand vom Morgen* (Stuttgart).

1934   CHRISTIE, DOUGLAS, *The Striking Force* (London).
       CURTIS, MONICA, *Landslide* (London).
       DALTON, MORAY, *The Black Death* (London).
       DAUDET, LÉON, *Ciel de feu* (Paris).
       MACILRAITH, FRANK, and CONNOLLY, ROY, *Invasion from the Air* (London).
       MOSELEY, MABOTH, *War upon Women* (London).
       PRESTRE, WILLY, *Tocsins dans la Nuit* (Paris).
       REID, LESLIE, *Cauldron Bubble* (London).
       SPENCER, D. A., and RANDERSON, W., *North Sea Monster* (London).
       TROUBETZKOY, PRINCESS P., and NEVINSON, C. R. W., *Exodus, AD: A Warning to Civilians* (London).
       WHEATLEY, DENNIS, *Black August* (London).

1935   BIALKOWSKI, STANISLAUS, *Krieg im All: Roman aus der Zukunft der Technik* (Leipzig).
       BROWNE, DOUGLAS G., *The Stolen Boat-Train* (London).
       CONNELL, JOHN, *David Go Back* (London).
       CORNWALLIS-WEST, GEORGE, *The Woman who Stopped War* (London).
       DETRE, PROFESSOR L., *Kampf zweier Welten* (Vienna); published in London (1936) as *War of Two Worlds*.
       DIVINE, DAVID (DIVINE, ARTHUR DURHAM), *They Blocked the Suez Canal* (London).
       EDMONDS, H., *The Professor's Last Experiment* (London).
       OHLINGER, ERNST, *Bomben auf Kohlenstadt* (Oldenburg).
       POLLARD, LESLIE, *Menace* (London).
       STOKES, SIMPSON, *Air-God's Parade* (London).
       STUART, FRANCIS (FAWCETT, FRANK DUBREZ), *The Angel of Pity* (London).
       WARD, RICHARD HERON, *The Sun Shall Rise* (London).
       WOOD, SAMUEL ANDREW, *I'll Blackmail the World* (London).
       WRIGHT, SYDNEY FOWLER, *Prelude in Prague: A Story of the War of 1938* (London).

1936   BARAUDE, H. (TUPINIER, BARON AUGUSTIN JOSEPH), *La Catastrophe* (Paris).
       BEVERLEY, BARRINGTON, *The Space Raiders* (London).
       BREHPOL, WILHELM, *Vom Ende der Tagen* (Essen).
       BURKE, NORAH, *The Scarlet Vampire* (London).
       ČAPEK, KAREL, *Válka s mloky (Prague); published in London (1937) as War with the Newts*.
       CHANNING, MARK, *The Poisoned Mountain* (London).
       DEVERDUN, P.-L, *Le 'Redoutable': journal d'un commandant de vedette* (Paris).
       GÉRARD, FRANCIS, *The Black Emperor* (London).
       JAEGER, MURIEL, *Retreat from Armageddon* (London).
       KOSSAK-RAYTENAU, KARL LUDWIG, *Lermontov vernichtet die Welt* (Berlin).
       MACLEOD, J. G., *Overture to Cambridge* (London).
       MACPHERSON, IAN, *Wild Harbour* (London).
       O'NEILL, JOSEPH, *Day of Wrath* (London).
       PHILLPOTTS, EDEN, *The Owl of Athene* (London).

TUNSTALL, BRIAN, *Eagles Restrained* (London).

WRIGHT, SYDNEY FOWLER, *Four Days' War* (London).

1937　ADAM, RUTH, *War on Saturday Week* (London).

BIALKOWSKI, STANISLAUS, *Der Radiumkrieg!* (Leipzig).

CAMPION, SARAH (COULTON, MARY), *Thirty Million Gas Masks* (London).

JONES, GLYN, *The Blue Bed* (London).

HAWKER, R. C., *The Great Peril* (London).

OPPENHEIM, E. P., *The Dumb Gods Speak* (London).

PAVLENKO, PETR, *Na Vostokye* (Moscow); published in London (1938) as *Red Planes Fly East.*

SHIEL, M. P., *The Young Men Are Coming* (London).

WRIGHT, SYDNEY FOWLER, *Megiddo's Ridge* (London).

1938　BEAUJON, PAUL (WARD, BEATRICE LAMBERTON), *Peace upon Earth: Dialogues from the Year 1940* (London).

CACAUD, MICHEL, *La Guerre des ailes . . . demain* (Paris).

DESMOND, SHAW, *Chaos* (London).

LINKLATER, ERIC, *The Impregnable Women* (London).

MARTIN, J. S., *General Manpower* (New York).

POLLARD, CAPT. A. O., *Air Reprisal* (London).

RADCLIFFE, GARNETT, *The Sky Wolves* (London).

RAMSEYER, EDWIN, *Airmen over the Suburb* (London).

SETON, GRAHAM (HUTCHISON, GRAHAM SETON), *According to Plan* (London).

YOUNG, ROBERT (PAYNE, P. S. R.), *The War in the Marshes* (London).

1939　CAZAL, CMDT. (DE LA HIRE, JEAN), *L'Afrique en flammes* (Paris).

CAZAL, CMDT. (DE LA HIRE, JEAN), *Batailles pour la mer* (Paris).

CAZAL, CMDT. (DE LA HIRE, JEAN), *La Fin par le pétrol* (Paris).

CAZAL, CMDT. (DE LA HIRE, JEAN), *La guerre! La guerre!* (Paris).

CAZAL, CMDT. (DE LA HIRE, JEAN), *Maginot-Siegfried* (Paris).

CHADWICK, PHILIP GEORGE, *The Death Guard* (London).

GRAIG, CHARLES WILLIAM THURLOW, *Plague over London* (London).

GEORGE, VERNON (VERNON, GEORGE S.), *The Crown of Asia* (London).

SCHUBERT, A., *Weltwende durch Gas* (Berlin).

SHUTE, NEVIL (NORWAY, NEVIL SHUTE), *What Happened to the Corbetts* (London); also published in New York as *Ordeal.*

VERDUN, COMDT., *L'Escadron cyclone* (Paris).

VERDUN, COMDT., *Face à l'ennemi* (Paris).

WHITE, A., *Attack on America* (Boston).

1940　BROWN, DOUGLAS, and SERPELL, CHRISTOPHER, *Loss of Eden* (London).

NELSON, A. D., *America Betrayed* (New York).

NOYES, ALFRED, *The Last Man* (London); also published in New York as *No Other Man.*

PRASSER, VIKTORIA, *Die Sage von der Zukunftsschlacht am Baum* (Berlin).

VAN LOON, H. W., *Invasion* (New York and London).

1941　NATHAN, ROBERT, *They Went on Together* (New York and London).

1942　BOSHELL, GORDON, *John Brown's Body* (London).

1942   DIVINE, DAVID, *Tunnel from Calais* (London).

JAMESON, STORM, *Then We Shall Hear Singing* (London).

MORTON, H. V., *I, James Blunt* (London).

NEWMAN, BERNARD, *Secret Weapon* (London).

SACKVILLE-WEST, VITA, *Grand Canyon* (London).

1943   ARMSTRONG, ANTHONY, and GRAEME, BRUCE (WILLIS, G. A. and JEFFRIES, G. M), *When the Bells Rang* (London).

BARJAVEL, RENÉ, *Ravage* (Paris); published in New York (1967) as *Ashes, Ashes.*

CHAMBERS, WHITMAN, *Invasion!* (New York).

HAWKIN, MARTIN (HAWKINS, MARTIN), *When Adolf Came* (London).

KENT, CLAUDE H., *Armistice or Total Victory?* (London).

MAUGHAM, ROBIN, *The 1946 MS* (London).

RUSSELL, ERIC FRANK, *Sinister Barrier* (London).

1944   BEYMER, WILLIAM GILMORE, *12.20 P.M.* (New York).

COLLINS, ERROL, *Mariners of Space* (London).

LEA, RICHARD, *The Outward Urge* (London).

LESSNER, ERWIN, *Phantom Victory: A Fictional History of the Fourth Reich 1945–60* (New York).

1945   FOWLER, SYDNEY (WRIGHT, SYDNEY FOWLER), *The Adventure of the Blue Room* (London).

1946   BAKER, GORDON, *None So Blind* (London).

JENKINS, WILL F., *The Murder of the USA* (New York).

KARIG, WALTER, CAPT., *War in the Atomic Age?* (New York).

NOYES, PIERREPONT B., *Gentlemen, You Are Mad* (New York); reissue of *The Pallid Giant.* (1927).

ROSE, FREDERICK HORACE, *The Maniac's Dream* (London).

1947   ELDERSHAW, M. B. (ELDERSHAW, F. S., and BARNARD, M. F.), *Tomorrow and Tomorrow* (Melbourne).

ENGEL, LEONARD, and PILLER, EMANUEL S., *World Aflame: The Russian-American War of 1950* (New York).

KEPPEL-JONES, ARTHUR, *When Smuts Goes* (London).

LEINSTER, MURRAY (JENKINS, W. F.), *Fight for Life* (New York).

MAXWELL, C. F., *Plan 79* (London).

1948   BARJAVEL, RÉNE, *Le Diable l'emporte* (Paris).

BORODIN, GEORGE (BANKOFF, GEORGE ALEXIS), *Spurious Sun* (London).

DAHL, ROALD, *Sometime Never* (New York).

DE CAMP, L. SPRAGUE, *Divide and Rule* (Reading, Pa.).

FARJEON, J. JEFFERSON, *Death of a World* (London).

FAULCONBRIDGE, PHILIP (pseud.), *Commissars over Britain* (London).

GIBBS, HENRY, *Pawns in Ice* (London).

GROOM, PELHAM, *The Purple Twilight* (London).

HUBBARD, L. RON, *Final Blackout* (Providence, RI).

NEWMAN, BERNARD, *The Flying Saucer* (London).

1949   BALINT, EMERY, *Don't Inhale It!* (New York).

DEMAITRE, EDMUND, and APPLEMAN, MARK J., *The Liberation of Manhattan* (New York).

FITZGIBBON, CONSTANTINE, *The Iron Hoop* (New York).

GRAVES, ROBERT, *Seven Days in New Crete* (London); also published in New York as *Watch the North Wind Rise*.

HEINLEIN, ROBERT A., *Sixth Column* (New York); published in London (1962) as *The Day After Tomorrow*.

HUXLEY, A., *Ape and Essence* (London).

JAMESON, STORM, *The Moment of Truth* (London).

LEINSTER, MURRAY (JENKINS, WILLIAM FITZGERALD), *The Last Space ship* (New York).

NEWMAN, BERNARD, *Shoot* (London).

ORWELL, GEORGE (BLAIR, ERIC), *Nineteen Eighty-Four* (London).

WILLIAMSON, JACK, *The Humanoids* (New York).

1950 ASIMOV, ISAAC, *Pebble in the Sky* (New York).

BRADBURY, RAY, *The Martian Chronicles* (New York); published in London (1951) as *The Silver Locusts*.

FISCHER, LEONARD, *Let out the Beast* (Toronto).

GOHDE, HERMANN, *Der achte Tag* (Innsbruck).

GUERARD, ALBERT JOSEPH, *Night Journey* (New York).

KUTTNER, HENRY, and MOORE, CATHERINE L., *Fury* (New York).

LEIBER, F., *Gather, Darkness!* (New York).

MERRIL, JUDITH, *Shadow on the Hearth* (New York).

REYNOLDS, PHILIP (pseud.), *Ce pourrait passer comme ça*. (Paris); published in New York (1951) as *When and If*, and in London (1951) as *It Happened Like This*.

ROBBAN, RANDOLPH, *Si l'Allemagne avait vaincu* (Paris).

WILEY, RAY. H., *On the Trail of 1960: A Utopian Novel* (New York).

1951 BRUCKNER, K. C., *Nur zwei Roboter?* (Berlin); published in London (1964) as *The Hour of the Robots*.

COLLIER'S, 'Preview of the War We Do Not Want', special issue for 27 October 1951.

DUBOIS, THEODORA, *Solution T-25* (New York).

EDMONDS, HARRY, *The Rockets (Operation Manhattan)* (London).

GIBBS, LEWIS (COVE, JOSEPH WALTER), *Late Final* (London).

HAMILTON, EDMOND, *City at World's End* (New York).

JONES, RAYMOND F., *Renaissance* (New York).

PILKINGTON, ROGER, *Stringer's Folly* (London).

RAYER, FRANCIS GEORGE, *Tomorrow Sometimes Comes* (London).

RUSSELL, ERIC FRANK, *The Star Watchers* (New York); published in London (1954) as *Sentinels from Space*.

SIMAK, CLIFFORD D., *Time and Again* (New York).

TUCKER, WILSON, *The City in the Sea* (New York).

WEST, ANTHONY, *Another Kind* (London).

VAN VOGT, A. E., *The House that Stood Still* (New York).

1951 WYLIE, PHILIP, *The Smuggled Atom Bomb* (New York).

WYNDHAM, JOHN (HARRIS, JOHN BEYNON), *The Day of the Triffids* (London).

1952 ANDERSON, POUL, *Vault of the Ages* (New York).

BERRY, BRYAN, *Born in Captivity* (London).

BLOCH-MICHEL, JEAN, *La Fuite en Egypte* (Paris); published in London (1957) as *The Flight into Egypt*.

CAMERON, BERL, *Cosmic Echelon* (London).

CALDWELL, TAYLOR, *The Devil's Advocate* (New York).

CONKLIN, GROFF, *Invaders of Earth (New York)*.

CONROY, RICK, *Mission from Mars* (London).

DUNCAN, RONALD, *The Last Adam* (London).

HAWKINSON, JOHN L., *We, the Few* (New York).

JONES, RAYMOND F., *This Island Earth* (New York).

KORRODI-WYLER, KARL, *Die drei grossen Weltkriege der Endzeit der christlichen Aera* (Zürich).

MACDONALD, JOHN D., *Ballroom of the Skies* (New York).

NORTON, ANDRÉ, *Star Man's Son* (New York and London).

SCOTT, WARWICK (SMITH, TREVOR DUDLEY), *The Domesday Story* (London).

SLATER, HENRY J., *The Smashed World* (London).

TUBB, E. C., *Atom War on Mars* (London).

TUCKER, WILSON, *The Long Loud Silence* (New York).

WARD, JULIAN, *We Died in Bond Street* (London).

WILLIAMS, ISLWYN, *Dangerous Waters* (London).

WOLFE, BERNARD, *Limbo* (New York); published in London (1953) as *Limbo '90*.

1953 BERRY, BRYAN, *From What Far Star* (London).

BERRY, BRYAN, *The Venom-seekers* (London).

BRADBURY, RAY, *Fahrenheit 451* (New York).

CAPON, PAUL, *The World at Bay* (London).

DIVINE, DAVID, *Atom at Spithead* (London).

ELLIOT, LEE, *Overlord New York* (London).

ELLIOT, LEE, *The Third Mutant* (London).

KORNBLUTH, C. M., *The Syndic* (New York).

LANG, GREGOR, *Terra* (New York).

MACINTOSH, J. T. (MACGREGOR, JAMES MURDOCH), *World Out of Mind* (New York).

MOORE, WARD, *Bring the Jubilee* (New York).

PADGETT, LEWIS (KUTTNER, HENRY), *Mutant* (New York).

RICHMOND, MARY, *The Grim Tomorrow* (London).

VANDEL, JEAN GASTON, *Attentat cosmique* (Paris); published in London (1954) as *Enemy beyond Pluto*.

WELLARD, JAMES, *Night in Babylon* (London).

WYNDHAM, JOHN (HARRIS, JOHN BEYNON), *The Kraken Wakes* (London); also published in New York as *Out of the Deeps*.

1954 BENNETT, MARGOT, *The Long Way Back* (London).

BLACK, DOROTHY, *Candles in the Dark* (London).

BOUQUET, MARCEL, *Et ce fût la guerre atomique* (Paris).

BURKE, JONATHAN (BURKE, JOHN FREDERICK), *The Echoing Worlds* (London).

CROWCROFT, PETER, *The Fallen Sky* (London).

DEXTER, WILLIAM (PRITCHARD, WILLIAM THOMAS), *World in Eclipse* (London).

GOLDING, WILLIAM, *The Lord of the Flies* (London).

GORDON, REX (HOUGH, STANLEY BENNETT), *Utopia 239* (London).

MCINTOSH, J. T. (MACGREGOR, JAMES MURDOCH), *Born Leader* (New York).

MACKENZIE, NIGEL, *Invasion from Space* (London).

RUSSELL, ERIC FRANK, *The Star Watchers* (London); also published in New York as *Sentinels from Space*.

SHAFER, ROBERT, *The Conquered Place* (New York).

TUBB, E. C., *World at Bay* (London).

WRIGHT, SYDNEY FOWLER, *Spider's War* (New York).

WYLIE, PHILIP, *Tomorrow!* (New York).

1955 ASH, ALAN, *Conditioned for Space* (London).

BARR, DENSIL NEVE (BUTTREY, DOUGLAS NORTON), *The Man with Only One Head* (London).

BOLAND, JOHN, *White August* (London).

BOUNDS, SYDNEY JAMES, *The Moon Raiders* (London).

BRACKETT, LEIGH, *The Long Tomorrow* (New York).

BURKE, JONATHAN, *Revolt of the Humans* (London).

CONQUEST, ROBERT, *A World of Difference* (London).

DEXTER, WILLIAM (PRITCHARD, WILLIAM THOMAS), *World in Eclipse* (London).

DEXTER, WILLIAM (PRITCHARD, WILLIAM THOMAS), *Children of the Void* (London); sequel to above.

ELLIOTT, H. CHANDLER, *Reprieve from Paradise* (New York).

ELTON, JOHN, *The Green Plantations* (London).

HOUGH, S. B., *Utopia 239* (London).

HUGHES, RILEY, *The Hills Were Liars* (Milwaukee).

MEAD, HAROLD, *The Bright Phoenix* (London).

KORNBLUTH, C. M., *Not this August* (New York; published in London (1957) as *Christmas Eve*.

MCCANN, EDSON (DEL REY, LESTER, and POHL, FREDERIK), *Preferred Risk* (New York).

MCINTOSH, J. T. (MACGREGOR, J. M.), *The Fittest* (New York).

MEAD, HAROLD, *The Bright Phoenix* (London).

REIN, HAROLD, *Few Were Left* (New York and London).

ROBERTS, TERENCE (SANDERSON, IVAN TERENCE), *Report on the Status Quo* (New York).

SAVAGE, RICHARD, *When the Moon Died* (London).

SOHL, JERRY, *Point Ultimate* (New York).

STORMONT, LAN, *Tan Ming* (New York).

TUCKER, WILSON, *Time Bomb* (New York).

1955   WYNDHAM, JOHN (HARRIS, JOHN BEYNON), *The Chrysalids* (London); also published in New York (1955) as *Rebirth*.

1956   BESTER, ALFRED, *The Stars my Destination* (New York); also published in London as *Tiger! Tiger!*.

BOUNDS, SYDNEY JAMES, *The World Wrecker* (London).

CAIDIN, MARTIN, *The Long Night* (New York).

CHRISTOPHER, JOHN (YOUD, CHRISTOPHER SAMUEL), *The Death of Grass* (London).

FRANK, PAT (HART, HARRY), *Forbidden Area* (Philadelphia); published in London (1957) as *Seven Days to Never*.

HERBERT, FRANK, *The Dragon in the Sea* (New York).

HOUGH, STANLEY BENNETT, *Extinction Bomber* (London).

JONES, RAYMOND F., *The Secret People* (London); published in Boston (1959) as *The Deviates*.

LOTT, S. MAKEPEACE, *Escape to Venus (London)*.

MARTINSON, HARRY, *Aniara: en Revy om Människan i Tid och Rum* (Stockholm); published in London (1963) as *Aniara: A Review of Man in Time and Space*.

MONSARRAT, NICHOLAS, *The Tribe that Lost its Head* (London).

RICHARDS, GUY, *Two Rubles to Times Square* (New York); published in London (1957) as *Brother Bear*.

WILLIAMS, NICK BODDIE, *The Atom Curtain* (New York).

1957   ADLER, ALLEN A., *Mach 1: A Story of Planet Ionus* (New York).

BANNISTER, MANLY, *Conquest of Earth* (New York).

BARLOW, JAMES, *One Half of the World* (London).

COLE, BURT, *Subi: The Volcano* (New York).

GAYLE, HENRY K., *Spawn of the Vortex* (New York).

KIRST, HANS HELLMUT, *Keiner kommt davon: Bericht von den letzten Tagen Europas* (Vienna and Munich); published in New York and London (1959) as *The Seventh Day*, and in Manchester (1960) as *No One Will Escape*.

MACKENZIE, NIGEL, *The Wrath to Come* (London).

MARS, ALASTAIR (GILLESPIE, ALASTAIR CAMPBELL), *Atomic Submarine* (London).

MOORE, C. L., *Doomsday Morning* (New York).

NORTON, ANDRÉ, *Sea Siege* (New York).

PADGETT, LEWIS (KUTTNER, HENRY), *Tomorrow and Tomorrow; and, The Fairy Chessmen* (New York); published in London (1963) as *Tomorrow and Tomorrow*.

POHL, FREDERIK, *Slave Ship* (New York).

POWYS, JOHN COOPER, *Up and Out* (London).

SCHMIDT, ARNO, *Die Gelehrtenrepublik* (Karslruhe); published in London (1979) as *The Egghead Republic: A Short Novel from the Horse Latitudes*.

SHUTE, NEVIL (NORWAY, NEVIL SHUTE), *On the Beach* (London).

SILVERBERG, ROBERT, *The Thirteenth Immortal* (New York).

SISSON, MARJORIE, *The Cave* (Hemingford Grey, Hunts).

1958   BRYANT, PETER (GEORGE, PETER BRYAN), *Two Hours to Doom* (London); also published in New York as *Red Alert*.

COON, H., *43,000 Years Later* (New York).

COOPER, EDMUND, *The Uncertain Midnight* (London); also published in New York as *Deadly Image*.

JONES, EWART, *Head in the Sand* (London).

JONES, MERVYN, *On the Last Day* (London).

RIGG, ROBERT B., *War—1974* (Harrisburg, Pa.).

RUSSELL, ERIC FRANK, *Wasp* (London).

WALLACE, DOREEN, *Forty Years On* (London).

WARD, H., *L'Enfer est dans le ciel* (Paris); published in London (1960) as *Hell's Above Us*.

WILLIAMS, ROBERT MOORE *Doomsday Eve* (New York).

YOUNG, A. M., *The Aster Disaster* (Ilfracombe).

1959   BARR, TYRONE C., *Split Worlds* (London).

BLISH, JAMES, and LOWNDES, ROBERT W., *The Duplicated Man* (New York).

BRUNNER, JOHN, *The Brink* (London).

CHAPKIN, P., *Light of Mars* (London).

CLARKSON, HELEN, *The Last Day: A Novel of the Day After Tomorrow* (New York).

COOPER, EDMUND, *Seed of Light* (London).

DESMOND, HUGH, *Suicide Fleet* (London).

FOSTER, RICHARD (CROSSEN, KENDALL FOSTER), *The Rest Must Die* (New York).

FRANK, PAT (HART, HARRY), *Alas, Babylon* (Philadelphia and London).

HEINLEIN, ROBERT, *Starship Troopers* (New York).

MILLER, WALTER M., *A Canticle for Leibowitz* (New York).

ROSHWALD, MORDECAI, *Level 7* (London and New York).

RUSSELL, ERIC FRANK, *Next of Kin* (London).

1960   ADAMS, JOHN, *When the Gods Came* (London).

BERRIAULT, G., *The Descent* (New York).

CASEWIT, CURTIS W., *The Peacemakers* (New York).

COPPEL, ALFRED, *Dark December* (Greenwich, Conn.).

FITZGIBBON, CONSTANTINE, *When the Kissing Had to Stop* (London and New York).

HARTLEY, L. P., *Facial Justice* (London).

KING-HALL, STEPHEN, *Men of Destiny* (London).

LYMINGTON, JOHN (CHANCE, JOHN NEWTON), *The Giant Stumbles* (London).

STURGEON, THEODORE (WALDO, EDWARD HAMILTON), *Venus Plus X* (New York).

SULLY, KATHERINE, *Skrine* (London).

VAN MIERLO, H. A., *By Then Mankind Ceased to Exist* (Ilfracombe).

1961   ANDERSON, POUL, *Twilight World* (New York).

ASTERLEY, H. C., *Escape to Berkshire* (London).

GALOUYE, DANIEL F., *Dark Universe* (New York).

GESTON, MARK S., *Out of the Mouth of the Dragon* (New York).

1961   HOUGH, S. B., *Beyond the Eleventh Hour* (London).
        JOHNSON, L. P. V. (LE ROY, P. V.), *In the Time of the Thetans* (London).
        LYMINGTON, JOHN (CHANCE, JOHN NEWTON), *The Coming of the Strangers* (London).
        PAPE, RICHARD, *And So Ends the World* (London).
        SMITH, GEORGE H., *The Coming of the Rats* (London).
        WILLIAMS, R. M., *The Day they H-Bombed New York* (New York).
        WILSON, ANGUS (JOHNSTONE, FRANK), *The Old Men at the Zoo* (London and New York).

1962   ANDERSON, POUL, *After Doomsday* (New York).
        BARRON, D. G., *The Zilov Bombs* (London).
        BRINTON, HENRY, *Purple-6* (London).
        BURDICK, EUGENE, and WHEELER, HARVEY, *Fail-Safe* (New York).
        CRANFORD, R., *Leave them their Pride* (London).
        DANVERS, JACK (CASELEYR, CAMILLE AUGUSTE), *The End of It All* (London).
        DEL REY, LESTER, *The Eleventh Commandment* (Evanston, Ill.).
        LYMINGTON, JOHN (CHANCE, JOHN NEWTON), *A Sword above the Night* (London).
        MACTYRE, PAUL (ADAMS, ROBERT JAMES), *Midge* (London); also published in New York (1962) as *Doomsday 1999*.
        MAINE, CHARLES ERIC (MCILWAIN, DAVID), *The Darkest of Nights* (London).
        MONSARRAT, NICHOLAS, *The Time Before This* (London).
        NEWMAN, BERNARD, *The Blue Ants: The First Authentic Account of the Russian–Chinese War of 1970* (London).
        OWEN, DEAN (MCGAUGHEY, DUDLEY DEAN), *End of the World* (New York).
        ROSHWALD, MORDECAI, *A Small Armageddon* (New York).
        SHECKLEY, ROBERT, *Journey Beyond Tomorrow* (New York).
        SCHOONOVER, LAWRENCE, *Central Passage* (New York).
        THÉRIAULT, YVES, *Si la bombe m'été contée* (Paris).
        VAN GREENAWAY, PETER, *The Crucified City* (London).

1963   ARISS, BRUCE, *Full Circle* (New York).
        DELANY, SAMUEL R., *Captives of the Flames* (New York); published in London (1968) as *Out of the Dead City*.
        GARDNER, ALAN, *The Escalator* (London).
        GEORGE, PETER, *Dr Strangelove; or, How I Learned to Stop Worrying and Love the Bomb* (London).
        GOLDSTONE, R., *The Shore Dimly Seen* (New York).
        GOOD, C. H., *The Wheel Comes a Turn* (New York).
        HOUSEHOLD, GEOFFREY, *Things to Love* (Boston, Mass.).
        INGREY, D., *Pig on a Lead* (London).
        MARTEL, SUZANNE, *Quatre Montréalais en l'an 3000* (Toronto); published in New York (1964) as *The City Underground*.
        NEWTON, JULIUS P., *The Forgotten Race* (London).
        PAINE, L., *This Time Tomorrow* (London).
        SMITH, GEORGE H., *Doomsday Wing* (Derby. Conn.).
        SUTTON, JEFF, *The Atom Conspiracy* (New York).

WYLIE, PHILIP, *Triumph* (New York).

1964   ALDISS, BRIAN, *The Dark Light Years* (London).

ALDISS, BRIAN, *Greybeard* (London and New York).

BRADDON, RUSSELL, *The Year of the Angry Rabbit* (London and New York).

DELANY, S. R., *The Towers of Toron* (New York).

DICK, PHILIP K., *The Penultimate Truth* (New York).

DONNE, MAXIM (DUKE, MADELAINE E.), *Claret, Sandwiches and Sin* (London).

HEINLEIN, ROBERT, *Farnham's Freehold* (New York).

LIVESEY, ERIC M., *The Desolate Land* (London).

MCCUTCHAN, PHILIP, *Bowering's Breakwater* (London).

MILLER, WARREN *The Siege of Harlem* (New York).

MINOT, STEPHEN, *Chill of Dusk* (New York).

PANGBORN, EDGAR, *Davy* (New York).

TABORI, PAUL, *The Survivors* (London).

TREW, ANTONY, *Two Hours to Darkness* (London).

1965   BALL, FLORENCE, *Zero Plus Ten* (New York).

BLACKER, IRWIN ROBERT, *Chain of Command* (London).

BRUNNER, JOHN, *The Day of the Star Cities* (New York).

BURNS, ALAN, *Europe after the Rain* (London).

COMPTON, D. G., *The Quality of Mercy* (London).

DAVENTRY, LEONARD, *A Man of Double Deed* (London and New York).

DELANY, SAMUEL R., *City of a Thousand Suns* (New York).

DICK, PHILIP K., *Dr Bloodmoney; or, How we Got Along After the Bomb* (New York).

DICK, PHILIP K., *The Zap Gun* (New York).

FENWICK, VIRGINIA, *America RIP* (Chicago).

GEORGE, PETER, *Commander-1* (London and New York).

GRIFFITHS, JOHN, *The Survivors* (London).

HALE, MARTIN, *The Fourth Reich* (London).

HERSEY, JOHN, *White Lotus* (London).

HILBURN, JOHN EDWARD, *The Last Days* (New York).

MCCUTCHAN, PHILIP, *The Man from Moscow* (London).

ROSS, JEAN, *A View of the Island: A Post-Atomic Fairy Tale* (London).

WYND, OSWALD, *Death the Red Flower* (London).

1966   ANDERSON, WILLIAM C., *Pandemonium on the Potomac* (New York).

DELANY, SAMUEL R., *Babel-17* (New York).

CARTER, MARY, *Minutes of the Night* (London).

DRURY, ALLEN, *Capable of Honor* (New York).

GORDON, REX (HOUGH, STANLEY BENNETT), *Utopia Minus X* (New York).

HARKER, KENNETH, *The Symmetrians* (New York).

JENKINS, GEOFFREY, *Hunter-Killer* (London).

JONES, D. F., *Colossus* (London).

MCCUTCHAN, PHILIP, *A Time for Survival* (London).

MERAK, A. J., *The Dark Millennium* (New York).

1966   MILTON, JOSEPH, *The Man Who Bombed the World* (New York).
       NUNES, CLAUDE, *Inherit the Earth* (New York).
       PANGBORN, EDGAR, *The Judgment of Eve* (New York).
       QUEST, RODNEY, *Countdown to Doomsday* (London).
       ROBERTS, KEITH, *The Furies* (London).
       SOUTHWELL, SAMUEL B., *If All the Rebels Die* (New York).
       ZELAZNY, ROGER, *This Immortal* (New York).

1967   ADAMS, JOHN, *When the Gods Came* (London).
       BORDEN, WILLIAM, *Superstoe* (London).
       COONEY, MICHAEL, *Doomsday England* (London).
       CORDELL, ALEXANDER (GRABER, GEORGE ALEXANDER), *The Bright Cantonese*
           (London); published in New York (1969) as *The Deadly Eurasian*.
       GRAY, MICHAEL WAUDE, *Minutes to Impact* (London).
       HOLM, SVEN, *Termush, Atlanterkavskysten* (Copenhagen); published in
           London (1969) as *Termush*.
       NEWMAN, BERNARD, *Draw the Dragon's Teeth* (London).
       NOLAN, WILLIAM, and JOHNSON, GEORGE CLAYTON, *Logan's Run* (New
           York).
       SUTTON, JEFF, *H-Bomb over America* (New York).
       TAYLOR, RAY WARD, *Doomsday Square* (London).
       THOMAS, LESLIE, *Orange Wednesday* (London).
       VORHIES, JOHN R., *Pre-Empt* (Chicago).
       WATKINS, PETER, *The War Game* (London and New York).

1968   ANTHONY, PIERS (JACOB, PIERS ANTHONY), *Sos the Rope* (New York).
       BARJAVEL, RÉNÉ, *La Nuit des temps* (Paris); also published in New York and
           London as *The Ice People*.
       BLISH, JAMES, *Black Easter; or, Faust Aleph-Null* (New York).
       BULMER, KENNETH, *The Doomsday Men* (London and New York).
       CORSTON, GEORGE, *Aftermath* (London).
       DELANY, SAMUEL R., *The Jewels of Aptor* (New York).
       DICK, PHILIP K., *Do Androids Dream of Electric Sheep* (New York).
       FAUCETTE, JOHN M., *The Age of Ruin* (New York).
       FENNERTON, WILLIAM, *The Lucifer Cell* (London and New York).
       HAY, JOHN, *The Invasion* (London).
       LEIBER, FRITZ, *A Specter is Haunting Texas* (New York).
       MASON, DOUGLAS RANKINE, *Ring of Violence* (London).
       SABERHAGEN, FRED, *The Broken Lands* (New York).
       STRUGATSKY, ARKADY, and STRUGATSKY, BORIS, *Prisoners of Power* (London
           and New York).
       WOUK, HERMAN, *The Lomokome Papers* (New York).
       ZERWICK, CHLOE, and BROWN, HARRISON, *The Cassiopeia Affair* (London).

1969   ALDISS, BRIAN, *Barefoot in the Head* (London).
       ALTER, ROBERT EDMOND, *Path to Savagery* (New York).
       BRUNNER, JOHN, *A Plague on Both Your Causes* (London).
       BUCHARD, ROBERT, *Trente secondes sur New York* (Paris); published in
           London and New York (1970) as *Thirty Seconds Over New York*.

CAIDIN, MARTIN, *The Mendelov Conspiracy* (New York).

CARTER, ANGELA, *Heroes and Villains* (London).

CORLEY, EDWIN, *Siege* (New York and London).

GARNER, WILLIAM, *The Us or Them War* (London).

GREENLEE, SAM, *The Spook Who Sat by the Door* (New York and London).

HURD, DOUGLAS, and OSMOND, ANDREW, *The Smile on the Face of the Tiger* (London).

KNEBEL, FLETCHER, *Trespass* (New York and London).

LAUDER, G. D. (DICK-LAUDER, SIR GEORGE), *Our Man for Ganymede* (London).

LESLIE, PETER, *The Autumn Accelerator* (London).

LESSING, DORIS, *The Four-Gated City* (London).

REED, KIT, *Armed Camps* (London).

RESNICK, MICHAEL, *Redbeard* (New York).

SALLIS, JAMES (ed.), *The War Book* (London).

SEYMOUR, ALAN, *The Coming Self-Destruction of the United States of America* (London).

SHAW, BOB, *Shadow of Heaven* (New York).

WISE, C., *The Day the Queen flew to Scotland for the Grouse Shooting* (London).

ZELAZNY, ROGER, *Damnation Alley* (New York).

1970   ANDERSON, POUL, *Magellan* (New York and London).

ATKINSON, HUGH, *The Most Savage Animal* (London).

AVALLONE, MICHAEL, *Beneath the Planet of the Apes* (New York).

BRUNNER, JOHN, *The Jagged Orbit* (London).

COOPER, EDMUND, *The Last Continent* (London).

CORLEY, EDWIN, *The Jesus Factor* (New York).

CRAIG, DAVID (TUCKER, ALLAN JAMES), *Contact Lost* (London).

EGLETON, CLIVE, *A Piece of Resistance* (London and New York).

FRAME, JANET, *Intensive Care* (New York).

GOULART, RON, *After Things Fell Apart* (New York).

MACDOUGALL, A. NEALE, *Attitude* (New York).

MANO, D. KEITH, *War is Heaven* (London and New York).

MILLIGAN, SPIKE, and ANTROBUS, JOHN, *The Bedsitting Room* (Walton-On-Thames).

MITCHELL, ADRIAN, *The Bodyguard* (London).

PAGET, JOHN, *World Well Lost* (London).

POYER, JOE, *North Cape* (London).

SELLINGS, ARTHUR (LEY, ARTHUR), *Junk Day* (London).

VALE, RENA, *The Day after Doomsday* (New York).

WILLIAMS, ROBERT MOORE, *Beachhead Planet* (London).

WILLIAMS, T. OWEN, *A Month for Mankind* (London).

1971   ARDIES, TOM. *Their Man in the White House* (New York and London).

BERK, HOWARD, *The Sun Grows Cold* (New York and London).

BLISH, JAMES, *The Day After Judgment* (New York).

BUNCH, DAVID R., *Moderan* (New York).

1971   CAIDIN, MARTIN, *Almost Midnight* (New York).
       COOPER, EDMUND, *The Overman Culture* (London).
       CRAIG, WILLIAM, *The Tashkent Crisis* (New York and London).
       DELANY, SAMUEL R., *The Fall of the Towers* (London).
       DICKSON, GORDON, *The Tactics of Mistake* (New York); first published in
           the *Dorsai* series.
       DONIS, MILES, *The Fall of New York* (New York).
       EGLETON, CLIVE, *Last Post for a Partisan* (London and New York).
       FAUCETTE, JOHN M., *Siege of Earth* (New York).
       GIBSON, COLIN, *The Pepper Leaf* (London).
       HARRISON, MICHAEL JOHN, *The Committed Men* (London and New York).
       HARRISON, MICHAEL JOHN, *The Pastel City* (London and New York).
       HILL, ERNEST, *The G.C. Radiation* (London).
       HURD, DOUGLAS, and OSMOND, ANDREW, *Scotch on the Rocks* (London).
       LANGE, OLIVER (pseud.), *Vandenberg* (New York and London).
       MOORCOCK, MICHAEL, *The Warlord of the Air* (London); sequels were *The
           Land Leviathan* (1974); *The Steel Tsar* (1981).
       MORGAN, DAN, *Inside* (London).
       PENDLETON, DON, *Civil War II* (New York).
       PURSER, PHILIP, *The Holy Father's Navy* (London).
       SHAW, BOB, *Ground Zero Man* (London).
       WINTON, JOHN, *The Fighting Téméraire* (London).
1972   ANTHONY, PIERS (JACOB, PIERS ANTHONY), *Var the Stick* (London).
       ARDIES, TOM, *This Suitcase is Going to Explode* (New York and London).
       BALL, BRIAN N., *The Regiments of the Night* (New York).
       BREGGIN, R. P., *After the Good War* (New York).
       CAIDIN, MARTIN, *When War Comes* (New York).
       COOK, GLEN, *The Heirs of Babylon* (New York).
       CREASEY, JOHN, *The Insulators* (London).
       EGLETON, CLIVE, *The Judas Mandate* (London and New York).
       MARTIN-FEHR, J., *The End of his Tether* (Chichester).
       MERLE, ROBERT, *Malevil* (Paris); published in New York (1973) and
           London (1974) as *Malevil*.
       MULLALLY, FREDERICK, *The Malta Conspiracy* (London).
       PRIEST, CHRISTOPHER, *Fugue for a Darkening Island* (London); also pub-
           lished in New York (1972) as *Darkening Island*.
       SPINRAD, NORMAN, *The Iron Dream* (Boston).
       TALBOT, G. E., *Glory to Ajela!* (New York).
1973   ALDISS, BRIAN, *Frankenstein Unbound* (London).
       ANDERSON, POUL, *There Will Be Time* (New York).
       BRUNNER, JOHN, *Age of Miracles* (London).
       BRUNNER, JOHN, *The Stone that Never Came Down* (London).
       CAIDIN, MARTIN, *Operation Nuke* (New York).
       CONEY, MICHAEL, *The Hero of Downways* (London).
       COOPER, EDMUND, *The Cloud Walker* (London and New York).

CORDELL, A. (GRABER, GEORGE ALEXANDER), *If You Believe the Soldiers* (London).

DRURY, ALLEN, *Come Nineveh, Come Tyre* (New York).

FARREN, MICK, *The Texts of Festival* (London).

GERROLD, DAVID, *Battle for the Planet of the Apes* (New York).

GORDON, STUART, *One-Eye* (London); first in trilogy.

GYGAX, GARY, and STAFFORD, TERRY, *Victorious German Arms: An Alternative Military History of World War Two* (Baltimore).

HARDY, RONALD, *The Face of Jalanath* (New York).

LANIER, STERLING E., *Hiero's Journey* (New York).

LEES, DAN, *Rape of a Quiet Town* (London).

LJOKA, DAN, *Shelter* (New York).

LYONS, VICTOR S., *The Unconquerable Survivor of 2055 AD* (New York).

MASON, COLIN, *Hostage* (London and New York).

PEREIRA, W. D., *Aftermath 15* (London).

SABERHAGEN, FRED, *Changeling Earth* (New York).

SNYDER, GUY, *Testament XXI* (New York).

1974   ALDISS, BRIAN, *The Eighty-minute Hour* (London and New York).

BELL, NEAL, *Gone to be Snakes Now* (New York).

BLACKDEN, PAUL, *Adam and Eve 2020 AD* (London).

CHARNAS, SUZY MCKEE, *Walk to the End of the World* (New York).

COHEN, GARY G., *Civilization's Last Hurrah* (Chicago).

COOPER, EDMUND, *The Slaves of Heaven* (New York).

FORSYTH, FREDERICK, *The Dogs of War* (New York).

GAWRON, JEAN MARK, *An Apology for Rain* (New York).

HAINING, PETER, *The Hero* (London).

HALDEMAN, JOE, *The Forever War* (New York).

HARRISON, M. JOHN, *The Centauri Device* (New York).

HOWELL, SCOTT, *Menace from Magor* (London).

JAKES, JOHN, *Conquest of the Planet of the Apes* (New York).

JONES, D. F., *Fall of Colossus* (London).

KESTEVEN, G. R., *The Pale Invaders* (London).

LYMINGTON, JOHN (CHANCE, JOHN NEWTON), *The Hole in the World* (London).

MOSKOWITZ, SAM (ed.), *The Raid of 'Le Vengeur'* (London).

POWE, BRUCE, *The Last Days of the American Empire* (New York and London).

POURNELLE, JERRY, *Escape from the Planet of the Apes* (New York).

ROBERTS, KEITH, *The Chalk Giants* (London).

SAUNDERS, JAKE, and WALDROP, HOWARD, *The Texas–Israeli War: 1999* (New York).

SCORTIA, THOMAS N., *Earthwreck!* (Greenwich, Conn.).

SOLDATI, MARIO, *Lo Smeraldo* (Milan); published in New York (1976) as *The Emerald*.

1974   VAN GREENAWAY, PETER, *Take the War to Washington* (London).

1975   ADAMS, ROBERT, *The Coming of the Horseclans* (Los Angeles); first in the
       Horseclans series.

       ANTHONY, PIERS (JACOB, PIERS ANTHONY), *Neq the Sword* (New York and
       London).

       BARRETT, G. J., *City of the First Time* (London).

       BEEVOR, ANTONY, *The Violent Brink* (London).

       BENOIST, ELIZABETH S., *Doomsday Clock* (San Antonio, Texas).

       BROWN, WILLIAM M., *The Nuclear Crisis of 1979* (Washington, DC).

       BRUNNER, JOHN, *Total Eclipse* (London and New York).

       CALLENBACH, ERNEST, *Ecotopia* (New York).

       CHRISTIAN, JOHN, *Five Gates to Armageddon* (London).

       CLÉMENT, FRANÇOIS, *Birth of an Island* (New York).

       CONRAD, PAUL, *The Slave Bug* (London).

       DRURY, ALLEN, *The Promise of Joy* (New York and London).

       EDWARDS, PETER, *Terminus* (London).

       GARDEN, DONALD J., *Dawn Chorus* (London).

       GILCHRIST, JOHN, *Birdbrain* (London).

       GORDON, STUART, *Two-Eyes* (London).

       LOPEZ, ANTHONY, *Second Coming* (London).

       MCINTYRE, VONDA, *The Exile Waiting* (New York).

       MOORCOCK, MICHAEL, *Before Armageddon* (London).

       O'BRIEN, ROBERT C., *Z for Zachariah* (New York and London).

       PANGBORN, EDGAR, *The Company of Glory* (New York).

       PENNY, DAVID G., *The Sunset People* (London).

       PITTS, DENIS, *This City is Ours* (New York); published in London (1976) as
       Target Manhattan.

       SHARLAND, MIKE, *Nervestorm* (London).

       TOFTE, ARTHUR, *Walls within Walls* (Ontario).

       WYATT, PATRICK, *Irish Rose* (London).

1976   BOVA, BEN, *Millennium* (New York).

       COULSON, ROBERT, *To Renew the Ages* (Toronto).

       DICK, PHILIP K., and ZELAZNY, ROGER, *Deus Irae* (New York).

       EDWARDS, PETER, *Terminus* (London).

       ERDMAN, PAUL E., *The Crash of '79* (New York).

       FOLLETT, JAMES, *The Doomsday Ultimatum* (London).

       FREEMANTLE, BRIAN, *The November Man* (London).

       GILCHRIST, JOHN, *The English Corridor* (London).

       GILCHRIST, JOHN, *Lifeline* (London).

       GORDON, STUART, *Three-Eyes* (London).

       HARRIS, LEONARD, *The Masada Plan* (New York).

       HERBERT, FRANK, *Children of Dune* (New York and London).

       MCGHEE, EDWARD, and MOORE, ROBIN, *The Chinese Ultimatum* (Los
       Angeles).

       PINCHER, CHAPMAN, *The Eye of the Tornado* (London).

       REEVES, L. P., *The Last Days of the Peacemaker* (London).

       SCHUTZ, J. W., *The Moon Microbe* (London).

SILVERBERG, ROBERT, *Shadrach in the Furnace* (Indianapolis).

STANLEY, JOHN, *World War III* (New York).

TREW, ANTONY, *Ultimatum* (London).

WILHELM, KATE, *Where Late the Sweet Birds Sang* (New York).

WILSON, STEVE, *The Lost Traveller* (London and New York).

1977   ASPRIN, ROBERT, *The Cold Cash War* (New York).

BOLAND, JOHN, *Holocaust* (London).

DELANEY, LAURENCE, *The Triton Ultimatum* (New York).

DUGGAN, ERVIN S., and WATTENBERG, BEN J., *Against All Enemies* (New York).

FREELING, NICOLAS, *Gadget* (London).

GOULART, RON, *Crackpot* (New York).

GREEN, MARTIN, *The Earth Again Redeemed: May 26 to July 1, 1984* (New York).

HALDEMAN, JOE (ed.), *Study War No More* (New York).

KILWORTH, GARRY, *In Solitary* (London).

MOORCOCK, MICHAEL, *England Invaded* (London).

NIVEN, LARRY, and POURNELLE, JERRY, *Lucifer's Hammer* (New York).

NOLAND, WILLIAM F., *Logan's World* (New York).

1978   ANTHONY, PIERS (JACOB, PIERS ANTHONY), *Battle Circus* (New York).

BALIZET, CAROL, *The Seven Last Years* (Lincoln, Va).

BIDWELL, SHELFORD (and others), *World War 3: A Military Projection Founded on Today's Facts* (London and New York).

BOVA, BEN, *Colony* (New York).

BRILEY, JOHN, *The Last Dance* (London).

CHARNAS, SUZY McKEE, *Motherlines* (New York).

DENIS, JOHN, *The Moscow Horse* (London).

DUNNING, LAWRENCE, *Keller's Bomb* (New York).

HACKETT, GENERAL SIR JOHN and others, *The Third World War: A Future History* (London).

MacDONALD, ANDREW (PIERCE, WILLIAM), *The Turner Diaries* (Washington, DC).

McINTYRE, VONDA, *Dreamsnake* (Boston and London).

PAGE, GORDON, and ASPLER, TONY, *Chain Reaction* (New York).

PANGBORN, EDGAR, *Still I Persist in Wondering* (New York).

SANDERS, LAWRENCE, *The Tangent Factor* (New York).

TOPOL, ALLAN, *The Fourth of July War* (New York).

TURNER, GEORGE, *Beloved Son* (London and New York).

VINGE, JOAN D., *The Outcasts of Heaven Belt* (New York).

YARBRO, CHELSEA QUINN, *False Dawn* (New York).

1979   ALEXANDER, PATRICK, *Show Me a Hero* (London).

BRADY, MICHAEL, *American Surrender* (New York and London).

COWPER, RICHARD (MURRY, COLIN MIDDLETON), *Profundis* (London).

DRAKE, DAVID, *Hammer's Slammers* (New York); first in a series.

ERWIN, ALAN R., *The Power Exchange* (Austin, Texas).

FANE, MICHAEL, *Revolution Island* (London).

1979   GRAHAM, DAVID, *Down to a Sunless Sea* (London).
         KILIAN, CRAWFORD, *Ice Quake* (London).
         MACAULEY, ROBIE, *A Secret History of Time to Come* (New York).
         PALUMBO, DENNIS, *City Wars* (New York).
         POURNELLE, JERRY, *Janissaries* (New York); first in a combat series.
         SABERHAGEN, FRED, *Empire of the East* (New York).
         WARREN, GEORGE, *Dominant Species* (Norfolk, Va.).
         WYNDHAM, JOHN (HARRIS JOHN BEYNON), *Web* (London).

1980   ABBEY, EDWARD, *Good News* (New York).
         ALDISS, BRIAN, *Moreau's Other Island* (London); published in New York (1981) as *An Island Called Moreau*.
         AMIS, KINGSLEY, *Russian Hide and Seek: A Melodrama* (London).
         ANVIL, CHRISTOPHER, *The Steel, the Mist and the Blazing Sun* (New York).
         BARNWELL, WILLIAM, *The Blessing Papers* (New York).
         COETZEE, J. M., *Waiting for the Barbarians* (New York).
         GARDNER, JOHN, *The Last Trump* (New York).
         HOBAN, RUSSELL, *Riddley Walker* (London and New York).
         JOLY, CYRIL, *Silent Night: The Defeat of Nato* (New York).
         MACDONALD, ANDREW, *The Turner Diaries* (Washington, DC).
         MCGHEE, EDWARD, *The Last Caesar* (Los Angeles).
         MACLENNAN, HUGH, *Voices in Time* (New York).
         MCQUAY, MIKE, *Lifekeeper* (New York).
         MONTELEONE, THOMAS F. (BISCHOFF, DAVID), *Guardian* (New York).
         MOORCOCK, MICHAEL, *My Experiences in the Third World War* (London).
         ROUCH, JAMES, *Hard Target* (London); first in *The Zone* series.
         SIMPSON, GEORGE E., and BURGER, NEAL R., *Fair Warning* (New York).
         SPINRAD, NORMAN, *Songs from the Stars* (New York).
         TAYLOR, CHARLES D., *Show of Force* (New York).
         TERMAN, DOUGLAS C., *Free Flight* (New York).
         WINGATE, JOHN, *Frigate* (London).
         WINGATE, JOHN, *Submarine* (London).

1981   AHERN, JERRY, *Total War* (New York); first in *The Survivalist* series.
         BAKER, F. ROBERT, *Warhead* (New York).
         BARNWELL, WILLIAM, *Imram* (New York).
         BARNWELL, WILLIAM, *The Sigma Curve* (New York).
         CARLSON, W. K., *Sunrise West* (New York).
         CHERRYH, C. J., *Downbelow Station* (New York).
         COPPEL, ALFRED, *The Apocalyptic Brigade* (New York).
         FORMAN, JAMES D., *Call Back Yesterday* (New York).
         GORDON, STUART (GORDON, RICHARD), *Smile on the Void* (London and New York).
         HALDEMAN, JOE, *Worlds* (New York).
         LOGSDON, SYDNEY, *A Fond Farewell to Dying* (New York).
         MONTELEONE, THOMAS F. (BISCHOFF, DAVID), *Ozymandius* (New York).
         POHL, FREDERICK, *The Cool War* (New York).

POTOK, CHAIM, *The Book of Lights* (New York).

SOMTOW, SUCHARITKUL, *Starship and Haiku* (New York).

TURNER, GEORGE, *Vaneglory* (London).

WILLIAMS, PAUL O., *The Breaking of Northwall* (New York); first in the *Pelbar Cycle*.

WINGATE, JOHN, *Carrier* (London).

1982   ALDISS, BRIAN, *Heliconia Spring* (London); first in the *Heliconia* trilogy.

ALLBEURY, TED, *All our Tomorrows* (London).

ANDERSON, POUL, *Maurai and Kith* (New York).

BOVA, BEN, *Test of Fire* (New York).

BRADLEY, JOHN, *The Illustrated History of World War Three* (London).

BRIGGS, RAYMOND, *When The Wind Blows* (London and New York).

CRISP, FRANK R., *The Brink* (London and New York).

DA CRUZ, DANIEL, *The Ayes of Texas* (New York).

HACKETT, GENERAL SIR JOHN and others, *The Third World War: The Untold Story* (London).

HARRIS, BRIAN (LUDLUM, ROBERT), *World War III* (New York).

HOGAN, JAMES P., *Voyage from Yesteryear* (New York).

HUBBARD, L. RON, *Battlefield Earth: A Saga of the Year 3000* (Los Angeles).

ING, DEAN, *Systemic Shock* (New York); first in the *Ted Quantril* trilogy.

JERSILD, P. C., *Efter Floden* (Stockholm); published in New York (1986) as *After the Flood*.

MALAMUD, BERNARD, *God's Grace* (New York).

MILLS, PAT, and BOLLAND, BRIAN, *The Cursed Earth* (London).

PIPER, H. BEAM, and KURLAND, MICHAEL, *First Cycle* (New York).

TURNER, GEORGE, *Yesterday's Men* (London).

WINSLOW, PAULINE GLENN, *I, Martha Adams* (London).

1983   ALDISS, BRIAN, *Heliconia Summer* (London); second in the *Heliconia* trilogy.

ANDERSON, POUL, *Orion Shall Rise* (New York).

BARTON, JAMES, *Wasteworld, 1: Aftermath* (London); first in the *Wasteworld* series.

BASILE, GLORIA VITANZA, *Eye of the Eagle* (New York).

BATCHELOR, JOHN CALVIN, *The Birth of the People's Republic of Antarctica* (New York).

BENFORD, GREGORY, *Across the Sea of Suns* (New York).

COPPEL, ALFRED, *The Burning Mountain* (New York).

DONOHUE, TREVOR, *Savage Tomorrow* (Victoria, NSW).

DUNSTAN, FREDERICK, *Habitation One* (London).

FRASER, GENERAL SIR DAVID *August 1988* (London).

FULLERTON, ALEXANDER, *Regenesis* (New York).

GEE, MAGGIE, *The Burning Book* (London).

GUHA, ANTON-ANDREAS, *Ende* (Taunus, Germany); published in London (1936) as *Ende: A Diary of the Third World War*.

HALDEMAN, JOE, *Worlds Apart* (New York).

ING, DEAN, *Pulling Through* (New York).

1983   JOHNSTONE, WILLIAM W., *Out of the Ashes* (New York); first in the *Ashes* series.

LANIER, STERLING E., *The Unforsaken Hero* (New York).

MCLAUGHLIN, JOHN C., *The Helix and the Sword* (New York).

O'HEFFERNAN, PATRICK and others, *The First Nuclear World War* (New York).

PAUSEWANG, GUDRUN, *Die letzten Kinder von Schewenborn: oder sieht so unsere Zukunft aus?* (Ravensburg); published in London (1988) as *The Last Children*.

POURNELLE, JERRY, and CARR, JOHN F. (eds.), *There Will Be War* (New York); first in series of collections.

PROCHNAU, WILLIAM, *Trinity's Child* (New York).

RHINEHART, LUKE (COCKCROFT, GEORGE), *Long Voyage Back* (New York and London).

SMITH, L. N., *Nagasaki Vector* (New York).

VARLEY, JOHN, *Millennium* (New York).

1984   ABE, KOBO, *Hakobune no Sakura* (Tokyo); published in New York (1988) as *The Ark Sakura*.

BASILE, GLORIA VITANZA, *The Sting of the Scorpion* (New York).

BENFORD, GREGORY, *Across the Sea of Suns* (New York).

BLOCK, THOMAS, *Airship Nine* (New York and London).

CLARK, WILLIAM, *Cataclysm: The North–South Conflict of 1987* (London).

COOK, PAUL, *The Ajendra Variations* (New York).

DRUMM, D. B., *First, You Fight* (New York); first in the *Traveler* series.

EDMONDSON, G. C., and KOTLAN, C. M., *The Takeover* (New York).

FORD, RICHARD, *Melvaig's Vision* (London).

FORMAN, JAMES D., *Doomsday plus Twelve* (New York).

FRANKLIN, H. BRUCE (ed.), *Countdown to Midnight: Twelve Great Stories About Nuclear Warfare* (New York).

HARDING, RICHARD, *The Outrider* (New York); first in the *Outrider* series.

HERBERT, FRANK, *Heretics of Dune* (New York).

HILL, DOUGLAS, *Alien Citadel* (New York).

JONES, DENNIS, *Russian Spring* (London).

JONES, GWYNETH, *Divine Endurance* (London).

KELLEHER, VICTOR, *The Beast of Heaven* (Brisbane).

LOVEJOY, JACK, *A Vision of Beasts*, Book 1: *Creation Descending* (New York).

LOVEJOY, JACK, *A Vision of Beasts*, Book 2: *The Second Kingdom* (New York).

MACE, DAVID, *Demon 4* (London).

MORRIS, JANET, and MORRIS, CHRIS, *The Forty Minute War* (New York).

PALMER, DAVID R., *Emergence* (New York).

ROBINSON, KIM STANLEY, *The Wild Shore* (New York).

STACY, RYDER, *Doomsday Warrior* (New York); first in the *Doomsday Warrior* series.

STRIEBER, WHITLEY, and KUNETKA, JAMES, *Warday* (New York and London).

SWINDELLS, ROBERT, *Brother in the Land* (Oxford).

TILLEY, PATRICK, *Cloud Warrior* (New York); first in the *Amtrak Wars* series.

VINGE, VERNOR, *The Peace War* (New York).

WHITMORE, CHARLES, *Winter's Daughter: The Saying of Signe Raghnhildsdatter* (New York).

ZAHN, TIMOTHY , *Cobra* (New York); first in series.

1985 ALDISS, BRIAN, *Heliconia Winter* (London); concludes the *Heliconia* trilogy.

AUSTIN, RICHARD (MILAN, VICTOR), *The Guardians* (New York); first in *The Guardians* series.

BEAR, GREG, *Eon* (New York).

BOVA, BEN, *Privateers* (New York).

BRIN, DAVID, *The Postman* (New York).

COOK, PAUL, *Duende Meadow* (New York).

COX, RICHARD, *Ground Zero* (New York).

DREW, WAYLAND, *The Gaian Expedient: Erthring Cycle Part Two* (New York).

FORSYTHE, FREDERICK, *The Fourth Protocol* (London).

FRAKES, RANDALL, and WISHER, BILL, *The Terminator* (New York).

HERBERT, JAMES, *Domain* (London).

ING, DEAN, *Wild Country* (New York); concludes the *Ted Quantril* trilogy.

JOHNSON, DENIS, *Fiskadoro* (New York).

JONES, DENNIS, *Barbarossa Red* (New York).

LAIDLAW, MARC, *Dad's Nuke* (London and New York).

LAWRENCE, LOUISE, *Children of the Dust* (New York).

LOVEJOY, JACK, *A Vision of Beasts*, Book 3: *The Brotherhood of Diablo* (New York).

MACKSEY, KENNETH, *First Clash: Combat Close-up in World War Three* (London and New York).

MASTERTON, GRAHAM, *Sacrifice* (London).

MAUDSLEY, JERE, *Hunter* (New York).

MAYHAIR, ARDATH, *The World Ends in Hickory Hollow* (New York).

MCMANUS, JAMES, *Chin Music* (New York).

MILAN, VICTOR, *The Cybernetic Samurai* (New York).

MILLER, WALTER M., and GREENBERG, MARTIN H. (eds.), *Beyond Armageddon* (New York).

MITCHELL, ELIZABETH (ed.), *After the Flames* (New York).

MORRIS, JANET (ed.), *Afterwar* (New York).

PARVIN, BRIAN, *The Singing Tree* (London).

POWERS, TIM, *Dinner at Deviant's Palace* (New York).

SERVICE, PAMELA F., *Winter of Magic's Return* (New York).

SHAW, BOB, *The Peace Machine* (London); revised version of *Ground Zero Man* (1971).

SHEFFIELD, CHARLES, *Between the Strokes of Night* (London).

SHIRLEY, JOHN, *Eclipse* (New York); first in *A Song Called Youth* series.

SILVERBERG, ROBERT, *Tom O'Bedlam* (New York).

STRIEBER, WHITLEY, *Wolf of Shadows* (New York).

1985   SWINDELLS, ROBERT, *Brother in the Land* (New York).
       TIRE, ROBERT, *Broken Eagle* (New York).
       VONNEGUT, KURT, *Galápagos* (New York).
       WESTON, SUSAN B., *Children of the Light* (New York).
       WHITE, ALAN, *Black Alert* (London).
       YATES, W. R., *Diasporah* (New York).

1986   AXLER, RICHARD, *Deathworlds: Pilgrimage to Hell too Late* (Toronto); first in the *Deathworlds* series.
       BARNES, JOHN, *The Man Who Pulled Down the Sky* (New York).
       BARRETT, NEAL, *Through Darkest America* (London).
       BENFORD, GREGORY, and GREENBERG, MARTIN H. (eds.), *Hitler Victorious: Eleven Stories of the German Victory in World War Two* (New York).
       BOVA, BEN, *Privateers* (New York).
       BROOKE-ROSE, CHRISTINE, *Xorandor* (London).
       CAIDIN, MARTIN, *Zoboa* (New York).
       CANAL, RICHARD, *La Malédiction de l'ephémère* (Paris).
       FISHER, LOU, *The Blue Ice Pilot* (New York).
       FOELL, EARL W., and NENNEMAN, RICHARD A. (eds.), *How Peace Came to the World* (Boston, Mass.).
       JAMES, DAKOTA, *Milwaukee the Beautiful* (New York).
       LA TOURETTE, AILEEN, *Cry Wolf* (London).
       LEM, STANISLAW, *Fiasko* (Warsaw); published in New York and London (1987) as *Fiasco*.
       MACLOY, JOHN (ed.), *Nukes: Four Horror Writers on the Ultimate Horror* (Baltimore).
       MARTIN, GRAHAM DUNSTAN, *Time-Slip* (London).
       MORRIS, JANET, and MORRIS, CHRIS, *Medusa* (New York).
       MORROW, JAMES, *This is the Way the World Ends* (New York).
       PRICE, E. HOFFMAN, *Operation Exile* (New York).
       PURSELL, J. J., *Okna* (New York).
       ROHMER, RICHARD, *Starmageddon* (Toronto).
       SARGENT, CRAIG, *The Last Ranger* (New York); first in *Last Ranger* series.
       SARGENT, PAMELA, *The Shore of Women* (New York).
       SERVICE, PAMELA E., *Winter of Magic's Return* (New York).
       VINGE, VERNOR, *Marooned in Real Time* (New York).

1987   ALEXANDER, DAVID, *Phoenix* 1: *Dark Messiah* (New York); first in the *Phoenix* series.
       ARMSTRONG, MICHAEL, *After the Zap* (New York).
       BEAR, GREG, *The Forge of God* (New York).
       BENFORD, GREGORY, *Great Sky River* (New York).
       BERMAN, MITCH, *Time Capsule* (New York).
       BILLIAS, STEPHEN, *The American Book of the Dead* (New York).
       BOWKER, RICHARD, *Dover Beach* (New York).
       BROWN, DALE, *Flight of the Old Dog* (New York).
       BUTLER, OCTAVIA, *Dawn* (New York); first in *Xenogenesis* trilogy.
       COYLE, HAROLD, *Team Yankee; A Novel of World War III* (Novato, Cal.).

DICKSON, GORDON R., *Way of the Pilgrim* (New York).
ELPHINSTONE, MARGARET, *The Incomer* (London).
FRIEDMAN, C. S., *In Conquest Born* (New York).
HINZ, CHRISTOPHER, *Liege-Killer* (New York and London).
HOGAN, JAMES P., *Endgame Enigma* (New York).
HOLT, ROBERT LAWRENCE, *Good Friday* (New York).
HOYLE, TREVOR, *Kids* (London).
JACKSON, WILLIAM, *The Alternative Third World War: 1985–2035* (London).
MCCAMMON, ROBERT, *Swan Song* (New York).
MCGOWEN, TOM, *The Magician's Apprentice* (New York); first in series.
MCLOUGHLIN, JOHN, *Toolmaker Koan* (New York).
PHILLIPS, TONY, *Turbo Cowboys: Jump Start* (New York); first in series.
POHL, FREDERIK, *Black Star Rising* (London).
POYER, D. C., *Stepfather Bank* (New York).
SEE, CAROLYN, *Golden Days* (New York).
SERVICE, PAMELA E., *Tomorrow's Magic* (New York).
SHEPARD, LUCIUS, *Life During Wartime* (London).
SIEGEL, BARBARA, and SIEGEL, SCOTT, *Firebrats: The Burning Land* (New York); first in series.
STOLBOV, BRUCE, *Last Fall* (New York).
WEAVER, MICHAEL D., *Mercedes Nights* (New York).
WILSON, HARRY, *A World for the Meek* (Albuquerque).

1988   BEAR, GREG, *Eternity* (New York).
BENFORD, GREGORY, and GREENBERG, MARTIN H. (eds.), *Nuclear War* (New York).
BRINKLEY, WILLIAM, *The Last Ship* (New York).
BROSNAN, JOHN, *The Sky Lords* (London).
BUTLER, OCTAVIA, *Adulthood Rites* (New York and London); second in *Xenogenesis* trilogy.
CLANCY, TOM, *The Cardinal of the Kremlin* (New York).
CROWDER, HERBERT, *Ambush at Osirak* (Novato, Cal.).
JONES, DENNIS, *Winter Palace* (New York).
LINAWEAVER, BRAD, *Moon of Ice* (New York).
MORAN, DANIEL KEYS, *Armageddon Blues* (New York).
REAVES, MICHAEL and PERRY, STEVE, *Dome* (London).
SHEFFIELD, CHARLES, *Trader's World* (New York).
TEPPER, SHERI S., *The Gate to Women's Country* (New York).
TILLEY, PATRICK, *Illustrated Guide to the Amtrak Wars* (New York).

1989   BARRETT, NEAL, *Dawn's Uncertain Light* (New York).
BENFORD, GREGORY, *Tides of Light* (London and New York).
BUTLER, OCTAVIA, *Imago* (New York and London); last in *Xenogenesis* trilogy.
CAIDIN, MARTIN, *Beamriders!* (New York).
CARD, ORSON SCOTT, *The Abyss* (New York).
CARD, ORSON SCOTT, *The Folk of the Fringe* (New York).
DALE, FLOYD D., *A Hunter's Fire* (New York).
OLAN, SUSAN TORIAN, *The Earth Remembers* (Lake Geneva, Wis.).

1989   ROBBINS, DAVID, *Blade: First Strike* (New York); first in *Blade* series.

SLONCZEWSKI, JOAN, *The Wall Around Eden* (New York).

WEAVER, MICHAEL D., *My Father Immortal* (New York).

WESTCOTT, C. T., *Silver Wings and Leather* (New York); first in *Eagleheart* series.

ZALOGA, STEVEN J., *Red Thrust* (Novato, Cal.).

1990   ABBEY, LLOYD, *The Last Whales* (New York).

ARMSTRONG, MICHAEL, *Agvig* (New York).

BEECHER, WILLIAM, *Mayday Man* (New York).

HOLT, ROBERT, and HOLT, FRANK, *Peace Maker* (New York and London).

McGANN, MICHAEL, *The Marauders*, 1 (New York); first in series.

McQUIN, DONALD E., *Warrior* (New York).

RODGERS, ALAN, *Fire* (New York).

TILTON, LOIS, *Vampire Winter* (New York).

WREN, M. K., *A Gift Upon the Shore* (New York).

Index

Abrechnung mit England, Die grosse 118, 125

Absolute at Large, The 152

Admiralty of the Atlantic, The 125

Aerostation . . . The Templar's Stratagem 7

Ailes repoussent, Les 140

Alas Babylon 187–8

Albert, Prince Consort 21, 22, 96

All the Year Round, on invasion dangers 29

America Fallen 2

American Surrender 183

Amis, Sir Kingsley 204

Anderson, Sir John, on first atomic bomb 163

Angell, Norman 111–13

Aniara 205–6

Anno Domini 2071 148

Annual Register, The 26, 29

Answers 59, 62

Anticipations (Wells) 87–8

Anticipations of the Future (Ruffin) 17–18

Anti-Gallican, The 14–15

Anymoon 143

Ape and Essence 171–3

Arago, Dominique, on peace and war 71

Arcadia, myths of 146–8

Armed Briton, The 12

Arms and the Man 112

Army Speech . . . dedicated to those who have been frightened by the Battle of Dorking 36

Arnold, General Henry Harley 166–7

Arnold, Matthew 25, 39

Arnold-Forster, H. O. 56, 58, 74–5

Artus, Louis 140

Auden, W. H., quoted 164, 190

August 1988 201

Bacon, Francis 68

Balance of Military Power in Europe, The 40–1

balloons, first ascents 7–8; fantasies of future developments 7–8, 49

Barbarossa Red 203

Barbusse, Henri 135–6

Barton, Samuel 43

Bataille de Berlin en 1875, La 34, 37

Bataille de Damvillers, La 101

Bataille de Dorking, La, preface on future war stories 144

Bataille de Londres en 188–, La 52

Battle of Dorking, The, see Chesney, Lt.-Col.

Battle of London, The 143

Battle of Port Said, The 73–4

Battle of the Swash, The 43

Begum's Fortune, The 66–7

Beresford, Lord Charles 99

Bernhardi, Friedrich von 139–40

Black Death, The 159–60

Black and White 62–3, 80, 118, 126, 129

Blackwood's Magazine 1–2, 27, 35, 40–1

Blake of the 'Rattlesnake' 77–8

Blatchford, Robert 125

Bleibtreu, Karl 10, 80–1

Bloch, Ivan S., forecasts war of entrenchments 114–15

Blunt, William Scawen, on German invasion 125

Bolingbroke, Henry St John, Viscount 5–6

Bomben auf Hamburg 139–40

Bowmen, The 92

Brackett, Leigh 207–8

Bradbury, Ray 188–9

Brave New World 152–3

Broken Trident, The 142

Brooke, Rupert 135

Bulletin of the Atomic Scientists, The 165

Bulwer-Lytton, Edward 49–50, 83

Burgess, Anthony 191

Burgoyne, A. H. 100

Burgoyne, Sir John 21, 24

Burton, F. G. 74–5

Butler, Lady, her military paintings 60

Butler, Samuel 49, 150
Bywater, Hector 139

Cambridge, Duke of, opposes Channel
    Tunnel 97
Campbell, Thomas 21
Canticle for Leibowitz, A 209
Cantril, Hadley, investigates Martian
    invasion panic 87
Čapek, Karel 148, 150–1
Captain of the 'Mary Rose', The 74–5
Carving of Turkey, The 41–2
Cayley, Sir George, on air warfarer 70,
    194
Cazal, Comdt. [Jean de la Hire] 140–1
Channel Tunnel, alarms and anxieties
    over 95–9, 140–1
Channel Tunnel, The 98, 105
Chesney, Lt.-Col. G. T. 1–3, 22, 26–35;
    Battle of Dorking, anti-Chesney stories
    35–7; Gladstone's criticism 34–5;
    influence of the story 33–6, 37–45,
    50–1; narrative methods of 30–4;
    originality of 32–4
Childers, Robert Erskine 15, 119–20
Chrysalids, The 212
Churchill, Winston 165
Cliffs, The 121
Clockwork Orange, The 191
Clowes, Sir William Laird 74–5, 100,
    109–11
Coeurderoy, Ernest 19
Coleridge, S. T., on invasion 15
Collapse of Homo Sapien, The 146
Collier's 166–8
Colomb, Admiral Philip 62, 80, 102
Coming Race, The 49, 83
Coming Waterloo, The 94
*Comment la France conquit l'Angleterre en
    1888* 53
Conan Doyle, Sir Arthur 90–1, 93, 134,
    156
Contemporary Review 128
Croly, David Goodman 149

Daily Mail 122–3
Daily News, on the danger of invasion in
    (1871) 36
Danger 90–1, 134
Dangin, Édouard 33, 37

Danrit, Capitaine (Driant, Émile) 76–7,
    81, 101–5, 107–8
Dans cent ans 149
Darwin, Erasmus 68–9
Darwinism 48–9, 50
Daudet, Léon 145–6
De Quincey, Thomas, his essay 'On War'
    132–3
Death of Grass, The 214
Debans, Camille 94–5
'Der des Der', La 145
Deroulède, Paul 102
Descente en Angleterre, La 9–10
Deutschland und der nächste Krieg 139
Deverdun, Pierre Louis 140
Discoveries . . . of the Nineteenth Century
    72–3
Dominio dell'aria, Il 153–5
Domvile, Sir Compton 91
Donnelly, Henry Grattan, *see* 'Stochastic'
Doomsday Clock 166, 216
Dooner, Pierton, *The Last Days of the
    Republic* 42
Dorking, *The Battle of, see* Chesney, Lt.-
    Col. G. T.
Doughty, Charles 121
Douhet, Giulio, on the command of the
    air 152–3
Down with England 87
Driant, Capitaine Émile, *see* Danrit,
    Capitaine
Du Maurier Guy 109, 116, 126–7
Dystopian fiction 149–53

Eastwick, James 77
Edelsheim, Freiherr von 119–20
'84. A Political Revelation 43
Einfall der Deutschen in England, Der 122
Eliot, T. S., quoted 144
Enemy in our Midst, The 124
Engel, Leonard 167–8
England's Peril 106
Englishman's Home, An 109, 116, 126–7
*Entscheidungsschlachten des Europaischen
    Krieges, 18–* 80–1
Erdmann, Gustav 39
Erewhon 49, 150
Ericsson, John 137–8

Fahrenheit 451 189–90
Fate of the Earth, The 4

Fictions guerrières anglaises 128–9
Fin de la Prusse, La 117
Final War, The 64, 104–5
Five Weeks in a Balloon 49
Fitzgerald, Admiral Penrose 91
Foch, Col. Ferdinand (later Marshal) 72
forecasting techniques 177–8
Forsyth, Frederick 182
Fourth Protocol, The 182
Frank, Pat (Harry Hart) 187–8
Frankenstein 149–50
Franklin, Benjamin, on air warfare 68
Frankreichs Ende im Jahre 19?? 129
Freneau, Philip Morin, on balloon battles 7
Fulton, Robert 8, 70, 194
future, tales of the 48–50

Galàpagos 5
Gas War of 1940, The 159
Gelehrtenrepublik, Die 204
Geoffroy, Louis, his alternative history 9
Gillray, James, his prophetic prints 13
Gladstone, William Ewart, on *Battle of Dorking* 1, 34–5
Glimpses of the future 149
Gobsch, Hans 140
Golding, William 191–2
Golz, Baron Colmar von der 72, 79, 119
Gooch, G. P. 88
Good Friday 203
Gopcevic, Spiridion 52–3
Gordievsky, Oleg 184
Gosse, Edmund, on war is good for you 134
Graves, Robert 135, 173–4
Great Illusion, The 112–13
Great Naval War of 1887, The 100, 105
Great Pacific War, The 139
Great Pirate Syndicate, The 107
Great Raid, The 126
Great War in England in 1897, The 58–9
Great War of 1892, The 62–3, 80, 174
Griffith, George 58, 107
Guerra del 190–, La 154
Guerre Anglo-Franco-Russe, La 2
Guerre avec l'Angleterre, La 116–17
Guerre au vingtième siècle, La 81–3
Guerre de demain, La 104, 107
Guerre en ballon, La 103

Guerre en forteresse, La 106–7
Guerre en rase campagne, La 103–4
Guerre fatale, La 107–8
Guerre! La Guerre!, La 140–1
Guerre microbienne, La 145
Guerre nécessaire, La 110
Guggisberg, Captain 113
Guirlanden um die Urnen der Zukunft 69

Hackett, General Sir John 198–201
Hakobune no Sakura 3
Haldane, Richard Burdon, on German spies 124–5
Harbour of Death, The 142
Harmsworth, Alfred 62, 109–10, 122–4
Harrison, Frederick, on German spies 124
Hay, William Delisle 54–6, 83
Helders, Major von [Knauss, Robert] 155–6
Hemingway, Ernest 135
Henderson, Admiral William 91
Henley, W. E., his prayer for war 102
Henty, George Alfred 131–2
Hindenburgs Einmarsch in London 129–30
Hiroshima, atomic bomb on 162–3
Hislam, P. A. 125
History of the . . . Invasion of England 22–3, 28
Hoban, Russell 209–10
Hohenlohe-Ingelfingen, Prince Kraft Karl zu 79–80, 112
Hommes frénétiques, Les 145
Hopkins Manuscript, The 161–2
How John Bull Lost London 98
Hugo, Victor, on coming world peace 4
Hunter, Lt.-Col. William 36
Hurrah!!! . . . Révolution par les Cosaques 19
Huxley, Aldous 147–8, 171–3

Idea of a Patriot King, The 5–6
Illustrated London News 21, 133, 137
Impregnable Women, The 160–1
In a Conning Tower 57, 58, 74–5
Inheritors, The 1, 192–3
Ini 69–70
Internationale Revue über die Gesamten Armeen und Flotten 52–3

Index

invasion, fantasies of, Napoleonic 8–16; in
    1850s 20–5; in 1870s 27–37; in 20th
    century 117–27
Invasion from the Air 160
Invasion from Mars, The 87
Invasion of 1883, The 33–4
Invasion of England, The (1803) 11
Invasion of England, The (1870) 28
Invasion of 1910, The 41, 122–4
Ireland's War 43

Jane, F. T. 77
Jenkins, Will F. 167
Joffre, Marshal, surprised by trench
    warfare 115
Joinville, Prince de 20–1

Kahn, Herman 178
Karig, Captain Walter 167
Keiner kommt davon 137
Kinder des Saturns, Die 141
Kirst, Hans 137
Koestler, Arthur 164
Krakatit 151
Krieg im Jahre 1930, Der 139
Krieg von 189–, Der grosse 52, 63
Kunetka, James 197–8

Lamszus, Wilhelm 112
Last Day, The 197
Last Days of the Republic, The 42
Last Man, theme of 144–7, 162, 184–5
Last Man, The 146, 162
Leers, Johann von 139–40
Le Queux, William 41, 58–9, 62, 106–7,
    122–4, 128
Lessing, Doris 191
Level Seven 186–7
Letters on Cavalry 80
Letzten Kinder von Schewenborn, Die 3,
    211
Liddell Hart, B. H. 153
Linklater, Eric 161
Lissa, Battle of (1866), and ramming
    action 75
Long Tomorrow, The 207–8
Lord of the Flies, The 192–3
Lowe, Charles, on war stories 128
Luftkrieg–1936 155–6

Macaulay, Lord, on marvels of science 65
McClure's Magazine 134
Machen, Arthur 92
Mackay, Charles 4
Malheurs de John Bull, Les 57, 94–5, 100
Manchurian Candidate, The 182
Marine Rundschau, Die, on British war
    stories 125
Martian Chronicles, The 188–9
Martinson, Harry 205–6
Maude, Col. F. 117
Maurice, Colonel J. F. 40–1, 60–1
Meillac, Charles 140
Menschenschlachthaus, Das 112
Mercier, Sebastien 69
Méric, Victor 145
Merril, Judith 197
Miller, Walter 209
Modern Warfare, or how our Soldiers Fight
    113
Monitor, The 21, 43, 137–8
Montgomery, Field-Marshal 185, 193
Moscow Horse, The 183
Mottram, R. H. 131
Muir, Edwin 211–12
Münch, Paul Georg 129–30
Munro, H. H. (Saki) 14
Murder of the USA, The 167
Murray's Magazine 58

Napoléon et la Conquête du Monde 19
Napoléon, Louis 21–2, 45
Napus, Le 144–5
Nation in Arms, The 72, 79, 119
*Naval Engineer and the Command of the
    Sea, The* 74–5
Naval War of 1887, The 2
Naviators, The 142
New Atlantis, The 68
New Battle of Dorking, The 37, 117
New Centurion, The 77–8
Nicolson, Harold 157–8
Niemann, August 108, 120–1
Nineteen Eighty-Four 169–70
1934: Deutschlands Auferstehung 139
Nineteenth Century, The, on Channel
    Tunnel 169–70
North Sea Monster, The 160
Northcliffe, Lord, *see* Harmsworth, Alfred
Not this August 203

Notes sur les Forces navales de la France 20–1

Noyes, Alfred 146, 161–2

'Offensive–Invasion' gegen England, Die 10
On the Beach 3, 177
Operation zur See 119–20
Origin of Species, The 48
Orwell, George 169–70

Paix sur la terre 140
Pall Mall Gazette 99
Palmerston, Viscount, on invasion 28; and Channel Tunnel 96
Partisan Leader, The 17–18
Pemberton, Max 105–6
People of the Ruins, The 144
Pérochon, Ernest 145
Piller, Emanuel S. 167–8
Plus d'Angleterre 53–4, 94
Plus encore d'Angleterre 53
Poisoned Bullet, The 62
Prisonniers français en Angleterre, Les 12–13
Pro Patria 105–6
Public Faces 157–8
Putnam, George, on *Battle of Dorking* 2, 37

Quarterly Review, on the 'German Peril' 125

Racconto di un Guardiano di Spiaggia, Il 38–9
Red Thrust 202
Redoutable, Le 140
Reed, Samuel Rockwell 43
Reign of George VI, The 5–7
Report on Non-military Defense 4
Revolution 143
Richards, Alfred Bates 28
Richet, Charles 149
Riddle of the Sands, The 15, 119–20
Riddley Walker 209–10
Rigg, Lieut.-Col. Robert R. 79
Roberts, Field-Marshal Lord, on conscription 41, 126
Robida, Albert 67, 78, 81–3
Roshwald, Mordecai 186–7
Ruffin, Edmund 17–18, 42

Ruh, A. K. 69
R.U.R. 148, 150–1
Ruskin, John, his lecture on 'War' 133
Russell, Lord John, on invasion 28

Sack of London in the Great French War of 1901, The 95
Saki, *see* Munro, H. H.
Sartre, Jean-Paul 193
Sassoon, Siegfried 135
Schell, Jonathan 4
Schlacht bei Châlons, Die 81
Schmidt, Arno 204
Secret of the Desert, The 147
Seekrieg im Jahre 1888, Der grosse 52–3
Seven Days in New Crete 173–4
Shadow on the Hearth, The 197
Shanks, Edward 144, 146–7
Shaw, George Bernard 112
Shelley, Mary 149–50
Sheriff, R. C. 161–2
Show of Force 202
Siege of London, The 52
Siege of Portsmouth, The 110–11
Silent Night 183
Siwinna, Carl, on future war stories 125–6
Smiles, Samuel 65–6
Soddy, Frederick 129, 156
Sommerfeld, Adolf 115
Songs of Distant Earth 214–15
Southey, Robert 16, 17
Spanner, E. F. 142
Spengler, Oswald 157
Stead, W. T., on state of Royal Navy 99
'Stochastic' (Henry Grattan Donnelly) 43–5
Stricken Nation, The 43–5
Strieber, Whitley 197–8
Surprise of the Channel Tunnel, The 98
survival, fantasies of 179, 204–14
Suttner, Bertha von 111–12
Swoop!, The 127
Szilard, Leo 157, 189

Team Yankee 203
technology, effects of technological development on the imagination 3–4, 8–9, 46–7, 68–9; military technology 25–6; naval technology 21–3

Tennyson, Alfred, poems on, the
    Volunteer Movement 25; the Fleet
    99; on war 194–5
Thiriat, Paul 129
Third World War, The 198–200
Third World War: The Untold Story
    200–1
Three Hundred Years Hence 54–6, 83
Three Men Make A World 147–8
Time Machine, The 83
Tocqueville, Alexis de 47–8
Toward New Horizons 166–7, 177–8
Tracy, Louis 54, 64, 104–5
Tucker, Nathaniel 17–18, 42
Twenty-fifth Hour, The 162

United States, early war stories, 17–19,
    42–5; post-1945 fiction 178–80

Vademecum für Phantasiestrategen 125–6
Valbert, Georges, on Channel Tunnel
    panic 95
Vansittart, Lord 163
Verne, Jules 49, 66–8
Victoria, HM Queen, on French danger
    22
Vom Krieg der Zukunft 139
Vonnegut, Kurt 5
Voss, Julius von 69–70

Waffen Nieder, Die 111–12
Wahn Europa 140
War Cruise of the 'Aries', The 77
War in the Air, The 43, 88–9
War in the Atomic Age? 194
War of 1886, The 46
War—1974 79
War of 1870 2–3, 25–6
War of the Worlds, The 84–7
Warday 5, 197–8
warfare: air 152–4; atomic 162–3, 164,
    186; civil war 142–4; complacent
    attitude to 71–3, 131–4; land 48–9;
    naval 22–5, 77–8, 139; post-1918

developments 138–40, 153–6; post-
    1945 developments 165–6, 186–7, 183
war-to-come, The tale of the: beginnings
    1–3, 5–6, 7–15, 22, 27–33, 39–42,
    45–7, 54–6; developments after 1880
    58–9, 76–8, 80–1, 93–5, 99–101, 120–8;
    after (1918) 130, 136, 138–9, 141–2,
    156–7; after (1945) 168–74, 184–7;
    espionage 125, 128, 180–2, 216; future
    wars with Germany 118–27; imagery
    of war 59–61, 67–8, 81–3, 133–4;
    influence of the *Battle of Dorking*
    59–61, 67–8, 81–3, 133–4; influence of
    contemporary political situations 21–3,
    26–7, 118–19, 121–2, 126–7, 174–5,
    177, 215–16; post-1945 developments
    195–6, 198–200, 210–11
Was England Erwartet 37
Watkin, Sir Edward, proposes Channel
    Tunnel scheme 95–6
We 150–1
Webb, Jane 43
Wehrlos zur See 39, 81, 118
Welles, Orson, his adaptation of the *War
    of the Worlds* 86–7
Wellington, Duke of, on invasion 20–1
Wells, H. G. 78, 82–90, 92, 163–4
Weltkrieg, Der 108, 118, 120–1
When William Came 14
Whitman, Walt, quoted 47, 66
Wodehouse, P. G. 127–8
Wolseley, Lord 97, 161
Woman who Stopped War, The 160
Wordsworth, William, poems on: invasion
    15; war 132
World Set Free, The 82–3, 89–90, 93,
    156–7
Wyndham, John 212

Yeats, William Butler, quoted 144
Yriarte, Charles, on *Battle of Dorking* 32,
    37

Zaloga, Stephen 202
Zamyatin, Yevgeny Ivanovich 150–1, 186